# Advertising on the Internet

## Second Edition

Robbin Zeff
Brad Aronson

**Wiley Computer Publishing**

**John Wiley & Sons, Inc.**

NEW YORK · CHICHESTER · WEINHEIM · BRISBANE · SINGAPORE · TORONTO

Publisher: Robert Ipsen
Editor: Cary Sullivan
Managing Editor: Brian Snapp
Associate New Media Editor: Mike Sosa
Text Design & Composition: Benchmark Productions, Inc.

Designations used by companies to distinguish their products are often claimed as trademarks. In all instances where John Wiley & Sons, Inc., is aware of a claim, the product names appear in initial capital or ALL CAPITAL LETTERS. Readers, however, should contact the appropriate companies for more complete information regarding trademarks and registration.

This book is printed on acid-free paper. ∞

Published by John Wiley & Sons, Inc.

Published simultaneously in Canada.

This publication is designed to provide accurate and authoritative information in regard to the subject matter covered. It is sold with the understanding that the publisher is not engaged in professional services. If professional advice or other expert assistance is required, the services of a competent professional person should be sought.

*Library of Congress Cataloging-in-Publication Data:*

Zeff, Robbin Lee.
  Advertising on the Internet/Robbin Zeff, Bradley Aronson. 2nd ed.
    p. cm.
  "Wiley Computer Publishing."
  Includes index.
  ISBN 0-471-34404-4 (pbk./website: alk. paper)
  1. Internet advertising. 2. Internet advertising Directories. 3. Internet advertising—Computer network resources. 4. Internet advertising—Rates. I. Aronson, Brad. II. Title.
HF6146.I58Z43   1999
658.8'0025'4678--dc21                                    99-21722
                                                          CIP

Printed in the United States of America.

10 9 8 7 6 5 4

# CONTENTS

# ACKNOWLEDGMENTS

Writing a book is an intimate experience between a person and the words they choose, but being able to gather the creative ideas and energy to produce the book takes a great deal of support. I have many to thank for their assistance and support.

I want to begin by thanking all those who contributed directly to this book by either writing an entire chapter or one of the editorial sidebars found throughout the book: Rochelle Blaustein, Andy Bourland, Rex Briggs, Ann Burgraff, Melinda Gipson, Ann Handley, Richard Hopple, Bob Ivins, Leslie Laredo, Tom Lix, Liddy Manson, Evan Neufeld, Ali Partovi, Katherine Randolph, Todd Tweedy, David Wamsley, Eric Ward, Tony Winders, and David Zinman.

For always providing me with a bottomless cup of coffee and a creative and supportive environment, I want to thank the regulars and staff at Metro 29 Diner and the Lyon's Village Starbucks.

I couldn't have finished this book and kept my business afloat without the help of my staff at The Zeff Group who assisted in researching this book: Jee Hyung Kim and Mimi Talamonti. As always, they produced A+ work.

I owe a great deal of thanks to the members of the online advertising and marketing community. This book would not have been possible without the generosity they shared in terms of information and ideas. I want to point out a few who went above and beyond the call of duty: ClickZ, FrankelBiz, the Internet Advertising Discussion List, Jupiter Communications, the Media Center, and the Online Advertising Discussion List.

I also need to thank the hundreds of students who have taken my Internet advertising class at ZDU (www.zdu.com). Their perspective from the four corners of the globe continually opens my eyes to the breadth and depth of this industry.

I must thank my publisher, John Wiley & Sons, Inc., for continually encouraging my publishing projects, especially my editor Cary Sullivan.

Writing a book is an exercise in fortitude, and I wouldn't have the stamina without the support of my friends and family. In writing this book Toby Dershowitz, Virginia Diamond, Matt Edelstein, Laura Kragie, Ronnie Levin, and Leon MacMullen were dear and patient friends. My family (my parents Jack and Debbie; my sister Tova, my brother Brick, and the entire Nadler clan—Jami, Zanni, Dustin, and Devon) deserve gratitude for always being there and never doubting that I would resurface when the book was done.

And finally, I lost a good friend during the writing of this book. I want to dedicate this book to Sammy; he never knew he was a cat.

*—Robbin Zeff*

I'm very fortunate in that I have always managed to have great friends, family, and colleagues.

The first thank-you is owed to my wife Mia. She did the majority of the work on the resources section of the book, and she was understanding of the hectic schedule as we brought the second edition of this book to a close. In general my schedule isn't usually normal, and she is always supportive.

I'd like to mention my parents Joe and Joan, my brother Rob (the investment wizard) and my grandparents Alva, Al, and Lucille. There is no substitute for a supportive family. All the articles I constantly receive from my grandparents are also better than any clipping service to which I could subscribe.

My uncle, Steven Krupnick, has always been a great advisor and the best landlord a company could want. Andy Ehrlich, who has an office in our building, has also been an excellent advisor. Both Steve and Andy have given their time generously to help me personally and to help in the growth of i-frontier.

I wrote a big portion of this edition while I was in Seattle, and I am thankful for the hospitality of my wife's family: Erik, Carol, Ike, and Erik. Even when I'm working in Seattle, if I'm visiting them, it feels like a vacation.

Folks from my office who contributed to the research and graphics include Paul Walcutt, Adam Embick, and Manlio Lo Conte. I'd also like to thank the rest of the hardworking people who have helped move i-frontier forward. Without a great team, I would never have had time to write the second edition. Those people include: Jeremy Lockhorn, Vincent Moos, Collie Andrews, Jodin Trocheck, Dan Hughes, Rob Aronson, Jennie Leigh, Frank Chiachiere, Raquel Torres Coates, Dan DaCosta. Others include Jon Hurwitz, Arvin Casas, Nathan Solomon, Jay Valinis.

Of course, I'd also like to thank Robbin Zeff, the co-author of this book. Her attention to detail is why no one will find a more comprehensive book about Web advertising. I hope we'll write a publication together again soon . . . after I have a little time to catch up on my sleep.

*—Brad Aronson*

# CHAPTER 1

# The Internet Advertising Landscape

S ince the emergence of modern advertising more than 70 years ago, members of the profession have recognized that it's a direct reflection of society at the time. "Day by day a picture of our time is recorded completely and vividly in the advertising in American newspapers and magazines," said a pamphlet produced in 1926 by the N.W. Ayer & Sons advertising agency. Today, the picture of our time would also be presented on a computer screen, with the sound of a modem connecting in the background.

## Setting the Stage

The Internet, the largest global network of networked computers, was founded in the spirit of free access to information. But with its transition from a platform used primarily by research, government, and educational institutions to a commercial entity, established business and entrepreneurial hopefuls have put up Web sites and begun using the Internet to make their mark—and their fortune—on the digital frontier. From established media companies like Time Warner to media companies that began as online business ventures such as Yahoo!, the Internet is following the American tradition of turning uncharted territory into opportunity. And, in the tradition of all great communication media, advertising has moved quickly to the forefront as a source for supporting online commercial ventures.

The first format of online promotion was the Web site itself. Then came advertisements—banners and buttons—whose goal it was to bring users from publishers' Web sites to the advertisers' Web sites. These ads followed the print model's standard of clearly defined borders. The limited screen real estate allotted for banners and buttons (less than 10 percent), as well as the advertisers' desire to reach more consumers without requiring users to come to their Web sites, inspired the development of new models. From sponsorships to interstitials to push technology, new online advertising models are blurring the lines between advertising and editorial, and providing advertisers with more obtrusive ads similar to television advertising.

By the end of 1998, online advertising had grown to a $1.8 billion industry, with revenue projections of almost $8 billion by the year 2002 (see Figure 1.1). Not bad for an industry that got its start just four years earlier in 1994. The Aberdeen Group (www.aberdeen.com) predicts that Internet advertising spending will reach $5.1 billion by the year 2000. It should be noted when evaluating online ad revenue figures that barter is a common practice in the North American online ad market and often miscounted as actual spending (see Figure 1.2).

In a February 1998 study conducted by the American Association of Advertising Agencies, 45 percent of those surveyed said Internet advertising already was or was expected to become a significant segment of their advertising budget. Of these, 23 percent said Internet advertising was already a major part of their advertising strategy, 50 percent projected that it would become so within two to five years, and the remaining 27 percent expected it to be within the next 5 to 10 years.

Indeed, with the growth in ad spending, we're also seeing a growth in the number of Web sites seeking advertising. According to AdKnowledge, in December 1998 there were 1,430 brand named sites seeking advertising that listed rate cards in AdKnowledge's database (see Figure 1.3). Since the AdKnowledge database primarily reflects major brands, the actual number is much higher. In reality, many more sites are accepting advertising. For example, LinkExchange alone has 400,000 members making the real number of sites seeking advertising more than a half million, with most of them small- to midsized sites.

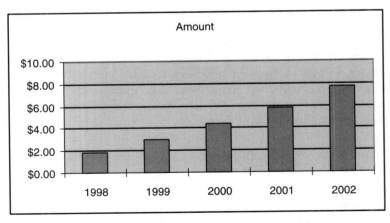

**Figure 1.1**   Web ad spending projections 1998–2002.

Source: 1998 Jupiter Communications (www.jup.com)

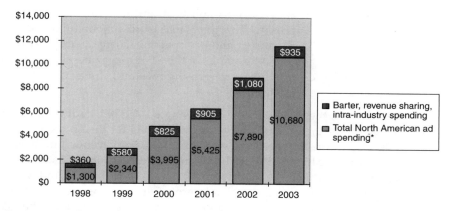

**Figure 1.2** The North American online advertising market.

Source: 1998 Forrester Research and Zenith Media (www.forrester.com)

Why is ad spending increasing? Because online buying is increasing. During the 1998 holiday shopping season, AOL members alone spent US $1.2 billion with online retailers. AOL sees great similarities between the online world and the offline world when it comes to reaching consumers. "Marketers either have to create their own shopping mall or buy space in somebody else's," says Bob Pittman, AOL president. "Traditional marketers know that building your own mall is harder." Indeed, on the Web it is easier and more efficient to advertise on someone else's site.

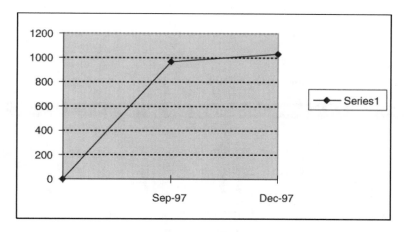

**Figure 1.3** Total number of Web sites seeking advertising.

Source: AdKnowledge, Inc. (www.adknowledge.com)

Note: Data reflects the total number of unique sites tracked and included in the AdKnowledge Planner database.

Of the hundreds of thousands of Web publishers, only a handful are generating significant revenues from advertising. This imbalance is not unique to the online world. It occurs in broadcast TV, magazines, and newspapers, where the majority of ad dollars go to a well-defined group. For example, of the 6,000 magazines in operation, only 31 receive in excess of $200 million in advertising revenues. Time Inc. alone commands one-third of the entire advertising market.

In many respects, the Web is merely following an age-old tradition whereby media buyers look for the biggest and most convenient bang for their buck. On the Web, the top 10 sites have attracted the lion's share of advertising revenue simply because they are the sites with the highest traffic. Traditional advertisers are accustomed to working with a mass-market medium, and high volume fits that profile. Today, the Internet does reach millions. According to Nua Internet Surveys (www.nua.ie), there were 87 million people in the United States and Canada online as of November 1998, for a worldwide total of 150 million users (see Table 1.1).

Will advertising be a viable revenue source for all Web sites big and small? Smaller sites will never be able to deliver the high-volume audience of major publishing sites, but they can deliver a targeted and loyal audience. It is this targetability and loyalty that will interest businesses in advertising on smaller sites representing niche markets.

And small sites are making money from advertising. Ray Owens, president of the "Joke a Day" humor mailing list (www.jokeaday.com), is proud to talk about how he turned telling old jokes via e-mail into "a $150,000 a year job, enabling me to spend my day sitting around in my bathrobe, surfing the Net, quitting my 'real job,' and generally living the 'American Dream.'" The "Joke A Day" site sells out its ad inventory six months in advance and is the largest daily humor mailing list in the world, reaching 115,000 people in 137 countries, with an average of 400 new people signing up for the list every day.

**Table 1.1**  Number of People on the Internet

| REGION | INTERNET USERS |
| --- | --- |
| Africa | 0.80 million |
| Asia/Pacific | 24.33 million |
| Europe | 32.76 million |
| Middle East | 0.78 million |
| Canada and U.S.A. | 87 million |
| South America | 4.5 million |
| **World Total** | **150 million** |

Source: Nua Internet Surveys (www.nua.ie)

**Table 1.2**   Internet Growth Rate in Relation to Other Media

| MEDIA | YEARS TO REACH 50 MILLION USERS |
|---|---|
| Radio | 38 |
| TV | 13 |
| Cable | 10 |
| Internet (estimate) | 5 |

Source: Morgan Stanley Technology Research

Many smaller sites are extremely attractive to major advertisers because of their ability to provide access and exposure to a defined online community, but the small publishers must generate enough traffic so that they have enough advertising inventory to sell. Most do not have the inventory to earn significant sums from selling advertising on a CPM (cost per one thousand times an ad is seen). The average CPM is around $30. This means that if a publisher sells all of his ad inventory he will be paid three cents for every time he can deliver an ad. At that rate, a fairly significant amount of traffic is needed to create a solid revenue stream. This is not to say that advertising is the only revenue model available to Web publishers. The revenue stream can include a combination of advertising, subscriptions, licensing content, and sales and merchandising.

The Internet is entering U.S. homes and spreading across the globe faster than any other medium in history (see Table 1.2). According to Geoffrey Ramse, Statsmaster at eMarketer (a Web site that tracks Internet statistics, [www.estats.com]), "The net is growing at a rapid pace. In America, 36 new, first-time users jump online every minute of the day—one new net user every 1.67 seconds" (see Figure 1.4). By the first quarter of 1999, AOL reported 15 million users on its service alone. Indeed, the Internet is substantially influencing how Americans spend their time.

At the end of 1998, America Online commissioned a study to help better understand the impact of the interactive medium. The America Online/Roper Starch Cyberstudy 1998 found that online communication is now permanently imbedded into how we communicate at work and at home. The study found that two-thirds of Internet consumers have been online three or more years, with three-quarters believing Internet services have bettered their lives. Nearly 90 percent responded that they would miss the Internet if it were no longer available. How valuable is the Net? When asked what they would prefer if stranded on a desert island, over two-thirds said a computer with Internet access, only 23 percent said a telephone, and barely 9 percent said a television. "My, how times have changed!" exclaimed Steve Case, AOL CEO in his Jan 8, 1999 letter to AOL members in reviewing the results of the study.

Other findings include these:

- Approximately 90 percent of online consumers regularly or occasionally go online to communicate with friends and family.

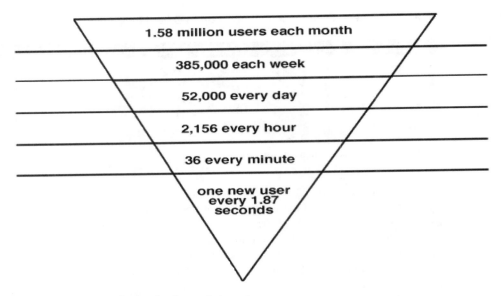

1.58 million users each month

385,000 each week

52,000 every day

2,156 every hour

36 every minute

one new user every 1.87 seconds

**Figure 1.4** Rate of growth of new Internet users.

Source: 1998 estats (www.estats.com)

- In the workplace, more than 50 percent of online consumers claim e-mail is their preferred mode of communicating with colleagues, clients, and customers.
- The majority of online consumers feel that the areas the Internet will most greatly affect are education, work, media, and entertainment.

The impact of the Internet today is remarkable—even more so when we recognize that only one-quarter of American households are online, with nearly two-thirds of these getting online for the first time within the past two years.

Indeed, advertisers are jumping online, but the industry has a long way to go before it will be a staple in the media budgets of big consumer brands. Many of the major advertisers are also the major publishers that advertise their sites to increase traffic to entice more advertisers; compare the top 50 online advertisers in June 1998 (see Table 1.3) with the top 50 online publishers (see Table 1.4).

Indeed, the only constant in the Internet has been its phenomenal growth, development, adoption, and acceptance. As the newest advertising medium on the block, the Web presents challenges from measurability to auditing to customized ad delivery, but what was promise and potential just months ago is now practiced with quantifiable results today. Every year brings significant technological developments. Every quarter sees rapid growth in the online population. Every month, new market leaders emerge in industry segments that did not exist before. And consumers are spending more and more time online. Internet usage has skyrocketed. The AOL members' daily usage has

**Table 1.3** Top 50 Advertisers Online (January–June 1998)

| RANK | ADVERTISER | YTD SPENDING |
|---|---|---|
| 1 | Microsoft Corp. | $ 17,230,670 |
| 2 | IBM Corp. | $ 14,864,940 |
| 3 | Digital Equipment Corp. | $ 5,565,804 |
| 4 | Excite Inc. | $ 4,918,606 |
| 5 | General Motors Corp. | $ 4,725,033 |
| 6 | InfoSeek Corp. | $ 4,515,489 |
| 7 | Netscape Communications Corp. | $ 3,767,448 |
| 8 | Lycos Inc. | $ 3,672,075 |
| 9 | 3Com Corp. | $ 3,493,988 |
| 10 | Datek Securities | $ 3,489,768 |
| 11 | AT&T Corp. | $ 3,438,059 |
| 12 | Intel Corp. | $ 3,349,221 |
| 13 | Walt Disney Co. | $ 3,330,960 |
| 14 | Compaq Computer Corp. | $ 3,314,658 |
| 15 | Yahoo Corp. | $ 3,148,160 |
| 16 | Barnes & Noble Inc. | $ 3,111,673 |
| 17 | Hewlett Packard Co. | $ 2,983,649 |
| 18 | CBS Sportsline USA Inc. | $ 2,563,586 |
| 19 | Honda Motor Co. Inc. | $ 2,511,553 |
| 20 | Sony Corp. | $ 2,442,539 |
| 21 | CDnow | $ 2,438,828 |
| 22 | i-Village | $ 2,402,210 |
| 23 | Toyota Motor Sales USA, Inc. | $ 2,284,458 |
| 24 | VISA International | $ 2,236,762 |
| 25 | Fidelity Investments | $ 2,099,978 |
| 26 | Sun Microsystems Inc. | $ 2,046,611 |
| 27 | Amazon.com Books | $ 1,997,383 |
| 28 | Ford Motor Co. | $ 1,969,524 |
| 29 | Charles Schwab Corp. | $ 1,907,353 |
| 30 | SPRINT Communications Co. | $ 1,903,749 |

*continues*

**Table 1.3** Top 50 Advertisers Online (January–June 1998) *(Continued)*

| RANK | ADVERTISER | YTD SPENDING |
|---|---|---|
| 31 | Preview Travel Inc. | $ 1,773,367 |
| 32 | OnSale | $ 1,698,380 |
| 33 | Procter & Gamble Co. | $ 1,637,977 |
| 34 | First USA Inc. | $ 1,592,040 |
| 35 | Egghead Inc. | $ 1,534,144 |
| 36 | American Express Co. | $ 1,531,462 |
| 37 | Bell Atlantic Corp. | $ 1,524,291 |
| 38 | Lotus Development Corp. | $ 1,489,550 |
| 39 | Ziff Davis Inc. | $ 1,476,981 |
| 40 | Hearst Corp. | $ 1,475,911 |
| 41 | Donaldson Lufkin & Jenrette | $ 1,465,012 |
| 42 | N2K Inc. | $ 1,452,203 |
| 43 | SAP AG | $ 1,420,033 |
| 44 | United Parcel Service of America | $ 1,416,423 |
| 45 | Consumerinfo.com Inc | $ 1,410,167 |
| 46 | Webnet Marketing | $ 1,390,208 |
| 47 | CNET Inc | $ 1,349,890 |
| 48 | Eastman Kodak Co. | $ 1,348,568 |
| 49 | Verio Corp. | $ 1,335,851 |
| 50 | Volvo North America Corp. | $ 1,310,878 |

Source: Jupiter Communications, 1998 (www.jup.com)

**Table 1.4** Top 50 Publishers, Ranked by Advertising Revenue (January–June 1998)

| RANK | PUBLISHER TITLE | YTD REVENUE |
|---|---|---|
| 1 | Yahoo | $ 54,161,508 |
| 2 | Excite Network–Excite.com and Webcrawler | $ 47,114,500 |
| 3 | InfoSeek | $ 33,640,584 |
| 4 | Lycos | $ 24,775,500 |
| 5 | Microsoft Network | $ 19,885,509 |
| 6 | Netscape | $ 18,962,508 |
| 7 | CNET | $ 18,584,000 |

**Table 1.4** *(Continued)*

| RANK | PUBLISHER TITLE | YTD REVENUE |
| --- | --- | --- |
| 8 | ZD Net | $ 17,948,239 |
| 9 | Altavista | $ 14,804,610 |
| 10 | CMP Net | $ 9,461,446 |
| 11 | CNN Interactive | $ 9,349,000 |
| 12 | Wired Digital | $ 9,092,875 |
| 13 | Sportsline | $ 8,547,500 |
| 14 | Wall Street Journal Interactive | $ 8,491,023 |
| 15 | IDG | $ 8,017,303 |
| 16 | Pathfinder | $ 6,688,000 |
| 17 | ESPN Sportszone | $ 6,117,331 |
| 18 | Weather Channel | $ 6,010,000 |
| 19 | Homearts Network | $ 5,760,000 |
| 20 | USA Today | $ 5,107,314 |
| 21 | Newspage (Individual Inc.) | $ 5,060,000 |
| 22 | AudioNet | $ 5,034,943 |
| 23 | GEOCITIES | $ 4,268,750 |
| 24 | New York Times | $ 3,251,000 |
| 25 | RealAudio | $ 3,246,000 |
| 26 | Disney Online | $ 3,130,300 |
| 27 | iVillage | $ 2,870,750 |
| 28 | Windows95.com | $ 2,717,395 |
| 29 | NBC | $ 2,635,000 |
| 30 | Warner Brothers | $ 2,430,000 |
| 31 | Quote.com | $ 2,312,500 |
| 32 | Tripod | $ 2,130,468 |
| 33 | Playboy | $ 2,074,544 |
| 34 | Discovery Channel Online | $ 2,015,000 |
| 35 | The Globe | $ 2,015,000 |
| 36 | Women.com | $ 1,967,050 |
| 37 | Riddler | $ 1,532,500 |
| 38 | Car and Driver | $ 1,509,115 |

*continues*

**Table 1.4** Top 50 Publishers, Ranked by Advertising Revenue (January–June 1998) *(Continued)*

| RANK | PUBLISHER TITLE | YTD REVENUE |
|------|------------------|-------------|
| 39 | Sony Station | $ 1,475,000 |
| 40 | Internet.com | $ 1,473,150 |
| 41 | Morningstar | $ 1,400,000 |
| 42 | MapQuest | $ 1,371,772 |
| 43 | Epicurious | $ 1,334,500 |
| 44 | E! Online | $ 1,307,500 |
| 45 | Los Angeles Times | $ 1,235,250 |
| 46 | Jumbo! The Official Web Shareware Site | $ 1,178,699 |
| 47 | Attitude Network | $ 1,113,016 |
| 48 | Stockmaster | $ 1,091,000 |
| 49 | PC Quote | $ 1,081,666 |
| 50 | Gamesville - Home of Bingo Zone | $ 1,055,000 |

Source: Jupiter Communications, 1998 (www.jup.com)

increased from 14 minutes per day in September 1996 to 45 minutes per day in July 1998 (see Figure 1.5).

The online mantra is supported in story after story in the press, with Web addresses plastered on everything and everywhere from billboards to beer bottles. Every movie, sports team, and beverage is marketing online. There is no question that Web advertising is starting to take center stage.

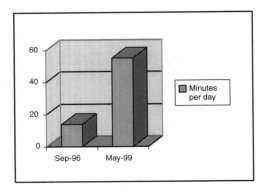

**Figure 1.5** AOL member's daily usage 1996–1998.
Source: AOL Company Reports, July 1998

# What Is Online Advertising?

Online advertising, like all advertising, attempts to disseminate information in order to affect a buyer-seller transaction. But Web advertising differs from other media by enabling consumers to interact with the advertisement. Consumers can click on the ad for more information, or take the next step and purchase the product in the same online session. Consumers can even purchase products from within Web advertisements.

On the Web, every element of the interactive canvas can be made into an ad, from product placement (a product name or logo used in text or in a display) to wallpaper designs (background images appearing behind editorial content) made up of a corporate logo or any other brand imagery. For example, Disney used a black and white spotted background on Yahoo! to promote the release of the remake of *101 Dalmatians* (the ad concept was developed by i-traffic [www.i-traffic.com]).

Web advertising gives advertisers the opportunity to precisely target an audience, enabling them to deliver advertisements that are customized to each user's particular interest and tastes. Other media offer targeting capabilities, but as you'll see later in this book, the Web offers a level of targeting that advertisers can't find anywhere else.

## Online Advertising and Traditional Advertising Vehicles

Can we compare online advertising to a television commercial or an ad in a magazine? Should a Web advertisement be compared to a direct mail piece or a roadside billboard? Should we look to the cable TV or direct response industry for historic precedence? Looking at online advertising in terms of traditional ad models will reveal the breadth and depth of this medium as an advertising vehicle. To that end, we'll discuss billboards, print, direct marketing, and television.

**Outdoor advertising: The Billboard.**  Web banner ads are often likened to roadside billboards. Like a billboard, which can refer passersby to an upcoming attraction or location, a banner ad may point Internet users to a Web site. But roadside billboards are static, whereas Web users can interact with a banner ad by clicking on the ad to get to other sites and more information. Some banners even allow consumers to take an action (like playing a game) without leaving the ad—a huge difference between banners and billboards. With a Web ad, an advertiser can measure exactly how many times a banner was clicked. Unless the billboard is a direct response campaign with a special phone number, there usually isn't an accurate method for determining how many people respond to it.

**Print advertising.**  In a newspaper or a magazine, a quarter-, half-, or full-page advertisement is clearly identifiable. Advertisements are formatted in a way that allows readers to easily separate them from the editorial content. If a magazine advertisement resembles editorial text, the magazine will place a banner across the top identifying the text as a "special advertising section." On the Web, banner advertising corresponds to the print model with its clearly recognizable borders.

Current screen real estate for banner advertising is limited—usually less than 10 percent of the viewable area. However, as you'll see in Chapter 2, Web advertising is not merely banners, and it is not always clearly identified as advertising; it can actually be quite difficult for a consumer to differentiate between advertising and editorial.

**Television advertising.** The 30-second television commercial is one of the premiere advertising formats. Television commercials allow an advertiser to "take over" the television screen completely, delivering a full-motion advertisement that can target a consumer's interests, needs, and even emotions.

Should a Web ad be more like a TV commercial? Some think so. The idea of an ad commanding the entire screen has inspired the development of ad models that are more dynamic and intrusive, as will be discussed in Chapter 2.

**Cable television advertising.** Cable television traded the reach and frequency of broadcast TV for better access to niche audiences. The cable audience is more upscale and extremely attractive to advertisers. Increased targeting has lead to specialized commercials with targeted and provocative messaging. Like cable, the Web offers many targeted ad buys, in addition to the buys that allow for massive reach.

**Direct marketing.** From direct mail to telemarketing, direct marketers can accurately track the number of people who respond to a specific promotion and use this number to determine the profitability of each campaign. The Internet's innate accountability has led advertisers to take a direct marketing approach to the Web—specifically, basing their campaigns on their cost per response.

# Internet Advertising—A Definition

Defining Internet advertising has almost become a sport within the industry. At first people defined it in terms of whatever industry they came from. If a person came from cable, then Internet advertising was like cable. If a person came from print, then Internet advertising was like print. Then the debate shifted to whether Internet advertising was more like traditional advertising, which focused on building brand awareness, or direct marketing, which sought to generate leads or execute sales.

The days of always having to compare the Internet with TV, cable, or print for credibility are over. This either/or definition has shifted to one of overlap and inclusion. Internet advertising is the convergence of traditional advertising and direct response marketing (see Figure 1.6).

The AOL advertising team takes the definition one step further. "We don't look at Internet advertising as just brand building or direct marketing," says Steve Keenan, VP of marketing and operations at AOL. "You can have branding like TV, radio, print. You can also get vast amounts of information to people like print or direct marketing. And you can also make a transaction happen; it's just like going to the store or calling an 800 telephone number." For AOL, Internet advertising is the convergence of branding, information dissemination, and sales transactions all in one place.

# Internet Advertising

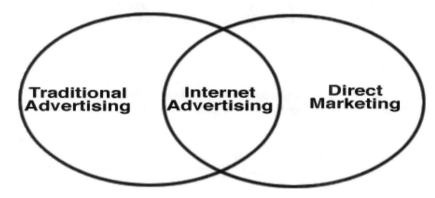

**Figure 1.6**    Internet advertising is the convergence of traditional advertising and direct response marketing.

Source: 1999 The Zeff Group (www.zeff.com)

## The Online Advertising Advantage

Online advertising holds four distinct advantages.

### Targetability

Online advertisers have an entirely new range of targeting capabilities They can focus on users from specific companies, SIC codes, or geographical regions and nations, as well as by time of day, computer platform, and browser. They can target using the databases that serve as the backbone of direct marketing. They can even target based on a person's personal preferences and actual behavior.

### Tracking

Marketers can track how users interact with their brands and learn what is of interest to their current and prospective customers. For example, a car manufacturer can track how a user progresses through its site to determine whether more users are interested in the safety information or the "extras" that come with a particular model.

Advertisers can also measure the response to an advertisement (through the number of times an ad is clicked on, the number of purchases or leads an ad generated, etc.), which is difficult to do with traditional television, print, and billboard advertising.

### *Deliverability and Flexibility*

Online, an ad is delivered in real time 24 hours a day, 7 days a week, 365 days a year. Furthermore, an ad campaign can be launched, updated, or canceled immediately. An advertiser can follow a campaign's progress daily, notice that a campaign is generating very little response in the first week, and replace it by week 2. This is a big difference from print, where an ad cannot be changed until a new edition of the publication is published; or TV, where the high costs of ad development make frequent changes prohibitive.

### *Interactivity*

An advertiser's goal is to engage the prospect with a brand or product. This can be done more effectively online, where consumers can interact with the product, test the product, and, if they choose, buy the product. For example, an advertisement for software can take a user directly to the location where a demo can be downloaded and tested immediately. If the consumer likes the software, he or she can purchase it right then and there. No other medium moves the consumer from information seeker to purchaser friction free.

## A Short History of Online Advertising

The history of online advertising spans a very short period of time, from the launching of the commercial online service Prodigy, through the so-called spam wars, and to the coming of age with the launch of HotWired, originally the online sister company of *Wired* magazine.

## In the Beginning

Long before the commercialization of the Web, Prodigy was testing the online advertising waters. When the service went live in 1990, it adopted advertising as a revenue source. Prodigy was the lone experiment in this area; the other commercial online services shied away from incorporating advertising into their content mix. CompuServe went online in 1979 but did not sell its first sponsorship until 1995. Likewise, America Online (AOL) did not start addressing advertising seriously until the fall of 1995. Today, many members of Prodigy's original online advertising sales team head up advertising sales efforts at the top sites.

## Setbacks: The Spam Wars

As Prodigy was testing advertising within the subscriber-only environment, others were exploring the commercial implications of Internet applications. In 1994, the law firm of Canter and Siegel thought they had discovered the silver bullet for tapping the Internet as a cheap marketing medium and posted an advertisement for green card assistance to over 7,000 newsgroups (Internet discussion areas). Internet etiquette, known as *netiquette*, dictates that discussion forums not be used to post blatantly commercial materials that have nothing to do with the subject of the discussion group. Such unrelated and commercial posts, as well as unsolicited commercial e-mails, became known as *spam*. Spam was disruptive to the discussion group, polluting the topic of conversation, and often resulted in large volumes of e-mail complaints, known as *flames* sent to the spammer and his Internet Service Provider (ISP).

Although Canter and Siegel did receive requests for green card assistance as a result of the posts, the resulting outrage hurt the firm's reputation within the online community. Canter and Siegel's ISP crashed 15 times under the flood of 30,000 flames in only 18 hours. Their ISP subsequently canceled their account.

Canter and Siegel next set up accounts at two other ISPs, insisting they would place even more advertisements. They received tremendous press coverage in print, but were blacklisted from the Internet community—ISPs dropped their accounts rather than face thousands of angry e-mails.

## Acceptance

The Canter and Siegel spam wars occurred just before *Wired* magazine launched HotWired (www.hotwired.com), a Web property with an advertising business model. Fearing backlash from the cyberspace community, HotWired reduced the on-screen dimensions it had originally planned to use for its first advertising unit, the banner ad.

HotWired signed its first ad contract with AT&T on April 15, 1994, and launched its site on October 27, 1994 (see Figure 1.7). Its inaugural sponsors represented a cross-section of the advertising community, from such blue chip advertisers as AT&T and IBM to Pepsi's alcoholic beverage Zima.

To HotWired's pleasant surprise, the only negative comments received were in response to portions of the Web site that were still under construction; no one criticized the advertisements.

Although HotWired hoped to profit from its advertising sales, it did not begin with a dedicated sales force. Instead, it used the national sales force for its print magazine *Wired*. This proved satisfactory because there were only two agencies buying the vast majority of online advertising: Modem Media (now Modem Media Poppe Tyson [www.modemmedia.com]) and Messner Vetere Berge McNamee Schmetterer (www.mvbms.com). Together, the clients of these two agencies accounted for almost half of HotWired's charter advertisers. "Our charter advertisers were visionaries," recalls Rick Boyce, vice president of advertising at HotWired. The story goes that the folks at Modem Media were so convinced of the significance of being a charter sponsor of HotWired that they bought ads before they had final approval from AT&T, since no one at AT&T was ready to take responsibility for online ad buying. Modem Media's gamble paid off: the charter sponsors received tremendous press coverage as part of the site's launch.

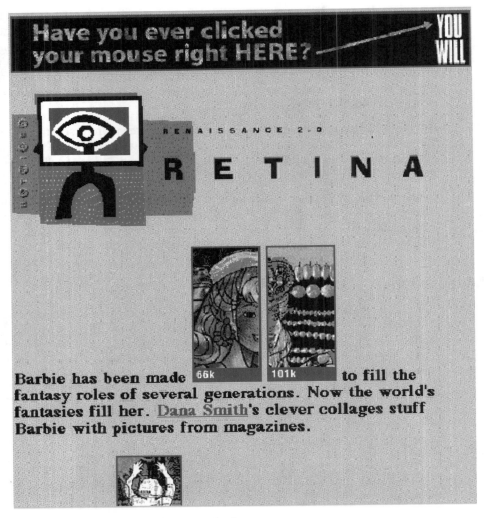

**Figure 1.7**   First banner ad on HotWired.
Source: HotWired (www.hotwired.com)

Word (www.word.com) was the second "zine" (Web magazine) to sign sponsors. It too received its first sponsorships—Zima and MasterCard—from the Internet advertising visionaries at Modem Media. Soon, other sites were scrambling to accept advertising, and today there are hundreds of thousands of sites that accept advertising.

## Wake Up, It's a Mass Market

From 1994 to 1996, some of the major advertising agencies on Madison Avenue maintained a wait-and-see attitude toward the importance and viability of Internet advertising. The joke used to be that the mantra on Madison Avenue was "wake me when it's a mass market." Madison Avenue is awake now.

Over time there have been pivotal events that have cemented a medium's place to a particular decade in the history of communication. For the 1920s, it was the radio delivering Calvin Coolidge's State of the Union addresses into the home. In the 1960s, it was the televising of the Nixon-Kennedy debate that completely changed politics and campaigning. And for the Information Age of the 1990s, the pivotal event will surely be the release of the Starr Report, where over a two-day period 24.7 million unique visitors used the Internet to view the text of the report. And the Start Report even became an advertising issue, because sites sold ad space next to this high-traffic-generating content.

The Internet started out as a medium used primarily by the infamous early adopters, those consumers who will spare no expense to have the latest electronic or computer gizmo. However, in 1998 the number of current users started to extend into mass market turf. Indeed AOL, with its 15 million users and climbing, is in the same league as TV mass marketing heavyweights (see Figure 1.8). Correspondingly, Internet users accept online advertising as they do advertising on all other media.

A report conducted by Opinion Research Corp. International in 1998 found that Internet brands such as America Online, Yahoo!, and MSNBC are recognized by at least half of America's adults, with brands such as Netscape, Amazon.com, and Priceline recognized by at least a quarter of U.S. adults. "The most valuable real estate in the world is screen real estate," says Brewster Kahle, president of Alexa Internet.

## Critics

Online advertising is not without its critics (see Table 1.5). There are several software products that block ads and promote themselves as speeding up Web page download time. These products include JunkBuster (www.junkbuster.com), @tGuard

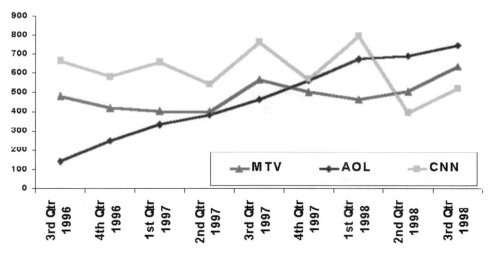

**Figure 1.8** AOL is now in the same league as TV mass market heavyweights.

**Table 1.5** Web Advertising Opinions

| | DISAGREE | AGREE |
|---|---|---|
| Advertising is needed to keep content free | 11% | 53% |
| Targeted ads are fine if site or ISP doesn't give out my info | 18% | 50% |
| Web ads are less obtrusive than direct-mail offers | 23% | 43% |
| Web ads are less obtrusive than TV commercials | 24% | 43% |
| Would pay extra to subscribe to site without ads | 37% | 22% |
| ISPs should be able to sell subscriber lists, like magazines do | 61% | 16% |

Source: 1998 INTECO survey of 2,500 U.S. adults.

(www.atguard.com), and WebWiper (www. webwiper.com), to name a few. Fortunately, these products are not taking off as vigorously as advertising. The online audience understands that there is a price to pay for free access to content, and that price is advertising support. Besides, the average consumer does not find Web advertising irritating enough to warrant taking the time to download and install software to block the ads.

# Players in the Internet Advertising Industry

The cast of characters in the Internet advertising industry can be divided into three camps: the sellers, the buyers, and the advertising infrastructure—those companies that make Internet advertising possible by developing the tools to deliver the ads, measure the ads, audit the ad campaigns, and complete the other tasks that make advertising on the Internet work.

It is important to note that in the online advertising world, the line between the buyers and the sellers is narrow: Many publishers buy ads to promote their Web sites, and advertisers develop Web sites to promote their products.

## The Sellers

The Web is now made up of hundreds of thousands of sites and the numbers are growing each minute. Young entrepreneurs, many of them college students with free Internet accounts, developed the first sites. Other early players were those folks ready to embrace technology or who looked to the Web as a place to express themselves.

### Web Site Publishers

Today, major publishers are media companies. Some sites are produced by a single company, like Washingtonpost.com, which is the online version of the *Washington Post* newspaper (www.washingtonpost.com). Other sites represent different channels of interest and are owned by one parent company such as Microsoft's Expedia (www.expedia.com) or Carpoint (www.carpoint.com). Still others are joint projects of two or more companies—for example, MSNBC (www.msnbc.com) is a joint project of Microsoft and NBC.

In 1997, AOL was limping into the advertising arena. But in 1998 alone, AOL had signed up more than 400 advertisers, with as many as 55 spending in excess of $1 million annually a piece. "Whether you're 6 or 60, we want you on AOL," says Steve Case, AOL Chairman. AOL hopes to sell advertising that targets a number of demographics—not simply the technically savvy males who were the majority of early Internet users. And though AOL was not the early leader in accepting advertising on online services, it currently dominates the advertising landscape.

### Sales Channels

In the seller's camp, the key players are indeed the publishers, who produce the sites with advertising space to sell; but the facilitators of the sales are equally important and include ad networks, representation firms, and ad auctions that sell advertising for the publishers.

**Ad networks.**   To assist sites in generating revenue from advertising, ad networks have formed to sell advertising. The ad network represents a slate of sites serving as a sales force for publishers who participate in their networks. These networks benefit the publishers by providing an aggressive and experienced sales force. Also, a publisher's inventory may be more difficult to sell individually than when it is part of a larger inventory pool. The networks make it possible for advertisers to extend their reach into a variety of sites with one media buy. In addition, advertising agencies are often more willing to meet with a network rather than have dozens of meetings with individual Web site publishers.

**Representation firms.**   Sites with advertising to sell can hire a firm to sell the ad space on their behalf.

**Auctions.**   Publishers can offer soon-to-expire ad space on the auction block for quick sale. There are also ad networks that allow publishers to sell their excess ad inventory in real time.

## The Buyers

The buyers consist of the advertisers who have products, services, or Web sites to promote. They are often represented by interactive or traditional agencies that design online advertising campaigns and the media buyers who actually purchase the ad space.

### Advertisers

The first advertisers to jump on the Web en masse were the Internet publishers themselves. In fact, the list of the top advertisers for 1998 reads similarly to the list of top publishers for that year (see Tables 1.3 and 1.4). Indeed, those with the most to gain from the growth of the Web invest the most money.

In 1998, one of the largest consumer advertisers in the world, Procter & Gamble, moved from the sidelines into the headlines. Procter & Gamble hosted a conference in Cincinnati to bring together major global advertisers, online publishers, interactive advertising agencies, leading technology companies, and others to discuss the best means to accelerate the growth and development of online advertising. Titled the Future of Advertising Stakeholders (FAST) Summit (www.fastsummit.com), the two-day meeting focused on three guiding principles:

> FAST will focus on developing action plans that accelerate the development and use of digital advertising models that are both effective and consumer-acceptable in order to enable interactive digital media to become more available, more useful, and more enjoyable for the end user/consumer.

> FAST must be driven by committed advertising, media, and technology firms determined to help achieve win/win solutions for the entire industry.

> FAST efforts will focus on both broadening acceptance of the current state of the space (through effective knowledge sharing) as well as accelerating the development of breakthroughs that will more rapidly enable its future potential.

> (Source: www.fastsummit.com/pages/index.cgi/principles)

The historic event resulted in the formation of the Fast Forward organization (www.fastinfo.org), a broad-based Internet industry coalition formed to accelerate development of online marketing with such committees as consumer acceptance, ad models, measurement, and media buying. Even more importantly, this event brought the major brand advertisers to the table to commit to investing in the Internet as an advertising medium, making advertising on the Internet part of every brand's marketing mix.

## Interactive Agencies

The link between the advertiser and the publisher is often the interactive agency. The birth of interactive advertising did not take place on Madison Avenue, the home of the ad agency. Instead, it bloomed in Multimedia Gulch in San Francisco and New York City's Silicon Alley.

In 1994, Ed Artzt, CEO of Procter & Gamble and president of the American Association of Advertising Agencies (a.k.a. 4As), scolded his association for not embracing the possibilities of the new technology. Though at the time Artzt was referring to interactive television, it soon became clear that the Internet was the dominant medium on the horizon. While traditional ad agencies took a wait-and-see approach to the Internet's potential, "boutique shops" pioneered online advertising. These shops did not look at online advertising as new wine in old bottles, but embraced the nuances of cyber culture, to make Web advertising a vehicle that worked.

Following in the tradition established by former P&G CEO Artzt, Denis Beausejour, vice president of advertising at P&G in 1998, proclaimed that in ten years there would be two kinds of agencies: digital agencies and dinosaur agencies.

Today's interactive agencies have their origins in Web site development, direct marketing, and traditional advertising agencies. The agencies that began as Web site development shops had strong technical backgrounds. These shops built the first corporate Web sites and brought in the marketing and advertising expertise to make their companies full-service operations later. Agencies that came from the world of direct response marketing reacted to the Web's remarkable ability to serve as a direct marketing vehicle. And finally, some interactive agencies were built by visionaries from the ad agency world who set up interactive divisions or formed their own boutique shops.

These early roots are quickly becoming a distant memory, as traditional advertising agency giants try to catch up. Some have set up interactive departments within the company. Others have spun off their own interactive shops. And others have merely acquired the expertise. Whichever the case, traditional ad agencies are now in the interactive business, trying to regain their attractiveness with advertisers as full-service providers.

# Advertising Infrastructure

A service and software solution infrastructure has formed to provide the tools to help publishers and advertisers deliver results through Internet advertising.

### Traffic Measurement

The Internet's keen ability to conduct in-depth measurement of Web site and advertising activity has given birth to an entire measurement industry that includes the counters, the auditors, and the comparative measurement researchers. Today, Web publishers can measure everything that occurs on a Web site and everything that occurs within a Web ad. In other advertising media, measurement is based on sample. On the Web, however, measurement is done by census, every impression is counted.

### Targeting and Personalization

Targeting and personalization are key advantages of Internet advertising and essential components of the advertising infrastructure for publisher and advertiser alike. The targeting and personalization software companies are central to the online advertising industry.

### Ad Management

Software solutions that coordinate the logistics of ad placement are available for the online advertising industry. The software takes care of the daily management of ad placement, rotation, reporting, and billing—all the required components of a Web advertising campaign.

The technological infrastructure of online advertising sets it apart from traditional advertising. Chapters 4 and 5 explain how these tools work. But before we jump into a discussion about the tools of the trade, we will examine the types of ad models that are in use today and being developed for tomorrow.

## It's That Simple. It's That Complex.

Tom Lix, President/CEO (tlix@newmarket.net)
NewMarket Network (www.newmarket.net)

The Internet is just like anything else, like print, like television, like radio, like billboards, like the insides of a book of matches. Except for one thing. People can talk back. They can have a conversation. They can ask questions. They can complain. They can compliment. They can suggest. And, they can demand. Not only "can" they do all these things, but they "will" do all these things and more, much more.

As marketers we've always talked about communicating with our customers, even in recent years when the mantra of "1 to 1 marketing" appeared. But in reality, we never really communicated with our customers. Rather, we talked "to" them—sometimes as a market, and sometimes as an individual—but always talking "to" them, not with them.

The Internet is changing all of that. While most people don't admit it, I'd venture a guess that most people in business are scared to death (by the way, my advice is, get over it real fast).

So here's the deal. Embrace this dialog; use it to your advantage and to your customer's advantage. Be willing to listen to all the problems, face the tough questions, deal with the irate customers, and use it to improve (just do it quickly).

Consider advertising as a means to talk with, not at your customers. Advertising is no longer a means to define or obfuscate your brand. It is no longer a manageable device to communicate "selected" attributes and benefits. Advertising is certainly not a simple tool to carefully portray or reinforce an image that "you" want to deliver. The Internet means we have to talk with our customers. We have to listen to them. We have to respond to them.

The Internet also means our customers not only talk to us, but they talk to each other quickly and in numbers that you never imagined. The old adage about dissatisfied customers telling ten of their friends is now about telling thousands. Traditional advertising just won't be adequate anymore. The only thing that will suffice is an open, honest dialog with our customers. It's that simple. It's that complex.

# Online Ad Models

The first form of Web advertising was the Web site itself. But as the Web became cluttered with commercial sites, simply building a Web site wasn't enough to reach Internet consumers. Advertisers needed a tool for driving users to their Web sites, and publishers needed a way to pay for their Web endeavors. The first Web advertising models were banners and buttons that resembled the traditional print advertising format by appearing within clearly defined borders. But, the limited screen real estate used for banners and buttons, along with an average click-through rate that is now under 1 percent (according to NetRatings [www.netratings.com]) inspired the development of new, more obtrusive types of Web advertising. In this chapter we'll examines the many advertising models used on the Internet today.

## Web Site as Ad

For many companies, the first foray into Internet advertising was building a Web site. These sites were usually built because the company thought the Web was "cool," having a Web site would make the company look "hip" or the company was too afraid not to have a Web site and appear behind the competition. The first sites ran the gamut from "brochureware," which was nothing more than print material reproduced online, to the opposite extreme—a site that employed every technological and design feature available.

Both tactics were disappointing in failing to deliver results and caused advertisers to rethink their use of corporate Web sites. Brochureware didn't take advantage of the depth of information that could be presented in a user-friendly manner through the Web, and so-called cool sites became prohibitively expensive to produce and lacked a clear objective other than showcasing new technology. Consequently, advertisers began to produce Web sites that contained product information potential customers actually needed. Web users are looking for information; when a person visits a company's Web site, that person expects product information. Buyers of large-ticket items—especially lifestyle items like cars and homes—usually want as much information as possible. This is not to say that advertisers are no longer trying to make these sites interesting and fun, but they are not investing hundreds of thousands of dollars in Web sites designed only to entertain and not educate the users on their wares. Web sites are required to fulfill clear business objectives.

Companies are learning to develop innovative Web strategies that move a potential customer from browser to buyer. For example, on the Cadillac site (www.cadillac.com), a consumer can plan every aspect of buying or leasing a new Cadillac through an interactive showroom. In the showroom, the consumer chooses the model of the car she is interested in and then the screen presents an image of that car. From that point, the user decides on the options she wants—from exterior color to interior design. Each time she chooses a feature, the sample car is redrawn on the screen to include the newly chosen option. After the user has composed her perfectly outfitted model, she is provided with a suggested retail price as well as financing options. From there the user can locate a dealer in her area. All of this is done in the comfort and privacy of the user's home; there are no set hours and no pushy car dealers.

Sometimes the product itself isn't conducive to a heavy information type site and a humorous approach works well. One of the first to succeed at this strategy was the Ragu spaghetti sauce site (www.eat.com). The site centers around Mama, the woman behind Ragu. The site offers humorous stories from Mama, interesting background information on Italy, and Italian lessons where Web-surfing parents can learn phrases such as "Clean your room, or no spaghetti for you tonight." The Ragu site was an instant hit receiving high traffic and tremendous publicity for blending content with the type of irreverent humor that the Internet audience adores.

The tradition of blending humor with information has progressed and we now have sites that are witty, informative, and successful. A good example of this genre is the Web site for the radio program Car Talk (www.cartalk.com). The Car Talk site uses irreverent humor to discuss the trials and tribulations of persistent car problems (see Figure 2.1a) as well as responding to letters from their audience (see Figure 2.1b). The site was designed and developed by Public Interactive (www.publicinteractive.com).

We're learning that brand credibility is most successful when the information offered is kept in context and on topic. An outstanding example of this is the site for Tide detergent, titled The Tide Clothesline (www.tide.com). One might think that there is little compelling content to place on a Web site for a laundry detergent. However, the designers of Tide kept clear of kitsch and instead came up with site features that have a high value to their customers. They start off by giving laundry tips and time-saving suggestions and then move on to one of the most valuable features of the site: "The Stain Detective" (www.tide.com/stainDet/) (see Figure 2.2). This page is a search

**Figure 2.1a** The Car Talk site uses humor to provide a wealth of information about "Lemon Laws."

**Figure 2.1b** Humor goes a long way in branding the Car Talk style of interacting with their customers.

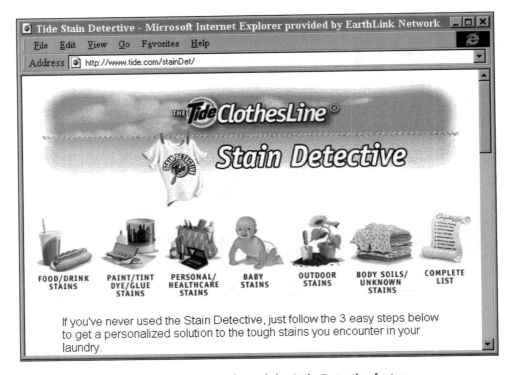

**Figure 2.2**    Tide adds value to its site through its Stain Detective feature.

engine providing extremely useful stain removal information, making the Tide site a valuable resource based on its own content alone.

Although our discussion has focused on Web site advertising, some brand/product sites fulfill other functions such as customer service. The Federal Express site (www.fedex.com), for example, does an excellent job of servicing its customers by offering package tracking; in that way, the site is an excellent tool for building brand loyalty and creating an image of a highly advanced delivery service—not to mention that the online service represents savings to the company (see Figure 2.3).

# Ad Models

Online advertising models make use of the Internet's two most popular applications: e-mail and the Web.

## Advertising via E-mail

What is the first thing people do after connecting to the Internet? They check their e-mail. Although e-mail is the most widely used Internet application, and an effective advertising vehicle, it is often overlooked by advertisers. When marketers hear about e-mail marketing, they often scoff at the idea, calling it spam. *Spam,* which is unsolicited

**Figure 2.3** | Federal Express makes customer service and ease of use top priorities.

e-mail messages and advertisements, is a dangerous marketing tactic that we do not recommend. However, there are many effective ways to use e-mail advertising, which we will discuss now, as well as in the next chapter, which covers Internet direct marketing.

## Sponsoring Discussion Lists and E-mail Newsletters

An e-mail newsletter is a publication created by a business or individual and then sent out to people by request. An e-mail discussion group, on the other hand, is made up of "conversations" that subscribers are having on a particular topic. Anyone who wants to contribute to the discussion sends a message to a moderator or an e-mail address that automatically sends the message to all subscribers. Most good e-mail discussion lists have a moderator who reviews all of the messages and decides which are appropriate to be sent to the entire list. This protects the list members from being inundated with irrelevant or unintelligible posts.

In most cases, subscribers to e-mail discussion lists can choose between receiving each message individually or receiving digests (compilations of all messages sent each day or week). There are currently thousands of niche discussion lists and newsletters on every subject imaginable. Table 2.1 lists directories of e-mail discussion lists and newsletters.

E-mail discussion lists and newsletters offer inexpensive and effective advertising opportunities for reaching a niche market. Advertisers can sponsor e-mail discussion lists for a week or month at a time.

**Table 2.1**    Directories of E-mail Discussion Lists and Newsletters

| DIRECTORY | URL |
| --- | --- |
| Yahoo List | (http://dir.yahoo.com/Computers_and_Internet/Internet/Mailing_Lists/Web_Directories/) |
| Liszt | (www.liszt.com) |
| Reference.com | (www.reference.com) |
| eGroups.com | (www.egroups.com/index.html) |
| The List of Lists | (http://tile.net/lists/) |
| Publicly Accessible Mailing Lists | (www.neosoft.com/internet/paml/) |

The benefit of sponsoring a discussion group or an e-mail newsletter is that it reaches a precisely targeted audience. Participants are not casual surfers checking out the content of a particular Web site; they are people who have taken action to subscribe to the list.

E-mail newsletters and discussion groups can be delivered as pure text or as HTML files, which allow messages to look like Web pages. Whether or not the recipient of the newsletter receives an HTML version depends on two things. First, the user needs to be using e-mail software that can read HTML e-mails. Second, the sender has to send HTML e-mails. Figure 2.4 shows an e-mail newsletter with text formatting, and Figure 2.5 shows an e-mail newsletter with HTML formatting.

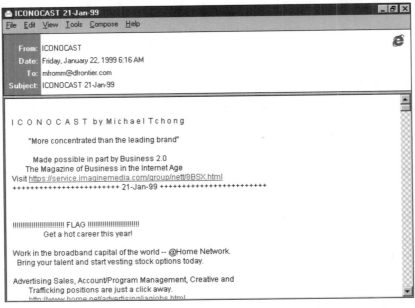

**Figure 2.4**    E-mail newsletter in text format. This is the beginning of the ICONOCAST e-mail newsletter.

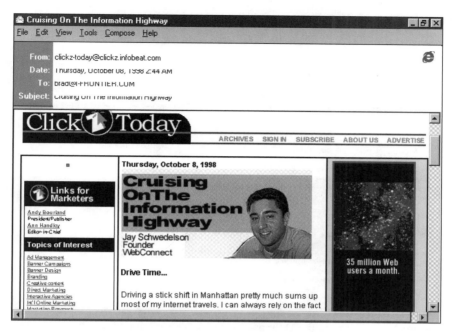

**Figure 2.5** E-mail newsletter as HTML, from ClickZ.

## Tips for Maximizing the Usefulness of E-mail Sponsorships

**Only sponsor moderated lists.** This increases the likelihood that your ad will not run alongside (and therefore be associated with) irrelevant posts to the list.

**Be introduced.** If you're sponsoring a moderated discussion list, ask the moderator to send out a note to the list introducing you as the sponsor. This tip comes from Richard Hoy, moderator of the Online Advertising discussion list (www.o-a.com). Figure 2.6 shows an example of a note that Hoy sends to his list to introduce a new advertiser.

**Request multiple placements.** In many cases an advertiser is the sole sponsor of a particular publication. If this is the case, the publisher of the list cannot place any other advertisers in the newsletters or discussion list posts that you sponsor. So, why not ask for multiple placements? Have different variations of your ad run in the beginning, middle, and end of the e-mail. You've just tripled your chances of getting a response.

**Make an offer.** Your ad is surrounding content that people want to read. A strong offer from a discount to a special give away will entice people to take action.

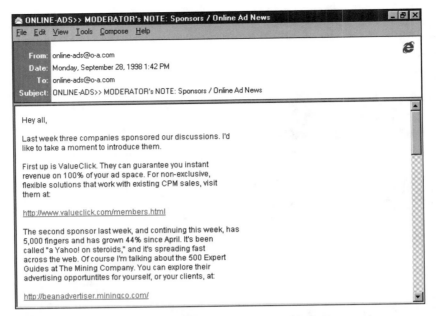

**Figure 2.6**   A note to the Online Advertising Discussion List sent by moderator Richard Hoy to introduce new advertisers.

When advertising in a text e-mail newsletter, the advertiser can know the total number of people who receive the e-mail message, because the sender can track exactly how many e-mails are sent. However, it is impossible to know how many people actually read the sponsorship text in the message. This is for two reasons. First, some people subscribe to a lot of newsletters and discussion groups that they don't read, because there isn't enough time in the day. And second, many people forward e-mail to others actually increasing the list's circulation. Another consideration is that in a text e-mail newsletter, an advertisement is plain text limiting the advertising to only a certain number of characters to convey its message. See Figure 2.7 for an example of a text sponsorship.

When you're sponsoring HTML e-mail, you can run the same banner and button advertisements that you run on the Web. Figure 2.8 shows an e-mail newsletter from Andover Update. This is an example of a banner ad within an HTML e-mail newsletter. There are benefits to sponsoring an HTML e-mail newsletter rather than a text newsletter. For starters, you can use a graphical advertisement, which will attract more attention than a text advertisement. Also, you'll know how many times the e-mail newsletter with your ad was opened. Every time an HTML e-mail is opened, the graphics are pulled from the publisher's ad server. By looking at the number of times your banner was pulled from the ad server, the publisher can give you an indication of the reach of your advertisement. (Text-based e-mail newsletters cannot provide this information, since they do not pull files from the server when the impressions can be counted.) On the

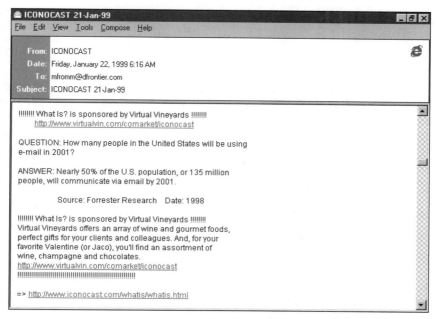

**Figure 2.7**  Virtual Vineyards e-mail sponsorships of ICONOCAST.

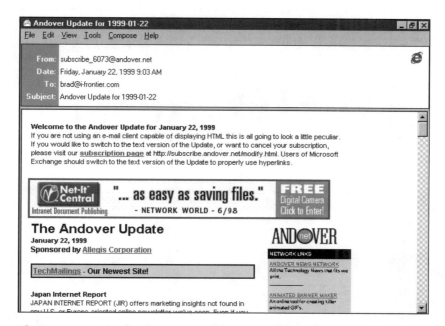

**Figure 2.8**  Example of an HTML ad in an e-mail newsletter.

other hand, HTML e-mail newsletters can be as cluttered as Web pages, making your ad less noticeable than an ad in a text-only newsletter.

### Direct E-mail

In addition to sponsoring discussion lists and e-mail newsletters, which usually give the advertiser only one or two lines of copy, advertisers are using direct e-mail. Early attempts at direct e-mail took the form of spam. Although companies are still using spam, it has proven to deliver extremely poor results (not to mention causing people to hate companies associated with spam). Acceptable direct e-mail advertising is sent to folks who have requested e-mail solicitations on a particular subject. A more thorough discussion of direct e-mail is provided in Chapter 3.

### Ad-Supported E-mail

Companies like Hotmail (www.hotmail.com), shown in Figure 2.9, Juno (www.juno.com), and USA.Net (www.usa.net) were some of the first marketers to offer free e-mail access to people who would use their e-mail readers, which display paid advertising. Now, most of the search engines and many additional Web sites offer free e-mail. For a list of free e-mail providers, you can visit:

http://dir.yahoo.com/Business_and_Economy/Companies/Internet_Services/
E-mail_Providers/Free_E-mail/

Most of these services require users to visit their Web site (and therefore have Internet access) to use the free e-mail. The exception is Juno. Juno provides complete Internet e-mail access (from the software to the dial-in connections) to anyone with a Windows-

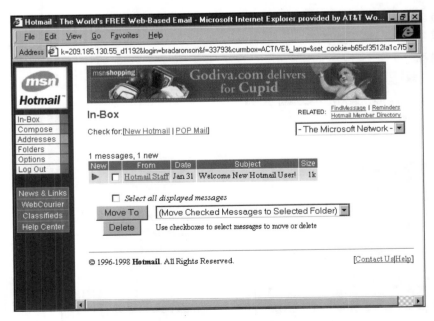

**Figure 2.9** Hotmail interface and advertisements.

compatible PC and a modem. No other software or Internet access is needed. To set up a Juno account, all a user must do is complete a demographic survey. And, of course, advertisers can target based on the answers. When the user sends and receives e-mail, Juno advertisements rotate on a timely basis (see Figure 2.10).

# Advertising via the Web

The bulk of online advertising is occurring on the Web. The Web, with its audio, video, and interactive capabilities, provides tremendous opportunity for effective and creative ad development.

## *Banners*

As we mentioned in Chapter 1, Web advertising began with banners, those rectangular graphics located on Web pages (Figure 2.11 displays a banner ad on PriceSCAN). Banners come in a range of sizes, but are usually around 7 inches wide by 1 inch deep or $468 \times 60$ pixels (see Figure 2.12 for a graphical representation of the standard banner ad units). Although advertisers and publishers have been saying that advertising must go "beyond the banner," this format currently receives the vast majority of Web ad spending and will continue to be a Web advertising staple for the foreseeable future.

The industry has now come to realize that we need banners; the key is to learn how to build better banners. There are three primary categories of banners: static, animated, and interactive.

**Figure 2.10**   Juno interface and advertisement.

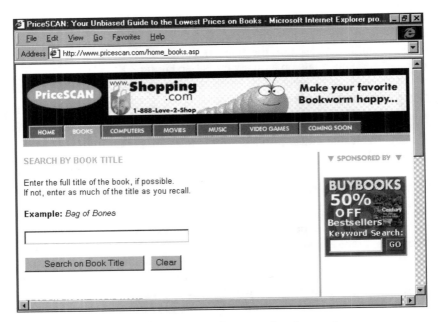

**Figure 2.11** PriceSCAN displaying a banner advertisement.

**Static banners.**   Static banners are fixed images on a site and were the first type of banner used in the early years of Web advertising. The advantages of a static banner are its ease of production and its universal acceptance by all sites. Its drawback is that with all the new innovations in banner ad technology, a static banner looks stale and boring. Additionally, static banners generate less user response than animated and interactive banners.

**Animated banners.**   These are banners that move or spin or have some form of action. They most often use GIF89 animation, which operates like the old flip books full of consecutive images. Most animated banners have from 2 to 20 frames. Animated banners are extremely popular, and with good reason. Animated banners pull higher click-through rates than static banners. With multiple frames, an animated banner can deliver more information and graphical impact than a static banner. Moreover, this type of banner is relatively inexpensive to produce and small in size, usually under 15 kilobytes.

**Interactive banners.**   When the call rang out for better banners, the interactive banner emerged. Interactive banners serve to engage the user in some way, either by playing a game, inserting information, answering a question, pulling down a menu, filling out a form, or making a purchase. These are ads that require direct interaction, which is more involving than a mere "click." Interactive banners are divided into two types: HTML and Rich Media.

**HTML banners.**   HTML banners are a low tech option that allows the consumer to enter data into the banner or make a choice from a pull-down or radio button menu

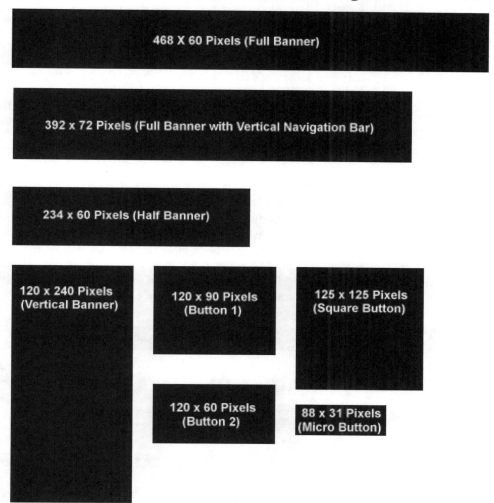

**Figure 2.12**    Graphical representation of the standard banner ad units.

within a banner. In our experience, HTML banners have had much higher response than animated banners. HTML banners allow a user to get involved: to choose which section of the site to visit, or to ask a question in the form, or to participate in a game (see Figures 2.13 and 2.14 for examples of HTML banners). This type of banner can be seen by a user with a low speed connection and an early version of a browser. The banner requires a few additional steps on the site's part to serve it up, but is quickly receiving broad acceptance.

**Rich media.**    This is the incorporation of advanced technology into the banner ad itself.

Stop the madness of searching online.

Find it here: [            ] Go

**Figure 2.13a** This is an HTML banner for the Internet portal site 4anything.com. The banner's text plays on the frustration of searching online and the graphic ties into 4anything's television advertising, which compares searching on most portals to a wild goose chase. In this advertisement, the user can type a search query into the banner, instead of having to click on the banner and start searching after arriving at the site. See Figure 2.13b to see what happens after a search query is entered.

## Rich Media Banners

When we wrote the first edition of this book, push (discussed later in this chapter) was the hot topic that everyone was discussing. As of the writing of this book, rich media is the current craze. Tom Hespos, media manager of K2 Design, defines rich media as: "any new technology that allows for either a more detailed advertising message to be presented, or for a higher level of interactivity than you might get in a standard GIF banner." Rich media is considered higher bandwidth advertising that delivers more of a brand impact than a GIF-animated banner advertisement.

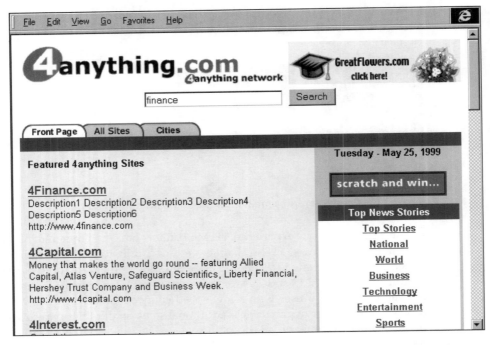

**Figure 2.13b** After typing in the query, the user goes to a search results page. This example is the search results page for "finance."

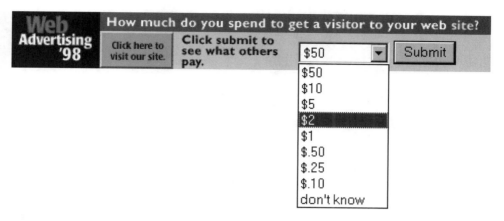

**Figure 2.14a**   This banner asks the question that is on the minds of many media buyers: "How much do you pay to get a vistor to your Web site? After the media buyer chooses an answer from a pull-down menu, she goes to a page that is a real-time tabulation of all the answers so far. Response rates can be high in a banner like this, because it allows for user interactivity.

Rich media banners allow a consumer to complete a transaction within the advertisement without ever leaving the publisher's Web site. A consumer usually visits a Web site to read the content, which makes it difficult to lure the consumer away—even with an enticing banner. However, if an advertiser can make a great offer in the banner, and

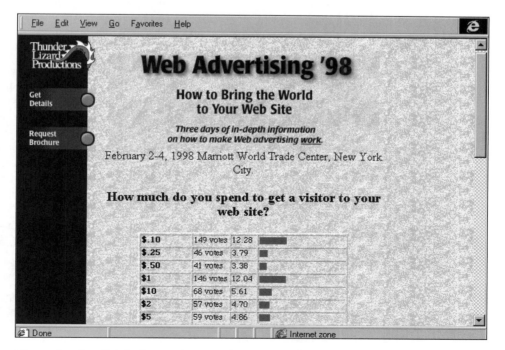

**Figure 2.14b**   This is the results page that a media buyer receives.

**Figure 2.15**  The Hewlett Packard Java pong game ad.

the consumer can complete a transaction or receive the entire advertising message through the banner without leaving the Web site, it seems logical that the consumer will be more responsive.  One of the early rich media banners used java programing to bring its banners to life and was developed for Hewlett Packard. The goal of the ad was to deliver the message: "HP is a high tech company that is on the cutting edge." To convey this message, HP didn't need to drive traffic to its Web site. HP created a banner advertisement that was actually the game Pong (see Figure 2.15). Consumers could play the game within the banner, which contained the HP logo. To our knowledge, HP's ad was the first banner that contained a game. The game was incredibly popular, and HP's target audience spent a lot of time playing this game and thinking about how "cool" HP was.

Java ad banners can also allow consumers to order a product from within the banner. This feature is ideal for taking advantage of consumers' impulse-buying habits by facilitating the entire buying process from the banner ad itself. Figure 2.16 is the Java banner for 1-800-FLOWERS that allows customers to order Mother's Day flowers directly through the banner ad.

Rich media as a general term is used to denote ads that make use of advanced technology. Let's look at some of the technology used to enhance banner ads.

### InterVU

Using InterVU (www.intervu.com) technology, a banner can display a short video clip from within a window in the banner. InterVU calls this its V-Banner. The looping video clips are usually 3 to 5 seconds. Despite the quality of the video, advertisers have found that InterVU banners can increase response rates; probably, this is because a video banner has the potential to stand out more than an animated banner. InterVU hosts these high bandwidth ads (and content) for Web publishers so that the publishers don't have slowdowns on their sites when a lot of people request high-bandwidth, rich media ads. Figure 2.17 shows an InterVU V-Banner for Cobra Golf. The right side of that banner has a video clip of a golfer swinging.

**Figure 2.16**  1-800-FLOWERS ad that allows consumers to order Mother's Day flowers through the banner.

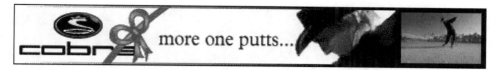

**Figure 2.17** InterVU V-Banner ad for Cobra Golf.

Another good example of an InterVU banner is the one that was developed for the movie *Air Force One*. The looping video on the right side of the banner catches the viewer's attention. The video certainly stands out more than any of the animated GIFs that might be on the page competing for the user's attention. It is important to note that InterVU banners are GIF banners that include a video portion. The video takes more time than a GIF to load. This means that even when users leave the site before the video in the ad has loaded, they will still see the GIF ad.

### RealAudio and RealVideo (www.real.com)

RealAudio and RealVideo (www.real.com) technology allow vibrant audio and video to be incorporated into the banner. Advertisers can use a variety of combinations of audio and video in these ads. For example, an advertiser can have the banner play audio when the a is downloading or after it is clicked. Figure 2.18 shows a RealAudio/Video ad developed by Modem Media.Poppe Tyson for Reebok. In the middle there is video of Allen Iverson playing basketball (something sure to attract the attention of surfers of NBA.com, which is where this ad ran). There is also audio of him talking about basketball with a commentator. The combination makes it enticing for a user to click through on the ad.

### Narrative Communications' Enliven Technology

Narrative Communications' Enliven technology (www.enliven.com) delivers a small Java applet allowing for transactions to be completed within a banner.

Figure 2.19 is a Hewlett Packard Enliven ad. This ad allows users to print out spec sheets for HP's LaserJet 3100. Figure 2.20a-b shows an Enliven ad used by Eddie Bauer. This ad allows a consumer to order from within the banner; the order is tied directly into Eddie Bauer's system.

One of the benefits of an Enliven ad is that surfers can complete a transaction (requesting something or even making a purchase) without leaving the content site, encouraging the consumer to buy on impulse. However, these banners can take a long time to load. Some publishers have even complained that ads like Enliven slow down their site. In any event, as the technology to make the downloads faster improves, this will be a great means of making banners more interactive.

### Macromedia's Flash

Macromedia's Flash (www.macromedia.com/software/flash) is a series of audio-visual players that allow a user to view streaming content, which means the user can

**Figure 2.18**    Reebok's RealAudio/Video banner ad.

see the ad as it is downloading instead of having to wait for the entire ad to download before seeing anything. Because the content is streamed, it doesn't take long to download the ad, so a banner ad that utilizes Flash will have more animation than an animated GIF that is the same file size. However, a user must have the plug-in to view this ad. As with other rich media ads, the publisher can serve the ad in such a way that only surfers who have the plug-in will receive the rich advertisement, while other folks will receive an advertisement that they can use with their plug-ins and browser.

### Thinking Media's ActiveAds

Thinking Media's ActiveAds (www.thethinkingmedia.com/activeads/activeads.html) allow advertisers to create banner ads with which users can have a high level of interactivity and complete transactions. ActiveAds banners can include features such as secure, in-banner credit card transactions, subscription forms, games, animation, and streaming audio—delivered in a basic "player" file of 5 KB. Thinking Media's Java-based ads can be created with a software developer kit (Sonata). Sonata consists of a number of reusable Java components for such features as text animation, image animation, streaming audio, real-time polls, real-time auctions, subscription forms, frequent flyer miles, SSL credit card transactions, decision trees in-banner, clickable news tickers, games, quizzes, and timers. Thinking Media also provides a tracking feature, ActiveTrack, which reports what happens *inside* the banner: how long a banner was visible to the user on the screen, how much time surfers actually spent on average interacting with it, as well as information specific to tracking an individual banner.

Figure 2.21 is an example of an ActiveAds banner for HomePC. The first frame is an offer for a free issue of the magazine. A user is instructed to drag the sticker to the other side of the banner. This makes the offer pop onto the screen, and then an order form appears. The user can order right from within the banner.

**Figure 2.19**    HP's Enliven banner, which allows people to print a spec sheet from the banner.

**Figure 2.20a** Eddie Bauer's Enliven banner presents the consumer with an offer to purchase pants within the banner.

| Eddie Bauer | Select Size and Quantity | | | |
|---|---|---|---|---|
| | Cut | Waist | Inseam | Quantity |
| CANCEL CONTINUE | ● Regular ○ Long Rise | 29 | 30 | 1 |

**Figure 2.20b** After a consumer clicks the banner, he can answer various questions within the banner to complete the purchase.

Figure 2.22 is an example of an ActiveAds banner from CDnow. This ad offers users a chance to win a $10 discount. As you can see from the pictures, users can choose a quiz category and answer the question in the banner. If they get the question right, the banner congratulates them and offers them a discount. If they get it wrong, they are encouraged to "try again." This is a fun banner that encourages people to interact with the advertisement. We think it's great for promoting a brand or service. However, e-commerce advertisers with the goal of selling products should test this carefully. The ad, while it can certainly be great for a branding experience, can create the appearance that there are additional barriers to overcome before simply purchasing a product; users may fear that they have to participate in a game or some other process, when they really want to take advantage of a discount and continue surfing.

## Both Sides of Rich Media

Many publishers and advertisers see rich media as the way to get more advertising dollars committed to the Web. These marketers have primarily expressed an interest in using rich media to improve Internet advertising's branding efforts. A banner is usually only the size of six postage stamps, and the file size is usually only around 10 KB. This doesn't leave much space for a message, or much KB size to use video or audio to better convey a message. Marketers often say that TV is much more powerful, because the full motion video and audio allow for more emotional advertisements. Marketers are

**Figure 2.21** ActiveAds banner for HomePC.

**Figure 2.22a**    ActiveAds banner for CDnow (introductory animation).

**Figure 2.22b**    ActiveAds banner for CDnow (quiz question).

**Figure 2.22c**    ActiveAds banner for CDnow (discount offer).

hoping that rich media will provide a step towards better branding opportunities through Internet advertising. Rich media's market penetration is growing, as presented in Table 2.2.

Rich media is not without its critics. There are many who feel that since most users still connect to the Internet through low bandwidth, the push toward rich media is premature. AOL, which connects more people to the Internet than any service in the world, refuses to use rich media for this very reason. Some interesting arguments for

**Table 2.2**    Rich Media Penetration

| PLAYER/FILE TYPE | PENETRATION | SOURCE |
| --- | --- | --- |
| Java (Director, Flash, Emblaze, Enliven, AdController, Microsites, etc.) | 76% | InterVU |
| QuickTime | 86% | Apple Computer |
| MPEG | 80% | Microsoft |
| AVI | 79% | Microsoft |
| RealPlayer | 65% | RealNetworks |
| Shockwave | 20% | Macromedia |
| Flash | 35% | Macromedia |
| Cosmo Player | 20% | Cosmo Software |

Source: Rich Media Handbook produced by InterVU, 1998

## Beware the Cost of Implementation

High technology banners, which use rich media, can be great for increasing response. However, a lot of time must go into technology-enhanced banners, and we're not just talking about the creation of the advertisements. Getting Web sites to display your advertisements correctly and getting their ad serving software to work with these ads is very time consuming. In some cases we've found that the cost of the additional time actually surpasses the value in the increased responsiveness from the ad.

Another note of warning is that many rich media ads require a user to have a particular plug-in. In those cases you want to make sure an alternative ad is delivered to the users who don't have the plug-in. Otherwise a good number of people may not see anything. Also be sure to check the download speeds of technology-enhanced banners. They're often much slower than is desirable. Keep in mind that few people will wait for an ad to download. To determine the percentage of sites that will take your rich media advertisements, look at Figure 2.23. This chart was created by AdKnowledge from their database of Web sites that accept advertising.

| Ad Technology | Accepting Sites |
| --- | --- |
| • Active Ads | 52 |
| • Enliven | 215 |
| • HTML | 606 |
| • Java | 535 |
| • JavaScript | 275 |
| • MicroSites | 66 |
| • RealAudio | 178 |
| • Shockwave | 304 |
| • V-Banner | 133 |
| • VRML | 87 |

Data from January 1999.

**Figure 2.23**   The ChannelSeven.com rich media Report Card provides a summary of Web sites and the rich media formats they accept. This information is provided by AdKnowledge, a directory of Web sites that accept advertising. The data is self-reported by the sites.

# Building Better Banners

Advertisers can precisely measure the response to their banner advertisements via the aforementioned click-through determinations. (Chapter 4 has more on Web measurement and tracking.) This tracking capability has led advertisers to continually test new banners to see if they will achieve higher response rates. Here are some hints for creating a responsive banner ad:

**Pay attention to placement.**    Some sites will outperform others for an advertiser. The more focused a site is on the target audience, the better the response. In addition to finding a focused site, advertisers should pay particular attention to finding the best pages within a site. Performance on two pages of the same site can differ enormously. As Kevin O'Connor, CEO of DoubleClick, an advertising network, points out: "The best-performing page on a poor-performing site will outperform the worst page on a good-performing site."

**Chart frequency—how often a particular user sees a particular ad.**    According to research performed by DoubleClick and I/Pro, users are most likely to respond the first one to two times they see a banner ad. Response drops significantly after the second time.

**Call to action.**    Why should users click on the banner? Do they win a prize? Receive a discount? Without a reason to click, there is no incentive for a user to leave a publisher's Web site. The incentive should be relevant to the site on which you're advertising. Obviously, a sports offer will work better on ESPN's Web site than on the Epicurious food Web site. "Free" works well, but you won't always get the most qualified audience.

**Add "click here" to your banners.**    Banners with "click here" consistently pull better than those without. There will always be new users of the Web, many of whom won't know where to click. This may also explain why some advertisements have a better response rate when there is hyperlinked text underneath the ad. Hypertext links signal to even the newest users that something is clickable.

**Create a sense of urgency.**    Give users a reason to "click now."

**Do not use too much text.**    Encourage users to look at the banner with a simple offer and design.

**Incorporate animation.**    The banner is a small portion of the Web page, and there are a lot of other graphics and text competing for a user's attention. Animation makes a banner stand out.

**Try HTML and rich media banners.**    Rich media banners tend to have higher click-through rates. So, if the sites on which you advertise accept rich media, give it a try.

**Make good use of colors.**    Use colors that stand out. These will differ depending on the colors used by the site on which you are advertising.

**Rotate banners.**    Using multiple banners throughout a campaign almost always increases response.

and against rich media are presented in the editorials at the end of this chapter by leaders in the online ad industry: Ali Partovi, product manager and original partner of LinkExchange, and Richard Hopple, chairman and CEO of Unicast Communications.

A nice resource for rich media information is ChannelSeven's TurboAds site (www. turboads.com/index.shtml). This site, which is built for the advertising community, has numerous case studies and information about rich media technologies.

### The Branding Power of Banners

The role of banner advertisements is changing. Banner ads used to be used for the sole purpose of getting a Web surfer to click and go to an advertiser's Web site. Consumer responsiveness to banners has been dropping. When we wrote the first edition of this book, the average click-through rate (the number of times someone clicks a banner ad divided by the number of times the ad is seen) was 2 percent. According to NetRatings (www.netratings.com), the click-through rate has been steadily dropping, and, as of this writing, it is below 1 percent. To maintain the effectiveness of their advertising, advertisers and agencies must either negotiate lower rates or find Web advertisements that will supplement banners to increase the overall response to a campaign. Advertisers have realized that they need to get a benefit beyond clicks from their banner ads.

Advertisers are now looking to derive a branding value from their ads. For example, most advertisers do (and all advertisers should) keep at least a corner of their banners for a brand image. This allows advertisers to deliver some sort of a message to those people who don't click! Advertisers have also begun to purchase more sponsorships and advertorials, which allows them to integrate their message or call to action within the content, and, in some cases, to deliver their message without forcing the user to leave the site. Studies, such as those conducted by Millward Brown Interactive (www.mbinteractive) and the Internet Advertising Bureau (www.mbinteractive.com/site/iab/study.html) are showing the strong branding ability of banners. And according to a 1999 study by Ipsos-ASI and AOL, consumers are as likely to remember an online banner ad as a television commercial.

## Testing

In the early days of banner development (1994 to 1995), very little was known about the dynamics of banner ads on the Web. The same banner would be sent to every site, though admittedly the list of sites was short. Today, the rigorous testing of banners by advertisers and publishers has helped maximize response rates. Rich Boyce, VP of advertising at HotWired, advises, "Be prepared to test, learn, and evolve. Make adjustments as needed. And remember that a Web advertisement is always a work in progress. It's a continual process of refinement. Unlike a television commercial that once produced is done, with Web advertising, the creative is never done."

One of the benefits of advertising on the Web is the ease, accuracy, and speed with which you can conduct a performance test. Ad management software facilitates real-time reporting for banner testing. Most banner campaigns begin with several ads that are tested over a 24-hour period before they are refined and tested again. Consequently, the resulting banners used in the full campaign have been well researched for maximum click-through effectiveness. Conducting banner ad testing is relatively inexpensive—a banner ad test costs a few thousand dollars, whereas a test of a TV commercial costs tens of thousands of dollars.

Banners only give advertisers limited space with which to promote their brands or sell their products, so it is essential to make the most of that real estate. No doubt we will continue to see major changes in banner creatives as advertisers strive to effectively use a banner's space. Advertisers will also begin to use other forms of advertising, such as sponsorship (which we discuss later in this chapter), that give them the opportunity to use more online real estate to promote their brands.

## Buttons

Buttons are small banner-type advertisements that can be placed anywhere on a page and are linked to the button sponsor. Buttons were embraced by consumers and advertisers throughout the Web faster than banner advertisements—probably because they always led to free downloadable software.

One of the first of these campaigns was the "Download Netscape Now" button. Scott Heiferman, CEO of i-traffic (www.i-traffic.com), helped get that campaign started, and brought a grassroots enthusiasm to the program. The i-traffic team surfed the Web for sites that posted text stating that they were "optimized for Netscape." Hundreds of sites with this listing were contacted by i-traffic and offered a T-shirt if they switched to the button. Hundreds of T-shirts later, the Netscape Now button is a standard on Web sites. If imitation is the greatest form of flattery, button campaigns are flattering indeed. Proof positive is that the Microsoft Internet Explorer launch had a strong "download button" component.

The benefit of buttons, especially download buttons, is that they are simple in what they offer. A person clicks on a download button because he or she wants to download the software immediately. And, since the Web community is a strong market for software, buttons have resulted in millions of software downloads.

Buttons can also help advertisers build brand awareness. The ubiquitous Download Netscape Now button not only led to large numbers of software downloads, but also helped familiarize Web users with Netscape and establish it as the first leader in browser market share.

Buttons are commonly used as a way to have a constant presence in specific Web content without paying the high fee of banner advertisements. Figure 2.24 shows a Lycos page with two buttons: one for CDnow and one for barnesandnoble.com. These ad placements work well for the publisher and the advertiser. The publisher can offer advertisers button ads on every page of the site. This builds a nice brand awareness for the advertiser, and with the correct offer, these buttons can generate high response

**Figure 2.24** Button ads for CDnow and barnesandnoble.com go down the right column of the page.

rates. The publisher can have multiple buttons on a page (since they don't take up a lot of space) and still have 100 percent of the banner inventory left to sell. To increase the response rate of button advertisements, advertisers often include text specific to the content alongside the button. For example, Figure 2.25 shows a button ad for Amazon on Yahoo! Above the button ad there is always text related to the search performed by the user. In this case, the Yahoo! search was for "goats" and the text above the button reads, "Buy Books on Goats." This type of customization based on the user's search query will significantly increase response rates.

Some button advertisements are large enough that they are the most noticeable advertisement on the page. Figure 2.26 shows a page from PriceSCAN (a price search engine). The button advertisement stands out more than any other element on the page. Not surprisingly, PriceSCAN said that their button advertisements are in higher demand than any of their other ad units. In general button advertisements are good for publishers because it gives them additional inventory to sell—another ad unit on each page. Of course, this has to be balanced with issues of page clutter and number of ads, both of which can reduce advertising effectiveness.

## Text Links

Text links are some of the least intrusive, yet most effective advertisements. In the online advertising industry most of the commotion is related to finding new ways to

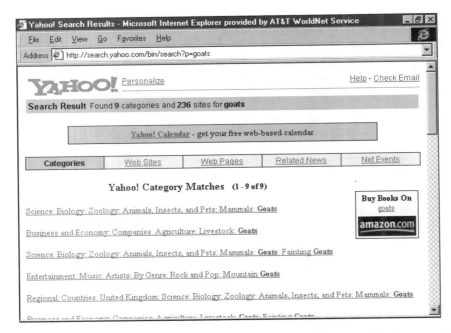

**Figure 2.25** Button ad on the right for Amazon.com with customized text on Yahoo!

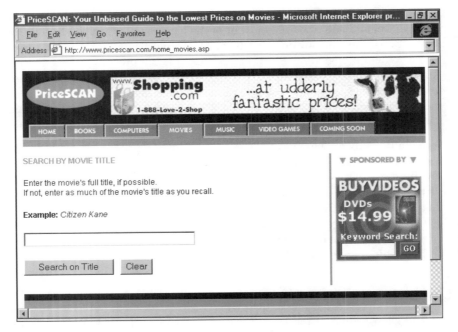

**Figure 2.26** PriceSCAN identifies its button ads as sponsors.

advertise at a higher bandwidth. However, sometimes the least bandwidth-intensive and simplest of advertisements can be most effective.

One example of a text link is Figure 2.27. Here you see an AltaVista search that was performed for the keyword "superman." To the right of the search results is a text advertisement paid for by the bookseller Amazon.com. The advertisement tells users to go to "Books about superman." Amazon has the text link change to match whatever search the user performs. The power of these text ads is that they can be tailored to any search a consumer performs on AltaVista; this would be impossible through a banner campaign. As we mentioned in the previous section, a button ad along with a text ad can also be very effective.

Another text link example is from the search engine Lycos. Lycos sells a text link that will appear as the first search result when someone performs a search. In Figure 2.28 we have performed a search for allergy medicine "Claritin." The text ad that pops up says, "Bullseye! The Claritin relief zone." This is a paid advertisement from Claritin even though it looks very much like it's the first text listing that Lycos found, rather than an ad.

Many folks in the online ad industry believe that this is a compromise of editorial integrity. We believe it will become commonplace as Web sites search for more advertising revenue streams and advertisers search for more effective means of reaching consumers.

**Figure 2.27**   A text ad from Amazon.com on AltaVista.

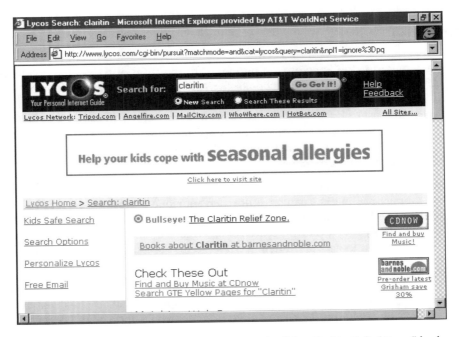

**Figure 2.28** The "Bullseye" text ad on Lycos for "The Claritin Relief Zone" looks very much like editorial content, which is why it is so effective.

Some sites sell text listings as one of their main advertising staples. One example is the Year 2000 Web site (www.year2000.com), which is published by the Tenagra Corporation. This site is a comprehensive resource for people who have to deal with the computer problems that will be caused by the Y2K. If you look at Figure 2.29, you'll see the extensive amount of text link advertisements that they sell; all of the listings on the left side of the Web page are paid advertising. These text ads serve as a resource for Web site users; folks visiting the Web site want to find computer companies that address the Y2K problem. If this resource list had been in a graphical format rather than a text format, it would have been much more difficult to use. This is, in effect, a directory like Yahoo!, but all listings are purchased.

## Sponsorships

Sponsoring a Web site can take many forms, most of which lead to placements that are beyond typical banner buys. Sponsorships allow an advertiser to have a successful ad campaign without necessarily having to drive traffic to its Web site. Consumers trust the brands that they visit repeatedly to get information. So, delivering your message within such trusted brands can often make that message more powerful. Indeed, sponsorships are on the rise.

An early, very effective sponsorship (an example from the first edition we couldn't possibly remove; it's one of our favorites) was Dockers' sponsorship on HotWired. HotWired was able to smoothly integrate Dockers' content into its Dream Jobs

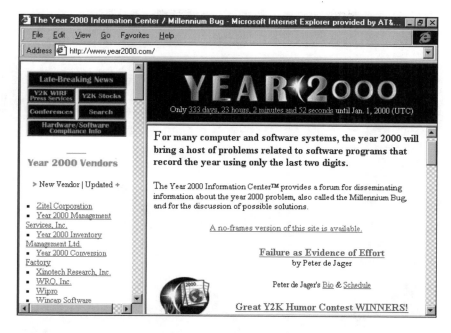

**Figure 2.29**    The Year 2000 Web site has text advertisements running down the left side of the page.

(www.dreamjobs.com) Web site. (Dream Jobs has since been fully integrated into the HotWired Web site.) Dream Jobs lists employment openings that are considered ideal for its hip, technologically savvy audience. Next to the job descriptions is a meter that rates the jobs based on the dress code. The meter includes the categories "cut off khakis," "stone-washed khakis," and "monkey suit." Dockers clearly conveys a message: Dockers are cool—at cool jobs you can wear them. Levi's doesn't need to drive anyone to the Dockers Web site to succeed with this campaign.

Many sponsorships relate to a specific aspect or feature of a site. Chapstick, a product associated with both cold and hot weather, sponsors the Intellicast Weather site (see Figure 2.30). Charles Schwab sponsors the personal stock tracker on Excite (see Figure 2.31). Excite lets users create their own home pages. Users can choose to have a number of stock quotes appear on their home pages. Those quotes will then appear as stock tickers incorporating advertisements for Schwab. This is a perfect placement; if a user sees that the stocks he is tracking are rapidly moving, he can click the Schwab link to open an account and start trading. Schwab is targeting folks at the point where they will be likely to switch from an imaginary portfolio to actual trading.

# Advertorial

An advertorial is a sponsorship that looks more like an editorial than like an advertisement. In print publications, advertisements that resemble editorials have a clear

**Figure 2.30** Chapstick sponsorship on the Intellicast Weather Site.

**Figure 2.31** Charles Schwab sponsorship of the stock ticker on Excite.

label that usually reads something along the lines of "special advertising section." On the Web, there is usually no clear indication that advertorial areas aren't editorial

Because consumers trust editorials, advertorials will often have a higher response rate than other Web advertisements. However, advertisers must be careful not to create a negative brand impression by causing consumers to feel deceived; they clicked on something that looked like editorial content, only to discover that it was actually an ad. (Publishers also need to be careful. You don't want to upset your greatest asset: the people who visit your Web site.) Advertorials will be very effective if they deliver the content a consumer expects to receive. On the other hand, if the consumer does not receive that content, the ads will backfire and probably cause a negative brand impression.

A great advertorial example is accessed when a user conducts an Infoseek search for the keyword "health"—and a link to go to the "health news and info" area on Infoseek appears (see Figure 2.32). This area has various text listings, including "Conditions A-Z" and "-in-depth reports" on specific problems. These all look like editorial links, but the links go to OnHealth (www.onhealth.com), a health site that advertises on Infoseek.

**Figure 2.32**   Results of a Search on Infoseek using the keyword "health."

Another example comes from Better Health (www.betterhealth.com, see Figures 2.33a and 2.33b). One editorial option on the Better Health site is "Skin care options for aging skin. . . ." Clicking on the link takes the user to a co-branded site that is actually sponsored by Renova, a product to help aging skin. The benefit to Renova is that it gets the credibility of teaming with the respected Better Health site, which already reaches its target market.

## Push Technology

Advertisements delivered through *push* technology are sent (usually with content) directly to a user rather than waiting for the user to appear. Push technology includes e-mail, which was already discussed in a previous section of this chapter. The push technology explored here includes other systems that enable Web users to sign up to receive information broadcast to their computers.

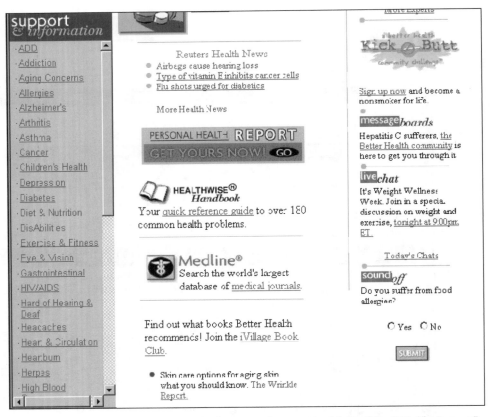

**Figure 2.33a**    Renova text ad on the bottom of Better Health for "The Wrinkle Report."

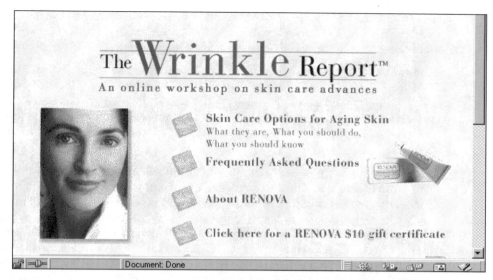

**Figure 2.33b** "The Wrinkle Report" is a Renova co-branded Web site on Better Health.

PointCast (www.pointcast.com) is one of the many players offering push technology. After downloading the PointCast client (software), users can request that PointCast send them news updates on specific topics. When they register, consumers choose what types of information are of interest to them (stock quotes, news headlines, etc.). Then, when the consumer's computer is idle, a PointCast screensaver appears, containing the information the consumer requested, along with advertisements. This system works best when the computer is always connected to the Internet, such as with a direct connection. But it can work on a dial-in basis.

The main problem some advertisers have with PointCast is that the ads only appear when a computer is idle, and an idle computer often means that the monitor is not being watched. On the other hand, the ad could be seen by many more people in the same office.

## Interstitials

Interstitials are advertisements that pop onto the screen and interrupt users. They are sometimes called "pop-ups," "e-mercials, or "intermercials." This ad model is similar to television ads in that the ad interrupts programming. Interstitials come in different sizes (taking up all of the screen or only pieces) and with different levels in interactivity, from static to fully animated productions. Users can sometimes dismiss the interstitial by clicking out of it (which they can't do with television ads), but there is no warning as to when the ads will appear or reappear.

Advertisers like the prospects of using interstitials because these advertisements are sure to be noticed. Indeed, every AOL user can attest to the fact that one can't help but notice the static pop-up ads that greet the user upon opening AOL (see Figure 2.34).

Some interstitials give advertisers an opportunity to use animated or full-motion video (full-motion video is usually limited to interstitials delivered through push vehicles). Advertisers certainly have a better opportunity to get their brand message across when they are not competing with anything else on the screen and can use more images and screen real estate (see Figure 2.35 for an example of an interstitial advertisement).

The downside to interstitials is that publishers and advertisers need to be very cautious not to upset consumers. The Internet began as a medium for the free exchange of information, and at the beginning, there were no advertisements. There's a small minority of people who feel that the commercialization of the Web is bad and that all advertising is bad. Those aren't the people we worry about (unless they're your target audience). We worry about the average consumers who are accustomed to controlling their Web experience; they choose what sites to visit and what to click. These consumers are often upset and bothered that a site and advertiser will force them to see an interstitial. To avoid this, many sites are now using interstitials that are daughter windows (small windows that pop up over the browser and only take up 1/8 of the screen).

Here are some rules that will help ensure that your interstitials don't upset consumers:

**Choose sites already using interstitials.** Interstitials usually have the best response when they're placed on a site that has run this type of advertisement in the past; con-

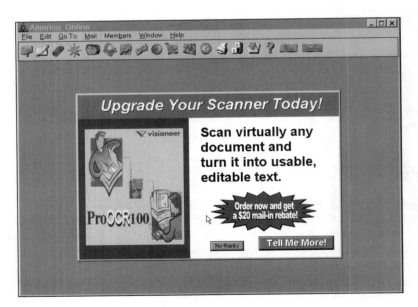

**Figure 2.34** Pop-up ad on AOL.

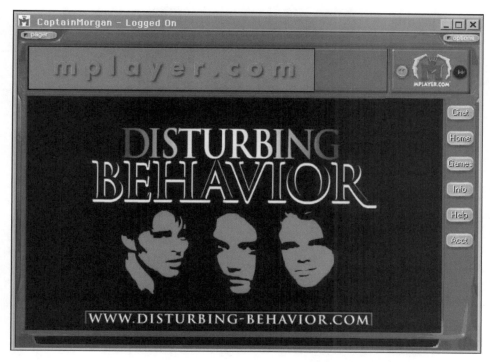

**Figure 2.35**   Interstitial for the MGM release of the movie *Disturbing Behavior* using MPath technology.

sumers are expecting them. For example, consumers know that Berkley Systems' "You Don't Know Jack" Web site has had interstitial ads since its inception, and interstitials are accepted there.

**Try interstitials that are smaller than a full page.** These are less obtrusive than a full-page interstitial and seem to be better received by consumers. These small pop-ups take only a quarter of the page and appear in a separate window on top of the browser.

**Use interstitials when a user's screen would otherwise be idle.**   The interstitial shown in Figure 2.36 appears while software is downloading. This eliminated negative feelings about the ad, because it was not preempting any content; it appeared while their screen was idle.

**Interstitials can be interactive.**   Unicast (www.unicast.com) is being used for some exciting interactive campaigns, from sample requests (see Figure 3.12) to other transactional pop-ups.

The interaction can be made into a game, as happens on BoxerJam, a game show site (www.boxerjam.com) where users actually compete against each other in a format

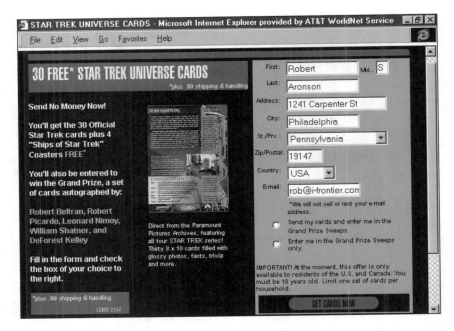

**Figure 2.36**  Star Trek Universe cards interstitial.

resembling a traditional TV game show. BoxerJam GameShow uses "intermercials" (another term used for interstitials) before the game and between rounds. The ads are used to build brand awareness, drive traffic to a site, and to offer the player an interactive experience through the ad, as demonstrated in Figure 2.37, an ad for Omaha Steaks on the BoxerJam site.

**Figure 2.37**  Omaha Steaks "intermercial" on the BoxerJam site.

# A Few More Ad Models outside the Box

Not all ad models can fit neatly into the categories we've listed in this chapter, so we've written this section to cover those new ad models that that are outside the current category box.

## New Screen Real Estate

The first ad model that breaks the mold is delivered through Alexa (www.alexa.com). Alexa is a Web navigation service that works with your browser and accompanies you as you surf, providing useful information about the sites you are viewing and suggesting related sites. Alexa isn't so much a new ad model as a redefining of available ad real estate. The Alexa toolbar travels with users as they surf the Internet. Alexa sells advertising on its toolbar, which is visible to users no matter what site they are visiting, giving advertisers a presence on any site on the Web (see Figure 2.38) In fact, using Alexa you can place your advertising "on" any site on the Web whether that site accepts advertising or not. "Alexa lets you do a competitive stealth play," explains Doug Hansen, Director of Advertising Sales with Alexa. "For example, if you're a major bookseller, you can advertise on your chief competitor's site by advertising on the toolbar

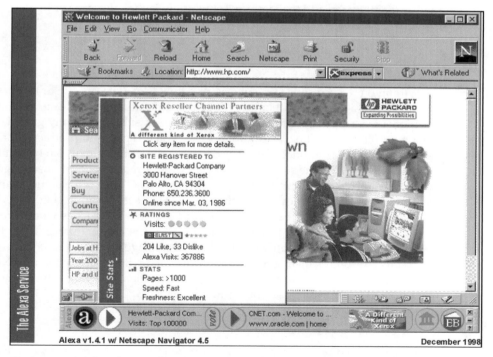

**Figure 2.38**  The Alexa toolbar lets you place advertising on any site on the Web.

just as the consumer is about to purchase a book. This advertising approach cannot be replicated in traditional site-based ad models." The only limit to the reach of Alexa is the number of people who use their service. As of the writing of this book, Alexa has said that over 1 million people have downloaded their software.

Another exploration of new real estate for advertising space comes from Aureate Media (www.aureatemedia.com), which puts banner ads on software programs themselves. Aureate also hosts the AdSoftware Network, which is composed of a group of software products that have the ability to display electronic advertising.

## Screensavers

The entire screensaver itself can be an advertisement. SaveScreen.com (www.savescreen .com) allows consumers to build their own personalized screensavers containing integrated advertising.

## Bookmarks and Toolbars

Bookmarks and toolbar buttons on the browser are now available for sale for advertising. Advertisers are paying for premium placement on a user's browser. Advertisers can also be found on browser toolbars. 100hot SurfBoard (www.web21.com/ surfboard/), a product of Web21 and AdNet Strategies, allows users to download a toolbar that they can add to their browser window (either Netscape or Explorer) which contains the advertiser's logo as a link (see Figure 2.39).

## Cursors

Everything on the screen is fair game as an ad vehicle. Even the cursor can be turned into an ad, for a unique form of branding. Comet Systems (www.cometsystems.com) has pioneered a way to customize the mouse cursor, substituting any graphic or animation for the conventional arrow. In this way, you can put your product's image on a user's browser for continual branding. For example, a flower shop can have its cursor be a flower, and when the cursor moves over flower arrangements, it can change to display special discounts. Another example, provided by Comet, is a weather map where the cursor changes as it moves over the map to reflect the weather conditions in each city (see Figure 2.40). The custom cursors will only work for users who have downloaded the Comet Systems software. The download is an easy process, but because users must download this software, it will be a challenge for Comet Systems to get significant reach—unless their software comes bundled with future versions of Netscape and Explorer. Once the software is on your system, you can see the advertising curser when you go to a site that uses the Comet curser.

## Undervalued Web Space

Nothing is wasted on the Web, not even a page that could be considered a dead end. Columbus Group (www.columbus-group.com), out of Vancouver, British Columbia,

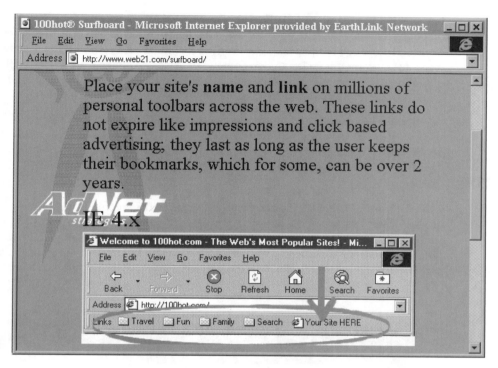

**Figure 2.39** 100hot SurfBoard lets an advertiser buy a link on a user's browser toolbar.

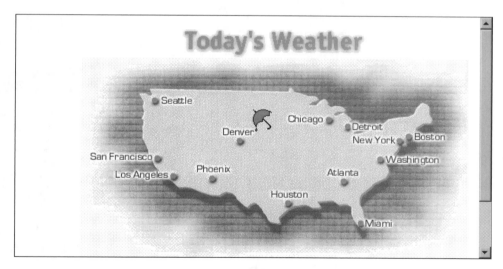

**Figure 2.40** A weather technology map using the Comet cursor displays an umbrella by Denver to denote rainy weather.

has a technique that they call "Dead End Advertising," involving the placement of ads on pages that are like dead ends for users navigating the Web, such as thank you pages or receipt-for-payment pages. "The user has just finished a task, and [is] now mentally ready to see something else and go somewhere else," explains Darren Zwack, Director of Online Advertising at Columbus Group. It is on this page that the user is presented with the ad, completely unobstructed by any other content except a link back.

Another variation of redefining the screen real estate is ZDNet's "extramercial," which uses a 3-inch-wide column to the right of a Web page. This screen real estate is available for use with Netscape Navigator 4.0 and IE 4.0 (see Figure 2.41).

## ISPs

Even ISPs are getting into the act. NetZero (www.netzero.com) is offering free Internet access for viewing ads. When a user signs up for the service, the demographic data collected will be used for ad targeting. Ads are served in a window that stays open whether the user is surfing the Web or reading e-mail. Figure 2.42 shows an example of an advertisement through the NetZero service.

**Figure 2.41**    Extramercial on ZDNet adds an extra column after the Web page for advertising space.

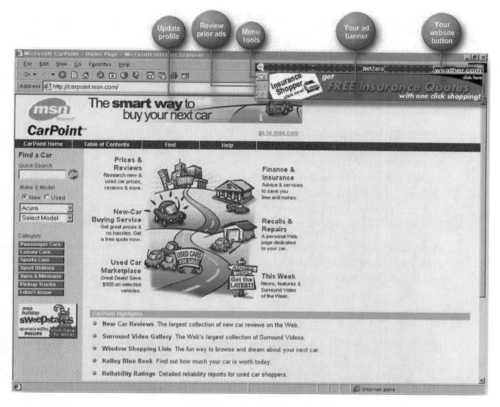

**Figure 2.42** NetZero offers free Internet access for the price of viewing ads.

## Other Formats

Online ads are moving to even smaller screens, the palmtops. Wired Digital has designed ads for PalmPilots and other Windows CE–compatible hand-held computers. With 13 million units in use by 2001, it makes sense that the ads could subsidize the content.

## Guarding Your Domain

"People treat their domain name as their brand," says Douglas Wolford, Network Solutions senior vice president of marketing. Indeed, a good domain is an ad; that's why some domains have been sold for hundreds of thousands of dollars. And, companies are taking seriously the risk that sites will be created to challenge their brand, by buying up possible domains of "anti" sites. For example, Bell Atlantic bought the domains bellatlanticsucks.com and bigyellowsucks.com. One of the earliest "anti" sites was www.aolsucks.com. How AOL would like that domain now!

## Resources for Reviewing Ads and Ad Campaigns

There are numerous resources online that highlight successful ads, review ad campaigns, and locate ad development shops. Microscope (www.microscope.com), a ClickZ network site, features a new ad campaign every week and invites leaders in the online ad industry to critique the ads themselves (see Figure 2.43).

ChannelSeven's network of sites (www.channelseven.com) cover a cross-section of the online creative industry. TurboAds (www.turboads.com/index.shtml) is a rich media ad resource. Ad/Insight (www.channelseven.com/adinsight/index.shtml), a section on the ChannelSeven site, provides a collection of ad campaign case studies. AdsGallery (www.adsgallery.com) is a visual yellow pages for creative resources in the online advertising industry and is comprised of a directory of agencies and contractors, as well as an interactive online portfolio of their work (see Figure 2.44).

Four Corners Effective Banners from White Palm (www.whitepalm.com/fourcorners) offers a look at various banners and their response rates. The site also suggests methods for improving responsiveness of banner ads.

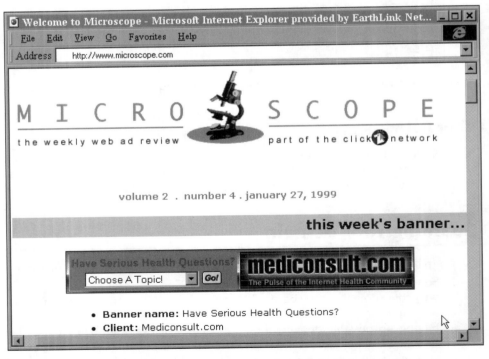

**Figure 2.43**  Microscope does a weekly review of web advertising campaigns.

**Figure 2.44**  AdsGallery is a virtual yellowpages for the digital advertising industry.

In this chapter we've discussed a lot of the different types of ads, from text to banners to sponsorships. Indeed, the types and formats that make up the matrix of online advertising are extremely exciting and dynamic, and constantly pushing the entire industry in new directions. Online users vary as to whether they find ads informative, entertaining, or irritating (see Figure 2.45). However, one thing is certain: online ads are here to stay.  In the next chapter, we're going to dive deeper into some of these models and see how they are being used by direct marketers.

|  | Banner | Shared Real Estate | Banner with DW | Interstitial |
|---|---|---|---|---|
| Like Very Much/Somewhat | 42% | 48% | 45% | 50% |
| Disliked Somewhat/Very Much | 8% | 14% | 18% | 18% |
| Irritating | 7% | 9% | 15% | 15% |

**Figure 2.45**  Percentage of surfers who find ads irritating.

Source: Study conducted by IPSOS-ASI 1998.

Note: Results aggregated from an online copy-testing survey of 180 ads.

## Think "Reach," Not "Rich"

Ali Partovi, Product Manager and Original Partner (apartovi@linkexchange.com)
LinkExchange (www.linkexchange.com)

Have you seen a "rich media" ad on your favorite Web site lately? Neither have I! If you're like the majority of users, your connection is not even fast enough for the practical needs of your busy day. You're frustrated and have no patience for an audio or Java ad distracting you from what you want to get done. Your favorite Web site probably knows this, too.

Web designers are finding that graphics-intensive, "beautiful" Web pages are less effective than light, simple ones. Sites like Yahoo! and Amazon that have focused on speed and simplicity have been rewarded with success, and others are now dropping their works of art for more functional designs. The same applies to advertising. Why try to force a multimedia ad on an audience that has clearly voted for simplicity and speed?

Web users are regular people, not technology enthusiasts. They're here to find things, learn things, buy things. They'd prefer to do so quickly and simply—without learning a new interface, without waiting for new technology to download. Every time we put new technology between our users and what they want to do online, we lose some users. So, think about the trade-off between rich media and reach. The smarter path is to aim for reaching the most people, even if we're not reaching them with as "rich" a medium as we'd like.

The vendors of rich media tools and software would like us to believe that rich media ads are the wave of the future. The technology enthusiast in me wishes this were true. However, in the meantime, fortunes are being won and lost on simple text and graphics. I'd rather have a text-only site with zillions of users today, than a "rich media" Web site with the hope of many users tomorrow. And I'd rather advertise with regular text or graphics ads and reach zillions of users, than shrink my advertising audience and impose a frustrating "rich media" experience on them.

People say that brand advertising is handicapped without video and audio, like TV. This might be true (and there are many ad agencies that hope it's true, as their business thrives on producing TV/radio ads). However, it's also true that the Web simply doesn't support rich media well. If your branding strategy is critically dependent on rich media, think about whether you can adapt your strategy for a world where zillions of users watch less TV and spend more and more time on simple text-and-graphics Web sites.

You don't need a rich audiovisual experience to influence consumer purchasing. The best form of advertising is word-of-mouth, and word-of-mouth can come in the form of a simple text-only e-mail. However, the Procter & Gambles of the world are holding their breath and holding their wallets while they wait for the Internet to re-create the rich audiovisual experience that made their TV branding strategy a success. How long can they wait?

# It's Just Better Advertising

Richard Hopple, Chairman and CEO, (rhopple@unicast.com)
Unicast Communications (www.unicast.com)

Many argue that the Internet and its users are simply not ready for "rich media," or a more sophisticated form of advertising, and that bandwidth remains . . . a major problem and the solution to today's online advertising needs is "smaller, less intrusive banners."

Smaller, less intrusive banners? Isn't that regressing back to a form of advertising that research has proven to be ineffective? Static Internet banner ads, as a standard, have actually depressed or at least delayed interest in investing from big name advertisers. Since advertising dollars makes the Internet economy go round, this solution needs to be rethought. Without big name advertising funds, the user will ultimately pay.

## We've Come Too Far

We've come too far to revert back to an advertiser's worst nightmare: a static banner delivering minimal information that many users choose to ignore. Let's take into consideration the progress that has been made in the world of Internet advertising. After years of skepticism, the Web has revealed itself as a viable medium to risk-averse, traditional advertisers—the advent the online ad industry has been awaiting. With the support of mainstream advertisers like Procter & Gamble, McDonald's, and Coke, the Internet as an advertising medium has the capability to deliver greater returns for both advertisers and publishers and maintain the delivery of free content to the user.

In addition, we've even come so far as to say that the bandwidth bottleneck is no longer an excuse for publishers to dismiss more attractive and effective advertising. Today, there are technologies that begin to solve this ever-vexing problem. In fact, some solutions enable the most innovative advertising concepts to be quickly delivered to users over a 28.8 modem.

## The Time Is Now

The time to "sit back and ponder" the medium has passed. It is time to take action and find a better, more effective form of advertising on the Net.

According to research conducted by Grey Interactive and ASI, larger, more complex and sophisticated online ad units are much more effective than standard banner ads. They are more memorable, have higher click-through rates, offer increased communication and the potential for branding.

Which leads us to a solution—the badly misnamed, and in some circles surprisingly controversial, rich media. Essentially, rich media gives the advertiser[s] the opportunity to begin using some of the creative techniques that have been successful for them in other media. It enables animation and sound to capture

## It's Just Better Advertising *(Continued)*

the nature of television advertising and the interactivity of the Web. It's not richer advertising. It's just better advertising.

Publishers should be working more aggressively to deploy the existing technologies, understand how they can best be used and how they can be improved going forward. It is in their interest to see that these solutions succeed.

Advertisers should begin paying at least as much attention to the creativity of the advertisements themselves as they have to the buying of the media—the kind of creativity that has powered the advertising industry in other media.

The technologies are here now. It is time to learn how to put them to best use . . . to begin pushing the creative parameters and show ourselves just how effective advertising on the Internet can be. If we don't learn to use them effectively, the big money will be left on the sideline . . . and that would be too bad for everyone.

# 3

# Internet Direct Marketing

Internet direct marketing is coming of age. The proof is everywhere, from the proliferation of online direct marketing campaigns to the formation of the Internet Direct Marketing Bureau (www.idmb.org), a trade association dedicated to servicing and building the industry (see Figure 3.1). Why is direct marketing on the Internet so appealing? Because the Internet can deliver everything traditional direct marketing delivers and more.

A 1998 study by Gruppo, Levey & Co. found that 73 percent of direct marketers now conduct transactions online, with an impressive 43 percent reporting a profit from their online campaigns. The study examined such direct marketing heavyweights as Avon and L.L. Bean. According to Gruppo, Levey & Co. vice president Karen Burka, "The Web really taps into the same type of direct-to-end-user marketing that direct marketers have always known how to do."

The basis for effective direct marketing is being able to sell products or services at a certain cost per sale. The Internet's ability to track purchases back to a specific ad on a specific site makes it very easy for direct marketers to use the Web; as with traditional direct response vehicles, they're able to evaluate every advertisement based on the number of sales it generates. From an ad pricing perspective, there are many great opportunities for direct marketers. Since many Web sites are struggling to generate adequate ad revenue, they will often sell ad space on a cost-per-action basis. This makes the buy very safe; the direct marketer knows exactly what the cost will be for every sale or lead.

In this chapter we're going to discuss the many forms of direct marketing on the Internet: direct e-mail advertising, banner advertising, loyalty programs, and more.

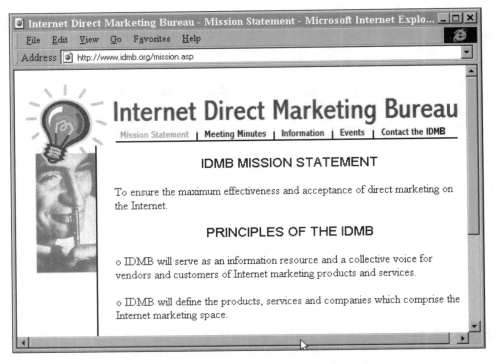

**Figure 3.1**    The Internet Direct Marketing Bureau was founded in 1998 to ensure the maximum effectiveness and acceptance of direct marketing on the Internet.

# Direct E-mail

Forrester Research estimates that about 55 million American homes now have e-mail and send over 150 million e-mail messages every day. Moreover, Forrester predicts that 50 percent of the U.S. population or 135 million people will communicate via e-mail by 2001. Indeed, more Americans use e-mail than surf the Web. The Web may be sexy, but e-mail reaches more and more people every day. To an advertiser, the bottom line is the results, and direct e-mail is producing results.

What advertisers are using e-mail? The travel industry, for one. Airlines and destination resorts are building e-mail lists to deliver messages regarding unsold rooms and last-minute deals on tickets. In fact, it is reported that Club Med is bringing in from $25,000 to $40,000 every month from its e-mail database of 34,000 people, who receive messages about last-minute specials (see Figure 3.2).

"Companies are increasing their e-mail marketing efforts because it clearly works," says William Park, president of Digital Impact (www.digital-impact.com). "Our clients are not only building brand loyalty with their e-mail marketing, but are also experiencing triple-digit ROIs and big click-through rates." A campaign that Digital Impact designed for ClickRewards resulted in an unprecedented 50 percent response rate to

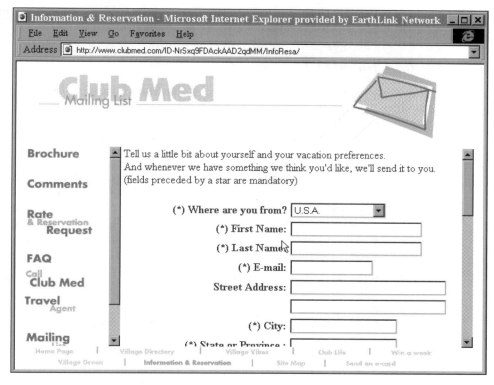

**Figure 3.2**   Sign-up page for Club Med's e-mail list.

opened HTML e-mails. "Our formula is to always personalize the content, customize the e-mail format to fit the software being used, and track everything that happens with each customer," explains Ray Kaupp, VP of marketing at Digital Impact.

And e-mail is not just in text and HTML format; there are even multimedia e-mail options, such as Mediasynergy's @loha e-mails (www.mediasynergy), that are veritable e-mail multimedia productions.

E-mail advertising is gaining strength around the globe. A 1998 user survey conducted by the Japanese company Nikkei Multimedia found that e-mail advertising has a high approval rating among Japanese online users: 74.3 percent of respondents had a positive attitude towards e-mail advertising, with over 50 percent rating e-mail ads as providing the necessary information and details about a product, and with 31.2 percent saying that links to Web sites in e-mail ads make them more useful than other forms of advertising.

## E-mail Lists

There are two ways to get e-mail lists. One option is to rent lists from list brokers. The other option is to develop a list yourself through a registration process on your own site, as was done by Club Med in the example mentioned above. The value of the do it yourself option is that the list becomes your in-house property.

## Renting E-mail Lists

The most important factor in renting an e-mail list is making sure the list is "opt-in." This means that everyone on the list has agreed that they want to receive e-mail solicitations. To make sure a list is opt-in, you should ask the list owner how the names were gathered. This is essential to avoid using a list put together by software that surfs the Web looking for e-mail addresses, exactly what you don't want.

You should also ask for references of other advertisers who have used the service. When you check with the references, you'll be able to confirm that the list is truly opt-in. If not, the advertisers probably would have received numerous angry e-mails from the folks to whom they sent e-mail advertisements. Sending e-mail advertisements to lists that are not opt-in is spam. Therefore, check list broker references to make sure you don't become a spammer because you chose a bad list.

Just to be on the safe side, when using a list for the first time, you should test a small direct e-mailing prior to e-mailing the entire list or a large part of the list. Although the references may be good, it's still better to be safe than sorry. See Table 3.1 for a list of list brokers that have opt-in lists. The bottom line is: rent lists from reputable companies.

## In-House Lists

In addition to renting lists, advertisers can build their own in-house lists for direct e-mailings. We strongly believe in the value of building your own e-mail list. Especially since it's so easy; all you need to do is invite people who visit your Web site to sign up for an e-mail newsletter or e-mail updates. Figure 3.3 shows how Tenagra (www.tenagra.com), an interactive agency, provides a way for people to sign up for their e-mail list. In addition to using these forms, any time someone enters a contest, purchases a product or requests information from your Web site, you can give them the

**Table 3.1**  E-mail List Brokers

| COMPANY | DESCRIPTION |
| --- | --- |
| BulletMail (www.bulletmail.com) | BulletMail offers targeted opt-in direct e-mail marketing services. |
| Direct Marketing Online (www.directmarketing-online.com) | Full array of online and off-line direct marketing services such as opt-in e-mail list rental. |
| PostMaster Direct Delivery (www.postmasterdirect.com) | Offers e-mail list rental, list management/brokerage, and e-mail list delivery. |
| Sift, Inc. (www.sift.com) | Sift's Net-Lists opt-in e-mail network allows clients to reach more than 3,000,000 recipients in thousands of categories—business-to-business or consumer. |

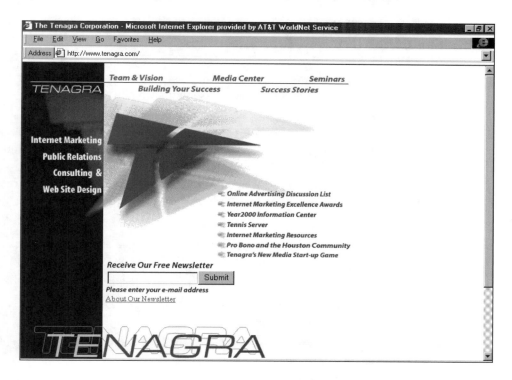

**Figure 3.3** Tenagra's home page, with a place for visitors to sign up for their e-mail list.

opportunity to join your e-mail list. Also, if you are in contact with your customers or prospects through retail locations, phone calls, or other means, you can use these opportunities to build your own e-mail list as well. Sending an e-mail solicitation to customers and prospects who specifically request the solicitations from you will almost always work better than using a rented list.

Sites can quickly build lists by offering visitors incentives. For example, Preview Travel (www.previewtravel.com) asks users when they register for an account if they want to "receive a variety of special e-mails designed to help you get the most for your travel dollar, and to make your travel planning easier" (see Figure 3.4a). In a campaign developed by direct e-mailing firm Digital-Impact (www.digital-impact.com), users then receive special e-mails that are customized to their travel interests and e-mail program type: if their e-mail program can only read text, then they receive text-only e-mail (see Figure 3.4b); if their e-mail program can read HTML, then they receive graphically enhanced e-mail (see Figure 3.4c).

You should not rent your in-house list to other marketers. Seth Godin, founder of Yoyodyne (an e-mail marketing company purchased by Yahoo!), looks at it this way: "Permission rented is permission lost." He feels that the value in these lists is that the users gave you permission to correspond with them, making this "permission-based marketing."

## Effective Direct E-mail Advertising Tips

- Check references to make sure your e-mail list source is providing names of folks who have asked to receive advertisements via e-mail.

- Have an interesting subject line. People get a lot of e-mail—especially people who are on direct e-mail lists. When these consumers look at their e-mailbox they see the subject lines of all of their e-mails. Come up with a subject interesting enough that it will make people open your mail. At the same time, make sure you're not being deceiving. You don't want to anger potential customers with misleading titles like, "information you requested."

- Keep your message short and to the point.

- Avoid sending attachments. People don't like to receive attachments unless they requested them.

- Make an offer. Consumers need a strong reason to respond.

- Provide the user a choice in how to respond: an e-mail address, a URL, a phone number, and a fax number.

- Code your URLs so that you know which e-mail list generated the most (and highest quality) responses.

- Test different offers to see what works best.

Managing an in-house mailing list can be done in-house or through a service provider. Table 3.2 provides a list of e-mail list management software, and Table 3.3 lists e-mail list management providers.

### Spam

E-mail direct marketing, done right, can be extremely effective. Done wrong, it can be worse than doing no advertising at all. In fact, it can ruin a company's reputation. That's why we're mentioning spam several times in this book. Spamming is considered a high crime by the online community, whose retribution can be firm and swift. On the most basic level, spammers lose customers. More directly, they can be blacklisted by the online community. Indeed, monitoring spammers is almost as old as spamming itself. The grand-daddy list of spammers is the "Blacklist of Internet Advertisers" (see Figure 3.5), which began in 1994 following the antics of Canter and Siegel (discussed in Chapter 1).

What exactly falls under the rubric of spam? In his article "It's a Fine Line Between Legitimate E-mail Marketing and Spam" published on ClickZ (www.searchz.com/clickz/051098.shtml), Cliff Kurtzman, president and CEO of Tenagra Corp., identified five categories of spam:

- Unsolicited advertisements distributed via e-mail (even if not mass e-mailed).

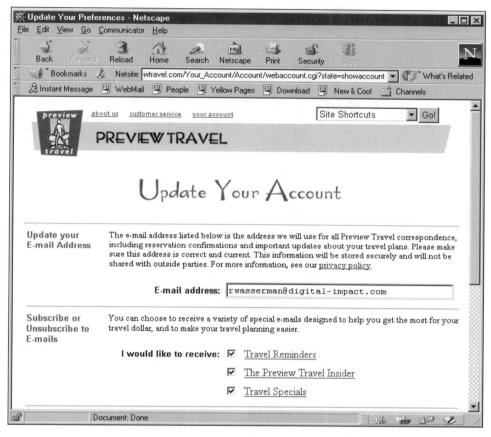

**Figure 3.4a** Preview account set up.

- An unsolicited mass e-mail (commercial or not).
- An out-of-context mail list, newsgroup, or forum posting.
- Using a mail list or newsgroup or forum in a manner that is outside of the volume or frequency that readers have signed up for.
- Putting users on a mailing list without their consent and requiring them to "opt-out."

Today, spamming is not only a violation of netiquette, but it is also a crime. For more on the legal aspect of spamming, see Chapter 13.

## Opt-in

The best way to avoid falling into the spam trap is to only use "opt-in" lists. "Opt-in" means that a person has to ask to receive the e-mails. At any time, that person can just as easily choose to opt out and stop receiving the e-mail messages.

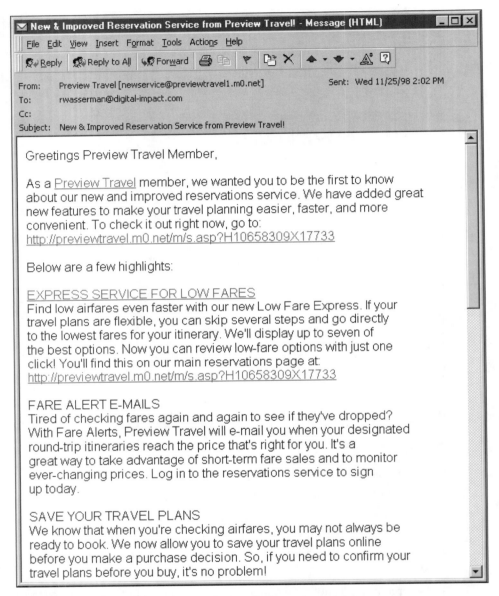

**Figure 3.4b** Preview Travel text-only e-mail of travel specials.

One of the largest e-mail direct marketers is NetCreations (www.netcreations.com), with its PostMaster suite of products and services. PostMaster Direct Response (www.postmasterdirect.com) targeted e-mail service now has 8 million e-mail addresses (more than 1.8 million unique names) in over 9,000 topical categories, from

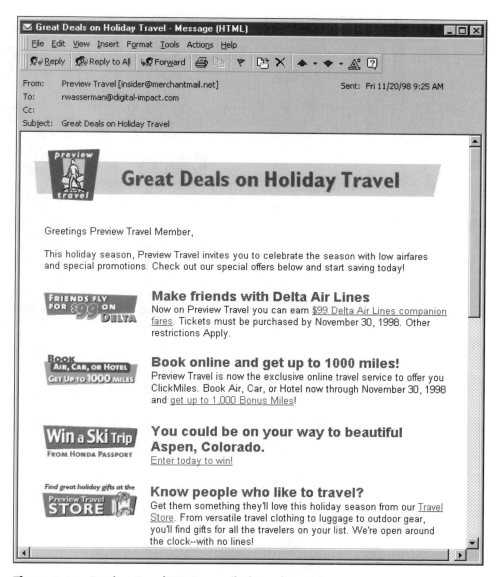

**Figure 3.4c** Preview Travel HTML e-mail of travel specials.

consumer lists to business-to-business. Their lists are opt-in only and they diligently protect list members' privacy by never releasing their names or e-mail addresses to the marketers who rent the lists.

PostMaster Direct places advertising on other Web sites to convince consumers to sign up to receive e-mail advertisements on topics of their choosing. Advertisers can then

**Table 3.2**  E-mail List Management Software

| COMPANY | DESCRIPTION |
|---|---|
| Cuenet (www.cuenet.com) | Provides list servers, auto-responders, document distribution, and other services. |
| LISTSERV (www.lsoft.com/listserv.stm) | System that allows the creation, management, and control of electronic mailing lists on corporate networks or the Internet. |
| Lyris (www.lyris.com) | Software for running Internet e-mail mailing lists, such as newsletters, announcements, and discussion lists. |
| MailKing (www.mailking.com) (owned by Revnet) | Offers an e-mail merge tool for Windows. It allows companies to open most popular databases directly, filter data into targeted e-mail lists, and then send personalized e-mail to members of the lists. |
| Revnet Express (www.revnetexpress.net) | Offers a full range of e-mail management and delivery functions, as well as advanced options, allowing companies to target demographic or interest groups, personalize messages, track click-through behavior, or deliver e-mail campaigns. |

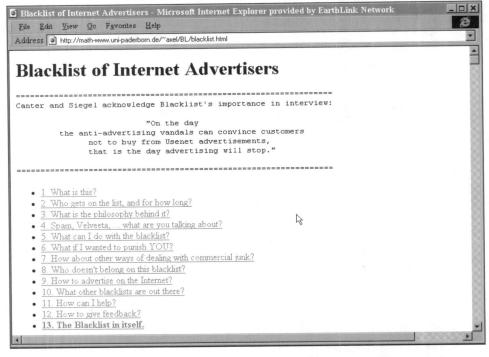

**Figure 3.5**  The Blacklist of Internet Advertisers, started in 1994, monitors spammers.

**Table 3.3**  E-mail List Service Providers

| COMPANY | DESCRIPTION |
| --- | --- |
| Acxiom DirectMedia (www.directmedia.com) | One of the largest list brokerage and management companies in the country. They offer off- and online solutions for direct marketers, including CatalogLink and E-mail Campaign Management. |
| CMG Direct (www.cmgdirect.com) | Provides database management services, analytical services, and targeted "opt-in" e-mail lists to clients. |
| Digital Impact (www.digital-impact.com) | Develops customized electronic marketing campaigns. |
| MatchLogic (www.matchlogic.com) | MatchLogic's DeliverE campaign management service includes fielding a target e-mail audience, coordinating the e-mail content and URLs, managing the campaign push, and monitoring the lifecycle of the campaign. |
| PostMaster Direct Delivery (www.postmasterdirect.com) | Offers e-mail list rental, list management/brokerage, and e-mail list delivery. |
| Revnet Express (www.revnetexpress.net) | Offers a full range of e-mail management and delivery functions, as well as advanced options, allowing companies to target demographic or interest groups, personalize messages, track click-through behavior, or deliver e-mail campaigns. |
| WebPromote (www.webpromote.com) | Sends clients' e-mail messages to a targeted list of individuals who have asked to receive announcements about sites that cater to their specific interests. |

## Tips for E-mailing Your In-House List

**Remind recipients that they requested the e-mail updates.**   People sign up for numerous e-mail lists, and often forget. You want to ensure that they don't think you're spamming them.

**In the beginning of the message, let people know that there will be instructions for getting off the list at the bottom of the e-mail.**   An automated procedure for getting off the list is important; otherwise you may be inundated with phone calls and e-mails from people who no longer want to subscribe.

**Provide some sort of value in every mailing—it can be a discount, great information, or something else.**   The point is to give people a reason to read the next mailing and feel good about your company.

**Keep it short.**   A person's attention is a valuable commodity online.

send their solicitations to different segments of the PostMaster Direct list. For example, a high-tech publication would probably be interested in sending subscription advertisements to anyone who signed up to receive e-mail advertisements related to year 2000 computer problems. PostMaster Direct usually charges between $.15 and $.20 per name. One of PostMaster Direct's big success stories was for ichat, as described in the section, "PostMaster Direct Helped ichat Ring Up $50,000 in Sales in 5 Hours."

In case you still don't believe what we've said about junk e-mail (spam), here's what your prospective customers say. In 1998, World Research conducted an online survey on junk e-mail (www.survey.com/junkresults.html). Some of the results are provided below.

How much junk mail have you experienced in your e-mail account?

| ANSWER | RESPONSE |
| --- | --- |
| None | 12.02% |
| Very Little | 20.41% |
| Some | 28.05% |
| Quite a bit | 23.95% |
| Tons | 15.55% |

How do you feel about the junk e-mail you get?

| ANSWER | RESPONSE |
| --- | --- |
| Hate it | 42.95% |
| It's bothersome | 24.90% |
| Don't care | 16.40% |
| It's O.K. | 8.68% |
| Love it | 7.04% |

On a scale of 1 to 5, how useful has junk e-mail been to you?

| ANSWER | RESPONSE |
| --- | --- |
| 1-Not useful at all | 68.43% |
| 2 | 16.93% |
| 3 | 8.37% |
| 4 | 2.02% |
| 5-Totally useful | 4.23% |

Do you feel that junk e-mail should be regulated in some way?

| ANSWER | RESPONSE |
| --- | --- |
| Yes | 66.60% |
| No | 33.39% |

## PostMaster Direct Helped ichat Ring Up $50,000 in Sales in 5 Hours

Selling on the Internet isn't easy, and nobody knows that better than Bruce Dietzen. That's why Dietzen, director of corporate sales for ichat, Inc. (www.ichat .com), a leading supplier of Web-based real-time communications software, turned to PostMaster Direct Response for help. Within four weeks of mailing to PostMaster Direct's 30,000-member Web Design and Promotion List, Dietzen saw ichat's sales quadruple.

"We sent out e-mail at 10 A.M. one day and, by 3 o'clock, we had hundreds of visitors on our site, where we interacted with them directly via our software and then called them immediately afterwards," Dietzen says. "In five hours' time, we closed $50,000 in sales, including a single order for $20,000."

For most companies trying to market products on the Internet, this kind of success is practically unheard of. "Simply having a great product is not enough," Dietzen says. "The key is well-targeted promotion, not spamming. E-mail lists that you choose must be select decision makers that have already indicated an interest in hearing about whatever it is that you are promoting."

Using PostMaster Direct, ichat was able to contact a highly qualified list of Web developers and Internet marketers that have "opted in" to receive commercial announcements. Ichat's first PostMaster Direct mailing yielded a 7 percent response. Subsequent mailings yielded 4 percent response rates. And, because PostMaster Direct lists are not only voluntary, but self-cleaning, the company's mailings generated little negative feedback from the Net community.

"At 15 cents a name, this is the best price/performance tool that I have ever encountered," Dietzen says. "There's another benefit, too. The time it takes to cycle a targeted e-mail marketing campaign is only two days. I was used to print marketing campaigns that took two months!"

Using direct e-mail, ichat can create a campaign one day and book orders the next. "Faster cycles at lower costs mean a lot more campaigns are possible," Dietzen says. "That's what drives sales growth."

## Banner Advertising

The banner ad model can be likened to a direct mail piece with the banner itself representing the envelope. Just as on an envelope, there is limited real estate on a banner. And, within that limited space, an advertiser needs to convince a consumer to take action. With a direct mail piece, that action is opening the envelope. With a banner, the

## Sample Direct E-mail Piece by PostMaster Direct for DELL Computers

Date: Wed, 15 Apr 1998 16:06:01 -0400
From: "DELL" <mailbox@netcreations.com>
To: <rosalind@netcreations.com>
Subject: Introducing the fastest PC ever from Dell - only $2499
——————————————————————————————————— ————

This mail is never sent unsolicited. This is a PostMaster Direct mailing! UNSUB
ALL: -forward- this entire message to deleteall@postmasterdirect.com (be sure to
*forward* the ENTIRE message, or it will not unsubscribe you!) To review your
subscription: http://www.postmasterdirect.com/review MAIL TO LISTS:
http://www.PostMasterDirect.com 100% OPT-IN(tm)
——————————————————————————————————— ————

——————————————————————————————

SPECIAL ** SPECIAL ** SPECIAL

——————————————————————————————

Dell Dimension(r) Desktops...The most award-winning line of desktops
PCs in 1997.(+)

Introducing the fastest PC ever from Dell—the NEW Dell Dimension(r)
XPS R-series. New leading-edge technology announced today from Dell at
aggressively low prices!

With the NEW Dell Dimension XPS R400, you get a powerful 400MHz
Intel(r) Pentium(r) II Processor, announced by Intel today. And, NEW
100MHz SDRAM memory which bursts data up to 50% faster than previous
66MHz SDRAM technology. With the Dell Dimension XPS R400, you get
system performance up to 33% faster than our Dell Dimension XPS D333.
Plus the largest EIDE hard drives—up to 16.8GB available—gives you
plenty of room to store your critical data. Order yours today!

DELL DIMENSION XPS R400

400MHz Pentium II Processor with MMX(tm) Technology
Mini-Tower Model
64MB 100MHz SDRAM Memory
512KB Integrated L2 Cache
8.4GB Ultra ATA Hard Drive (9.5ms) with Disk Performance Driver
1000LS 17" (15.9" vis) Monitor
NEW Diamond Permedia 2 8MB 3D AGP Video Card
32X Max.* Variable CD-Rom Drive

3.5" Floppy Disk Drive
NEW Turtle Beach Montego A3D 64 Voice PCI Sound Card
Altec Lansing ACS-90 Speakers
Microsoft(r) Office Small Business Edition plus Bookshelf 98
McAfee VirusScan
Microsoft Windows(r) 95
FREE Microsoft Windows 98 Upgrade Packet(1)
Microsoft Internet Explorer 4.0
Dell QuietKey(r) Keyboard
Microsoft IntelliMouse(r)
3-Year Limited Warranty(2) / 1-Year Next-Business-Day On-Site
Service(3) 24-Hour Toll-Free Telephone and Online Technical Support

Order Code 590423
$2499
$95/36 MO. BUS. LEASE(4)

Recommended Upgrades:
Upgrade to 128MB 100MHz SDRAM Memory, add $199
Upgrade to a NEW 16.8GB Ultra ATA Hard Drive (9.5ms), add $299
Upgrade to a 1200HS 19" (17.9" vis, .26dp, 95KHz) Monitor, add $289
*32X Max/14X Min.

To customize this system to your exact needs and to order online,
visit http://www.dell.com/smallbus/hotprice6.htm or give us a call at
1-888-617-9680 and mention keycode 61622.

IF YOU'RE IN BUSINESS YOU SHOULD BE DOING BUSINESS WITH DELL.
(+)According to the top 4 PC publications. Promotional pricing is not
discountable. Prices and specifications are valid only in the U.S. and
are subject to change without notice. (1)Each Dimension XPS R-series
with Microsoft Windows 95 factory installed, shipped after 4/1/98 and
prior to 7/31/98 will be eligible for a free upgrade to Microsoft
Windows 98 when available, subject to terms and conditions contained
in Microsoft Windows 98 upgrade packet shipped with system. Length of
offer subject to change. (2)For a complete copy of Guarantees or
Limited Warranties, please write to Dell, One Dell Way, RR1 Box 12,
Round Rock, TX 78682, Attn: Warranty. (3)On-site service guarantee
provided pursuant to a service contract an independent, third-party
provider. May not be available in certain remote areas. (4)Business
leasing arranged by Dell Financial Services, L.P., an independent
entity, to qualified customers. Lease payments based on 36-month

## Sample Direct E-mail Piece by PostMaster Direct for DELL Computers *(Continued)*

lease, and do not include taxes, fees, shipping charges; subject to availability. Lease terms subject to change without notice. Dell, the Dell logo, QuiteKey, and Dell Dimension are registered trademarks of Dell Computer Corporation. Intel, Pentium, and the Intel Inside logo are registered trademarks and MMX is a trademark of Intel Corporation. Microsoft, Windows, MS and IntelliMouse are registered trademarks of Microsoft Corporation. Other trademarks and trade names are the property of their respective owners. ©1998 Dell Computer Corporation. All rights reserved.

## Seven Tips to Get Users to Fill Out Forms

Like the *BYTE* magazine example, many Internet direct response campaigns are focused on getting users to fill out forms and order products. Below are some tips for improving the number of people who fill out your forms.

**Make your privacy stance clear.** People will be more likely to give you information if they know that you will not rent or resell their names and addresses.

**Be clear and explicit that you won't rent or resell e-mail addresses.** Otherwise, people may provide incorrect e-mail information.

**Ask as few questions as possible.** Unless there is some benefit to the consumer (for example, they'll get detailed health information if they fill out a lengthy profile), every additional question you ask the user will decrease the number of completed forms.

**Explain why you need the information.** Next to each question you should explain how providing this data benefits the consumer.

**If this is an order form, also offer phone and fax numbers as contact options.** Many consumers are fearful of ordering online.

**If your offer is open to international customers, make sure they can fill out the forms.** Either have fields that accept international addresses, or provide additional language versions. See Chapter 12 for a full discussion of the value of translation and localization.

**Have a "thank you" page.** After users fill out a form, they should go to a page that indicates that their form was received. Otherwise, they may submit their form numerous times to make sure it gets through. This causes added work for you and frustrates the users.

action is either clicking on the ad or interacting with the ad. The site on which the banner is placed is similar to a mailing list. With a direct mail piece, you mail the letter to the list. With a banner ad, the people who come to the site represent the list. Clicking the banner is the equivalent of opening the envelope. A prospect is transferred to a Web site or mini-Web site or page (a stand-alone Web page developed just for a specific ad campaign) that is serving the same role as a traditional direct response piece; it is designed to entice prospects to take a particular action (buy a product, sign up for a sample, etc).

Depending on the type of banner advertisement, some banners can even serve as the envelope and the mail piece. Rich media banners (discussed in Chapter 2) allow prospects to complete a transaction—from filling out a form to ordering a product—within the advertisement.

## Banner to Web Site or Mini-Page

When the action is linking to a Web page, the page needs to convince the consumer to take a specific action.

An example of a direct response banner campaign is one that i-frontier developed for *PC Computing* magazine. The purpose of the campaign was to generate magazine subscriptions. Once people clicked on the banners, they went to a form that resembled the magazine's direct mailer (see Figure 3.6). The campaign was paid for on a cost per subscriber basis, which meant that the advertiser only paid Web sites that generated subscriptions—a very safe type of campaign for the advertiser. However, paying on a cost per subscription basis will limit the number of sites on which the advertising can be placed. First, not all sites accept cost per action campaigns. And second, advertising can be pre-empted by CPM (cost per thousand) paying advertisers, which is what most publishers prefer since the publisher is only responsible for delivering an audience, not results.

**Figure 3.6**   The banner ad leads users to this form to fill out to receive a trial magazine subscription.

First name ▢  Last Name ▢

Catalog Request Form   Address ▢   Next ▼

**Figure 3.7**   Lands End banner invites users to request a catalogue.

# Banner as Direct Response Piece

Some direct marketers use the banner as the entire direct marketing piece. Figure 3.7 shows a banner used by Lands End to get customers to request a catalogue without ever leaving the banner. Figure 3.8 shows a banner ad in which a sale can be completed.

# Loyalty Programs

What is one of the most valuable marketing resources for an airline? Its rewards program. Frequent flyer programs sell tickets and keep customers coming back to a particular airline. Understandably, loyalty programs are jumping online, mirroring their off-line counterparts. See Table 3.4 for a list of online loyalty programs.

One of the first loyalty programs to hit the Web was Cybergold (www.cybergold.com). Nat Goldberg, founder and CEO, made an early discovery that one of the most valu-

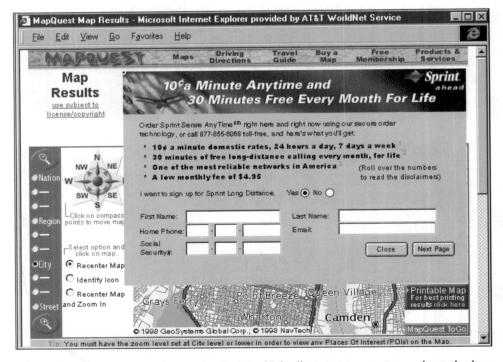

**Figure 3.8**   E-commerce banner for Sprint which allows consumer to purchase the long-distance service from within the banner without having to go to a Web site.

**Table 3.4** Loyalty Programs

| COMPANY | DESCRIPTION |
|---|---|
| AOL Rewards (www.aol.com) | Gives members points—redeemable for products from AOL merchant partners—when they view ads or purchase products. |
| Cybergold (www.cybergold.com) | Allows marketers to pay consumers for viewing ads and promotions, visiting a Web site, or purchasing a product. |
| ClickRewards (www.clickrewards.com) | Allows members to earn ClickMiles for shopping at their network of retail sites. ClickMiles are redeemable for miles on leading airlines and other rewards. |
| FreeRide (www.freeride.com) | Members collect points, redeemable for free Internet access and other products and services, by browsing sponsor Web sites, answering surveys, and shopping sponsors' stores. |
| BonusMail/MyPoints (www.intellipost.com) | BonusMail allows companies to send targeted e-mail offers and Rew@rds points to an opt-in audience of consumers. Rew@rds points may be redeemed for frequent flyer miles and name brand merchandise. <br><br> MyPoints members earn points by filling out surveys, visiting Web sites, reading and replying to e-mail, making purchases, and more. The points are redeemable on the Internet for merchandise, travel, and entertainment. |

able commodities online was a person's attention. He recognized that an efficient way to secure this attention was to pay for it directly. Cybergold members get paid for viewing ads, making purchases, or visiting sites of program partners.

One of the most basic programs is AOL Rewards. AOL automatically enrolls every one of its members in the program. Members get points for buying products and responding to advertisements. These points are redeemable for items from designated AOL merchants.

ClickRewards (www.clickrewards.com) is a travel-oriented program. Members earn ClickMiles through purchases from partnering merchants and can redeem points at participating airline, hotel, and car-rental agencies (see Figure 3.9). ClickMiles are good towards the frequent flyer programs of most major airlines, as well as Marriott Hotels and Resorts, National Car Rental, and others. Sites that offer ClickMiles include 1-800-FLOWERS, barnesandnoble.com, Microsoft Plaza, and Preview Travel. Another varia-

**Figure 3.9** ClickRewards lets you earn points for airline tickets or hotel rooms by making purchases from partnering merchants.

tion is FreeRide (www.freeride.com), which offers points for visiting sites or making purchases at partner sites (see Figure 3.10).

What is the value of these programs? The value of these programs to the users is clear—if they purchase from particular merchants, they will earn points redeemable for merchandise or frequent flyer miles. The value to an advertiser is to grow a loyal customer base through incentives.

As in all online categories, a whole host of players have emerged in the loyalty arena. Slowly, merger mania is creeping in and consolidation is building marketing leaders.

## Coupons

Many people receive the Sunday newspaper for one reason: the coupons. Discount coupons drive traffic to retail stores and motivate purchases. Online couponing is making its mark through its ability to target customers by geographic location, interests, and tastes.

Online coupons are everywhere. Sites now offer printable coupons. For example, if you go to the Lane Bryant (women's clothing) site, your reward for filling out a survey is a 15-percent-off coupon.

**Figure 3.10**   On FreeRide, you earn points for visiting sites or making purchases.

There are online only-coupon ventures such as Coupon Central (www.couponcentral .com, an online site for local and Internet coupons) and CoolSavings (www.coolsavings .com, see Figure 3.11).

Direct marketing coupon giant Val-Pak (www.valpak.com) is now online and allows users to search for coupons for local products and services by business name, location, and keyword. Val-Pak mails to some 40 million people and sees its Web presence as complementary to direct mail by expanding the company's ability to reach consumers everywhere they go. See Table 3.5 for a list of online coupon companies.

Online coupons can help a retail store reach its local audience online. For example, JCPenney lacked a means for customers to purchase directly online through their site, so their interactive agency, Proteus (www.proteus.com), designed a campaign that included coupons customers could use at Mid-Atlantic stores. The campaign goal was to drive traffic to the stores, and the coupon gave the advertiser a way to measure success.

## Free Samples and Trials

Earlier in this chapter we discussed using banner advertisements to get users to request products or free samples. In this section we're going to go into a little more detail regarding generating free sample requests online.

For starters, there is a large risk that you will generate free sample requests from thousands of unqualified people. There are hundreds of Web sites and a number of e-mail

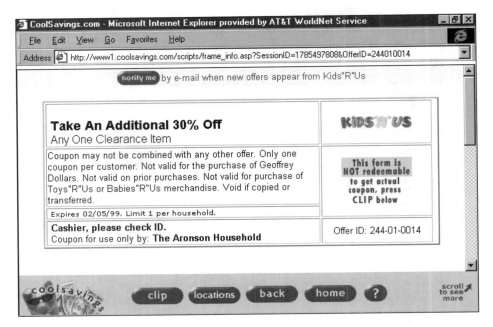

**Figure 3.11** CoolSavings lets you print coupons right off your printer.

**Table 3.5** Online Coupon Companies

| COMPANY | ONLINE ONLY | COUPONS AVAILABLE ONLINE AND OFF-LINE |
|---|---|---|
| Val-Pak (www.valpak.com) | | X |
| America's Coupon Explorer (www.couponx.com) | X | |
| Action Pack of America (www.actionpack.com) | | X |
| E-centives (www.e-centives.com) | X | |
| CouponClipper.com (www.couponclipper.com) | X | |
| Coupon Central (www.couponcentral.com) | X | |
| Internet Coupon directory (www.coupondirectory.com) | X | |
| CoolSavings (www.coolsavings.com) | X | |
| Storecoupon.com (www.storecoupon.com) | X | |
| ValuPage (www.valupage.com) | X | |
| PlanetU (www.planetu.com) | X | |

newsletters that are centered around distributing information about free stuff that is available on the Internet (samples, contests, etc). And, these information vehicles are powerful. We've seen thousands of responses generated from mentions in these publications. So, you need to be careful—if you offer something free, you may have to deal with throngs of respondents just after the free product with no intention of ever being a future paying customer.

There are a number of ways to reduce the problems associated with unqualified respondents. For starters, you could offer a freebie that would not be of interest to those outside of your target audience. If you give away a $50,000 prize, it's something that pretty much everyone will sign up for. Then, if you ever want to use the list of entrants for a direct mailer, you could have a pretty hard time figuring out which folks are actually qualified.

On the other hand, if you're reaching a niche audience, you can have a niche giveaway. The Alexander Hamilton Institute (www.ahipubs.com), a publisher of information for business managers, is an example of finding qualified respondents and limiting fulfillment costs for a campaign. The Alexander Hamilton Institute offers a series of free reports (samples of the high quality information that they publish), including "Conducting the Disciplinary Interview" and "Top Tips for Avoiding Performance Appraisal Mistakes."

As you can imagine, only their target audience would be interested in receiving these reports. To get the reports, a prospect must submit name, address, and other information that helps this company qualify a prospect. Then the prospect can download the report as a PDF (Acrobat) file, which eliminates shipping and handling costs.

Of course, not all free samples or trials are as focused on a niche audience as this example. Many are interested in general branding—trying to reach as wide an audience as possible. This was the case for a campaign by Unilever for Mentadent toothpaste. Using Unicast ad technology (www.unicast.com), Modem Media.Poppe Tyson created a direct response campaign using a transitional pop-up ad that resulted in an impressive 10% click-through for product sample requests (see Figure 3.12).

## Contests and Games

Contests and games are popular online, and some marketers are using them as a means to generate traffic to their Web site. These contests can be both Web- and e-mail–based. Yoyodyne, now part of Yahoo!, was an early producers of custom e-mail games for companies to help build brand and generate site traffic. Webstakes (www.webstakes.com) produces contests that drive traffic to sites. See Table 3.6 for a list of companies that build online contests.

Some have tried to use contests to generate leads, and this can be risky. Many consumers enter contests just to win and are not interested in the sponsor. For this reason, contests can be a poor tool to build a targeted mailing list.

Games are also used a great deal and can double as a brand-building tool. For example, an ad campaign developed by Ketchum Advertising for Zippo lighters has a game

**Figure 3.12** Transitional pop-up using Unicast ad technology to collect product sample requests for Mentadent toothpaste.

Source: Courtesy of Chesebrough-Pond's USA Co.

**Table 3.6** Companies That Build Online Contests

| COMPANY | DESCRIPTION |
| --- | --- |
| Yoyodyne Entertainment (www.yoyo.com) (acquired by Yahoo!) | Produces online sweepstakes and contests to drive consumers to client Web sites. |
| Webstakes (www.webstakes.com) | Webstakes' member-based site features a Prize and Savings Club with 11 targeted consumer channels. Webstakes members receive exclusive savings, special offers, discounts, and samples through the Savings Club, while Prize Club gives consumers the chance to win gift certificates, shopping sprees, and new products. |
| Pickem Sports (http://corp.pickem.com) | Creates interactive contests and games as promotions or engaging new content to add to Web sites. |
| Prizes.com (www.prizes.com) (RealTIME Media) | RealTIME Media develops online sweepstakes and also operates prizes.com. Prizes.com was launched in 1994 and receives millions of visitors each month. They offer members the opportunity to win cash and prizes. |
| High Altitude Promotions | Can manage all aspects of sweepstakes and contests via any medium. |

**Figure 3.13** Zippo game, which serves as a brand building tool.

that runs on the AdSmart Network. The game, created with Java, has players match up different Zippo lighters (see Figure 3.13). At the end of the game users are linked back to the Zippo site (www.zippo-usa.com), where they can fill out the sweepstakes registration form. "This campaign targeted the 18- to 24-year-olds," says Patrick Grandy, manager of Zippo Marketing Communications. "It's a brand-building tool that builds on the concept that this younger age group responds best to interactivity."

## Internet Direct Marketing Agencies

As Internet direct marketing grows and expands, a new breed of agencies are emerging that specialize in designing and implementing these campaigns. Some of the early leaders include WebPromote (www.webpromote.com), Webconnect (www.webconnect .com), and InterActive agency (www.i-agency.com).

## The Web vs. Other Media

David Zinman, Founder, Director of Business Development
(dzinman@adknowledge.com)
AdKnowledge (www.adknowledge.com)

The Web became a $2 billion medium in 1998? *Big deal.* That's only 1% of the $200 billion media pie in the U.S. What's the Web going to do to the other $198 billion? Now that's a question worth pondering. A new medium always forces change upon existing media. Radio redefined itself with the rise of television advertising. The Web will be no exception.

It's already becoming clear why ad dollars are flowing to the Web. The biggest reason is accountability. Using tools available today, marketers can track exactly how much it costs to generate a lead or sale. E-commerce marketers, the drivers in this new medium, are aggressively pursing Web advertising because the return is easy to calculate. What does this mean for some familiar traditional media?

Direct mail: The biggest loser. The Web offers all the accountability with no postage or printing costs. Direct marketers will simply compare returns from direct mail with that of Web advertising. Direct mail will shift to focus more on the less affluent, as the Web begins to offer comprehensive coverage of higher incomes. Don't hold your breath for a moratorium on catalogs and credit card weighing down your local postal carrier. Much of the Web's growth is likely to come at the expense of direct mail, however. Greenpeace will learn to love the Web!

Television: Television advertising is driven largely by branding needs, and will therefore be most insulated from the Web's initial impact. The effects of branding on the Web are still difficult to gauge and largely unproven. With 98% household penetration, and full motion video to paint a picture, television's appeal for advertisers will not fade soon.

Magazine: A true battleground media. They are geared to affluent audiences and relying on considered purchase advertising will find the Web a daunting competitor. Just flip open *Business Week* to see a list of advertisers that will find a huge percentage of their audience online. Another subtle strength of the Web is that its audience is not passive, but information hungry. How many of those *Business Week* advertisers can afford to ignore such an audience when they are in the information seeking mode?

Should the folks at Publisher's Clearinghouse start jumping out of windows? Hardly. They should just take their act online. How about the media barons of print? Do they need to swallow the dangerous end of a revolver? We've seen many new media evolve this century. It's an incontrovertible fact, however, that no new media has ever killed an old one. If radio can survive the advent of television, existing media should find their places alongside the Web as well. It's clear that no one can afford to ignore the impact of the Web, though, and that's saying a lot for 1%.

# The Art and Science of Web Measurement

T he growth of the Web advertising industry is closely tied to the development of tools for measuring audience size, behavior, and demographics. In traditional advertising, the measurement unit used to determine the cost of reaching an audience is CPM (cost per thousand), based on circulation for print media and projected viewing audience for television. With the Web, the number of times an ad is delivered and clicked is not projected—it is fairly accurately measured. The Web can measure audience behavior by counting the number of times an advertisement is seen, as well as the number of times an ad is clicked.

This chapter will cover the cornerstone of Web advertising, its measurability: what can be measured, how this measurement is conducted, and the products and services available for measurement, as well as the obstacles to effective measurement.

A common myth about the Web is that everything is measurable. As you'll learn in this chapter, the Web is far from the perfectly measurable medium people claim, but it is certainly more accurate than all other media.

## Building Blocks

The foundation of Web measurement comes from the information captured by the computer housing a Web site—the server. When you visit a Web site, your browser has a "conversation" with the site's server, and much of that conversation is recorded by the server in a log file. Your browser first requests the HTML page from the server. The code in the HTML page directs the browser as to which graphics it should also request, and from where those graphics should be received. The server records the following user information from each request:

- Date and time of the request.
- What was requested: a specific GIF, HTML page, etc.
- IP number of the computer making the request.
- Browser used by the surfer: Netscape 4, Internet Explorer 3.0, etc.
- Computer platform used by the surfer: Macintosh, PC, etc.
- Referring URL: If you clicked on a hyperlink to get to the Web site, the site from which you came will be recorded in the log files.

A log file records one line for every request. So, if you visit a home page with five graphics, there will be six requests recorded in the log file—one request for the HTML page and one for each of the graphics. For each request the log file records the IP number, specific item requested, browser used, time and date of request, and so on. As you can imagine, since all of this information is recorded for every request, log files become quite large. A busy Web site can generate many megabytes of data in the daily log file alone.

A lot of very useful information is housed within Web site log files. Figure 4.1 shows a raw log file, which should give you an idea of the difficulty of gleaning useful infor-

## What Is an IP Number?

An IP (Internet Protocol) address is a numeric code that uniquely identifies a particular computer on the Internet. An IP address is static. An IP number, on the other hand, can be dynamically generated for an Internet user by an ISP (Internet service provider). Every surfer on the Internet has an IP number that is recorded in the log files of the sites that surfer visits. Here's how a surfer's IP number is determined:

- Surfers using an ISP have IP numbers dynamically assigned to them by the ISP each time they dial in. Suppose your ISP is AOL. You dial into AOL to access the Internet. AOL has a batch of IP numbers that are assigned to customers as they dial into AOL. Now when you surf the Web, you are identified in log files by the IP number you were just assigned. Every time you dial into AOL, you can be assigned a different IP number from AOL's batch of numbers.

- If the surfer is accessing the Internet through a direct connection, the surfer's computer will have an IP address. The IP address is static; every time that computer is used to access the Internet, the same IP address is recorded in log files.

- If the surfer is accessing the Internet through a server at the office (which is how most business users access the Internet), the office server (like AOL) will dynamically assign an IP number to the office worker. It is important to note that folks accessing the Net through a company connection or an ISP may be going through a proxy server. Depending on how the proxy server is set up, it can assign each user an IP number, and/or all users can be given the same IP.

```
marco2.riccione.net - - [01/Feb/1999:04:54:51 -0500] "GET /advertising/newadbook.jpg HTTP/1.0" 200
marco2.riccione.net - - [01/Feb/1999:04:54:49 -0500] "GET /advertising/resources.html HTTP/1.0" 20(
sdn-ar-002varestP286.dialsprint.net - - [01/Feb/1999:05:03:41 -0500] "GET / HTTP/1.1" 200 - "-" "M(
sdn-ar-002varestP286.dialsprint.net - - [01/Feb/1999:05:03:44 -0500] "GET /finally.gif HTTP/1.1" 3(
sdn-ar-002varestP286.dialsprint.net - - [01/Feb/1999:05:03:45 -0500] "GET /clearpixel.gif HTTP/1.1"
sdn-ar-002varestP286.dialsprint.net - - [01/Feb/1999:05:03:45 -0500] "GET /Home_GreenButtonOn.gif ]
sdn-ar-002varestP286.dialsprint.net - - [01/Feb/1999:05:03:45 -0500] "GET /Services_GreenButton.gi:
sdn-ar-002varestP286.dialsprint.net - - [01/Feb/1999:05:03:45 -0500] "GET /Events_GreenButton.gif ]
sdn-ar-002varestP286.dialsprint.net - - [01/Feb/1999:05:03:45 -0500] "GET /Publications_GreenButto:
sdn-ar-002varestP286.dialsprint.net - - [01/Feb/1999:05:03:45 -0500] "GET /Classes_GreenButton.gif
sdn-ar-002varestP286.dialsprint.net - - [01/Feb/1999:05:03:46 -0500] "GET /About_Us_GreenButton.gi:
sdn-ar-002varestP286.dialsprint.net - - [01/Feb/1999:05:03:46 -0500] "GET /Contact_GreenButton.gif
sdn-ar-002varestP286.dialsprint.net - - [01/Feb/1999:05:03:46 -0500] "GET /zdu60.gif HTTP/1.1" 304
sdn-ar-002varestP286.dialsprint.net - - [01/Feb/1999:05:03:46 -0500] "GET /button.gif HTTP/1.1" 30'
sdn-ar-002varestP286.dialsprint.net - - [01/Feb/1999:05:03:46 -0500] "GET /a_bottomGreenLine.gif H'
sdn-ar-002varestP286.dialsprint.net - - [01/Feb/1999:05:04:12 -0500] "GET /wiley HTTP/1.1" 301 242
sdn-ar-002varestP286.dialsprint.net - - [01/Feb/1999:05:04:13 -0500] "GET /wiley/ HTTP/1.1" 200 59'
sdn-ar-002varestP286.dialsprint.net - - [01/Feb/1999:05:04:14 -0500] "GET /icons/blank.gif HTTP/1.:
sdn-ar-002varestP286.dialsprint.net - - [01/Feb/1999:05:04:14 -0500] "GET /icons/back.gif HTTP/1.1'
sdn-ar-002varestP286.dialsprint.net - - [01/Feb/1999:05:04:14 -0500] "GET /icons/dir.gif HTTP/1.1'
sdn-ar-002varestP286.dialsprint.net - - [01/Feb/1999:05:04:24 -0500] "GET /wiley/chap_2_graphics/ j
sdn-ar-002varestP286.dialsprint.net - - [01/Feb/1999:05:04:25 -0500] "GET /icons/blank.gif HTTP/1..
sdn-ar-002varestP286.dialsprint.net - - [01/Feb/1999:05:04:25 -0500] "GET /icons/back.gif HTTP/1.1'
sdn-ar-002varestP286.dialsprint.net - - [01/Feb/1999:05:04:25 -0500] "GET /icons/image2.gif HTTP/1
```

**Figure 4.1**    The contents of a log file.

mation by just looking through the unformatted text. Fortunately, special analysis tools will crunch all of this data to produce Web site activity reports.

# Key Terminology in Web Measurement

Before we dive into the different types of log analysis reports and how they can help you, we will review some of the common terms that you'll see in Web site analysis reports. This new vocabulary blends technology and traditional advertising terms. The following are some of the key terms that will serve as the foundation for understanding the language of Web measurement. For a comprehensive assessment of the concepts and metrics in Web ad measurement, see this book's companion Web site, which includes a reprinting of the Internet Advertising Bureau's "Metrics and Measurement" white paper compiled by the Media Measurement Task Force. This white paper is a fantastic resource when it comes to explaining the intricacies and problems of Internet advertising measurement and reporting.

**Ad request.**    The request of an ad from the server. This happens when someone visits a Web page that has an advertisement and the surfer's browser asks the server to deliver the ad. For a variety of reasons, the ad may not always be successfully served.

**Ad view.**    Technically, the delivery of an ad by the server.

**Cache** (pronounced *cash*).    The temporary storing of a Web page on a user's computer following the page downloading. This speeds up downloading on repeated use, so that the next time you request that page, it is accessed from the cache on your computer instead of from the Web server. Proxy servers and ISPs also cache pages to make access easier for their customers, and to reduce their bandwidth expenses (they don't have to use extra bandwidth every time a page is requested if they have cached that page).

**Click rate.**   Clicks divided by ad requests.

**Click-throughs.**   The number of times an ad is clicked.

**Domain name.**   A naming system that translates the IP number given to computers on the Internet into user-friendly addresses. Domain names are read from left to right, going from specific to general. For example, the domain name for Yahoo! is www.yahoo.com, of which *www* indicates the type of server (World Wide Web), *yahoo* is the general domain name for Yahoo!, and *com* is the top-level domain (commercial). There are two types of top-level domains: categories (com, edu, org, etc.) and countries (uk-United Kingdom, au-Australia, etc.).

**Exposures.**   The number of times that an advertisement is viewed. "Exposure" is commonly used interchangeably with "impression."

**Gross exposures, ad views.**   These are advertising terms that denote the total number of times an ad is seen.

**Hit.**   A hit is a record of each time a file is requested from a server. If a home page consists of eight graphics, nine hits would be recorded each time the home page is requested (one hit for the HTML text and eight for the graphics). Ten people going to that home page would result in 90 hits. Obviously, hits do not reflect the number of people viewing the site, just the number of files requested. Moreover, an increase in hits may be the result of more material on a site (let's say, a redesign of the home page added three new graphic elements) rather than an increase in users visiting the site. Sites still boast about their number of hits, but this basic unit of measurement isn't something that advertisers regard seriously.

**Impressions.**   The number of times an ad is delivered. When an advertiser buys advertising on a CPM basis, the advertiser is paying for every 1,000 impressions that the site can deliver. Different sites measure an impression differently. Some sites count an impression when an ad is requested; others count an impression only when an ad is fully downloaded; and there are other definitions that are used as well. Savvy advertisers will ask the publishers how they define impressions.

**Log file.**   This records all activity on a server. It records the items that are requested (Web pages, graphics, etc.), at what times they are requested, the browser used by the surfer, and other information. Traffic analysis software crunches log files to produce reports that are easy to understand and use as a basis for measuring Web site success.

**Page view.**   This is commonly referred to as viewing all of the elements that comprise a Web page (graphics, text, etc.). It is generally agreed that if someone looks at a Web page that has frames, a page view will be looking at all of the elements of the page. However, some advertisers will count each frame as a separate page view to boost their level of traffic. Number of page views is a common metric for measuring traffic.

**Response rate.**   The number of times an ad is clicked divided by the number of impressions that ad received.

**Visitor.**   A person who goes to a specific Web site. Sites often define their traffic levels in terms of the number of visitors they've had in a given time period.

**Visits.**   This is another term for comparing and measuring Web site traffic. A visit is activity on a Web site from a specific individual. That activity usually counts as a new visit if the individual has been away from the Web site for a period of thirty minutes or longer.

# What Can Be Learned from Log Analysis

Marketers can use Web site analysis software that they either purchase or custom build, or they can use a third-party service to take all of the data in their log files and produce analysis reports. The reports can be used to understand how customers are using the Web site and to help determine action items for improving the effectiveness of the Web site. Successful Web advertising goes hand in hand with an effective Web site. Below are some of the reports that can come from Web site analysis and how we suggest using those reports to improve your Web site.

## Most Frequently Requested Pages

This can indicate a few things. First, you may discover that there are certain placements of navigational links that increase traffic to specific sections of your Web site. For example, we have seen that the highest traffic pages are often the ones that are the first navigational options listed on the home page, or those with buttons that are above the fourteen-inch point on the screen. The fourteen-inch point is the place where even material on the screen is visible even on a fourteen-inch monitor (one of the smaller desk top size monitors in use). Buttons above the 14-inch point have worked better than lower placements on the page, because they are seen by the greatest number of people. As we've seen time and time again in focus groups, Web surfers rarely scroll. Almost all Web users (even those with small monitors) can see everything within the first 14 vertical inches of the screen. This can be likened to putting the most important news above the fold on a newspaper

Assuming that the different sections of your site have equally prominent navigational options, you can use this statistic to learn what is most interesting to your audience. It's probably a good bet that your hot content could generate great ideas for advertisements to which your target audience would respond well. You'll also know what content is worth adding to and where you shouldn't be allocating your resources.

If some pages deep within your site have unusually high traffic, you should consider pushing these pages more towards the front of the site. If they have significant traffic when they're buried, imagine what would happen if they were easier to access.

## Number of Visits

This gives you a general idea of your traffic levels; it's a good benchmark of your site's popularity. A visit is most often defined as activity on your Web site from one IP address. If the IP address is not active on your Web site for a period of thirty minutes, then any new activity from that IP address will be counted as a separate visit. Since IP addresses are dynamically assigned by ISPs and proxy servers, and more than one person can have an IP at the same time, activity from one IP can actually be from a variety of folks.

## Pages Viewed Per Visit and Length of Visit

This gives you an idea of how interested users are in your content. The number of visitors in a given time period is a good benchmark of overall traffic, but you need to know if you're actually getting good traffic—people who are interested in the content. For example, if 50 percent of your visitors look at one page of your site and then leave, you're in trouble. Watching these numbers will also be a good measure of the effect of new content and redesigns. If redesigns and new content increase the number of pages viewed, then you're succeeding at interesting people in what you're offering.

It's important to note that the length of visit can be deceiving. If your server is slow, visit length may go up because surfers have to wait longer for your content to download. Also, an increased visit length can sometimes be the result of a poor redesign that makes it harder for users to find the content that interests them. Of course, these increases in visit length would be far from an indication that the quality of your site is improving, so it's important to carefully determine why changes in the visit length occur.

## Distinction Between First-Time and Repeat Visitors

This measurement is not going to be accurate unless folks have to register at the site or the site employs cookies (both cookies and registration will be discussed later in this chapter).

## Most Popular Usage Times

This lets you know at what time a daily update is early enough to reach the most users. It also tells you the best times to perform server maintenance (when you have the least traffic). You can also learn about your consumers. Is your site receiving its heaviest traffic during business hours or on weekends and evenings?

## Popular Paths Followed through the Site

This gives you a framework for testing navigational changes that influence how a surfer uses your site. You can answer questions like, "if I move the 'current news' button to the top of the page, will there be a greater number of people clicking that option?" This is great for determining what navigational options and copy will influence the path users take through the site.

## Click-through Rate

This provides you with data to give to advertisers. Although the click-through rate isn't as important as actually reaching the right audience, a majority of advertisers use click-through rate to measure success, so this is an important measurement. You'll be able to see how different placements and navigational changes affect your click-through rate. You'll also notice what types of ads work best for your audience.

## Browser Used

This will help you to determine what design elements are appropriate. If you want to use Java, you want to make sure that a majority of your Web users are using browsers that work well with Java. You should test-view your Web site with the various browsers that your consumers are using.

# Referring URL

This tells you where your users are coming from, which is a good way to track the effectiveness of link trades and advertising. High referrers that are not from advertising are usually sites worth investigating for advertising opportunities. Many marketers think it isn't worthwhile to advertise on sites that deliver them a lot of traffic, because they're already getting that traffic for free. But we've seen that the increase in response from actual advertising usually makes the ad buy well worth the investment.

# Domain and Host of the User

Log analysis software can use the IP address that is recorded in your log files to figure out the actual domain and host name. In the case of AOL, the name is www.aol.com. An IP address coming from a direct connection at IBM would be www.ibm.com.

Marketers can obtain good information from this data. For example, for one of our U.S.-based clients we found high amounts of traffic from countries outside the United States. In particular we noticed a lot of traffic from Brazil (.br). To accommodate the Brazilian customers, we recommended modifying the order page to make it easier for taking Brazilian orders. The orders from Brazil rolled in, and the client was glad we had uncovered this traffic pattern from their log files.

# User Computer Platform

This provides valuable information for computer or software vendors and manufacturers.

# User Entrance Page

This lets you know which pages need to serve a home page function and offer the look and feel of a "welcome." Users will not always enter through your home page, and knowing where they do enter will alert you to design those pages in a manner that draws users deeper into the site.

# User Exit Page

It's important to know the last page your users view before leaving. These are pages that you want to redesign to keep users from leaving.

# Web Measurement Tools

As we've mentioned, the information contained in log files is presented in a raw format. The ability to organize this information into actionable reports is a function of a variety of software solutions. There are three options available. The first is to build the measurement software yourself. This is what many of the early sites had to do before there were commercial products available. Today, the products are so good that this is relatively uncommon. The second option is to purchase the software and manage the process in-house. And the third option is to outsource the entire process. We will discuss the in-house management and outsourcing options below.

## Third-Party Outsourcing

Web publishers with a bank of servers or with servers in different geographic locations can save considerable time and effort by hiring a firm to analyze all of their Web site usage data. Such vendors collect and process the data from a company's server logs to generate analysis reports off-site. The leading company for outsourcing Web measurement is I/PRO (www.ipro.com, see Figure 4.2). Using a third party for the time-consuming usage analysis leaves your company more time to focus on other aspects of the business. And, in addition to traffic reports for your own site, I/PRO provides reports on how your traffic growth and patterns compare to the Internet at large. This is useful for determining if your site's growth is faster or slower than the growth of the Internet as a whole. Moreover, many advertisers like the appearance of objectivity that comes from outsourcing to a third party. Since log files are just text file, one could easily tamper with the file. Having a third party handle the analysis places an extra layer between the publisher and the report.

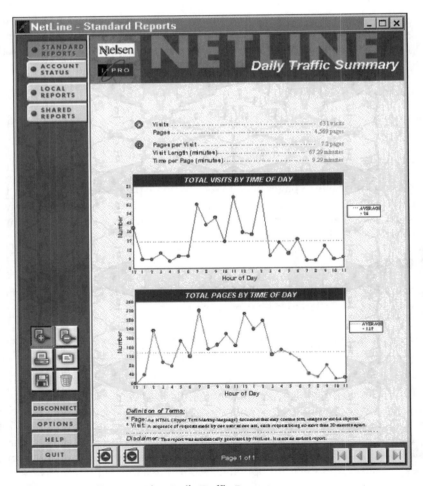

**Figure 4.2**   I/PRO NetLine Daily Traffic Report.

The disadvantages of using such a service are that Web publishers lose control of their usage information. When using a vendor for measurement, a publisher contracts for services on a monthly basis. Payment models vary based on size and frequency of reporting requirements.

## In-House Management of Software

Publishers can also purchase their own tracking software. Table 4.1 provides a list of leading Web measurement software solutions. Almost all of these companies will let you download a free trial version of the software from their Web sites, which is a great way to figure out which software will work best for you. Some of these products can service the smallest sites, and others can provide the horsepower to measure traffic on large commercial ventures. Off-the-shelf versions of the software can cost as little as $300. For example, WebTrends Log Analyzer is a popular choice for small businesses on a limited budget (see Figure 4.3). WebTrends Log Analyzer is easy to operate and does not require that the software reside on the server. Instead, the log file is downloaded to the user's computer and the reports are generated there.

**Table 4.1**  Web Measurement Software

| COMPANY | PRODUCT LINE | SAMPLE CLIENTS |
|---------|--------------|----------------|
| Marketwave (www.marketwave.com) | Hit List Pro Hit List Commerce Hit List Enterprise Hit List Live | Microsoft, Intel, IBM, Apple, Disney, AT&T |
| I/PRO (www.ipro.com) | NetLine | Dell, InfoSeek, NBC, USA Today, Excite, Netscape, Geocities, Kraft |
| net.Genesis (www.netgenesis.com) | net.Analysis | Lucent, Sun, 3Com, Xerox, Astra |
| WebTrends (www.webtrends.com) | WebTrends Log Analyzer (popular inexpensive product) WebTrends Enterprise Suite WebTrends Professional Suite WebTrends for Firewalls and VPNs | IBM, Netscape, Microsoft, Compaq, Novell |
| Andromedia (www.andromedia.com) | Aria 2.5 | U.S. Postal Service, 3Com, Sony Online, Earthlink |
| Accrue Software Inc. (www.accrue.com) | Accrue Insight 2.5 | Warner Bros., Hearst New Media, FedEx, Sun, Qualcomm, Motorola |

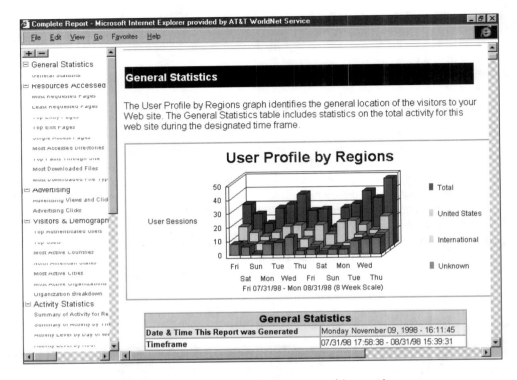

**Figure 4.3** WebTrend's report of User Profile by Geographic Location.

For higher traffic sites, the cost can be thousands of dollars. Leaders in this industry include software from Accrue, Andromedia, Marketwave (see Figure 4.4), net.Genesis (see Figure 4.5), and WebTrends.

Significant resources are needed for in-house reporting for Web sites that generate a high volume of traffic, including enough disk space to maintain log files, the computer to run the analysis, and someone to manage the software and the process. The process becomes even more complicated when a Web site is spread over several servers across the country.

## The Problems with Web Measurement

As a new and rapidly growing industry, it is only natural that there are some problems with Web measurement. One challenge is a technological hurdle—certain developments in this area can skew the accuracy of numbers. Problems also arise as a result of the lack of standardization in the industry, which can cause measurement numbers to be misunderstood and difficult to compare.

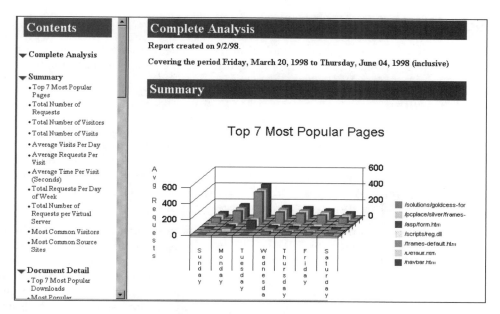

**Figure 4.4**    Marketwave's Hit List Pro report of most popular pages on a site.

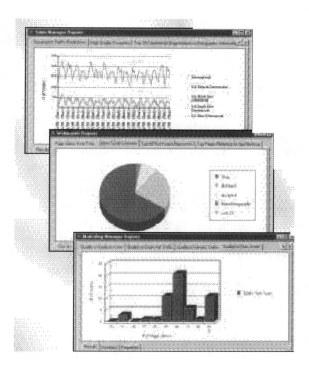

**Figure 4.5**    net.Genesis's net.Analysis series of Web site usage reports.

# Technological Hurdles

Some of the very same technological developments that assist in speeding up Web delivery and facilitating corporate security can skew measurement numbers.

## Caching

Caching describes the process of storing Web pages on a hard disk or server to decrease the download time; it eliminates the need to download the same pages each time they are requested. Most browsing software caches recently viewed pages on a user's hard disk, and the larger commercial online services and ISPs, such as AOL, store particularly popular Web pages on their server to expedite the loading of those sites for its members. This also occurs at many large corporations.

Although this process allows users to access information more quickly, publishers cannot track the usage of their Web sites when that usage occurs on someone else's server. For example, thousands of AOL users can surf a Web site, but if it is cached on AOL's servers, the publisher would not know about this activity. This is a problem for two reasons. First, the publisher does not have the correct usage data of the Web site. Second, if the publisher is selling advertising based on impressions, he or she is unable to charge for impressions delivered through cached pages, because no record exists of the impressions in the log files. Note that although impressions aren't recorded, clicks are—when someone clicks a banner it triggers a script that runs through the publisher's server, so sites that are cached will report inflated click-through rates.

The caching server does keep usage records of sites it has cached; this information is recorded in the caching server's log file. Publishers are not against caching, but they would like to have access to the log files of cached sites so they can accurately measure the activity on their Web sites. Help is on the way. There are now software products, such as MatchLogic's TrueCount (www.matchlogic.com), that can measure impressions even when caching occurs.

## Proxy Servers and Multiple Users of One Machine

In an effort to maintain security on corporate computer systems, proxy servers act as the gateway from inside a company's firewall to the outside world. Requests for information from the Internet generated inside the firewall must first go to the proxy server, which then gathers the material from the Internet. Proxy servers usually use only one IP address, though larger systems may use several. The result is that a publisher's log file may have identified only one user (the proxy server) when in fact hundreds of computers at a company requested information from the site. This obstacle will be hard to overcome for obvious security reasons.

Another similar situation occurs when several people share a machine. This happens at businesses, academic institutions, and in home environments. For example, at a small company, only one computer may be connected to the Internet, and all employees wishing to surf the Web have to use that machine. This also occurs in an academic setting where many students may use the same computers in the school's computer lab. And, in the home, every member of a family might use the same PC. The result is that the same IP address will appear several times, giving the impression that one person was returning to the site (or visiting a lot of pages) when in fact it was several. This demonstrates the shortcoming of defining a user by unique IP; the IP identifies the computer, not the user. Also, as we mentioned earlier, proxy servers cache publishers' pages.

## Robots

Whereas caching and proxy servers can deflate the true number of requests, robots can inflate the traffic numbers. A robot can be programmed to request a site hundreds or thousands of times a day. A robot may also be a search engine that requests every page of a Web site in order to add those pages to its database. Fortunately, most measurement analysis software is sophisticated enough to identify this measurement aberration for known spiders (the ones used by the major search engines). However, if someone is tracking your site through a spider or an unknown search engine is spidering your site, it can be difficult to detect.

## Industry Standards

Without a doubt, one of the growing pains of any industry is that standardization comes on the heels of invention. And in many respects, Web measurement—from terminology to technology—is still developing. With new measurement software coming on the market virtually every month, the lack of industry-wide standards accentuates the confusion. And this confusion extends from terminology to design to pricing structures.

In terms of reporting, standards are needed so advertisers can compare ad performance reports from different publishers. As Richy Glassberg, VP/general manager of Turner Interactive Marketing & Sales and founding member of IAB, puts it, "Standardizing Web measurement in general will make it easier for agencies and clients to buy so that everyone does well."

Any growth industry generates its own terminology, and the Internet is no exception. The Internet has a vocabulary for applications, procedures, and products. Though terms exist to describe the processes and procedures in Web advertising, what is lacking is industry-wide acceptance of the meanings of those terms. Fortunately, organizations like the Internet Advertising Bureau (IAB) (ww.iab.net) have developed standards for Web terminology. Unfortunately, not everyone uses their metrics yet.

One example of a term with different meanings is "impression," which is the basis of a majority of ad buys. The methodology for measuring impressions actually differs from site to site. Some sites count an impression as every time a request is made of the server for an advertisement, whereas others count impressions only if the ad is actually delivered. Also, some sites might have ads rotate while the consumer is on the page. In that case, an impression on one site may be a presence on the page for 10 seconds, whereas on other sites an impression is the ad's presence on the page for the user's entire time spent on that page.

## Cookies

A discussion about Web measurement isn't complete without a discussion about cookies. This is a topic about which many people fuss, but with which few are actually familiar.

A cookie is text that can be written to a text file on the user's hard drive when visiting a Web site. In most cases, that text will be a unique string, allowing the person to be identified.

Earlier in this chapter we talked about the discussion that a browser has with the server when someone visits a Web site. That discussion can entail the server asking the browser if the user has a cookie from the Web site. If the user has a cookie, the browser will present that information to the server. (Please note that the server can only access cookies that it has placed; it cannot access cookies from other servers.) If the user doesn't have a cookie, the server will try to place one in the user's cookie file (see Figure 4.6 for a look at an actual cookie file).

For example, a site may assign you a cookie with the text string "123." Every time you access a page on the site, the server can request the cookie it placed and recognize that "123" is back again and track where "123" goes on the site. Maximum information can be gained by using cookies in conjunction with a database. For example, the site that

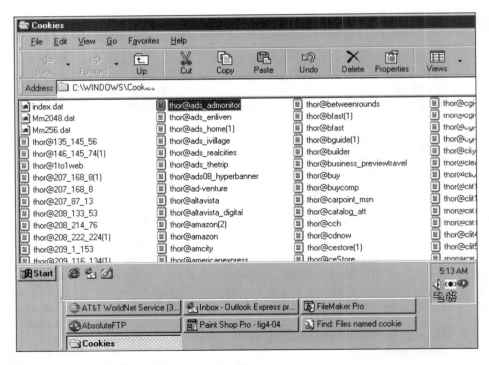

**Figure 4.6** A Windows folder of cookie files.

gave you the "123" cookie may have a corresponding "123" record in a database. Every time you do something on the site, your actions can be recorded in the database.

People are often against cookies, because they believe that cookies are an invasion of privacy. In reality, a cookie can't find out anything about you unless you give that information to the Web site. The site knows that "123" is visiting, but not who "123" is or your address unless you provide that information. As we mentioned earlier, there can be a back-end database that is tied to your cookie ID. Then, each time you click on an advertisement or fill out a survey, enter a contest, or otherwise interact with a site, the actions can be recorded in a database as those performed by "123." But unless you fill out a form with your address, the site can't use a cookie to figure out who you are. And, if you fill out a form, the site will know who you are even if it isn't using cookies. The cookie ID tag resides on your hard drive, so the next time you visit the site, that information can be used again.

There are clear benefits for advertisers and publishers to using cookies. For example, if a publisher checks an ID tag, and discovers that according to its database the user visited the auto section of its Web site three times, the publisher can deliver an advertisement to the user for a car manufacturer. To take that scenario a step further, if the user then clicks on the ad and goes to Ford's Web site, Ford can place its own cookie (containing a unique ID) on the user's drive. If Ford enables users to design their dream car on its Web site, and a user chooses to do so, Ford can record that user's

## What Determines If a Cookie Is Placed?

Cookies are supported by most browsers, from Netscape 1.1 to more current software. The full specifications on using cookies are provided in a document from Netscape titled "Persistent Client State HTTM Cookies": it is available at www.netscape.com/newsref/std/cookie_spec.html. Although the server can try to set a cookie, there are situations in which the cookie cannot be placed on the user's hard drive.

The latest browsing software can block cookies. The press has been reporting that cookies invade a user's privacy by clandestinely placing a file on the user's hard drive (we disagree, as we discuss in the text). To address the concerns of users in this regard, both Netscape 3.0 and Internet Explorer 3.0 offer users the option to block cookie files. These browsers also have a feature that alerts users when a cookie is being attached.

Users can manually delete cookie files. As noted, cookies are text files that usually reside on the hard drive in the same directory as the Internet software. All you have to do is delete the text within the file, or delete the entire file, and you remove the cookie.

Proxy servers may preclude cookie use. These computers, which serve as gateways between the company's internal network and the Internet, do not always allow cookies to be placed on individual computers.

dream car in a database record that corresponds to the user's cookie. Then, the next time the user visits, the server can recognize the user based on the ID tag in his or her cookie and deliver an advertisement with the user's dream car. The possibilities for such targeting are obvious.

A publisher using cookies can record when a specific unique ID number saw an advertisement, and use that information to ensure that the same ad is not delivered multiple times to the same browser. This also gives advertisers an opportunity to deliver a series of advertisements to a particular user. After a user sees the first ad in a series, it is recorded in a database. The next time the server recognizes that user, it delivers ad number 2, and so on.

And finally, cookies can also retain other information about users that might be useful. For example, when a user registers at a Web site, the cookie can retain the user name and password so that registration is required only once. When the user returns to that site, the server will automatically check the cookie it gave to that user to determine his or her name and password. A cookie can also remember the items a user placed in a shopping cart. In this way, cookies help create a relationship between the content, the advertiser, and the visitor, without forcing the visitor to repeatedly fill out forms. However, cookies are far from perfect.

### When the Cookie Crumbles

Unfortunately, the cookie picture is not all rosy. There are a number of reasons why a server cannot place cookies on a user's hard drive. In fact, only about eight out of ten Internet users can be cookied.

Moreover, cookies are mapped to the browser, not to the individual. The hard drive on which cookies are placed may be used by several people, thus opening the door for profile distortions. For example, at a college computer center where many students may be accessing a particular Web site through the same computer, the first time a student accesses the site from that computer, the computer will receive a cookie file. (In this case we'll assume that the publisher placed a unique ID in the cookie file, to learn more about the user.) Unfortunately, what the publisher thinks is one user is actually 100 different students using the same machine. The same problems (although to a lesser extent) are also caused by family computers that are used by more than one person.

## Auditing of Web Site Traffic

Like any other advertising medium, Web advertising needs impartial third-party verification of numbers. Independent third-party audits will provide the foundation for confidence in the Web as a legitimate advertising medium. Web measurement is the timely tracking of all activity on a particular site. At this stage of the Web's evolution, there are a multitude of Web measurement solutions available, and most folks are using them. However, auditing Web measurement reports is mostly being done only by the large commercial sites with blue chip advertisers.

When advertisers are considering a site for ad placements, the advertisers want to know about the site's traffic. As an example, a site might say that it has 30 million page views each week. How does the advertiser know that this is a true number? How does the advertiser know that the site is actually counting page views correctly? We have seen that sites both purposely and accidentally miscount traffic numbers, which is why audits are important. Audits are also important simply because advertisers are accustomed to receiving them from other advertising vehicles. Currently, most advertisers and their agencies aren't demanding audits, but we think that audits will be expected as the Internet advertising industry matures.

An audit usually tells an advertiser the total traffic of the site as well as the traffic the advertiser's ads receives (see Figure 4.7). An audit will also define the terms as the publisher's site uses them so that an advertiser can be certain what an impression really is. If an advertiser uses third-party ad serving, which we mentioned earlier in this chapter, the advertiser will have a third-party measurement of impressions and clicks, but will not have an audit of total site traffic. Just because something is done by a third-party does not mean it was audited. Also, auditors look for foul play, such as programs that will click on all advertisements to increase click-through rates.

The following are the main audit services currently available for Web sites:

**Audit Bureau of Verification Services, Inc.** (ABVS) (www.abcinteractiveaudits.com) was established on January 1, 1996. It is a wholly owned subsidiary of the Audit

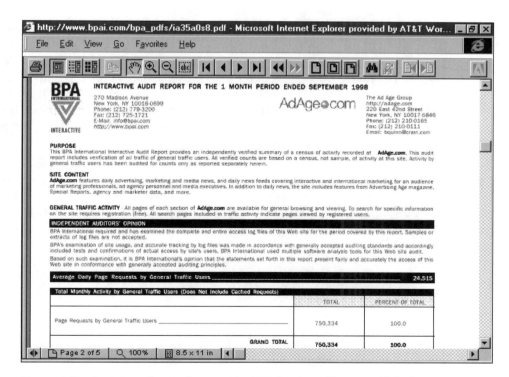

**Figure 4.7**   An Interactive Audit report by BPA for the AdAge.com Web site.

Bureau of Circulation (ABC). ABC—with over 82 years of circulation auditing experience—formed ABVS "to provide verification requirements of new and nontraditional advertiser-supported media."

**BPA International** (www.bpai.com), a global leader in magazine auditing since 1931, established an interactive auditing division because "as advertising on the Web grows into a commercially viable medium, advertisers need to know they are buying 'cyberspace' on the basis of accurate numbers that have been verified by an independent third party."

**Nielsen**, the television rating firm, has teamed with I/PRO (www.ipro.com) to offer a Web site analysis service for auditing and reporting Internet activity.

# Rating the Web One Click at a Time

In advertising, broadcasters sell time or space to advertisers to disseminate their message to a particular medium's viewership. And, every medium—print, TV, radio, and so on—has a means to judge this viewership. Viewership is determined through ratings; that is, the number of people exposed to the message. Ratings equal the percentage of a given population group (for example, U.S. households for television) engaged with a medium at an identifiable moment in time.

There is nothing dull about rating Web sites. Whether you are referring to the act of profiling site audiences or to the firms that rate the sites, this is a field full of surprises. In 1998, the rating field shrank from four players to only two teams as the result of mergers. The two biggest players in the field, Media Metrix and RelevantKnowledge, merged into a new bionic Media Metrix ("The Power of Relevant Knowledge") (www.mediametrix.com). The other team consists of the strategic alliance between Nielsen Media Research (www.nielsen.com), the company that owns TV ratings, and NetRatings (www.netratings.com).

How are sites rated? Media Metrix offers coverage of over 15,000 Web sites and online properties, with monthly, weekly, and real-time data reporting, from a representative sample of over 40,000 people measured at home, work, and school. Media Metrix uses a suite of patented software "meters" placed on participants' computers to measure actual Internet and digital media audience usage behavior. The meters capture real-time, actual behavior of Internet users at the time it occurs—minute-by-minute, page-by-page, click-by-click. Tables 4.2–4.6 present the top 25 Web sites in a variety of categories, from Media Metrix. These ratings reflect the integration of the Media Metrix and RelevantKnowledge samples following the merger.

**Table 4.2**   Top 25 Web Properties
Media Metrix, Inc.
November 1998 Measurement Period
(11/1/98 through 11/30/98)

| RANK | WEB PROPERTY | % REACH | UNIQUE VISITORS (000) |
|---|---|---|---|
| | Total Web Universe | 100.0 | 56,781 |
| 1 | AOL Websites | 53.5 | 30,350 |
| 2 | Microsoft Sites | 48.9 | 27,751 |
| 3 | Yahoo Sites | 48.0 | 27,283 |
| 4 | Lycos | 45.2 | 25,656 |
| 5 | GeoCities | 32.0 | 18,158 |
| 6 | The Excite Network | 30.0 | 17,015 |
| 7 | Netscape | 29.9 | 16,987 |
| 8 | Disney Online | 25.6 | 14,510 |
| 9 | Infoseek | 20.2 | 11,488 |
| 10 | Altavista Search Services | 19.2 | 10,907 |
| 11 | Time Warner Online | 18.6 | 10,580 |
| 12 | Bluemountainarts.com | 16.0 | 9,087 |
| 13 | Xoom Sites | 15.4 | 8,759 |
| 14 | Amazon | 13.8 | 7,812 |
| 15 | RealSite Portfolio | 12.9 | 7,326 |
| 16 | ZDNet Sites | 12.6 | 7,170 |
| 17 | BroadCast.com Consolidation | 11.8 | 6,691 |
| 18 | CNET | 11.7 | 6,670 |
| 19 | LookSmart | 10.5 | 5,982 |
| 20 | Snap.com Search Services | 9.5 | 5,377 |
| 21 | Switchboard Network | 9.2 | 5,218 |
| 22 | Infospace Impressions | 8.0 | 4,554 |
| 23 | eBay | 7.7 | 4,382 |
| 24 | Viacom Online | 7.7 | 4,374 |
| 25 | Go2Net Network | 7.5 | 4,263 |

**Table 4.3**   Top 25 Web Sites
Media Metrix, Inc.
November 1998 Measurement Period
(11/1/98 through 11/30/98)

| RANK | WEB SITE | % REACH | UNIQUE VISITORS (000) |
|---|---|---|---|
| | Total Web Universe | 100.0 | 56,781 |
| 1 | aol.com | 48.7 | 27,630 |
| 2 | yahoo.com | 47.0 | 26,690 |
| 3 | msn.com | 32.7 | 18,544 |
| 4 | geocities.com | 32.0 | 18,158 |
| 5 | netscape.com | 29.9 | 16,987 |
| 6 | excite.com | 25.1 | 14,237 |
| 7 | lycos.com | 23.2 | 13,192 |
| 8 | microsoft.com | 22.9 | 12,991 |
| 9 | infoseek.com | 19.3 | 10,963 |
| 10 | Altavista Search Services | 19.2 | 10,907 |
| 11 | tripod.com | 18.5 | 10,488 |
| 12 | angelfire.com | 16.8 | 9,533 |
| 13 | hotmail.com | 16.7 | 9,509 |
| 14 | bluemountainarts.com | 16.0 | 9,087 |
| 15 | xoom.com | 14.6 | 8,280 |
| 16 | amazon.com | 13.8 | 7,812 |
| 17 | real.com | 11.7 | 6,647 |
| 18 | zdnet.com | 10.8 | 6,112 |
| 19 | hotbot.com | 10.4 | 5,898 |
| 20 | Snap.com Search Services | 9.5 | 5,377 |
| 21 | switchboard.com | 9.1 | 5,156 |
| 22 | Disney Online | 8.6 | 4,875 |
| 23 | icq.com | 8.5 | 4,850 |
| 24 | simplenet.com | 8.5 | 4,846 |
| 25 | msnbc.com | 8.3 | 4,693 |

**Table 4.4** Top 25 Web Properties
Media Metrix, Inc.
November 1998 Measurement Period
(11/1/98 through 11/30/98)

| RANK | TOP 25 WEB PROPERTIES—AT HOME WEB PROPERTY | % REACH | RANK | TOP 25 WEB PROPERTIES—AT WORK WEB PROPERTY | % REACH |
|------|--------------------------------------------|---------|------|--------------------------------------------|---------|
| 1 | AOL Websites | 49.2 | 1 | Yahoo Sites | 49.6 |
| 2 | Yahoo Sites | 43.7 | 2 | Microsoft Sites | 48.7 |
| 3 | Microsoft Sites | 43.1 | 3 | Lycos | 39.3 |
| 4 | Lycos | 39.1 | 4 | AOL Websites | 36.3 |
| 5 | GeoCities | 27.9 | 5 | Netscape | 36.0 |
| 6 | The Excite Network | 25.0 | 6 | The Excite Network | 27.5 |
| 7 | Netscape | 24.8 | 7 | GeoCities | 24.2 |
| 8 | The Walt Disney Company Online | 21.0 | 8 | The Walt Disney Company Online | 23.8 |
| 9 | Infoseek | 15.8 | 9 | Altavista Search Services | 21.8 |
| 10 | Altavista Search Services | 15.3 | 10 | Infoseek | 20.4 |
| 11 | Time Warner Online | 14.5 | 11 | Time Warner Online | 19.5 |
| 12 | Bluemountainarts.com | 14.1 | 12 | Amazon | 14.4 |
| 13 | Xoom Sites | 13.3 | 13 | ZDNet Sites | 14.0 |
| 14 | Amazon | 10.8 | 14 | RealSite Portfolio | 12.4 |
| 15 | RealSite Portfolio | 10.3 | 15 | Bluemountainarts.com | 11.5 |
| 16 | ZDNet Sites | 10.1 | 16 | CNET | 11.4 |
| 17 | BroadCast.Com Consolidation | 10.1 | 17 | Xoom Sites | 10.1 |
| 18 | CNET | 9.7 | 18 | BroadCast.com Consolidation | 9.7 |
| 19 | Snap.com Search Services | 8.6 | 19 | Weather Channel | 9.3 |
| 20 | LookSmart | 8.5 | 20 | LookSmart | 9.3 |
| 21 | Switchboard Network | 7.2 | 21 | Switchboard Network | 8.3 |
| 22 | Viacom Online | 7.1 | 22 | Infospace Impressions | 7.6 |
| 23 | eBay | 6.7 | 23 | Snap.com Search Services | 7.4 |
| 24 | Go2Net Network | 6.3 | 24 | Miningco.com | 7.1 |
| 25 | Infospace Impressions | 6.2 | 25 | eBay | 7.0 |

**Table 4.5**   Top 25 Web Properties
Media Metrix, Inc.
November 1998 Measurement Period
(11/1/98 through 11/30/98)

| TOP 25 WEB SITES—AT HOME | | | TOP 25 WEB SITES—AT WORK | | |
|---|---|---|---|---|---|
| RANK | WEB SITE | % REACH | RANK | WEB SITE | % REACH |
| 1 | aol.com | 44.5 | 1 | yahoo.com | 48.9 |
| 2 | yahoo.com | 42.8 | 2 | netscape.com | 36.0 |
| 3 | geocities.com | 27.9 | 3 | aol.com | 34.0 |
| 4 | msn.com | 27.7 | 4 | msn.com | 32.0 |
| 5 | netscape.com | 24.8 | 5 | microsoft.com | 24.6 |
| 6 | excite.com | 20.8 | 6 | geocities.com | 24.2 |
| 7 | microsoft.com | 19.4 | 7 | excite.com | 22.8 |
| 8 | lycos.com | 18.6 | 8 | Altavista Search Services | 21.8 |
| 9 | tripod.com | 16.3 | 9 | lycos.com | 20.9 |
| 10 | hotmail.com | 15.7 | 10 | infoseek.com | 19.7 |
| 11 | Altavista Search Services | 15.3 | 11 | amazon.com | 14.4 |
| 12 | angelfire.com | 15.0 | 12 | zdnet.com | 13.2 |
| 13 | infoseek.com | 15.0 | 13 | tripod.com | 12.5 |
| 14 | bluemountainarts.com | 14.1 | 14 | hotmail.com | 12.2 |
| 15 | xoom.com | 12.7 | 15 | real.com | 11.6 |
| 16 | amazon.com | 10.8 | 16 | bluemountainarts.com | 11.5 |
| 17 | real.com | 9.3 | 17 | cnn.com | 10.8 |
| 18 | Snap.com Search & Services | 8.6 | 18 | angelfire.com | 10.1 |
| 19 | hotbot.com | 8.3 | 19 | msnbc.com | 9.5 |
| 20 | zdnet.com | 8.3 | 20 | weather.com | 9.3 |
| 21 | icq.com | 8.2 | 21 | hotbot.com | 9.3 |
| 22 | simplenet.com | 7.2 | 22 | xoom.com | 9.2 |
| 23 | Disney online | 7.2 | 23 | switchboard.com | 8.3 |
| 24 | switchboard.com | 7.0 | 24 | infospace.com | 7.6 |
| 25 | ebay.com | 6.6 | 25 | espn.com | 7.4 |

**Table 4.6** Top Shopping Web Sites
Media Metrix, Inc.
WWW Audience Ratings
November 1998

| RANK | DOMAIN NAMES | % REACH | UNIQUE VISITORS (000) |
|------|--------------|---------|------------------------|
| | total Web users | 100.0 | 56,781 |
| | Shopping | 62.7 | 35,583 |
| 1 | bluemountainarts.com | 16.0 | 9,087 |
| 2 | amazon.com | 13.8 | 7,812 |
| 3 | ebay.com | 7.6 | 4,327 |
| 4 | Barnes & Noble | 6.6 | 3,769 |
| 5 | CNET Software Download Services | 5.9 | 3,327 |
| 6 | etoys.com | 5.2 | 2,957 |
| 7 | cdnow.com | 4.5 | 2,539 |
| 8 | columbiahouse.com | 4.5 | 2,536 |
| 9 | musicblvd.com | 4.0 | 2,262 |
| 10 | valupage.com | 3.7 | 2,109 |
| 11 | classifieds2000.com | 3.6 | 2,018 |
| 12 | coolsavings.com | 3.3 | 1,851 |
| 13 | spree.com | 3.0 | 1,718 |
| 14 | bmgmusicservice.com | 2.5 | 1,445 |
| 15 | onsale.com | 2.4 | 1,359 |
| 16 | 123greetings.com | 2.3 | 1,296 |
| 17 | beyond.com | 2.2 | 1,277 |
| 18 | CNET Commerce Services | 2.2 | 1,251 |
| 19 | netmarket.com | 2.1 | 1,202 |
| 20 | surplusaction.com | 2.1 | 1,180 |
| 21 | qvc.com | 2.0 | 1,148 |
| 22 | wal-mart.com | 2.0 | 1,131 |
| 23 | carpoint.com | 1.9 | 1,076 |
| 24 | freeshop.com | 1.9 | 1,075 |
| 25 | ezspree.com | 1.9 | 1,067 |
| 26 | egghead.com | 1.8 | 1,003 |
| 27 | reel.com | 1.8 | 995 |
| 28 | outpost.com | 1.7 | 939 |

**Table 4.6**    *Continued*

| RANK | DOMAIN NAMES | % REACH | UNIQUE VISITORS (000) |
|------|--------------|---------|------------------------|
| 29 | messagemates.com | 1.6 | 913 |
| 30 | cdw.com | 1.6 | 910 |
| 31 | priceline.com | 1.5 | 880 |
| 32 | tucows.com | 1.5 | 851 |
| 33 | bestbuy.com | 1.4 | 809 |
| 34 | landsend.com | 1.4 | 809 |
| 35 | autoweb.com | 1.3 | 763 |
| 36 | mypoints.com | 1.3 | 758 |
| 37 | firstauction.com | 1.3 | 747 |
| 38 | egreetings.com | 1.3 | 739 |
| 39 | supermarkets.com | 1.3 | 712 |
| 40 | ubid.com | 1.2 | 691 |
| 41 | winfiles.com | 1.2 | 660 |
| 42 | warehouse.com | 1.1 | 628 |
| 43 | autobytel.com | 1.1 | 625 |
| 44 | surplusdirect.com | 1.0 | 595 |
| 45 | netgrocer.com | 1.0 | 575 |
| 46 | jcrew.com | 1.0 | 554 |
| 47 | netcart.com | 1.0 | 545 |
| 48 | ezbid.com | 0.9 | 520 |
| 49 | worldremote.net | 0.9 | 520 |
| 50 | filez.com | 0.9 | 516 |

**Chart definitions:**

**Top 25 Web Properties:**  The top 25 World Wide Web properties are based on unduplicated audience reach. "Web Properties" include the largest single Web site brands as well as consolidations of multiple Web domains that fall under one brand or common ownership.

**Example of "Web Properties":** An example of a "Web Property" (i.e., one that offers more than one site) is the Excite Network, which encompasses city.net, excite.com, mckinley.com, and webcrawler.com.

**Top 25 Web Sites:** The top 25 Web sites are based on unduplicated audience reach. Top sites are from Media Metrix's At Home and At Work samples.

**Reach definition and example:** The percentage of Web-active individuals (i.e., individuals in the Media Metrix sample) that visited a site once in the given month. Individual visits are unduplicated (not counted twice).  For example, if a site has a 2% reach, that means that 2% of Web-active individuals visited that site within the given month.

**Unique visitors:** The actual number of total users who visited the Web site once in the given month. All Unique Visitors are unduplicated (only counted once) and are in thousands.

## Questions to Consider before Choosing a Web Measurement Solution for Your Company

What information do you want to track? Factor in the goals you have set for your Web site, the needs of your advertisers, and the reporting needs of upper management, to determine what information a measurement solution must provide.

Is it more efficient to perform the analysis in-house or should you outsource the process?   In-house analysis is less expensive if you have a low to medium traffic site. If, on the other hand, your Web site generates high volume traffic, you need appropriate resources: disk space, adequate computer capabilities, and staff to generate reports. Moreover, the solution must be scalable for continued growth. Note that you need not only enough disk space for your current log file, but enough to archive log files so you can generate long-term trending reports.

What is the volume of traffic at your site? Can the products or service bureau handle it?   Specifically, ask software vendors how much disk space and what type of a process you need to generate reports from log files to accommodate the traffic level (usually you will be asked to provide your log file size in megabytes).

How sophisticated does your traffic analysis need to be?   Consider your current and future needs in your decision-making process.

How frequently do you need reports?   Every day, every week, every month? Daily reports can be expensive when provided by a third-party provider. Also, if you do reports in-house, do you have the staff to put the reports together?

How many different departments need to use the data (marketing, IT, financial, etc.)? Does each department need different report configurations?   It is a mistake not to check with all of the departments that will need reports before choosing a solution provider. If they all have different needs, and you learn what they are, you have a better chance of finding a product that meets all or most of them.

**What reports will your advertisers need?** If you're a publisher, before you invest in a measurement solution, make sure it meets the needs of the companies footing the bill—your advertisers. Advertisers usually want to know how many times each creative is seen and how many times each is clicked. Advertisers prefer to get these statistics daily so they can tweak their campaigns to get maximum response rates (for example, daily reports will allow an advertiser to drop a poorly performing creative at the beginning of the campaign). Advertisers also want to compare how their ads perform on different pages of your Web site. Please note that unless your site is fairly low in traffic, you will benefit significantly from using adserving software rather than log analysis software to track advertising.

**How private do you want to keep your tracking information? Will you allow your traffic statistics to be used in aggregate for industry-wide analysis by the tracking company?** If you use a third party to generate traffic usage reports, your data is often used in aggregate for industry-wide analysis, such as I/PRO's analysis of click-through rates.

**Will you need to have your reports audited?** If so, check with the company that you want to perform the audits. They may recommend a measurement solution that makes the auditing process easier.

After you've considered these questions, you can conduct further research to ensure that you're making a smart purchasing decision. Find out whether any of the measurement solutions you're considering are already serving members of your industry. Ask how the solutions are working. Another alternative is to download a demo or trial version of the software. This gives you a chance to see how products work and how easy it really is to generate the reports you need.

# CHAPTER 5

# Ad Management

T he ad management landscape can be dissected into a continuum of features that go from the most basic to highly complex and sophisticated. The first feature is advertising inventory rotation software. The next concerns reporting on ad delivery with the differentiation among products on the issue of fixed report templates or report customization capabilities. The third feature is optimization for advanced technical delivery options such as delivering rich media ads or delivering geographic targeting. And the final feature is profiling where the ad management is married with personalization and targeting such that clickstream data and demographic data is combined to deliver the right ad, to the right person, at the right time.

The key to choosing ad management technology is knowing the features available and putting together the package that best fits the needs of your company. The difficulty in differentiating products and services in the ad management arena is that it is not uncommon for every product to claim it can do just about everything. The differentiation is in the details.

When you talk about ad management, it's important to be specific as to which hat you are wearing. Ad management is an issue for publishers on the one side and agencies and advertisers on the other. The tasks and tools are driven by different immediate questions and concerns, although the goals are the same—delivering online ads efficiently, accurately, and cost effectively to achieve a campaign's objective. This chapter will look at ad management from both sides. First we'll examine ad management and how it services publishers. Then we'll look at how ad management services the agency community.

# Ad Management for Publishers

When we were researching the first edition of *Advertising on the Internet*, we were told a story by a major Web publisher that demonstrated the importance of ad management tools. It turns out that in this publisher's early days they used to manage their ads by making a yellow Post-it note for each ad that was supposed to run and placing the Post-it on a big whiteboard that served as the schedule for ad flights (placement and length of run for each ad). This worked fine until they started running dozens of ads, each for different numbers of impressions and lengths of time.

One day they found a Post-it on the floor behind a chair and discovered that it represented an ad that was supposed to have run weeks before for one of their major sponsors. Now they were going to have to confess that the ad never ran. They couldn't fake it because every ad run had a report showing its activity, and this one obviously didn't. That's all it took for this site to take down the whiteboard and develop an ad server/management tool to automate and organize the process so that no ads could get lost because a yellow sticky fell on the ground.

Publishers realized that they needed a tool to help them manage ad inventory. They also realized they needed software that could tell them how many impressions they had to sell and organize the delivery and rotation of the ads. In the Internet industry, if there is a need, it is not too long before there are many software options.

Publishers now have two approaches they can take in dealing with serving and managing their ad inventory: they can mange their ad inventory in-house or use a third-party outsourcing solution. We will cover the full range of options, whether you are a small site or a large commercial venture, and whether you have a budget of $50 or $50,000 to invest in managing your ad inventory.

## In-House Ad Management

There are a number of choices for in-house ad serving software, and they differ greatly in terms of ease of use, price, and features (see Table 5.1).

For those with more time than money and who have the technical know-how to use bare-bones options, there are freeware and shareware banner rotation scripts available. Scripts such as Bannermatic (www.getcruising.com/crypt/banmat.html) and WebAdverts (www.awds.com) can do the job of rotating banners, but require a great deal of technical competency to set up and maintain. This is a popular choice for the small site on a tight budget.

The second option, popular with small to mid-size sites, is inexpensive ad serving software such as Ad Café Professional (www.infohiway.com/adcafe) and Central Ad PRO (www.centralad.com). These software options manage ad inventory, rotate ads, and provide ad delivery reporting. They can cost from $200 to $1,000, depending on features.

For the large sites, more robust and feature-intensive ad management solutions are needed. These tools don't just traffic your ads, making sure the right ad goes up for the right amount of time; but the software also reports on the activity of the ad (number of impressions and click-throughs). Products in this category include NetGravity's AdServer (see Figures 5.1 and 5.2), the Accipiter line from Engage Technologies (see Figure 5.3), and Real Media's Open AdStream. They are used by major commercial Web sites that are some of the highest trafficked sites on the Internet, and deliver thousands of ads per hour. These companies, of course, offer extensive customer support.

Purchasing software for in-house use is much less expensive than buying both the software and management services of a third party, but the savings must be balanced against the cost of staffing the management and operation of the software in-house. Both the largest and smallest sites have chosen to manage the ad delivery process on their own.

## Ad Management Service Bureaus

A site can choose to outsource the delivery of its ads to a service bureau (see Table 5.2). This option allows the publisher to delegate the entire ad servicing process, allowing him to focus on the business of running the site.

One of the leading Web-based services for delivering ads is DoubleClick's DART (www.doubleclick.com) (see Figure 5.4). This service manages all ad serving and reporting functions for a site and runs the entire process through DoubleClick's central servers. This means that a site has two T3 lines, with redundant service providers delivering ads,

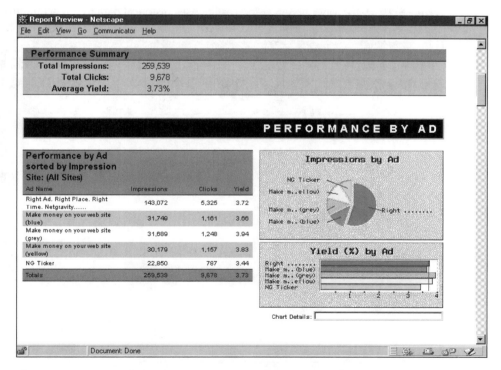

**Figure 5.1**    NetGravity's AdServer 3.0 gives advertisers insights into their ad performance.

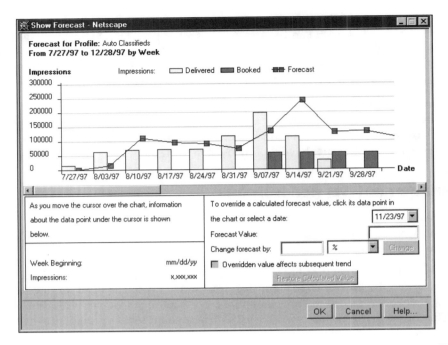

**Figure 5.2**    NetGravity's AdServer forecasting uses historical data to project traffic growth.

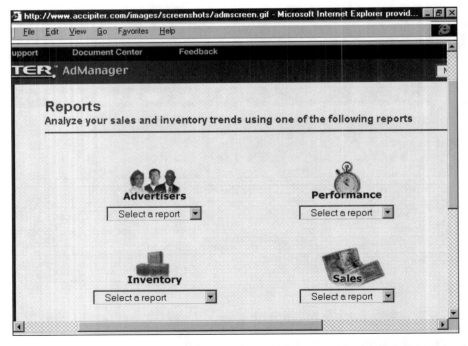

**Figure 5.3**    Accipiter's system assists you in analyzing your sales and inventory needs and trends.

**Table 5.1** Ad Server In-House Software Options

| | FREEWARE OR SHAREWARE | INEXPENSIVE OPTION | FULL-SERVICE SOLUTION |
|---|---|---|---|
| Bannermatic (www.getcruising.com/ crypt/banmat.html) | X | | |
| WebAdverts (www.awds.com) | X | | |
| Ad Café Professional (www.infohiway.com/adcafe) | | X | |
| Ad Juggler (www.adjuggler.com) | | X | |
| Central Ad PRO 3.0J (www.centralad.com) | | X | |
| Engage Accipiter (www.accipiter.com) | | | X |
| NetGravity AdServer (www.netgravity.com) | | | X |
| Real Media Open AdStream (www.realmedia.com) | | | X |

not to mention a setup that is expensive and complicated, and outside of the capabilities of many sites. The technical benefits to the publisher are the following:

- No hardware or software installation, just the addition of a few lines of HTML
- Delivery of rich media creatives
- Delivery of multiple ads per pages and different ad sizes

Indeed, for some sites, the convenience of outsourcing is well worth the price of the service.

# Ad Management for Advertisers

Ad management is also very much an issue for agencies and their advertisers. An agency needs to know who saw the ad, if that person clicked on the ad, and if any further action was taken. Agencies have two options: they can evaluate the ad campaign themselves or use a third-party ad management solution.

What does it mean for an agency to do it in-house? It means dealing with each site individually for all requests, from flighting creatives to making changes to collecting reports. For example, if your ads are running on 12 sites and you need to change one banner on each, you'll have to e-mail each of the 12 sites with a request to change the ad

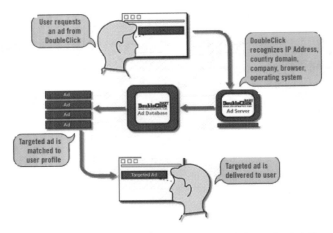

**Figure 5.4** How DoubleClick's DART Web-based ad delivery service goes from request to delivery.

**Table 5.2** Ad Management Service Bureaus

| SERVICE | FUNCTION | PRICING | SELECT CLIENTS |
|---------|----------|---------|----------------|
| Accipiter's AdBureau | Service includes all hardware and soft-ware to serve and track ads 24 hours a day. Does not aggregate click-through data. | Based on number of ads served each month | Microsoft; ChannelOne; BabyCenter; Bank Rate Monitor; Tripod; WebTV; ZDNet; WiseWire; Prodigy; Policy.com |
| NetGravity's AdCenter | Full-service ad serving solution for small and mid-size sites. | Monthly usage cost based on number of ads served | N/A |
| AdForce's AdForce | Full-service ad management solution for ad networks and large Web sites. | Based on ads delivered | AdAuction; FortuneCity; TN Technologies; Modem Media.Poppe Tyson; Eisenberg Communications; GeoCities; Netcom; Hachette Filipacchi |
| DoubleClick's DART | Web-based service; allows a site to manage all of its ad serving and reporting functions using DoubleClick's central servers. | Based on ads served | Wall Street Journal Interactive; NBC; Excite Europe; Reader's Digest; RealNetworks |

Source: 1998 Jupiter Communications

and so on. It also means gathering ad campaign reports from dozens if not hundreds of sites and evaluating the effectiveness of the campaigns. In many cases, this becomes a case of comparing apples and oranges. Indeed, one of the many hurdles in front of the online ad industry is developing standards in ad delivery reporting.

There are several agencies who have developed excellent in-house tools for ad serving: Thinking Media (www.thethinkingmedia.com) developed ActiveTrack; Modem Media.Poppe Tyson and TN Technologies developed TNToaster; Organic Online (www.organic.com) developed Borscht; and ORB Digital Direct (www.orb.net) developed ORBit3.0. Some of these agencies are even selling their ad servicing technology commercially, as i33 (www.i33.com) is doing with their AdMaximize product.

# Third-Party Ad Management

A more popular option is to use a third-party ad management solution that facilitates the buying, placement, and analysis of the campaign. This allows advertisers to have consistent reports, a single source for managing ads on every site on which they advertise, and more control over targeting. For example, if an advertiser is running advertisements on Yahoo! and using her own ad management option, she can have the ad server deliver different advertisements to users depending on whether they are from an educational institution or a business. These services save the agencies headaches and significant amounts of time.

Moreover, ad management tools are also taking the next step and facilitating ad planning, processing the insertion orders, and performing post-buy analysis. For example, AdKnowledge's Planner automates the entire Web advertising process from pre-planning to billing. AdKnowledge has a suite of products that includes Planner, a solution for researching and planning online media campaigns (see Figure 5.5a); Campaign Manager, for trafficking, reporting, and post-buy analysis of media campaigns as well as one-to-one database marketing (see Figure 5.5b); and Administrator, which integrates Web ad buy data and performance analysis with agencies' existing accounting and billing systems (see Figure 5.5c).

The costs of these services can be up to $2 CPM on the impressions you deliver through their service, plus additional fees for special services.

Before you make a long-term commitment to use one of the ad management services, be sure to test them. Some may have problems working with the sites on which you advertise and may not be able to serve ads perfectly.

## *Closed Loop Reporting*

In addition to factors measuring Web advertising effectiveness (such as the number of times an ad is served and the number of times the ad is clicked), an advertiser needs to know deeper measures, such as which ads drove the people who purchased a product, requested a catalog, or looked at four pages. This is known as *closed loop reporting* because it goes beyond the measurement of clicks—closing the loop to measure actual effectiveness.

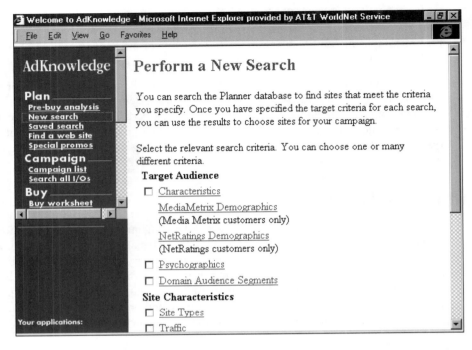

**Figure 5.5a** AdKnowledge's Planner lets you search their database to find the best sites for your campaign.

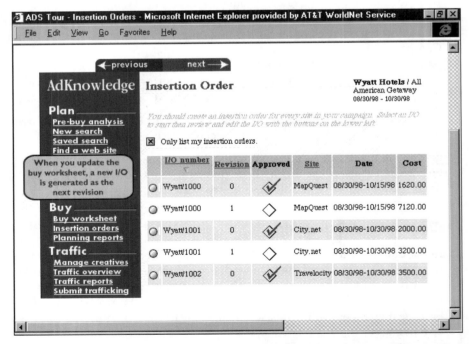

**Figure 5.5b** AdKnowledge's Campaign Manager assists in placing insertion orders.

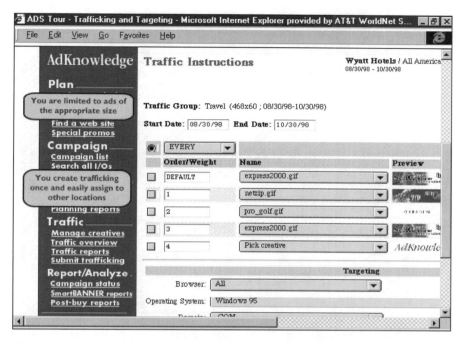

**Figure 5.5c**    AdKnowledge's Administrator manages the flight dates of each ad.

Many companies develop custom closed loop reporting solutions. For those who can't or don't want to develop their own solutions, there are some third-party services that offer closed loop reporting, such as AdKnowledge (www.adknowledge.com) and MatchLogic (www.matchlogic.com) (see Figure 5.6).

# Products for Both Publishers and Advertisers

When you line up all the products and services on the market for ad management, it's clear that the movement is to have products from one company that can meet the needs of publishers and advertisers alike. Having one company with products that can wear both hats eliminates compatibility and comparability issues. One company moving in this direction is AdForce (www.adforce.com) (see Figure 5.7).

**Advisor Post-Click Report**

**Client: ABC (identity concealed)**
**Campaign: XYZ (identity concealed)**
**Period: Oct. 1 - Oct. 10, 1998**

| By Site/Location/Creative | Ad Views | Clicks | Click rate | # of Post-Click Events | | | | Conversion Rate (Events per) | | |
|---|---|---|---|---|---|---|---|---|---|---|
| | | | | Bridge Page | Product Info | Send me info | Thank You | Bridge Page | Product Info | Send me info |
| **News Site** | | | | | | | | | | |
| Finance news | | | | | | | | | | |
| It's Fun! | 25172 | 179 | 0.71% | 159 | 68 | 47 | 27 | 0.63% | 0.27% | 0.19% |
| Free! | 25021 | 181 | 0.72% | 163 | 61 | 43 | 25 | 0.65% | 0.24% | 0.17% |
| Runs anywhere | 46357 | 422 | 0.91% | 363 | 111 | 90 | 55 | 0.78% | 0.24% | 0.19% |
| Easy to use | 27658 | 155 | 0.56% | 134 | 43 | 51 | 24 | 0.48% | 0.16% | 0.18% |
| Good service | 25211 | 125 | 0.50% | 119 | 38 | 38 | 22 | 0.47% | 0.15% | 0.15% |
| Finance news totals | 149419 | 1062 | 0.71% | 938 | 321 | 269 | 153 | 0.63% | 0.21% | 0.18% |
| **News Site totals** | 149419 | 1062 | 0.71% | 938 | 321 | 269 | 153 | 0.63% | 0.21% | 0.18% |
| **Search Engine A** | | | | | | | | | | |
| Keywords | | | | | | | | | | |
| It's Fun! | 14234 | 106 | 0.74% | 89 | 35 | 25 | 19 | 0.63% | 0.25% | 0.18% |
| Free! | 14082 | 85 | 0.60% | 79 | 31 | 16 | 12 | 0.56% | 0.22% | 0.11% |
| Runs anywhere | 27588 | 281 | 1.02% | 149 | 60 | 41 | 23 | 0.54% | 0.22% | 0.15% |
| Easy to use | 14141 | 70 | 0.50% | 64 | 21 | 17 | 8 | 0.45% | 0.15% | 0.12% |
| Keywords totals | 70045 | 542 | 0.77% | 381 | 147 | 99 | 62 | 0.54% | 0.21% | 0.14% |
| News | | | | | | | | | | |
| It's Fun! | 5381 | 32 | 0.59% | 24 | 9 | 8 | 7 | 0.45% | 0.17% | 0.13% |
| Free! | 5321 | 35 | 0.66% | 29 | 9 | 3 | 4 | 0.55% | 0.17% | 0.06% |
| Runs anywhere | 10688 | 112 | 1.05% | 67 | 10 | 5 | 3 | 0.63% | 0.09% | 0.05% |
| Easy to use | 5565 | 28 | 0.50% | 22 | 4 | 1 | 1 | 0.40% | 0.07% | 0.02% |

**Figure 5.6**  MatchLogic closed loop reporting gives a comprehensive analysis of a campaign's performance on each site.

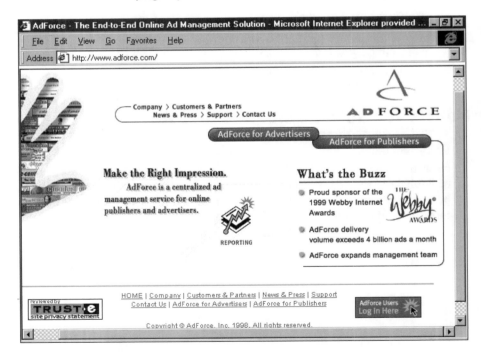

**Figure 5.7**  AdForce offers their suite of products to both advertisers and publishers for added compatibility and comparability of reporting.

# Objects Are Closer Than They Appear

Rex Briggs, Vice President, (rex@mbinteractive.com)
Millward Brown Interactive (www.mbinteractive.com)

The advancements I'll refer to come with a warning similar to the one on an automobile's side-view mirror: Objects are closer than they appear. Translation: We will soon see highly precise systems that will allow marketers and e-commerce sites to accurately assess the impact of their messages.

The way it stands upon the writing of this book is that marketers have a lot of loosely associated information, but nothing that helps them track marketing effectiveness from beginning to end. This is a *big* problem. Most of us expect marketing to be as predictable as a science; after all, you'd think that when you visit a company's Web site and enter your name or when you make a purchase from a company using your credit card that this information would be organized in the database, ultimately making the entire process more efficient and customer support more effective. While this technology exists, the follow-through has been lacking.

Today, the bits of information that marketers have gathered look more like an abused hallway closet: You open the door cautiously, so as not to disturb all the stuff that is precariously stacked. A lot of so-called marketing databases look like that dreaded hallway closet—plenty stuffed into it but rarely organized to find anything useful when you need it. But the good news is that those loosely associated bits of marketing data—ad exposure, visitation to a store, purchase of a product, etc.—are getting tied directly together in a tightly defined profile of purchase flow. This is not about advertising versus direct marketing; it's about selling and relationship management. The new tools will organize the information and put the data to use to make the marketing systems more efficient and effective.

This means marketers will have a meticulous scorecard letting them track their messages from establishing the stage in which creative is tested, to understanding how consumers are processing the message psychologically, all the way to determining what percentage of the people who saw an ad for a specific product actually purchased it. Marketers will be able to track not only who purchased their products and services once, but those who purchased repeatedly over a longer period of time; this means they will be able to treat the consumers who are most profitable differently than those who are less profitable. And beyond measuring online purchases, off-line purchases will be measured as well. Systems like Millward Brown Interactive's VOYAGER Profile, DoubleClick's Closed Loop, and AdKnowledge's Advisor are here, but in their infancy. As marketers become accustomed to these more precise systems at their disposal they will be able to more accurately assess the impact of their marketing—both on- and off-line.

# 6

# Targeting—The Online Advertising Advantage

For a long time Internet advertisers dreamed of delivering the right ad to the right person at the right time. In the early days of online advertising, the realization of this dream was touted as the true promise and potential of the industry. What was once just promise is now a reality. Various strategies are now readily available to capture the demographics, tastes, and preferences of users to better target content and advertising. In a broadcast television campaign, advertisers can target by geographic location, time of day, and the audience watching a particular show. With a direct mail campaign, marketers can target as finely as Fortune 500 employees who have attended safety and health conferences. Internet advertising can offer an advertiser all the targeting capabilities of other media plus a lot more. Indeed, on the Internet an advertiser can finally target every ad so that it goes out to just the right prospective customer at precisely the right time.

Advertisers use targeting to ensure the efficiency of their campaigns. Online publishers have a variety of targeting options to offer their advertisers (see Figure 6.1). In fact, online targeting moves up a continuum from the most basic means of reaching a customer up to extremely technologically sophisticated methods of learning about customers. The continuum starts with ad placement based on content and context. Next comes targeting gleaned from information received from the users themselves through site registration systems. Then there is targeting based on information available through Web measurement and ad serving tools. Targeting also occurs through database mining, collaborative filtering, behavioral analysis, and personalization tools. Today, these advanced tools are readily available and remarkably accurate. Advertisers are taking advantage of these targeting options to increase the effectiveness of their online ad campaigns.

The industry's intense interest in targeting rests on its benefits. First, targeting eliminates wasted impressions by only delivering ads to interested persons or those in the

# The Road to Customization and Personalization

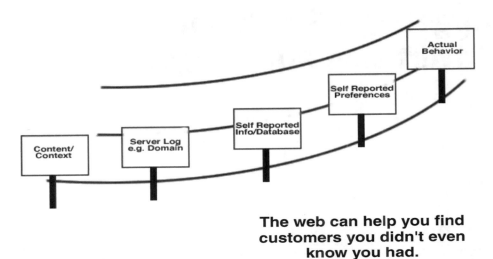

The web can help you find customers you didn't even know you had.

**Figure 6.1**  Internet advertising targeting continuum.

right target audience. Second, an ad is not considered a nuisance when it is information a person wants. Targeting ads to the right people increases interest and response.

How does the ad targeting actually occur? Targeting is facilitated through ad serving solutions. In the early days of targeting, the ad servers were separate from the targeting technologies, especially those providing personalization and customization. In 1998, these tools began to merge and form alliances to better facilitate ad delivery. In this chapter we're going to discuss the targeting continuum and demonstrate how targeting is the online advertising advantage.

## Targeting Based on Content and Context

The most basic form of targeting is through content and context. This is how the bulk of targeting is done in traditional media. In magazines an advertiser can appeal to a particular gender or age group or niche market, by advertising in *Sports Illustrated* or *Teen People* or *Cat Fancy*. Using context to target, you can take your targeting a step further—for example, by advertising a car dealership on the classified ad page listing automobiles for sale, or a sporting goods store in the sports section of the newspaper.

This also holds true for radio, broadcast TV, cable, and even billboards. Targeting through content and context, of course, is also an option for online advertising.

On the Web there are thousands of content sites from which advertisers can choose. And, each of these sites offers a variety of targeting opportunities. There are probably few Web sites as good for reaching sports enthusiasts as ESPN (www.espn.com). And, if advertisers wants to further target within ESPN they can do so. For example, Mercedes-Benz runs advertising in the golf area instead of the basketball area (Figure 6.2 shows a Mercedes ad running in the golf section of ESPN and targeted towards golfers).

Similarly, advertisers can target through keywords on search engines. This is a much more focused buy than simply running an advertisement across a search engine.

Another example of content and context targeting is advertising for Prilosec on the health site InteliHealth (www.intelihealth.com). Although the entire site is about health, it is much more effective for Prilosec, a drug for persistent heartburn, to run advertisements in the heartburn area rather than throughout the site. Figure 6.3 shows the ads running in the targeted heartburn section.

## Targeting Based on Registration Information

The simplest and often most accurate way to find out about a user is to ask the user directly. The key here is that users need to provide that information. The publisher

**Figure 6.2**   Mercedes-Benz ad on ESPN targeting the high-income demographic of golfers.

**Figure 6.3** Prilosec targets its banner ads for heartburn medication in the "Digestive Disorders" section of InteliHealth.

may be able to get users to provide personal information by offering the opportunity to customize the Web site, enter a contest, receive a discount, or some other means. Basically, the publisher needs to give the user a very good reason to provide demographic data. If the Web surfer provides that data, the ad server can work in conjunction with the database that stores customer profiles and targets ads accordingly. For example, if a pet site asked users to register for a drawing for a year's supply of pet food and the consumers list their type of pet, the dog food makers would know they weren't wasting advertising inventory; they could target only those people who said they had dogs as pets. (Often, if a publisher can get the user to provide a zip code for customized news, weather, or other information, other demographic data can be pulled based on the zip code.)

One of the main misconceptions in the use of ad serving software is that publishers believe the software will make this type of targeting a reality. The software will enable this type of targeting, but the publisher needs to collect the data from the consumer to make it work.

Since targeting can always be improved with user-supplied information, we thought we'd go through some tips for getting your customers to give you that information.

**Provide value.** In general, users have expressed that they do not want to provide information to Web sites. However, they will provide information, if there is value. In Figure 6.4 users are asked to submit their zip code to The Weather Channel

**Figure 6.4** Weather.com provides customized weather reports to users who supply their zip code.

(www.weather.com) to get customized weather information. Most visitors to weather.com will probably provide this information, because they want the weather for their geographic area. After getting zip code information, weather.com can use a database to determine the household income, geographic area, and basic demographics about the user.

**Tell people how they will benefit from providing you information.** MSNBC also requests a zip code for news, sports, and weather. Instead of simply saying "customize this site," MSNBC entices the user by explaining the benefits of customization as the carrot for providing information. If your site asks for multiple pieces of information, it is good to explain how each piece of user-provided information will improve the user's experience on the site.

**Only ask users to provide information that will play a part in delivering them value.** The more a site asks of a consumer, the less likely the consumer will be to provide information. Therefore, if a question you ask isn't absolutely critical to your business or to providing value for the consumer, don't ask it.

It is interesting to note that there are some exceptions to this rule. We have found specifically that consumers visiting healthcare sites, when given an option, will choose to fill out a long form over a short form, if they think it will help them get information that is more customized to their needs.

**Ask consumers for information in a fun way.** The Excite home page often asks an interesting poll question. Users can enter their answer and then go to a page to see the cumulative tally from everyone who has answered the poll. In Figure 6.5 you can see a sports poll. This is fun for users, who are voicing their opinions, probably without even realizing that this can add to the user profiles that the site is building based on their behavior and answers to poll questions.

**Privacy statement.** Consumers are very concerned with what will happen to their information after they provide it. Response rates will improve if you have a clear privacy stance linked from every page on which the user is asked for data. The Direct Marketing Association provides resource information on building a privacy statement (www.dma.org).

**Give users a reason to be truthful.** This goes back to providing value. If each question doesn't lead to value for consumers, it is very likely that many of the responses you receive will be lies.

In trying to gather consumer data, it's important to keep in mind how the consumer feels. A 1998 Jupiter/NFO Interactive survey of consumers found that only 16 percent of respondents reported that they were "very likely" to register at a site that requires registration. The study went on to ask what factors would encourage them

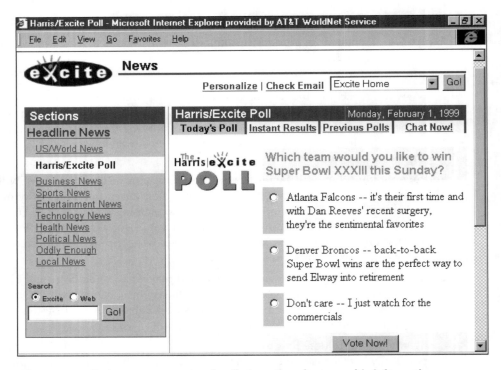

**Figure 6.5** Excite uses surveys and polls to gather demographic information.

to fill in a registration form (see Figure 6.6). Over half of the consumers (56 percent) said that their willingness to register would increase greatly with a guarantee that their personal information would not be misused. Other reported important factors included content of higher value (41 percent) and a less time-consuming registration process (32 percent). Incentive programs ranked lower in this survey, with only 23 percent saying affinity points would serve as an enticement, and 21 percent that sweepstakes would.

In addition to putting up a registration page, there are software options like Lead Spinner 2.0 (www.leadspinner.com), which tries to make the registration process more friendly for consumers. The software installs a program so that when the site is loaded, visitors receive a message on the screen that asks them if they wouldn't mind if their visit was logged. If they accept, then the data about the user is sent via e-mail into a database. If the user says no, then nothing is taken and the user can continue through the rest of the site without any further bothers. "As you can see, this is a great tool and service for people to use to find out 'who' is visiting the site as well as turn visitors into potential sales," says Brian Kilcrease, vice president of Glass Spider Designs, Inc.

## Using Cookies for Targeting

In the conversation between browsers and servers, cookies can be exchanged, which makes them useful for targeting. As we mentioned in Chapter 4, cookies are a way to identify browsers on a Web site. (A brief refresher: a server can place a cookie on a hard drive. The cookie most often contains a unique string of text that allows the user's browser to be recognized if the user returns to the Web site.) A cookie can track what visitors do on the site and target accordingly. For example, site visitors that go to the sports section numerous times could be "tagged" as sports people and delivered an NFL ad the next time they came back to the Web site.

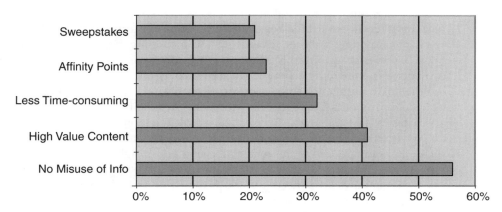

**Figure 6.6**  Factors that would greatly increase an online user's willingness to complete an online registration form.

Cookies can be used to facilitate user behavioral targeting. Behavioral targeting entails having enough content on your site that you can determine a user's preferences based on his or her actions on your site. For behavioral targeting you can create rules. For example, if a user goes to hiking content, that person should be profiled as an outdoors person. Or behavior-based targeting can be controlled by the software, which gauges a user's likeliness to want certain content or click particular ads based, for example, on the actions of previous users who took similar navigational paths.

An interesting use of cookies for behavior-based targeting is through a service that builds a user profile across those Web sites that use the service. There are a number of ad serving services that cookie users and track them across all participating sites. As users make decisions about what ads to click, or fill out registration forms, the software builds profiles that advertisers can use for targeting. A service like MatchLogic, which tracks users across high-traffic sites like Excite and WebCrawler, can generate a very large database of profiles, which will help advertisers deliver ads to the right people. As of the writing of this book, Engage Technology, another targeting service, had 30 million profiles. When advertisers or publishers deliver an ad through one of these services, they can target based on these profiles. In the future, this type of targeting will allow non-targeted buys to become targeted. For example, an advertiser could run an advertisement on Yahoo! and ask that the ad be delivered to users who request gardening information and who live in zip codes that indicate a certain income level. Later in this chapter we'll mention other companies that provide this type of targeting. It's important to note that a company like MatchLogic can only get registration information if that information is shared by the site on which they're delivering the ads. In the case of Excite, since the company owns MatchLogic, it's clear that the two share data.

## Targeting through Database Mining

Combining ad management software solutions with consumer profiling technology is a hot targeting technique that appeared on the scene in late 1998. One example, NetGravity's Global Profile Service (www.netgravity.com), enables advertisers and publishers to target Internet advertising and marketing messages based on comprehensive consumer profiles. NetGravity is working with such industry-leading data providers as MatchLogic (www.matchlogic.com) and Aptex (www.aptex.com) to build a flexible and anonymous consumer profile data source. "By aggregating multiple data providers," says Rick Jackson, vice president of marketing at NetGravity, "NetGravity's Global Profile Service will enable the thousands of Web sites powered by NetGravity to better understand their audience, and target advertisements and direct marketing offers with greater precision and insight." The Global Profile Service is based on using cookies to recognize users and build profiles of their interests. The service allows advertisers to unlock the value of their inventory by analyzing and segmenting audiences more acutely. "Precision Internet marketing and targeting requirements differ greatly from site to site and advertiser to advertiser. Since no two customers require the same data, a flexible solution is required," said Mark Peabody, a senior analyst with Aberdeen Group.

# Targeting through Profiling and Personalization

Now we're going to discuss technologies that usually work in conjunction with an ad server to help profile prospects and deliver them customized advertisements or content (see Table 6.1).

## Recommendations as Ads

Creating profiles to personalize content and make recommendations to consumers helps sites to secure sales, especially retail sites like CDnow and Amazon.com. The better these sites can service the customer by recommending appropriate products, the more likely the customer is to purchase. Retailers like these can use engines that make recommendations based on previous inquiries and purchases. The engines can also make recommendations by asking users about their tastes. For example, CDnow has incorporated NetPerception's (www.netperceptions.com) recommendation engine into its site. Users are asked to provide a a list of artists they like. The engine then searches its database for people who listed the same artists and recommend their recent purchases. If consumers rate a list of products, they can get recommendations when the engine cross-references their ratings with other users. Engines can also make recommendations by tracking what the user does on the site and comparing it to rules developed by the publisher or to other visitors.

**Table 6.1**  Personalization Companies

| COMPANY | COMPANY TAG LINE | SELECTED CLIENTS |
| --- | --- | --- |
| Art Technology Group (ATG) (www.atg.com) | Manages online relationships from advertising to commerce through personalization technology. | BMG Music, Kodak, Newbridge Networks, Sony, Sun Microsystems |
| BroadVision (www.broadvision.com) | Internet application solutions for one-to-one relationship management across the extended enterprise. | American Airlines, Liberty Financial, Softbank, Sony Communication Network, Sun Microsystems, US West |
| Net Perceptions (www.netperceptions.com) | Developer and supplier of real-time recommendation solutions. | Amazon, CDnow, E!online, Ticketmaster |
| GuestTrack (www.guesttrack.com) | Tailors content "on the fly" based on the interest profile of each member of the client's audience. | |

# Personalization

Personalization helps a company send relevant messages to different target audiences that are visiting their Web site. For example, age-sensitive ads can be dynamically delivered to customers fitting the age profile. And this is exactly what American Airlines is able to do using Broadvision's (www.broadvision.com) Dynamic Command Center. Once American Airlines knows that a user on its site is over 21 years of age, a beer or wine ad can be shown. Another use of personalization is through action-based targeting to offer purchasing incentives. For example, if an online shopper places an item in a shopping cart and then removes that item, you can offer a discount when she comes back to that item as an incentive to complete the purchase. By knowing the customer's activity history, you can move browsers into buyers.

Art Technology Group's (www.atg.com) Ad Station uses sophisticated behavior tracking to create a profile on each visitor, and uses this profile to deliver targeted and compelling ads (see Figure 6.7). "In the Internet business world, time, ease of use, accessibility, and performance is everything," says Nancy Morrisroe, Director of Public Relations, at Art Technology Group. "We created the Personalization Control Center so that business users don't have to rely on programmers to specify targeting rules for personalization."

Another personalization option comes from Net Perceptions (www.netperceptions. com). Their Ad Targeting technology can be deployed from within the framework of most leading ad server platforms and starts learning about each site visitor's interests and tastes from the first visit and keeps learning with every repeat visit. Tracked variables include recency/frequency, behavioral information, page ID, time of day, demographic information, keywords entered into search engine, and other categorical information. "This product increases Web site advertising revenues by increasing click-throughs for advertisers," says Steve Larsen, Net Perceptions' VP of marketing and business development. "It does this by automatically learning the individual interests and tastes of site visitors, then putting the right ads in front of each visitor in real time." The software deploys different ad targeting technologies at different times, so that it dynamically adjusts between new visitors, about whom it has minimal information, and repeat visitors, about whom it has learned much more. According to Larsen,

## Benefits of Personalization and Customization

**Segmenting users.** You can segment your users into affinity groups for better targeting of promotions.

**Matching promotions to users.** You can match time-sensitive and topic-specific promotions to users.

**Integrating legacy systems with current customer databases.** You can customize every contact a user has with your company.

**Tailoring the Web site.** You can customize a Web site to each user's interests and tastes.

**Tailoring the sales copy.** You can customize sales copy to each user's interests and tastes.

"Targeting gets increasingly personalized as the software continually learns about each visitor's individual interests and tastes." Although speaking for his own company, Net Perceptions, Larsen is really talking about the goal of all the services we've discussed in this chapter.

Net Perceptions' software learns continually and gets smarter with each customer interaction. Like most software of this kind, NetPerceptions can also integrate user-provided information (as in the cases of Amazon.com and Cdnow who both use Net-Perceptions) to customize their content. Net Perceptions' recommendation engine works like a salesperson, recommending products that match a person's tastes and interests (see Figure 6.8a and 6.8b).

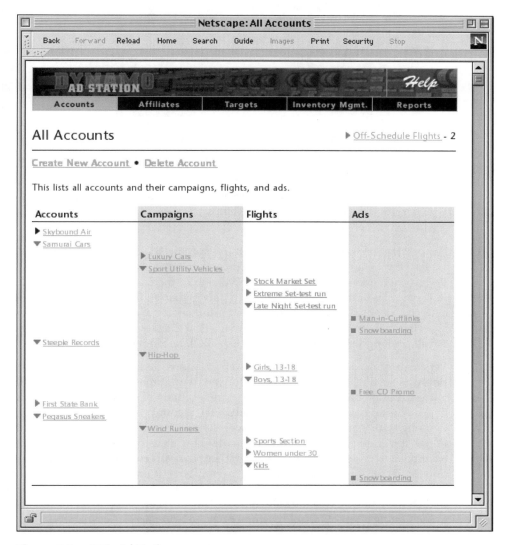

**Figure 6.7** ATG's Ad Station.

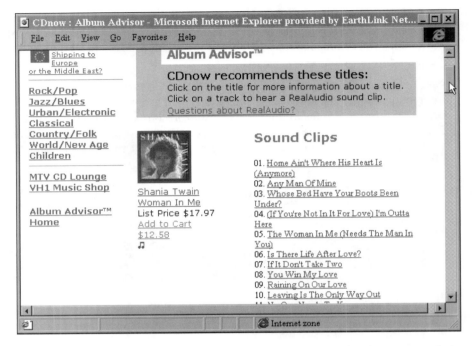

**Figure 6.8a** CDnow's "Album Adviser" uses the Net Perceptions' recommendation engine. The "Album Adviser" asks a customer to supply names of three of their favorite artists or albums.

Personalization is not language- or cultural-specific. BOL uses Net Perceptions' software extensively as an online bookseller to consumers in the United Kingdom, Germany, France, Netherlands, and Spain (each version of the site in the appropriate language). BOL employs both implicit and explicit data gathering in order to generate highly specific customer ratings. The site offers customers an array of personalization choices, allowing them to get ratings quickly with a *Book Chooser* function, and then continues to develop a long-term relationship using the BOL Recommendation Center.

Personalization doesn't stop on the Web; it is moving off-line as well. Personalization products such as BroadVision's One-to-One (www.broadvision.com) can be integrated with corporate data warehouses that store all kinds of customer information. One-to-One can be accessed by a corporate call center, account executives, or sales staff, whether working with a customer online or over the phone. With this system, the personalization that started online continues no matter how a customer contacts the company. For example, when a customer calls the company, the call center operator can access the customer's record, which lists what that person bought online and the customer's entire contact and purchasing history. This eliminates the need for customers to begin from scratch each time they contact the company. BroadVision sees personalization as a means of integrating all the available customer data to better service customers.

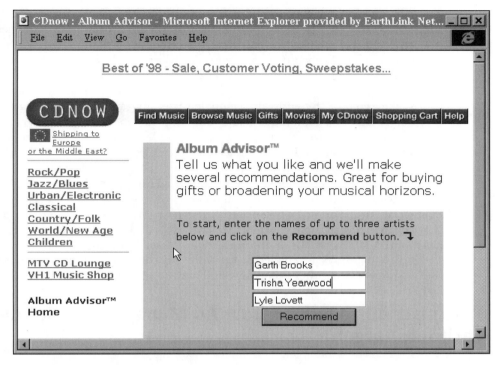

**Figure 6.8b** The "Album Adviser" then makes recommendations of other artists and albums.

## Collaborative Filtering

Another type of personalization is based on collaborative filtering. The company who perfected this technique is Firefly (www.firefly.com). A Firefly-enhanced site works by offering users the option to get a "passport." Users who register for a passport provide personal information building a personal profile. Drawing on each user's profile, Firefly can make recommendations based on its knowledge of passport users with similar profiles. Businesses can then leverage this information to provide each individual with highly personalized service and customized ads. Sites can also use Firefly to build community; users with similar profiles can find and communicate with one another. Users have an incentive to use their passports because it will mean customized content and recommendations. Sites that use Firefly can choose to have a passport exclusively for their site or to be part of the network of passport sites sharing profile information.

## Behavioral Targeting

And finally, the last stage on the continuum is targeting based on a person's actual behavior at any moment in time. One of the companies offering this services is Aptex (www.aptex.com) with its SelectCast for AdServers. SelectCast acts as an "intelligent observer," mining the context and content of all actions—including clicks, queries, page views, and ad impressions. No explicit user feedback or "taste" judgments are ever required. No cookies are used and the information is not captured or saved. SelectCast unobtrusively profiles all user actions, learning the detailed interests of each user, and applying this knowledge to every ad selection. Designated ads can be delivered consistently to selected groups, and new audiences can be automatically identified as they emerge. By correlating updated user and audience profiles against ad inventory, SelectCast continuously fine-tunes ad delivery. Aptex also offers products that help to personalize a Web site by using profiles to deliver custom content and e-commerce promotions. In short, SelectCast compiles demographic and taste information without registration or database mining. Sites that utilize SelectCast have become the secret weapon for successful banner ad campaigns for such noted interactive agencies as Anderson & Lembke and Left Field. Brent Hall, Internet Active Media Planner at Anderson & Lembke says "I use it on the majority of my campaigns." Infoseek uses SelectCast for its UltraMatch service and Brian Monahan of Left Field has found that placing ads on Infoseek's UltraMatch has resulted in better targeting making all their buys as targeted as keyword buys. In short, SelectCast can help you find customers you didn't even know you had.

## Putting It All Together: How Ad Management Solutions Facilitate Targeting

As we mentioned in Chapter 4 on Web measurement, information is shared between a site's server and the user's Web browser. Advertisers use this information for ad targeting. As a brief refresher, here are some of the targeting abilities that result from this technology-based conversation:

- IP address: domain and host (once the company name is determined, some services allow for SIC and revenue targeting).

- Geographic location: national, local, etc. (For issues regarding local targeting, see Chapter 11.)

- Browser used: Internet Explorer 4, Internet Explorer 3, Netscape 4, etc.

- Date and time of request.

- Computer platform: Mac or PC, and version of operating system.

Ad management server software now integrates targeting with ad delivery. Below is a list of the ways ad management software integrates targeting into the delivery of ads.

**Frequency capping.**   An ad server can limit the number of times an ad is seen by the same person (usually through the use of cookies). Along those lines, an ad server can also manage the delivery of a sequence of advertisements.

**Targeting based on the standard industry code (SIC) of the browser.**   The SIC represents the sector of the economy in which a company falls. For example, there is an

SIC for ad agencies. When a user goes to a Web site, the browser reveals its IP number. The SIC can be determined by looking up the company at the IP number (let's say it's i-frontier) and then determining that company's SIC from a database (in this case, advertising agency). The same system can be used to target by company size and revenues.

**Profiling/personalization.**   As we mentioned earlier, this allows the advertiser to target based on the user's behavior (what content he chooses to view, etc.) or user-provided registration (or customization) data.

**Profiling base wider than site.**   Some services build profiles of users from all of the sites that use their programs or services. Advertisers can benefit from profiles that have already been developed across other sites.

**Research company partner.**   Many of the services have partnered with database firms to bundle already existing customer databases and database profiles with information gathered online.

**Closed loop reporting.**   A system to provide advertisers with a means for measuring which ads produce specific results.

**Auditing.**   If you're a publisher and you want to provide audited numbers to your advertisers, all of these services can be tied into audits.

**Types of ads that can be delivered.**   We haven't included this information in Table 6.2, because it is constantly changing. However, it is important to make sure that your service can deliver the types of ads you want to use. For example, currently, not all services can deliver all types of rich media ads.

# Privacy

As we mentioned earlier in this chapter, a strong privacy policy is important for getting users to provide information. Here is Firefly's privacy policy:

**Firefly Network Privacy Policy**

Your e-mail address will not be shared outside of the Firefly Network for marketing purposes without your consent.

Profile information will be used to create personalized content, services, and advertising on sites in the Firefly Network. In addition, Firefly and third-party licensees may use your profile to generate aggregate reports and market research.

You may inform Firefly Network, Inc. at (www.firefly.com) at any time if you would like to cancel your account and have your contact information deleted from Firefly's records.

In addition to the Firefly Network Policy, we also take the following steps to ensure your privacy on sites operated by Firefly Network Inc.:

1) Firefly Network Inc. does not require an end-user to provide a name and address to use the service.

**Table 6.2** Ad Management Targeting Capabilities

| COMPANY, TECHNOLOGY NAME | NAME OF SERVING SOFTWARE THAT CAN BE INSTALLED | NAME OF SERVING SERVICE | PROFILING/ PERSONALI- ZATION | PROFILE BASE WIDER THAN SITE | RESEARCH PARTNER FOR ANALYSIS | CLOSED LOOP REPORTING | COMMENTS |
|---|---|---|---|---|---|---|---|
| AdKnowledge (www.adknowledge.com) | Not offered | SmartBanner | Yes | Yes | Yes | Yes | For advertisers and ad agencies. Also offers functionality that assists an advertiser in planning an ad campaign and executing a buy. |
| Double Click (Doubleclick.com) | DART | DART | Yes | Yes | Harris Black International | Yes | Offers a service for tracking e-mail advertising. |
| Engage Technologies (www.engage.com) | Engage Technology | Accipiter AdBureau | Yes | Yes. They currently have 30 million profiles. | VOYAGER Profile from Millward Brown Interactive | No | Over 2000 Web properties currently use Engage, allowing for an extensive profiling base. |
| AdForce | Not offered | AdForce | Starpoint | Yes | VOYAGER Profile from Millward Brown Interactive | Yes | |
| MatchLogic (www.matchlogic.com) (owned by Excite) | Not offered | MatchLogic | Yes | Yes | Harris Black International | Yes | Offers unique technology for counting cached impressions. |
| NetGravity, AdCenter (www.netgravity.com) | NetGravity AdServer | NetGravity AdCenter | Yes | Yes | Yes | Yes | Gets their profiling information from MatchLogic and Aptex. Plans to use other vendors as well. |

2) All profile data stored by Firefly Network Inc. has been entered solely by the respective end-user.

3) End-users can modify registration data associated with their account, and can control the amount of this information that is disclosed on their member page.

4) Firefly Network Inc. does not provide functionality to perform "reverse searches" which find individual names from address, e-mail, or phone number information.

5) Conversational transcripts of online chat are not retained except for moderated chat sessions.

6) Firefly Mail communications are only accessible by the designated recipients, except that Firefly Network Inc. personnel involved in maintenance of the system may have access to e-mail communications.

7) Recommendations are generated solely based on an end-user's rating preferences and the preferences of other end-users, and are not generated by Firefly Network Inc. or its advertisers.

Some Web sites that use Firefly include barnesandnoble.com, Ziff Davis, and Yahoo! Figure 6.9 shows a page where users of the Barnes and Noble site can sign up to get a passport. After they receive their passport, users can enter titles of books they've enjoyed and books they haven't liked. Based on that information, a user's profile

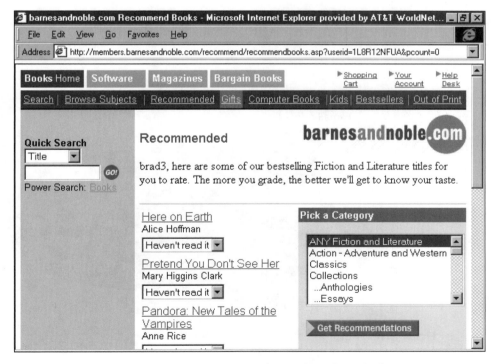

**Figure 6.9**  Barnesandnoble.com recommendations based on Firefly.

will be compared to those of similar users to determine other books that the user would enjoy.

Privacy is a big concern when it comes to personalization issues. When BOL (the online book-selling venture of Bertelsmann AG) decided to employ Net Perception's personalization technology for its European customer base, it had to address the heightened privacy concerns of European customers. The site developed a unique privacy policy element to allow customers to update their personalized profiles as well as their BOL purchasing history, making the customer master of his profile information. For a full discussion of privacy issues, see Chapter 13.

## Keeping Customers Is a Continuous Process

Interestingly enough, companies will develop very sophisticated personalization systems like the ones we mentioned in this chapter, but fail to take the time to respond to customer e-mails. Ken Allard, group director at Jupiter Communications, notes that companies often make sizable investments in personalization technology to derive what users want and then ignore the users when they communicate directly with the company to tell them. In a 1998 study Jupiter found that only 38 percent of major sites respond to customer inquiries within a day (see Figure 6.10). Personalization means being able to reach a person and retrieve an answer, not just fancy profiling systems.

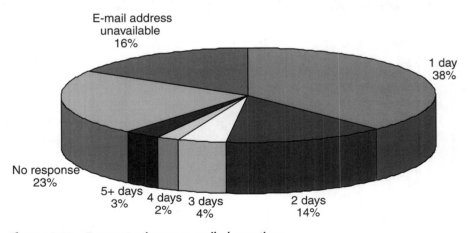

**Figure 6.10**    Response time to e-mailed questions.

## Interactive Marketing: An Unparalleled Opportunity to Reach the Right Customers at the Right Time

Ann Burgraff, Director of Corporate Marketing (ann@netgravity.com)
NetGravity, Inc. (www.netgravity.com)

1998 saw the Internet universe mature dramatically. For online advertising—everywhere, not just in Silicon Valley—there was a revolution. With more and more eyes on the Internet each day, major brands began to recognize the tremendous potential of online advertising to drive online business. Some trends that emerged were partnerships to create standards; initial public offerings; ad agencies taking more control over their online advertising campaigns; and publishers, merchants, and agencies demanding a range of solutions, both service and software, to fit their specific online advertising management needs, and maximize their efforts.

If 1998 was the year of revolution, 1999 will be the year of evolution. The Web has become a 24/7 customer interaction channel capable of delivering a personalized and targeted individual experience for each customer. It is closer to in-person interactivity than any other marketing channel and needs to be treated as such. We see online advertising expanding to tap into this opportunity. Mere online advertising will not be enough. Interactive marketing will be the demand for an even better approach to reach the right people at the right time. Interactive marketing will introduce the need for a whole new set of requirements to meet the needs of publishers, merchants, and ad agencies:

**The right fit.** It will be key for online marketing solution providers to provide the most appropriate solution for each customer, whether it be a customized solution for a market segment, software, service, or the ability to migrate from software to a service.

**Customer intelligence.** Offering the means to pinpoint the most profitable audience will be critical in ensuring that our customers' business is successful. It is our job to provide publishers, merchants, and ad agencies with the ability to collect different categories of data, both implicit and explicit, integrate a solution with existing corporate data, and offer the tools to analyze the data and make intelligent decisions based on the results.

**The ability to meet the needs of the Global 2000.** This means having unlimited scalability, global operations, full range of service, and enterprise-level partners. Interactive marketing will be a critical element of successful Internet strategies.

With interactive marketing maturing, we can begin to see the Internet for what it really is—an unparalleled opportunity to reach the right customers at the right time.

# CHAPTER 7

# Pricing Online Ads

The Web was born into a dichotomous environment: the Internet culture was founded on free access to information, but its content is extremely expensive to produce, especially if it is expected to rival TV, radio, and print for the public's attention. In the United States, commercial broadcast TV and radio are supported 100 percent by advertising, newspapers 80 percent, magazines 63 percent, and cable TV 50 percent. Naturally, Web publishers are hoping that advertising will cover the lion's share of the costs for their publishing ventures (and ideally even generate some profits). The results look promising—top publishers are beginning to tally significant ad revenues (see Table 1.4), and advertisers are concomitantly increasing their Web advertising budgets each year (see Table 1.3).

When advertising on the Web first began, no one knew how to price. The only known figure was the fee HotWired decided to charge for its first ads in 1994: $30,000 for banner advertising that ran for 12 weeks. "It was a bottom-up approach," recalls Rick Boyce, VP of advertising for HotWired. The figure was derived from the amount of revenue HotWired needed to generate. At that time, there was no pricing model and no precedent, so other sites quoted that same amount.

Modem Media, an interactive agency (now known as Modem Media.Poppe Tyson) based in Norwalk, Connecticut, was one of the first agencies to begin placing banners on Web sites. John Nardone, director of Media and Research Services at Modem Media, was not satisfied with the unaccountable pricing structure, so he developed his own method for calculating an online advertisement's value, which he called the Internet Reach and Involvement Scale. Word spread about Nardone's system, and soon he was getting a dozen calls a day asking him to help determine costs. Nardone remembers, "What I used to tell people was that I'll help you price your ad if you give my client

Zima.com an ad for half price. It was a really fun time. We were out on the Internet frontier." Before long, his scale had become the de facto pricing model.

But as more ad models developed, different pricing structures rapidly evolved with them. Currently, pricing models range from flat-fee to paying for the number of times an ad is seen to paying for the number of people who clicked on the ad to paying on a cost-per-lead or cost-per-purchase basis. The purpose of this chapter is to explore all of these models in use today.

# Pricing Models

Current pricing models are as varied as the ads themselves. As an industry, Web advertising is looking to other industries for role models; direct parallels cannot always be drawn, but in general, both a mass market and a direct marketing approach apply. The Internet can still be measured based on impression, just as TV, radio, and print can, but many believe that the Internet is actually more applicable to direct marketing, where clicking on an online ad can be likened to opening a direct mail envelope.

## CPM

The most dominant pricing model, which has been briefly mentioned throughout this book, is cost per thousand, or CPM. CPM delineates the price charged for displaying an ad one thousand times. This is the unit of measure used in traditional advertising, which is why advertisers and agencies are comfortable with a CPM model.

The calculation to determine CPM is:

- Price ÷ (number of impressions ÷ 1000)

For example, if a site charges $10,000 per banner and guarantees 500,000 impressions, the CPM is $20 ($10,000 divided by 500).

But how do you determine the appropriate CPM for an online ad? Is it $1, $10, $30? Internet advertising CPMs range from $1 all the way up to $200. The price for Web advertising varies across sites, but, in general, similar types of sites are charging rates in the same general range. The types of sites we're going to cover in this chapter include search engines, content sites, online services, and ad networks.

Keep in mind that prices are constantly changing, so the figures you read here should be regarded only as "ballpark" for different sites. Figure 7.1 shows the average CPMs over time from AdKnowledge, a company that maintains a database of sites that accept advertising. As you can see from the chart, ad rates varied significantly during the time period covered by this chart. And, these are gross prices; usually, advertising agencies receive a 15 percent discount off gross prices, paying the *net price*. Publishers are constantly adjusting their rate cards, and prices also fluctuate depending on the number of impressions purchased and over what time period they are delivered. To look at some actual rate cards, refer to information in the accompanying Web site at www.wiley.com/compbooks/zeff.

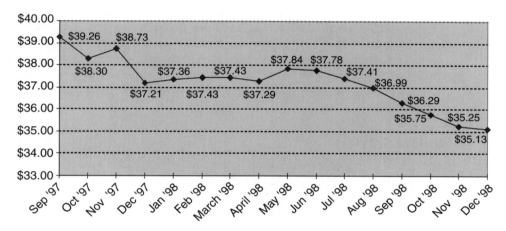

**Figure 7.1** Average CPM rate chart from AdKnowledge.

Source: AdKnowledge, Inc.

## Search Engines

Search engines and directories are receiving a large portion of advertisers' budgets; in fact, according to Jupiter Communications (see Table 1.4), the top four Web publishers by ad revenue are search sites. It is easy for advertisers to spend a large chunk of money on a high-traffic search engine rather than spreading the ad budget among many smaller sites that will deliver the same audience. The ad buyer only has to deal with one person instead of negotiating with multiple sites, sending ads to each of the sites, and so on. Search engines offer several pricing categories, each distinguished by its level of targetability.

**General rotation.** A banner will randomly appear during searches. General rotation prices usually range from a $15 to $25 CPM. On buys over $50K advertisers can sometimes get rates in the single digits.

**Run of category.** Advertising will rotate throughout a category such as arts, entertainment, or sports. Yahoo! (www.yahoo.com) charges a $20 CPM for run of category with a minimum of 500,000 impressions. It is interesting to note that Yahoo! is one of the few sites that does not offer a discount to advertising agencies.

**Keyword targeting.** Search engines also allow advertisers to "buy keywords"; this means the banner appears only when a user searches using specific keywords. Because the audience is more highly targeted, the CPM is higher. For example, the search engine Excite (www.excite.com) charges a $24 CPM for general rotation, a $60 CPM for advertising in a specific Excite channel, and a $70 CPM for keyword targeting. Keywords are in limited supply (unlike general rotation impressions) and in high demand by advertisers. Therefore, many of the search engines charge an additional fee to have exclusive rights to a keyword. (For example, at the time of this writing, the search engine Snap! (www.snap.com) charges a $1,000 fee for exclusivity for a keyword.) In many instances, the exclusive right to a keyword also means that the advertiser has the first right to purchase future inventory of that keyword.

As we mentioned under "Text Links" in Chapter 2, the search engine Lycos (www .lycos.com) has created additional keyword inventory by charging for the banner impression as well as a text impression; this is an ad placement that they recently developed. Because of the high demand for keywords, we think keyword prices will continue to rise faster than any other ad inventory (Excite is already at a $70 CPM), and we will see more sites following Lycos's lead and developing additional keyword type placements.

## Online Services

AOL offers a variety of CPM rates based on ad placement. At AOL, rates for run of service are a $30 CPM (250,000 minimum impressions). AOL sells much of its advertising inventory in packages. One type of package they offer is an industry package—an ad buy that they recommend for a specific industry. For example, AOL has packages for parenting, real estate, shopping, and sports. The price for these packages ranges from a $13 to a $17 CPM, with costs from $9,000 to $24,000 for one month. These buys will include some non-targeted placements. AOL also has targeting of specific site areas like movie reviews, record labels, and game shows online. The CPM for these buys is about $60.

## Content Sites

Content site advertising typically costs more than search engine general rotation because the audience is more targeted; users are interested in the specific content that is presented. For instance, ESPN's SportsZone (www.sportszone.com) sells a promotional package that costs $100,000 for 1.2 million impressions per month ($83.33 CPM). A targeted sports package is $250,000 and includes sponsorship of the area of choice and a guaranteed delivery of 1 million impressions ($25 CPM). A general rotation through SportsZone costs $15,000 per month for 500,000 impressions ($30 CPM). Content sites generally charge a $20–$45 CPMs. However, if the content is of a general nature, or it is not high quality, CPMs could drop below that price point. And, ad sites that are extremely targeted can charge more than the $45. An example is ClickZ, a site targeted toward media buyers, which charges up to a $70 CPM.

## Ad Networks

DoubleClick (www.doubleclick.net) is an example of an advertising network (see Table 10.2 for a list of ad networks). A media buyer can make one purchase with DoubleClick and have an ad placed on dozens of sites. For example, an advertiser who purchases impressions in DoubleClick's Sports/Leisure/Entertainment affinity would be able to run banners on the various sites that DoubleClick represents in this category. Put another way, a network gives an advertiser much greater reach than most individual sites. The CPMs for the DoubleClick network run from $30 to $70 depending upon the category. Technology is at the high end, with a $70 CPM, and the entertainment affinity is at the low end, with a $30 CPM. For an additional price, advertisers can also target by geography, domain name, SIC code, and company name and size.

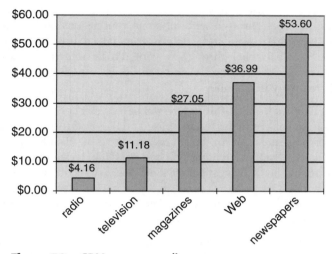

**Figure 7.2** CPMs across media.
Source: AdKnowledge, Inc.

## CPM Comparisons

How do these prices compare to the CPMs of traditional media? Take a look at Figure 7.2, and you'll see that Web CPMs tend to be higher. There are two justifications for this: not only is this is a new industry with no fixed market rate, but more importantly online advertising allows for a sophisticated level of targeting as demonstrated in Chapter 6. On the Web, advertisers can target by keyword, SIC code, company, geographic location, and time of day. Advertisers also have opportunities to target by preferences. Indeed, prices will continue to fluctuate as new targeting opportunities and new advertising units are developed.

# Click-Through

The term *click-through* refers to the action of a viewer clicking on an ad. Paying per click-through is one of the pricing models derived from a direct marketing perspective.

Advertisers and publishers began debating the merits of the click-through model when, in late spring 1996, Procter & Gamble (P&G) negotiated with Yahoo! to purchase ads for five P&G brands on a click-through basis. This was a big move because it negated the value of Web advertising for brand building and put all the weight in Web advertising's direct marketing appeal. In effect, P&G was saying two things: first, that there was no value to simply having its banners seen—no brand-building value; they were putting a premium only on getting clicks. And second, that the burden of getting a banner clicked was on the publisher as much as on the creative. The online advertising world took notice because P&G is the nation's largest advertiser, and prior to its move, most pricing was CPM-based. Furthermore, the model held publishers accountable for response, but the publishers weren't producing the creative; and wasn't there some branding value in having a user see a banner?

According to John Nardone of Modem Media, Yahoo! did not simply agree to P&G's new model of paying per click-through without some concessions on P&G's part as well. P&G agreed to give Yahoo! input and veto power on the creative P&G submitted. Since Yahoo! was responsible for click-through, it wanted to be able to modify the banner ads if necessary to ensure their success. And by this time, Yahoo! knew a great deal about what worked creatively in a banner ad.

The ability to accurately measure click-through response to Web banner advertising has led many advertisers to push for pricing models based on these performance measures. The benefits of click-through are clear for the advertiser. The advertiser knows from the start what the Internet advertising campaigns will cost per click. "A saving grace for our small-site online advertising has been cost per click model," says Scott Sizemore of New Media Consulting. "Without arguing the merits and drawbacks between CPC [cost per click] and CPM, it has been our experience that many clients feel more comfortable beginning paid advertising campaigns in the Cost Per Click arena."

The benefit to publishers using click-through pricing is not always so clear. Some say that the advantage is that a pay-per-click model entices advertisers who otherwise wouldn't place ads on their site. However, the concept of paying per click-through has met with harsh criticism by many publishers for several reasons:

- A click-through pricing structure requires publishers to rely on the quality of advertisers' creatives to generate revenues. Traditionally, the role of a medium is to offer access to an audience, not to share in the responsibility for the quality of the advertisement itself. Since many advertisers are new to the medium, the publishers are being asked to gamble on the advertisers' learning curve, a burden Web publishers are reluctant to take on.

- This model encourages a publisher to run a banner until the advertisement receives the number of clicks an advertiser purchased. This could result in a publisher compromising its inventory and ultimately the user's experience on the site.

- This model completely dismisses a banner as having brand-building value.

The pricing for cost per click can run anywhere from $2 to five cents. As an advertiser, it's nice to buy on a cost-per-click basis because you have some level of security. However, advertisers need to remember that a click probably isn't the real goal, so they've got to come up with a metric to determine the quality of those clicks. For publishers it's important to maintain the right to veto creatives for cost-per-click campaigns. Publishers will know what works best on their site, and there is no reason to accept a creative that will have a low response rate for a cost-per-click campaign.

For those advertisers who are interested, there are some Web properties that generally accept advertising on a cost-per-click basis. One is the ad network ValueClick (www.valueclick.com). ValueClick has more than 10,000 member sites, and sites are generally paid fifteen cents per click by ValueClick (which of course then charges advertisers a higher rate). Advertisers can target based on affinities to better qualify their prospects (for example, targeting sports sites that are members of the network). ClickTrade (www.clicktrade.com) is a program in which advertisers can post the cost-per-click advertising for which they would be willing to pay. Then sites that are part of the ClickTrade network can decide if they want to accept that deal. ClickTrade manages the process and charges a 30% fee on top of the price set by the advertiser. ClickTrade also offers cost-per-order and cost-per-lead advertising options. We discuss ClickTrade in more detail later in this chapter under "Affiliate Programs." Figure 7.3 is an offer as it would appear to a ClickTrade member site deciding what advertisements to accept.

GoTo.com (www.goto.com) is a pretty interesting cost-per-click search engine. Advertisers can buy keyword advertising on a cost-per-click basis. The advertiser who pays the most has her listing appear first. The interesting thing is that next to each search engine result, GoTo.com lists the amounts that the various advertisers have offered to pay per click to come up first. So, anyone using the search engine can see who is paying to come up early in the search results and how much they are paying. Figure 7.4 shows the search results on GoTo.com for the phrase "Star Trek."

There are many cost-per-click opportunities on the Web, but it's not always easy to find them. Mark Welch's Web Site Banner Advertising site (www.markwelch.com/bannerad/baf_click.htm) has a page where many cost-per-click opportunities are listed and evaluated (see Figure 7.5).

## Flat Fee

Some publishers are charging a flat fee for advertising—a set amount charged either monthly or yearly for ad placement on a site. Thus, the fee is tied to a time period, not impressions or visitor activity. Flat-fee pricing is used in several circumstances.

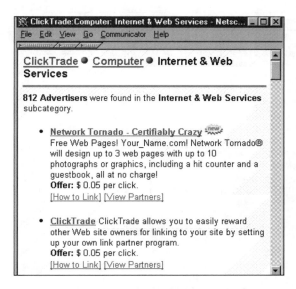

**Figure 7.3**    An offer as seen by a ClickTrade member site.

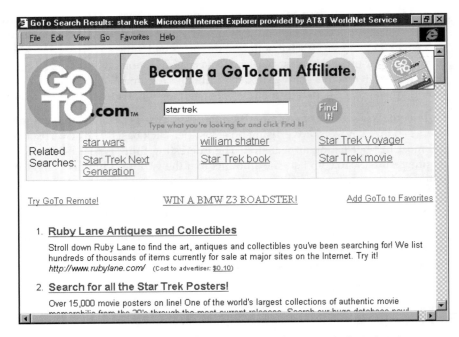

**Figure 7.4** GoTo.com search results show users how much the advertiser pays for each click.

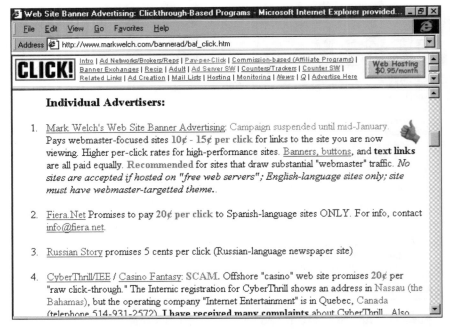

**Figure 7.5** A page from Mark Welch's Web site on banner advertising.

**Seed money.** Flat fees are often used when a publisher needs seed money, in which case the publisher often determines rates based on the amount of money needed. Clearly, this was the reason HotWired charged what it did for its first ads back in 1994. PriceSCAN (www.pricescan.com), a search engine that finds the lowest prices on goods, will often add new categories of products when an advertiser comes to them and offers sponsorship money in return for creating the content. Since Price-SCAN does not know the traffic of the category they are adding, they charge the sponsor an amount that will cover the cost and that they think will be reasonable given past traffic patterns. If the sponsor had not come forward, that specific category would not have been placed in the front of the development schedule.

Sites that are developing new content areas also charge a flat fee for seed money. These properties need to sell sponsorships before they know the amount of traffic the site will generate. Advertisers run the risk of paying a lot of money for a low volume of traffic, but there is also the potential to receive much more traffic than anticipated. Also, if the advertiser has a good relationship with the publisher that is creating the new content area, the advertiser can often get make-goods if the new property underdelivers on expectations.

**Low pricing.** The Year 2000 site (www.year2000.com), which covers the information systems problems that are predicted to arise when we reach the year 2000, is commercially supported by advertising that is bought on a flat fee. On the Year 2000 site, a large number of sites pay a low fixed price. The site is designed in frames, and each advertiser is given a text link on the home page in a sponsorship frame; the 100 advertisers are accessible on the home page, as shown in Figure 7.6. The Year 2000

**Figure 7.6** The Year 2000 site uses flat rate pricing.

site has three packages, which range from $2,000 to $6,000 per year, depending largely on the type of link provided. The full package, which is the most popular, offers a link directly to the advertiser's home page. For clients without a home page or on a limited budget, there are less expensive options that offer links to mini-pages with an e-mail link. Charging a yearly fee reduces the time the site needs to administer the accounts. The effort to deliver traffic reports, renew, and bill advertisers on anything less than a yearly basis is not worthwhile when the advertising rate is so low (it would only be $166 to $500 per month). By implementing pricing policies in a manner that precludes significant administrative labor, the Year 2000 site can also charge less money. "We have been on solid financial ground since day one," reports Cliff Kurtzman, CEO of Tenagra, publisher of the site. The Year 2000 format generates a high volume of advertisers at a low fixed rate.

**Premium placements.** Flat-fee pricing is also used for premium placements on a particular Web site. For example, Netscape charges a search engine a flat fee to have a search listing on its popular search page. The amount, a dollar value over $5 million (both cash and barter), is now the norm for such high-profile premium placement opportunities.

## Pay Per Viewer

Another model is to charge advertisers every time a user interacts with their brand. The new services that sell this type of advertising offer users money and other incentives, often similar to frequent flyer miles, to read advertisements and participate in interactive experiences with the advertiser's brand. Users can get paid for everything from visiting advertiser sites to filling out surveys to purchasing products. The philosophy is that the most valuable commodity on the Web is a person's attention and that the best way to acquire that is through direct incentives.

## Pay Per Purchase

Taking the payment-per-response model one step further, some advertisers have negotiated to pay only when purchases result from their advertising. This places publishers at the mercy of both the ad creatives supplied and the consumers' interest in purchasing a particular product. This arrangement can be favorable to both the advertiser and the publisher in a few situations when the item is highly targeted, but in most cases, this model clearly benefits the advertiser. The publisher assumes all risk for the advertiser's campaign, and there is no value placed on the brand exposure that advertisers receive through ads that aren't clicked. But, if the advertiser has to choose between no ad revenue and pay-per-sale ad revenue, the pay-per-sale model isn't all that bad.

In 1996, Orb Communications & Marketing, an interactive agency in New York, negotiated one of the first large-scale pay-per-purchase deals, for Nabisco Direct. The arrangement placed advertising for four Nabisco holiday gifts: Oreo and Mr. Peanut cookie jars, a holiday gift basket, and chocolate-covered Oreos. The advertising ran on such sites as Excite (www.excite.com), as well as on entertainment sites like MovieLink (www.movielink.com), Comedy Central (www.comcentral.com), and Entertainment

Drive (www.edrive.com). Nabisco paid only a percentage of sales generated by each publisher's site.

Publishers are reluctant to accept this type of deal because they feel that it underestimates the brand-building capabilities of advertising on the Web, but some sites will accept a pay-per-purchase negotiated price.

## Affiliate Programs

Another variation of this model is paying per sale through affiliate programs. Affiliate programs go by numerous names, including *partner* and *associates* programs, but they are most commonly referred to as affiliate programs. The typical affiliate program is run by an advertiser who would like publishers to run advertising on a cost-per-action basis. Instead of a usual ad buy that is negotiated on a site-by-site basis, most affiliate programs are automated. A publisher will go to a merchant site, fill out a form to become an affiliate, and then have access to instructions for how to set up links, ads, or a virtual storefront that points toward the merchant. Figure 7.7 shows a sign-up page for an affiliate program. The merchant tracks the success of the advertising, and pays the participating publishers accordingly. The process is automated, so that the advertiser can have thousands of sites promoting his business, without having to invest the resources in negotiating with each site. To publicize affiliate programs, advertisers will often run an advertising campaign. They will also list their affiliate programs on the sites that have directories of these opportunities (see Table 7.1).

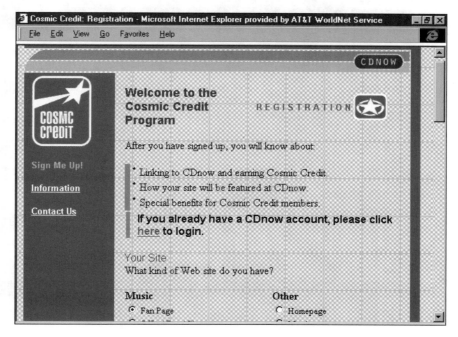

**Figure 7.7**   A sign-up page for the Cosmic Credit affiliate program.

Members of an affiliate program most often get paid a percentage of sales. This is a great way for advertisers to extend their reach with very little expense; advertisers only pay for orders that are generated. Also, the products can be sold within context. For example, a newspaper that belongs to Amazon.com's affiliate program can allow consumers to purchase a book right after they read the review. The newspaper will receive a percentage of the sale, and Amazon will probably successfully sell books through that type of contextual advertising.

"Affiliate marketing is simply direct marketing. In the cyberworld it allows marketers to be much more one-to-one, and products are marketed in context," says Gordon Hoffstein, COO of affiliate software maker Be Free. "There's no overhead. If it doesn't work, you don't pay."

However, advertisers must be aware that when publishing sites become affiliates, they can start to play a hand in promotion. The affiliate will try to promote the advertiser's store or products by running various ads. Instead of a logical link from a book review to purchasing the book, a site may place Amazon.com logos all over their site, and run Amazon.com banners that they create, to help generate more revenue. Since most merchants view sales as their primary objective, this isn't usually a problem, but the merchants must be prepared to occasionally have their brand advertised in a manner that they wouldn't choose themselves. As we mentioned in the newspaper example, affiliate programs usually go beyond a publisher simply running adver-

**Figure 7.8** Amazon.com affiliate store within the Women.com site.

**Table 7.1** Affiliate Program Resources

| SITE | DESCRIPTION |
|------|-------------|
| ChannelSeven's Ad-Guide (www.ad-guide.com/Affiliate_Programs/) | Directory of advertising affiliate programs |
| Mark Welch's Web Site Banner Advertising (www.markwelch.com/bannerad/baf_commission.htm) | An annotated list of all affiliate programs, both domestic and international |
| ClickQuick (www.clickquick.com) | A listing of affiliate and pay-per-click programs |
| Associate Programs.com (www.associateprograms.com) | Directory of associate programs |
| Revenue Avenue (http://revenue.linkexchange.com) | Listing of affiliate programs |

tisements. Publishers often create their own store within their site for the merchant. For example, Figure 7.8 shows the Women.com site, an affiliate of Amazon.com. Women.com built a store within their site. As you can see, the promotion is especially effective, because the advertisements are for books that are going to be of interest to Women.com viewers. Also, the site has the Women.com brand on it serving as a direct endorsement of the books.

The first granddaddy of all affiliate programs (and of of the very first) is online bookseller Amazon.com. They offer 15 percent of sales on most books and 5 percent of sales on out-of-print books and other items. Like most affiliate programs, Amazon.com provides the graphics and technology for publishers to set up their own bookstores. Information on Amazon.com's affiliate program is available at www.amazon.com (click on the "join associates" link).

Some affiliate programs pay on a sliding scale. Bookseller Barnes and Noble (www.barnesandnoble.com) pays commissions between 3 and 7 percent depending on the amount of sales an affiliate site generates. Table 7.2 provides some examples of affiliate programs. A list of affiliate programs resource sites is available in Table 7.1.

We've listed some of the larger affiliate programs in Table 7.2, but there are literally thousands of affiliate programs with all sizes of sites and all types of product offerings.

There are hundreds of topic-specific affiliate programs: everything from Lobsternet (www.thelobsternet.com) (see Figure 7.9) to Viagra sales at KwikMed (http://kwikmed.com/viagra/101985/affiliate.html) (see Figure 7.10). For example, CarPrices (www.CarPrices.com/join.html) has an affiliate program for cars price quote requests, insurance quote requests, and other inquiries. They pay between $1 and $12.50 per information request or information purchase. A complete breakdown of CarPrices' pricing is given in Table 7.3.

**Table 7.2** Sample of Affiliate Programs

| COMPANY | DESCRIPTION | COMPENSATION PROGRAM (PERCENTAGES OF SALES UNLESS OTHERWISE SPECIFIED) |
|---|---|---|
| Amazon.com (www.amazon.com) | You can build a virtual bookstore based on each section, and recommend books, music, and magazines. | 5%–15% |
| (www.barnesandnoble.com) | You can build a virtual bookstore based on each section, and recommend books, music, and magazines. | 3%–7% |
| beyond.com (www.beyond.com) | An online software superstore. They have a large section of educational software to which you can link and recommend specific titles for specific curriculums, or even offer a "recommended tutorial" list for parents. | 5%–10% |
| ClickTrade (division of LinkExchange) (clicktrade.linkexchange.com) | Offers a unique program where you can actually get paid for simply sending visitors to another site. ClickTrade will serve up the ads of the partners you choose and track how many visitors from your Web site clicked on the ad. They also pay on a per-lead and per-sale basis. | Varies depending on the company, ranging from $0.01 per click to $0.25 per sale or click. |
| Cyberian Outpost (www.outpost.com) | "The world's largest online computer store." They sell hardware, software, and associated technologies. | Terms are discussed after they review the site and are assured of a demographic fit. |
| Etoys (www.etoys.com) | Toys, toys, and more toys. This online toy store is growing in popularity. | They pay a huge 25% commission. |
| FileSafe (www.filesafe.net) | Online filing of your IRS returns for a low price. The site is known to be very safe and secure. | Variety of plans, $4.00 and up for referrals. |

**Table 7.2**    (Continued)

| COMPANY | DESCRIPTION | COMPENSATION PROGRAM (PERCENTAGES OF SALES UNLESS OTHERWISE SPECIFIED) |
|---|---|---|
| iPrint (www.iprint.com) | Online ordering for stationery, business cards, and printed novelty items. Lower cost than many local quick print stores, and you can do some amazing fine-tuning of the images and text online. | 4%–8% |
| LandscapeUSA (www.landscapeusa .com) | Grow your garden online? Not exactly, but everything you need to plan, and plant, and grow your garden can be purchased here. | 8% of total sale (average order is $65, some over $500, according to the site) |
| MapQuest Map Store (www.mapstore.com) | The people who developed the most popular online map system also sell maps of all shapes and types, including USGS topographic maps, historic maps, and maps of planets and countries. | 8% of sales during clicked session (program in transition) |
| Music Boulevard (www.musicblvd.com) | They sell . . . music.  A large site dedicated to selling CDs online. Since Amazon also sells books, you may want to focus your efforts on the one-stop shopping of Amazon, but this could be a good alternate resource if there are not contract conflicts. | 5%–15% depending on the method by which you link them, and the item itself |
| Reel.com (www.reel.com) | This site sells and rents movies. | 8% of gross revenue (probably more likely on net revenue after they remove credit card fees, shipping, etc.) |
| Seattle's Finest Gourmet Coffee (www.seattlesfinest.com) | Buy Seattle's Finest coffee online. | 20% |

*Continues*

**Table 7.2**    Sample of Affiliate Programs *(Continued)*

| COMPANY | DESCRIPTION | COMPENSATION PROGRAM (PERCENTAGES OF SALES UNLESS OTHERWISE SPECIFIED) |
|---|---|---|
| SportsSite.com (www.sportsite.com) | An online superstore of sporting goods. | 20% (program in transition) |
| Wall Street Journal Online (www.wsj.com) | Offers some special promotional programs where they will provide you with access to news elements to keep your site up to date daily, while also providing a revenue opportunity to you for referring customers to them for their subscription service. | $5.00 for every trial subscription you generate that results in a subscription |
| Ziff Davis University (ZDU) (www.zdu.com) | This online distance learning service focuses on high technology and other training programs. Some courses are independent training programs and others are instructor-led. | 10% referral fee for those who sign up for one year of unlimited training |

Source: 1998 InternetAdvocate.com (www.internetadvocate.com)

**Figure 7.9**    Lobster Net is one of the many affiliate programs available to publishers.

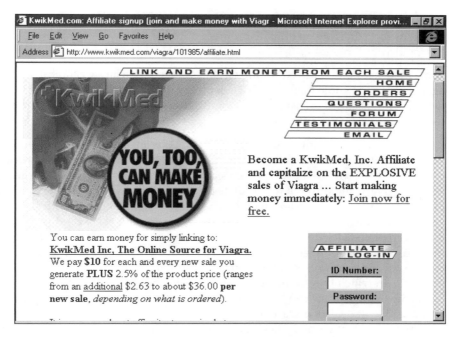

**Figure 7.10** The screen to sign up for the KwikMed affiliate program for Viagra. The program pays $10 per order and 2.5% of the product price for a new sale.

## Managing an Affiliate Program

To implement an affiliate program, publishers need software that (in addition to other capabilities) will manage the process of tracking orders, leads, or clicks back to a specific referring Web site. The ideal software package will also calculate how much each site is owed, handle the addition and subtraction of affiliate

**Table 7.3** CarPrices Affiliate Payment Rates

| ITEM | COST TO USERS | YOUR COMMISSION |
|------|---------------|-----------------|
| Insurance Quote | Free | $1 |
| Finance Quote | Free | $1 |
| New Car Price Quote | Free | $3 |
| Used Car Purchase Request | Free | $0.80 |
| Personal Credit Check | $10.95 | $1 |
| Warranty Purchase | Varies | $12.50 |
| Car Title Check | $12.50 | $1 |
| Custom Window Sticker | $12.95 | $0.75 |
| Car Secrets Book | $27.95 | $4 |

sites, and other tasks associated with running an affiliate program. There are several solutions for managing an affiliate program outlined below. A comparison of features is provided in Table 7.4.

Some folks use home-brewed solutions. Unless you have a large technical staff or an ad agency that can handle this type of development, you're better off using packaged software. It's almost always cheaper, and it will allow you to focus on getting orders rather than on software development.

ClickTrade (www.clicktrade.com) (see Figure 7.11) is an affiliate manager that matches buyers and sellers of Web advertising (ClickTrade is part of the LinkExchange, now owned by Microsoft). Web advertisers can place cost-per-click, cost-per-lead, or cost-per-sale advertising through this affiliate program. An advertiser begins by signing up at the ClickTrade Web site and then entering information about the affiliate offer. For example, a merchant might list $10 per sale as the amount she would want to pay for the advertising. ClickTrade charges a 30 percent commission, so in addition to paying the sites a $10 fee for every sale, she'd pay a $3 fee to ClickTrade. ClickTrade lists the offer in their database of ad offers. Sites go through the database and choose affiliate programs in which they want to participate. If the advertiser chooses, the system can be set up so that after the site chooses a specific advertiser, the advertiser has to approve the site. ClickTrade tracks the clicks, orders, or leads. The advertiser pays ClickTrade in advance, and ClickTrade pays the sites. There is no sign-up fee for Click-Trade's affiliate program. They do ask that advertisers make a minimum $100 deposit for starting a pay-per-click program and $500 if they are starting a pay-per-lead/sale program. ClickTrade has affiliates generate revenue through banners, buttons, and text links that drive traffic to the merchant's site. The advertiser can send an e-mail to publishers (who choose to receive it) through ClickTrade's interface; the advertiser does not have direct contact with the publishers.

All ClickTrade advertisers automatically get featured in Revenue Avenue (http://revenue.linkexchange.com), a directory of revenue-generating offers from Web merchants. In addition, ClickTrade delivers information about the offer to over 50,000 sites who participate in their affiliate programs.

If a Web site wants to participate in an affiliate program run by ClickTrade, the site will sign up with ClickTrade and then be able to choose the affiliate program that is of interest. Participation entails placing merchant banners, buttons, and text links on their site.

LinkShare (www.linkshare.com) manages the entire process for sites and their affiliates. They have software that merchants install on their e-commerce engine. As with ClickTrade, merchants can benefit from having their affiliate program broadcast to LinkShare's network of affiliate sites. Merchants who use LinkShare pay a $5,000 setup fee and 2–3 percent of revenues from sales. The merchant sets up various stores from which the affiliate can choose. The affiliate can also choose a specific product, if there is one that the affiliate decides is best suited for his audience. This allows the merchant some control over how the affiliate's store will look. This differs from ClickTrade in that affiliates can set up complete stores, instead of using only banners, buttons, and text links.

**Figure 7.11**    The ClickTrade affiliate program network.

LinkShare's clients range from the largest e-commerce retailers like 1-800-FLOWERS (www.800flowers.com) to smaller retailers like Bulldog Store (www.bulldogstore.com), which sells products for bulldog owners. The advantage for merchants using LinkShare is that they are able to control how the Web sees their brand. The merchant, and not the affiliates, serves the banners and whichever store the affiliate chooses through Link-Share's service. This ensures that the merchant can remove old creatives and offers from affiliate sites. When a merchant signs up affiliates, the affiliates join the LinkShare network and then they can join the merchant's program. This means that as with Click-Trade, the merchant's affiliates will be exposed to many offers.

Be Free (www.befree.com) manages the enrolling, supporting, and tracking of affiliate networks. Be Free functions a little differently than LinkShare and ClickTrade: when an affiliate joins the network, that affiliate can either sign up through the merchant or through Be Free. If the affiliate signs up through the merchant, Be Free receives no information regarding that affiliate. Be Free generally charges 2 percent of affiliate sales revenue for these services, and focuses on large and medium-sized commerce sites. Clients include barnesandnoble.com, American Greetings, and GeoCities.

Be Free lists two components to its affiliate software: Be Free Affiliate Serving Technology (BFAST) and Be Free Intelligent Targeting (BFIT). BFAST manages the process of enrolling, supporting, tracking, and managing affiliate networks. BFIT is an engine that tracks sales from the advertisement to the point of purchase. If merchants want, they can also pay Be Free to manage the payment of affiliate sites.

**Table 7.4** Comparison of Affiliate Vendor Features

|  | BE FREE | LINKSHARE |
|---|---|---|
| Key Clients | barnesandnoble.com, Travelocity, Reel.com | Cyberian Outpost, FAO Schwartz, Clinique |
| Number of Clients | 30 | 100 |
| Setup Fee | $5,000 to $7,500 for one-year contract; free of charge for three-year contract | $5,000 |
| Percentage of Transaction | 2–3 % | 2–3% |
| Affiliate Outreach | Merchants receive 5,000 affiliates free of charge; fee of $14 for each additional affiliate Be Free generates for you. | 6,326 affiliates; merchants have free access to all affiliates |
| Allows CPM Payment | Yes | Yes |
| Allows Click-through Payment | Yes | Yes |
| Allow Bounty Payment | Yes | Yes |
| Allow Loyalty Points (Click Rewards, My Points) Payment | No, but in development | Yes |
| Allow Hybrid Payment | Yes | Yes |

Source: 1998 Jupiter Communications (www.jup.com)

With hundreds of affiliate programs out there, it is difficult to determine the right price to pay affiliates. Merchants generally give their affiliates a 5–15 percent revenue share. If there are a lot of merchants in your category, you will want to offer a higher revenue share to encourage sites to join your affiliate program instead of your competitions' affiliate programs. If you're a merchant of a very high-priced product (like a car), you might want to give a flat fee per car sold rather than a commission.

## Auctions

Auctions are big on the Internet and are a good place to buy and sell excess ad inventory. Because the auctions are selling excess inventory, advertisers can usually get pretty good prices on well-recognized sites. For publishers it's a way to generate revenue on inventory that would otherwise go unsold.

The leader in this area is Adauction.com (www.adauction.com, see Figure 7.12). "Adauction.com is building a Web-based exchange for buying and selling media," says David

## Tips for Running a Good Affiliate Program

**Research pricing of other merchants in your market and be competitive. If you don't pay enough money, you won't have a high number of respondents.**

**Payments should be sent in a timely manner. When affiliates receive checks, they remember you and work harder to promote your offer. Remember, they can quadruple the sales they generate for you by giving you better positioning on their site. They often just need to know that they'll get paid.**

**Provide an area for affiliates to download advertisements that they can use to promote your merchandise. You know what works to help sell your products. And, the affiliates may not run their own advertisements to promote the special offer because they don't have time to design the ads. If you provide the ads, affiliates are usually happy to run them in an effort to generate more revenue.**

**Help your affiliates sell. In addition to providing graphics, work with them to create promotions and to teach them what helps sell your products. This can be done through an e-mail newsletter that reaches all of your affiliates, or a special Web site. Barnesandnoble.com has set up a Web site to help affiliates succeed, at www.affiliate.net.**

**Give affiliates a way to check the status of the revenue they've generated through online reporting. It is a nice bonus.**

Wamsley, CEO and president. It's "an online marketplace where price is determined dynamically based on a real-time supply and demand model." Adauction.com:

- Creates an alternate channel for media companies to move additional inventory without conflicting with direct sales.

- Evolves from auction to exchange—rather than participating in periodic events, advertisers around the globe can always find quality inventory at the best price possible.

- Offers just-in-time buy opportunities based on selling media days before it expires.

- Attracts buyers—large and small—with a valuable price proposition.

Some of the sites that auction inventory through this service are Yahoo!, Netscape, E! Online, Jumbo, and TUCOWS. Advertisers who purchase inventory have a choice of serving ads through AdForce or DoubleClick's DART. As of the writing of this edition, Adauction.com was auctioning CPM buys and had plans to start offering cost-per-click, sponsorship, and package buys. Adauction.com gives sites a means to sell excess inventory; they sell ad campaigns that begin the month after the auction (if the auction is in January, the flight is in February).

"Adauction.com has earned high marks for uniquely offering much-needed help to Web publishers in optimizing banner inventory. We are committed to using their service to generate revenue which we'd otherwise forfeit," said Ruth Chang, of Student Advantage Network (www.studentadvantage.com).

There are three ways to buy at Adauction.com:

**Tune-In.** Topic-specific auctions (finance, women's interests, travel, computers, etc.) two or three times each week. This is targeted inventory, featuring exclusive packages and special inventory for the target- and the brand-focused buyer.

**MarketPlace.** Features 15 categories and over 100 million impressions for sale, held the third week of each month. Great values on ROS inventory.

**LastCall.** For the buyer looking for plenty of eyeballs. A network buy at low CPMs. The biggest bang for the buck for broad reach and frequency.

The Internet ad auction has gone so well that Adauction.com is launching a similar trading platform for auctioning ad space for print, radio, cable, and infomercials.

## Real-Time Ad Buying Through Networks

Auctions are not the only means for real-time buying. Flycast (www.flycast.com), an ad network with over 700 sites that reaches more than 12 million people each month, also sells ads in real time. Unlike ad networks like DoubleClick, Flycast does not focus on branded high-end CPM sites. Instead, they've amassed a large number of sites, and they're focused on selling this low-priced inventory to direct marketers. Buys on the Flycast network fall into four categories: Run of Network (all sites), Run of Category (specific affinity), Category Select (affinity and additional targeting like geographic area), or Site Select (choosing a specific site).

**Figure 7.12** The Adauction.com bidding floor.

The Flycast philosophy, according to their Web site, is as follows:

> We begin with what we call zero-based media planning. This is where we use the actual results from a campaign, run without any targeting considerations, to create a response baseline. This baseline is used to determine where on the Flycast Network the ad campaign should be focused. The results from this first level of optimization form a behavioral targeting model. These real-time advertising responses provide our media consultants with the behavioral results to continue to optimize as needed to maximize the success of your campaign.

The run of network rate card price is a $6 CPM, and there are additional costs as advertisers choose more targeting options. Flycast's proprietary ValueTrack software enables advertisers to track the performance of a campaign from banner serve, to the "click," and then through to any type of back-end transaction, such as registrations, orders, or downloads.

Advertisers can negotiate with a Flycast representative and buy inventory weeks or months before a campaign begins, or buy inventory in Flycast's real-time bidding for space. In the real-time bidding, the site sets the minimum bid on the inventory, and the price increases if an advertiser needs to bid higher than someone else to secure the space. The real-time bidding usually occurs 48 hours before the ad buy will commence, so an advertiser has to be flexible; however, since this is a last-minute buy of inventory that would not otherwise be sold, the price is often reduced as much as 75 percent from rate card.

A Flycast network site can use Flycast's Site Registry to register the site and control what inventory is available on the Flycast Network, and at what price. The site can also control what types of ads it will accept (rich media, GIF, etc.). Plus, publishers can block any advertisers they do not want on their site.

Here is how Larry Braitman, vice president of business development and co-founder of Flycast, explains the system:

> At the top of every Web page is code that directs the server on how to fill the page. Every Web page that carries advertising is delivered with one or more holes in it. Code at the top of the page tells the site to fill the hole with a banner ad that has been purchased in the up-front market. If no banner ad has been sold up front, additional code tells the ad server to fill the hole with a banner ad that's sold in the real-time market, via an ad network like Flycast. If no one buys a banner to serve on that page in real time, a PSA (public service announcement) or other default banner can be served.

Like Adauction.com, Flycast is a good way for publishers to sell inventory that would otherwise go unused; for the sites who use these services, it's better to get something for these ad spaces rather than nothing.

# Hybrid

Because online advertising can achieve various ad campaign objectives, many publishers are finding that a tiered pricing model makes the most sense. For example, a site could offer one price for impressions, a higher price for click-through, and an even higher price if an advertiser pays only when the click-through results in a sale. If publishers offer only one model, they are going to lose those advertisers who are determined to use a different one. A hybrid of these models is one solution. Often a Web site will charge a low CPM as well as a cost per action. This is a compromise that will often make both sides happy.

# Trends in Pricing

Since the first edition of this book was published, we have seen several significant pricing trends. Prime real estate is costing a lot more than it ever has, and less desirable ad inventory is cheaper than ever. As we mentioned earlier in this chapter, keywords are an example of prime inventory. The price for keywords has more than doubled on many sites over the past year. And, some search engines will only allow advertisers purchasing a certain level of advertising to purchase some of the most popular keywords. Hot, well-targeted content sites have also been able to command very high prices. iVillage is one example; their network of Web sites will rarely allow advertisers who won't commit to spending $100K or more on their site.

On the other hand, non-targeted sites that reach the same audience as a search engine have had real difficulty in maintaining their pricing. An untargeted buy of $50K on a search engine can get a CPM as low as $5. Search engines have enough excess inventory that they can offer these low CPM deals to entice advertisers. This makes it difficult for smaller sites to charge high rates. Unless they're very narrowly targeted, how can they justify to advertisers charging more than what the advertisers would pay to run on a search engine?

# Problems with Comparing Value

Some of the same problems that impact Web measurement also stymie advertisers who try to compare the value of advertising on different Web sites.

One problem that must be solved is really one of semantics: There must be consistency in the definitions used by publishers' sites. For example, it is difficult to compare impressions when one site counts an impression only when the ad is fully downloaded before the user leaves the page, another site counts an impression when a user accesses the page (regardless of whether the ad is fully downloaded), and yet another counts an impression when an ad has been on the page for 8 seconds before another ad is rotated into its position.

There is also little comparative demographic data available, which makes it difficult to distinguish among the audiences of different Web sites. For example, what distinguishes users of the search engine Yahoo! from users of the search engine Excite? When buying traditional media, an advertiser knows the profile of the target audience—from age, gender, and zip code to such detailed information as single mothers in their thirties with average incomes over $50,000. At this point, Web publishers are only beginning to learn about their audiences. Moreover, these audiences are growing at such a quick rate that even accurate data seem outdated as soon as they are published.

# Flexibility Is the Key

The slate of pricing models conforms to the specific goals of an advertiser's campaign. There is no one pricing model that is the best; instead, the model should reflect the campaign's objective and the site's revenue needs. The rule of thumb in ad pricing, as in everything Internet, is to be flexible.

## How Much Do You Need to Spend on an Ad Campaign?

People are always trying to figure out how much they should budget for Internet advertising. Is $5,000 enough? Is $50,000 a month the magic number? The answer lies in your goals.

If you're trying to sell products or generate leads, there is no minimum budget. You can run a month-long test for as little as $1,000 to $5,000. Then you can use results to determine your cost per lead or cost per sale. If your cost per sale is lower than for your other media channels, you should start ramping up your advertising spending. However, keep in mind that as you increase spending, you need to watch your buys carefully to make sure your conversion rate doesn't decrease.

The determination of your budget will be based on the number of sales or leads you want to generate (assuming you have the budget to reach those goals). The cost per lead or sale will also determine if you should move some of your traditional advertising dollars to the Internet. This strategy also works if your goal is to build traffic.

If you are doing a serious direct marketing campaign to a very specific niche audience, you should expect to pay $10,000–$20,000 per month, buying on a cost-per-click and low CPM basis.

If you're doing a branding campaign to a small niche audience, you can do so with a budget of $150,000–$200,000 per year (we'd also recommend some print and direct mail to deliver your message).

If you're trying to reach a large consumer audience, that budget should be increased to $100,000 per month at the minimum.

If you want to dominate a specific category or appear under keyword placements, you'll have to spend more money. Many of the major search engines require minimum buys of $4,000 to $5,000 per month to purchase keywords. In general, branding campaigns take large amounts of money. A major branding campaign across the Web, buying premium CPM, can run from $250,000 to $600,000 a month.

If your budget is small—under $5,000 for the entire year—buying ads may not be the best use of your money. A better strategy would include banner exchanges and other more grassroots methods such as those discussed in Eric Ward's special section in this book, "How to Advertise for Free or Almost Free."

## Challenges Dictating Our Long-Term Success

Liddy Manson (mansonl@washpost.com), VP of Advertising and Marketing
Washington Post Newsweek Interactive (www.washingtonpost.com)

In the online news world, we are watching advertising demand explode, as advertisers and agencies become more strategic and varied in their approach to media placement. As a medium we are discovering that the Web works extraordinarily well as a promotional and branding vehicle for a broad range of businesses from construction companies to diamond dealers to car dealers to employment agencies. We currently face several challenges that will dictate our long-term success in a highly competitive and innovative market:

1. Our single challenge as a medium is to perfect the art of matching buyers with sellers. The accountability and trackability of Internet advertising combined with the newness of the medium puts significant pressure on our medium to deliver measurable results in a quick time frame. One result of this trend is a rapid proliferation of advertising products, and I expect that this creativity will continue for quite some time.

2. Currently advertising supply outpaces demand by a factor of roughly 50 to 1. As a result, pricing is extremely volatile, buyers have a tremendous amount of power, and sites without renowned brands are struggling to survive. My prediction is that there will be a shakeout in 1999 of those less well capitalized sites, whose staying power will start to fade.

3. The medium is advancing so quickly, both creatively and technically, that media sales reach far beyond devising creative advertising solutions in a static world; sales reps must reach beyond what is possible today, and devise new products and services in order to stay on the forefront of the industry.

# CHAPTER 8

# Market Research—Information Is Your Competitive Advantage

What's the value of market research? It's critical. "You wouldn't go sailing across the ocean without a map," says Evan Neufeld, director of Online Advertising Strategies at Jupiter Communications. "When it comes to making online advertising decisions, market research is an essential aspect of charting a road map for any campaign."

Information is power in conducting an effective and successful online advertising campaign. The technology, which serves as the very essence of the Internet, is the tool that allows the Internet to be information rich, both in the dissemination and the collection of data. In developing an advertising and overall marketing program for your site, it is essential to keep abreast of new technologies, techniques, and tactics. Equally important is monitoring the changes in the online audience in terms of gender, income, interests, language, and location. And finally, it's imperative to continually evaluate the programs and strategies of your competition. As Neufeld puts it, "Fortune favors the bold, and the bold do their homework with market research."

There are a multitude of resources both online and off that assist the online advertising professional to stay abreast of all elements affecting the industry and to gauge the online audience. These include the sites that list facts, statistics, and industry figures, and the bound reports compiled by market research firms. There are e-mail discussion lists galore for observing or conversing with others in the industry as well as conferences and seminars for face-to-face interactions.

A quick caveat: The only thing that grows and changes faster than the industry that covers and studies the Internet is the information itself. Indeed, surveys and studies are almost out of date a month after they're published. Keep in mind that the specific survey findings presented in this chapter will be outdated long before the concepts and techniques presented in this book outlive their usefulness. Therefore, we recommend using the specific data presented in this chapter as examples of the types of information available and where to go to keep up to date on a continuing basis.

# Building Your Body of Knowledge

To begin building your body of online advertising knowledge, there is no better place to start than by subscribing to some of the industry's e-mail lists. There are three types of lists. The first are discussion lists, where participants pose questions and comments and members of the community respond freely (see Table 8.1). These lists are moderated to keep the conversation rolling in a friendly and productive manner. The second type of lists are the newsletters, where the editor puts the information together and distributes it via e-mail (see Table 8.2). And the third type are specialty newsletters and lists on very specific industry topics such as building better banners or search engine registration (see Table 8.3).

# Industry Events: Where the Hunters and Gatherers Meet

With the Internet's global reach, an advertiser can be in one country, the agency in another, and the site on which the advertising is being placed in a third location. The geographic neutrality of the Web is great for getting work done, but nothing is better than face-to-face interactions for networking. The primary places people in the online advertising industry go to network are the myriad of conferences and seminars. A list of key online advertising events is presented in Table 8.4.

Conferences are also held outside the United States. A good global listing of conferences and trade shows can be found in The Internet Times (www.euromktg.com/eng/ed/it/current.html). The Internet World (events.internet.com/) series is held in most major countries and always has sessions on Internet advertising and marketing. Moreover, Jupiter Communications (www.jup.com) hosts events in Europe.

# Trade Associations

You know an industry has come of age when it has a handful of trade associations. Online advertising has reached this first stage of maturation. The development of the industry's trade associations started with special working groups from already established organizations, such as CASIE (Coalition for Advertising Supported Information and Entertainment, www.casie.org) and the New Media Federation of the Newspaper Association of America (www.naa.org). Then came the formation of an association out of the online advertising industry itself, the Internet Advertising Bureau (IAB) (www.iab.net). Now we have a host of associations addressing key issues and concerns of the industry, from privacy and taxation to measurement and reporting standards. Moreover, the associa-

**Table 8.1**  E-mail Discussion Lists

| LIST | MODERATOR | DESCRIPTION |
|---|---|---|
| Internet Advertising Discussion List (www.internetadvertising .org) | Adam Boettiger ia@eyescream.com | An e-mail discussion list focusing specifically on Internet advertising, Internet marketing, and the successful promotion of businesses on the Internet. Over 5,000 subscribers in 72 countries around the globe receive the list. |
| Internet Link Exchange Digest (www.ledigest.com) | John Audette ja@ledigest.com | A moderated discussion list meant to provide meaningful and helpful information to those engaged in building traffic to their Web sites. Discussions center on Web site promotion on the Internet and World Wide Web, which will of course include banner advertising. |
| Online Advertising Discussion (www.o-a.com) | Richard Hoy richard@tenagra.com | Focuses on professional discussion of online advertising strategies, results, studies, tools, and media coverage. The list also welcomes discussion on the related topics of online promotion and public relations. The list encourages sharing of practical expertise and experiences between those who buy, sell, research and develop tools for online advertising, as well as those providing online public relations and publicity services. The list also serves as a resource to members of the press who are writing about the subject of online advertising and promotion. |

tions are funding important research in the interest of the entire industry. Table 8.5 presents a list of online advertising trade associations.

# Market Research Firms

Market research firms are conducting studies to help define, analyze, and understand the inner workings and implications of this medium. These studies include online and

**Table 8.2** E-mail Newsletters

| LIST | DESCRIPTION |
|------|-------------|
| ChannelSeven NarrowCast Newsletter (www.channelseven.com) | Covers Internet advertising news and commentary. |
| ClickZ (www.clickz.com) | Daily newsletter with links to articles written about Internet advertising and marketing. |
| ICONOCAST (www.iconocast.com) | A free weekly e-cast (mail list) that chronicles the Internet's impact on traditional marketing. It contains data-rich market overviews designed to help readers understand key trends, plus "The Jacobyte," an insider column. |
| Web Digest for Marketers (www.wdfm.com) | A fortnightly review of about 15 marketing sites. |
| Internet Advertising Report (www.internet.com) | A weekly update on Internet advertising news. |

telephone surveys as well as industry trend analysis and forecasting. Market research firms actively conduct and publish studies and reports on some aspect of the Internet, including demographic information, usage patterns, and ad spending projections. Table 8.6 provides a listing of the market research firms specializing in the Internet and the online audience.

To keep up on the volumes of new research being conducted, there are a host of sites that consolidate the findings. Table 8.7 lists some of the sites most applicable to the online advertising industry.

Table 8.8 compiled by eStats demonstrates how different research firms can have different numbers for the same topic, such as Web advertising projections. The November 16, 1998, issue of the *Industry Standard* offered a brutally honest quote from journalist Evan Schwartz on the widely varying predictions of Internet research companies: "We know that there's a lot of hocus-pocus involved in those numbers, but they're better than nothing."

# Stats, Facts, and Figures

If we were to describe the average Internet user prior to 1998, it would have been a college-educated, financially comfortable, 34-year-old U.S. male with a strong technology comfort level. But these "early technology adopters," who were the majority of the Net population until now, are quickly being edged out by a user base that more accurately reflects American society. A study released in September 1998 by Market Facts (www.marketfacts.com) reported that American Internet users and the general Ameri-

**Table 8.3** Specialty Topic Newsletters and Listservs

| NAME | MODERATOR | DESCRIPTION | SUBSCRIPTION PROCESS |
|---|---|---|---|
| Banner Tips (www.whitepalm .com/fourcorners) | n/a | Monthly newsletter of information on how to increase site traffic by making a more clickable banner. | To subscribe, send mail to: BannerTips-request@lists.best.com with the body of the message as: Subscribe yourName@yourDomain.com |
| FrankelBiz (www.robfrankel.com/ frankelbiz/fbintro.html) | Rob Frankel | Listserv devoted exclusively to doing business on the Web, instead of talking about it. List members exchange discounts, offer business leads, and do business with each other. Sponsors offer products and services at discounts to members. | Subscription form available at www .robfrankel.com/frankelbiz/form.html |
| i-sales (www.mmgco.com/isales/) | John Audette | Formed in November 1995; the goal of the Internet Sales Moderated Discussion List is to provide a forum for meaningful and helpful discussion of online sales issues by those engaged in the online sale of products and services. | Subscription form available at www.mmgco.com/isales/ |
| Search Engine Report | Danny Sullivan | An e-mail companion to the site Search Engine Watch (searchenginewatch.com), which keeps you informed of how you can improve your Web site's listings in search engines. | Subscription form available at home page at searchenginewatch .com/sereport/ |
| WEBCMO DIGEST (www.webcmo.com/ mis/disc.htm) | | The digest covers three main themes: Web marketing strategy, Web marketing research, and free Web marketing research software. | To subscribe, send an e-mail to: subscribe@webcmo.com |
| Web Marketing Today | Dr. Ralph Wilson | Contains articles about Internet marketing and doing business on the Web. | www.webmarketingtoday.com |

**Table 8.4** Key Online Advertising Events in the United States

| CONFERENCES IN THE USA | PRODUCER | DATE AND LOCATION | DESCRIPTION |
|---|---|---|---|
| @d Tech | ConEx (www.ad-tech.com) | Held multiple times each year. | Several events rolled into one, with tracks on public relations, advertising creative, media, etc. |
| Advertising & Marketing on the Internet | The Zeff Group (www.zeff.com) | Held in cities around the country. | A one-day regionally focused event on Internet advertising and marketing. |
| AdWeek Forum at Internet World | AdWeek (www.adweek.com) and Internet World (events.internet.com/) | Held in conjunction with the NYC (fall) and Los Angeles (spring) Internet World conferences. | A two-day event of sessions covering the hot topics in online advertising. |
| Camp Interactive (www.4interactive marketing.com/camp99/index.html) | Interactive Marketing (www.4interactive marketing.com) | Held in the summer. | Following the philosophy that as much happens outside of the session rooms as inside, this event brings industry professionals together to schmooze in the great outdoors. |
| Ebiz (www.4interactive marketing.com/ebiz/) | Interactive Marketing (www.4interactive marketing.com) | Held once a year in a different location each time. | Focuses on e-commerce perspectives and solutions for interactive marketers. |
| Online Advertising Forum | Jupiter Communications (www.jupiter.com) | Usually held once a year in August in NYC. | The oldest of the online advertising events. This is the place were the CEOs go to see and be seen. A very high-level event both in terms of sessions and attendees. |
| Variety's Interactive Marketing Summit | Interactive Marketing (www.4interactive marketing.com) | Held in the spring. | Focuses on online marketing and advertising to and by the entertainment industry. |
| Web Advertising | ThunderLizard Production (www.thunderlizard.com) | Held once a year in a different location each time | A nationally focused training-style conference on Web advertising. |
| Web Marketing | ThunderLizard Production (www.thunderlizard.com) | Held various times a year in different locations. | A nationally focused training-style conference on Web marketing. |

**Table 8.5** Online Advertising Trade Associations

| ASSOCIATION | CONTACT INFORMATION | MEETINGS | MISSION STATEMENT |
|---|---|---|---|
| Internet Advertising Bureau (IAB) www.iab.net | Barbara Sweetman IAB Administrative Director c/o 38 Tyler Circle Rye, NY 10580 (914) 921-6988 (914) 967-2538 | West Coast Meeting (spring) East Coast Meeting (fall) | Global association devoted exclusively to maximizing the use and effectiveness of advertising on the Internet. |
| Internet Direct Marketing Bureau (IDMB) www.idmb.com | Note: voluntary organization with no official headquarters. | Currently meets in conjunction with other major advertising events. | Association ensures the maximum effectiveness and acceptance of direct marketing on the Internet. |
| FAST www.fastinfo.org | Note: voluntary organization with no official headquarters. | Currently meets in conjunction with other major advertising events. | A coalition formed as a result of the FAST Summit hosted by Procter & Gamble (Aug. 1998), with four primary working groups: advertising models, media buying, measurement, and consumer acceptance. |
| Direct Marketing Association (DMA) www.the-dma.org | 1120 Avenue of the Americas New York, NY 10036-6700 Phone: 212-768-7277 Fax: 212-302-6714 | NetMarketing held in spring. | Serves as the primary trade association for the entire direct marketing industry. |

**Table 8.6** Market Research Firms

| COMPANY |
| --- |
| Market Facts (www.marketfacts.com) |
| Aberdeen Group (www.aberdeen.com) |
| ActivMedia 'Net Marketing Research (www.activmedia.com) |
| Cowles/Simba Net (www.simbanet.com) |
| Cyber Dialogue (www.cyberdialogue.com) |
| Jupiter Communications (www.jup.com) |
| Laredo Group (www.laredogroup.com) |
| Matrix Information and Directory Services, Inc. (MIDS) (www.mids.org) |
| MBInteractive (www.mbinteractive.com) |
| WebCMO (www.webcmo.com) |
| Zona Research (www.zonaresearch.com) |

can consumer population are now mirroring one another in most buying habits, behaviors, and attitudes. The study concluded that the two populations are finally corresponding because 30 percent of the U.S. population that is 16 and older is online. "People using the Internet today are no longer just a group of early adopter techies," comments Wally Balden, vice president, ISG. "They are clearly more mainstream, everyday people." Let's take a look at the face of the online audience in terms of gender, age, race, language, income level, and usage patterns to get a more up-close-and-personal view of the online audience (see Table 8.9).

**Table 8.7** Information Consolidator Sites

| SITE | DESCRIPTION |
| --- | --- |
| CyberAtlas (www.cyberatlas.com) | The first site to provide short summaries of Internet advertising and marketing studies. |
| eStats (www.estats.com) | Compares the figures and statistics compiled by all the top Internet marketing firms. |
| ICONOCAST (www.iconocast.com) | Consolidates industry studies and research in its weekly newsletter. |
| The Industry Standard (www.thestandard.com/metrics/) | The online version of the weekly magazine. |
| Nua (www.nua.ie/surveys) | Ireland firm that is not United States–centric in its numbers and monitors Internet user numbers around the globe. |

# Why Study Findings Differ

As Mark Twain is quoted as having said, "There are three kinds of lies: lies, damn lies, and statistics." It is not unusual for studies on similar subjects to produce different results, especially in the Internet industry. Many factors contribute to this phenomenon. First and foremost is the time frame of the study. The rapid growth of the Internet has resulted in different sampling groups almost every 90 days, a particularly problematic element in any Internet study. Second, studies that examine the entire Internet universe will expose findings very different from those that focus only on Web users. Third, the answers received are a reflection of the questions asked, and even slight differences can result in widely variant answers. Fourth, bias can't be overlooked. As the site eMarketer (www.estats.com/estats/welcome.html) explains:

> Any research firm reporting statistics on the Internet will have built-in biases, not to mention methodological weaknesses. Figures pertaining to the size of the Net, for instance, are often inflated by research outfits which have received funding from companies who, in turn, have a vested interest in hyping the numbers (big numbers attract big dollars).

And finally, it must be taken into account that people do not always answer questions truthfully when filling out a survey or even an online registration form. People admit that they sometimes provide misinformation for reasons ranging from security (women who are single report they are married) to issues of social status (men report earning higher incomes).

**Table 8.8**   Comparison of Web Ad Revenues Projects Through 2002 (in millions)

| YEAR | 1996 | 1997 | 1998 | 1999 | 2000 | 2001 | 2002 |
|------|------|------|------|------|------|------|------|
| IDC | 260 | 550 | 1200 | 2000 | 3300 | NA | NA |
| Forrester | NA | 500 | 1000 | 1750 | 4100 | 5600 | 8100 |
| Cowles/Simba | 236 | 597 | 976 | 1580 | 2460 | NA | NA |
| Jupiter | 301 | 940 | 1900 | 3000 | 4400 | 5800 | 7700 |
| ActivMedia | NA | 400 | 1700 | 4700 | 11200 | 23500 | 43300 |
| IAB | 267 | 906 | NA | NA | NA | NA | NA |
| Yankee Group | 220 | 630 | 1200 | 1820 | 2200 | 3800 | 6500 |
| eStats | 175 | 650 | 1500 | 2200 | 3800 | 6500 | 8000 |
| Global Internet Project | 310 | NA | NA | NA | 5000 | NA | NA |

Source: eStats (www.estats.com)

**Table 8.9** Ongoing Internet Surveys

| |
|---|
| GVU User Surveys (www.cc.gatech.edu/gvu/user_surveys/User_Survey_Home.html) |
| Internet Domain Survey (www.nw.com/zone/WWW/top.html) |
| Survey-Net (www.survey.net/) |
| The Netcraft Web Server Survey (www.netcraft.co.uk/survey/) |

## Academic Studies

Among the longest running surveys of online users are those conducted by the Graphics, Visualization, & Usability Center (GVU) at Georgia Tech University (www.cc.gatech.edu/gvu/user_surveys/). Begun in January 1994, the surveys have been running continuously, with the tenth survey results announced in January 1999. The GVU surveys track usage patterns, interests, and demographic shifts over time. Each survey has approximately 10,000 participants. To be a part of the most current survey, register on the GVU survey site (www.gvu.gatech.edu/user_surveys/). For consistency, GVU survey results will be used as the benchmark for most of the demographic information in this chapter because of the program's longevity, reliability, and size of participation pool.

Another center for academic studies on online marketing is Project 2000 (www2000 .ogsm.vanderbilt.edu), directed by Professors Donna Hoffman and Tom Novak. Founded in 1994 as "Research Program on Marketing in Computer Mediated Environments" at the Owen Graduate School of Management, Vanderbilt University, to study the marketing implications of commercializing the World Wide Web, today this scholarly effort has emerged as one of the premiere research centers in the world for the study of electronic commerce.

## Psychographic Studies

Psychographic analysis attempts to segment consumer lifestyles into identifiable characteristics. One of the first major consumer segmentation systems was developed by SRI in 1978 and is known as VALS (Values and Lifestyles). In 1989 VALS 2 (http://future .sri.com/vals/vals2desc.html) was launched, modifying the segmentation system to incorporate more contemporary lifestyle trends, and improving the survey's applicability for advertising and marketing purposes. As a marketing tool, VALS can assist a company in finding out:

- Who to target
- What the target group buys and does
- Where concentrations of the target group lives
- How best to communicate with the target group
- Why the target group acts the way it does

There is now an Internet VALS (iVALS) to better understand the psychographics of the online consumer (http://future.sri.com/vals/iVALS.index.html). To participate in the survey and find out your VALs type, visit (http://future.sri.com/vals/ques-nt.html).

Another company doing important lifestyle segmentation is Claritas. The Claritas PRIZM lifestyle segmentation system defines every neighborhood in the United States in terms of 62 demographically and behaviorally distinct clusters. PRIZM offers an easy way to identify, understand, and target consumers down to the block level. Claritas introduced its PRIZM lifestyle segmentation system in the 1970s and has continued to update and refine its segmentation systems so that today marketers can combine detailed demographics with product, media, and lifestyle preferences to create a complete portrait of their target to answer the important marketing questions:

- Who are my customers?
- What are they like?
- What do they buy?
- Where can I find them?
- How can I reach them?

Claritas has both a direct dial-in online service and the Web-based Claritas Connect service (see Figure 8.1). Claritas Connect offers 127 different profiling reports. For example, a business can get a demographic report of a five-mile radius of a new store location. All this can be done over the Internet. "The design of the architecture of Claritas Connect,"

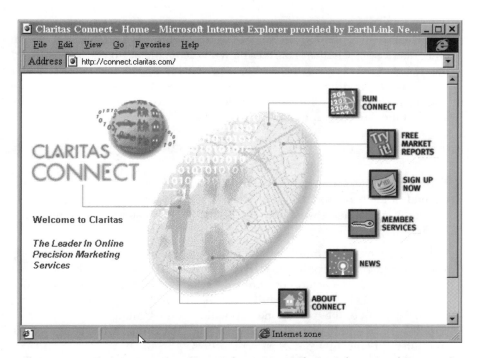

**Figure 8.1** Claritas Connect offers Web access to Claritas' demographic reporting capabilities.

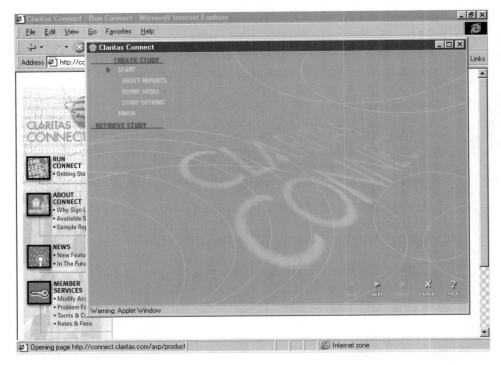

**Figure 8.2**  Claritas Connect offers a variety of reporting options through its Web site.

says Heather Oles, senior director of Claritas, "is to have the ability to partner with other databases." Claritas is partnering with Media Metrix to add Web rating data into the mix. At $195 per year, the service is reasonably priced, making it accessible to the small business; and signing up for the service can be done online in a matter of minutes. "The idea is to make it affordable, flexible, and easy to use," says Oles. See Figure 8.2 for a look at the different profiling report options.

# Age

The average Internet user in 1998 was 35 years old, putting the Net generation at the tail end of the baby boomers. When the first GVU survey was conducted in 1994, 56 percent of respondents were between 21 and 30. Eight surveys later, the average rests at 35 (see Figure 8.3).

What has changed the most over the past four years is the age spread (see Figure 8.4). There are more seniors online than ever before. According to a study conducted in 1998 by SeniorNet (www.seniornet.com) and Charles Schwab Inc. (www.schwab.com), there are over 13 million U.S. adults over the age of 50 with Internet access, representing 16.5 percent of the total online population in the United States. This random telephone survey found that 40 percent of all U.S. adults over the age of 50 have a computer at home, up from 29 percent in 1995.

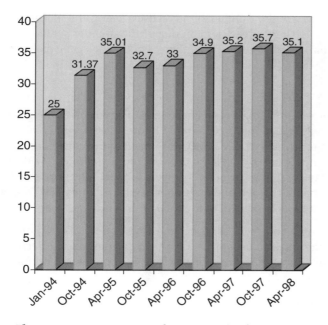

**Figure 8.3** Average age of net user over time

What do seniors do online? The study found that 72 percent use e-mail, 59 percent conduct research, 53 percent access news and current affairs, 47 percent make travel arrangements, and 43 percent check the weather. And sites that cater to the senior

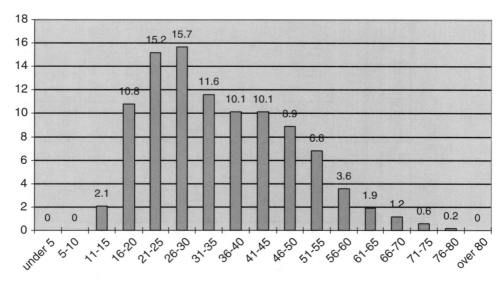

**Figure 8.4** Age distribution of Internet users.

audience are growing, as are the number of advertisers using the Net to reach this audience. Just look at the list of advertisers on one of the premier senior sites, Third Age (www.thirdage.com), to see that reaching seniors online has gone mainstream.

# Gender

The gender of the Internet is shifting as fast as the technology itself (see Figure 8.5). In 1994, the first GVU survey found only 5 percent of Internet users were women. By 1996 that number was 38 percent, with the majority of women using consumer online services like AOL and CompuServe. By 1998 the number rapidly climbed, with the GVU study finding that 41.2 percent of its respondents were female. All signs point to a continuing rise in the number of women online. Jupiter predicts that by 2000 the number of women online will jump to 44 percent of the total online audience (see Figure 8.6).

This proliferation of online users is contributing to a boom in e-commerce. It is believed, since female heads of household are the primary purchasing decision makers, that the increase in women has had a great effect on the increase in online sales.

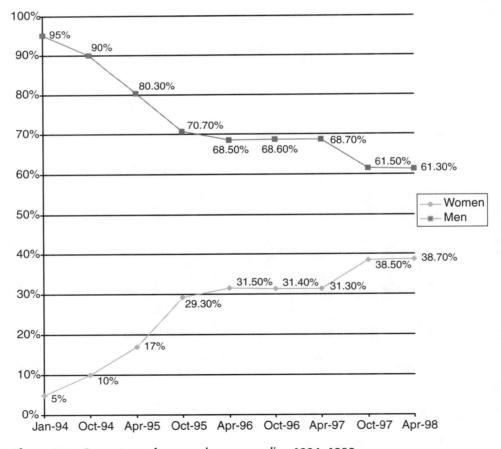

**Figure 8.5**   Percentage of men and women online 1994–1998.

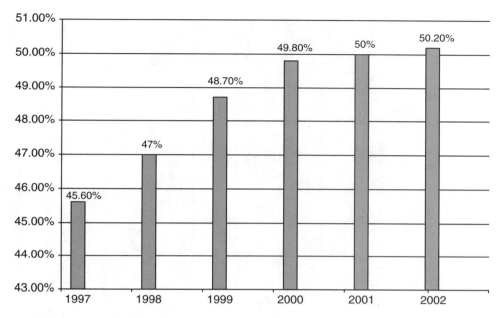

**Figure 8.6**   Number of women on the Internet.

A 1997 study by NetSmart Research on "What Makes Women Click" profiled the average women online as:

- 41 years old
- Household income of $63,000
- Online 6+ hours each week

The report summarizes that women go online because it is convenient, empowering, and fun.

By 1998, the number of women and their effect on the growth of Internet shopping demonstrated that there is economic power when women click. Sites that cater to the female audience are on the rise. From women.com (www.women.com), the first major site directed toward women, to Womenconnnect Online (www.womenconnect.com) for businesswomen, to the entire iVillage channel of female-oriented sites, women are a very important segment of the Net user population.

## Race

Internet use has not achieved a racial balance, and it looks like such balance will be slow in coming. The 9th GVU Survey distribution is presented in Figure 8.7 and reflects that the majority of Internet users (87 percent in 1998) continue to identify themselves as "Caucasian/White." It should be noted that the GVU surveys are beginning to show that younger Internet users are more racially diverse.

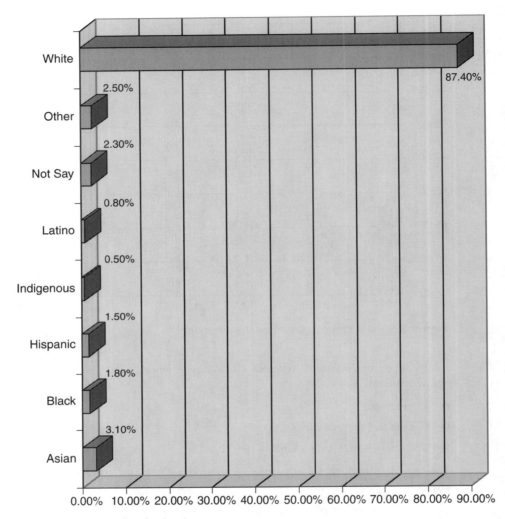

**Figure 8.7** Race distribution in U.S. Internet users.

The Internet may not be racially balanced, but, as we said before, it works well to reach niche markets, no matter how large or small. Much of the issue of race comes down to the issue of accessibility and acceptance. Internet access is dependent on PC availablity. If one can't afford a computer or the monthly service charge for an ISP, then Internet access is inaccessible, making economics a part of the accessibility equation.

Equally important, the Web is becoming more accessible in terms of multicultural content. Different ethnic groups are finding content and community of interest online. There are now a host of sites and services for the African-American community, from portal type sites like NetNoir (www.netnoir.com) and Black Voices (www.black-voices.com) to e-mail lists like Unity First (an outgrowth of the weekly newspaper

*Unity First News*, published in Boston), which is one of the direct e-mail news services targeting an ethnic group.

The Latino online community is also growing and producing its own sites. For example, LatinoLink (www.latinolink.com) services the Hispanic community and distinguishes itself with its bilingual approach to content and e-mail.

Asian Americans as well have a whole host of sites. For example, for Chinese-speaking Americans, there is Chinese.yahoo.com or Chinese Cyber City (www.ccchome.com).

## Language

The majority of users who access the Internet are English speakers, but this is rapidly changing. Just as the age and gender of the Internet is changing, so too are the language preferences. According to the figures put together by the firm Euro Marketing (www.euromktg.com), as presented in Figure 8.8, 75 million people access the Internet in languages other than English. See Chapter 12 for an overview of the international online landscape.

## Household Income

As the Internet comes to reflect more of the general population, the average household income is decreasing from the early Net days of primarily high income users to the 1998 GVU Survey results of $52,000, a slight decrease from the 8th Survey of $53,000. Figure 8.9 shows the GVU findings of average household income across gender, location, age, and Internet experience.

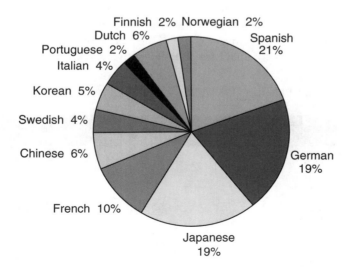

**Figure 8.8**  75 million people online who access the Internet in other languages.

Source: Global Reach (for latest update to this chart, go to glreach.com/globstats/).

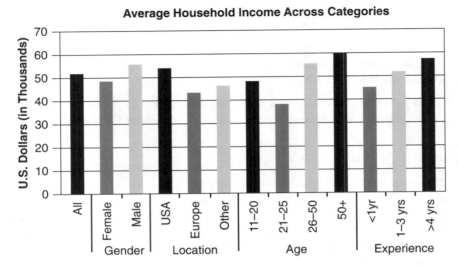

**Figure 8.9** GVU findings of average household income across gender, location, age, and Internet experience.

## Usage Patterns

No matter the source of the study, all agree that the usage patterns are pretty much the same: the majority of Net access occurs at home, with the primary uses of the Net for gathering information, whether news or personal. Figure 8.10 shows the primary uses of the Net, and Table 8.10 shows Internet usage patterns 1997–1998.

One doesn't need to be a scientist to realize that the larger the online user base and the more time that community spends online, the less time they are spending at other activities. In 1998, a series of studies were released investigating if online users were spending less time watching television as a result of the Net. Veronis, Suhler & Associates reported that consumer use of television in the past five years has dropped 9 per-

**Table 8.10** Internet Usage Patterns 1997–1998

| STATISTIC | GVU 9 (APRIL 1998) | GVU 8 (OCT. 1997) | GVU 7 (APRIL 1997) |
|---|---|---|---|
| Primary place of Web access: Home or Primarily Home | 62.6 | 65.2 | 60.4 |
| Frequency of Web Use: Daily | 87.9 | 85.4 | 85.2 |
| Hours of Web Use: >20 hrs. per week | 26.4 | 23.7 | 22.2 |

Source: GVU Survey Results

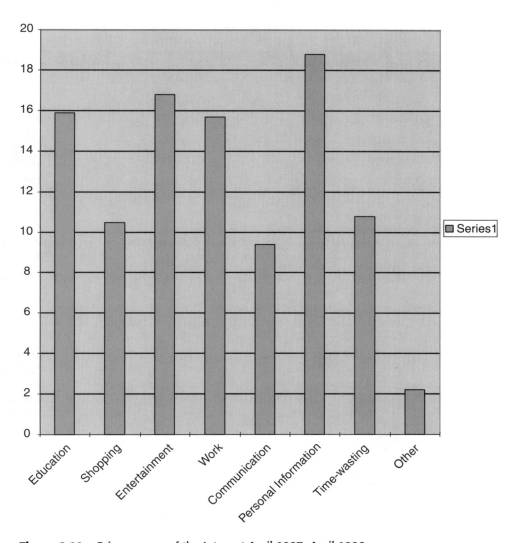

**Figure 8.10** Primary uses of the Internet April 1997–April 1998.

cent, while cable TV and online services have gained 33 percent. But the one-to-one correlation between online use and the decline in TV audience is not so clear. A December 1998 Nielsen Media (www.nielsenmedia.com) study concluded that the Internet does not affect TV viewing habits. The study found that U.S. households that go online were already light TV users before they gained Net access. eMarketer (www.e-land .com/e-stat_pages/usage_net_vs.html) reviewed several studies and found that in most cases Net users actually read more magazines and newspapers than their non-Net-user counterparts. ICONOCAST put all the studies together into one table to show the variation of results (see Table 8.11).

**Table 8.11**   Percent of Users Who Spend Less Time Watching Television

| STUDY | STUDY DATE | DECLINE |
|---|---|---|
| Nielsen PC Ownership Study | Jun. 1998 | 4%* |
| Nielsen/America Online | Aug. 1998 | 6%* |
| ICONOCAST | Sep. 1998 | 17% |
| Hambrecht & Quist/LinkExchange | Mar. 1998 | 22% |
| PricewaterhouseCoopers | Oct. 1998 | 34% |
| GVU9 | Apr. 1998 | 36%** |

Source: Table by ICONOCAST (www.iconocast.com)
* In primetime viewing.
** Use the Web instead of watching TV at least once a day.
So far only one survey, the Nielsen/Discovery Communications study, found television use actually rose 2% [ICONOCAST 30-Sep-98] in online households. While the media tide is unquestionably shifting, there seems to be an insatiable appetite for swimming against the current.

How do users find out about Web sites? The conventional wisdom is that search engines direct all traffic. But no one medium exists in a vacuum, and people use information gained through one source for another. A study conducted by NetSmart in July 1998 found that users learn about sites online and off (see Table 8.12). There is no better example of this than the flood of TV commercials, radio ads, direct mail, bus signs, billboards, and print ads for Web sites. Moreover, simultaneous use of the computer and TV is growing. According to a report by Media Metrix released in November 1998, 47 percent of PC Windows homes have a television set in the same room as the computer, and in most cases both are running simultaneously. This is up from 40 percent in 1997. In fact, we can say that Net users are often multimedia taskers (Table 8.13).

## General Online Advertising Resources

The online advertising industry now has a whole host of sites that cater to the online advertising and marketing professional providing a variety of resources from data-

**Table 8.12**   How Users Learn about Sites

| METHOD | PERCENT |
|---|---|
| Search engines | 56% |
| Magazines | 38% |
| Newspapers | 36% |
| TV news | 26% |

Source: July 1998 NetSmart IV

**Table 8.13**   Multimedia Tasking—Juggling Other Communication Media While Online

|  | MEN | WOMEN |
|---|---|---|
| Listening to the radio | 66% | 62% |
| Watching TV | 49% | 47% |
| Talking on the phone | 46% | 53% |
| Doing household chores | 22% | 32% |
| Paying bills | 24% | 18% |

Source: July 1998 Yankelovich Partners

bases of interactive agencies to case studies of ad campaigns. Table 8.14 includes a list of these valuable resource sites, which should be bookmarked by everyone involved in buying and selling online advertising.

**Table 8.14**   General Online Advertising Resource Sites

| SITE | DESCRIPTION |
|---|---|
| Ad Resource (www.adresource.com) | A collection of Web advertising and promotion resources. |
| Channel Seven Network (www.channelseven.com) | This site is a bit of everything for Internet development, marketing, and advertising executives. |
| ClickZ Network (www.clickz.com) | A network of Internet advertising and marketing sites. Three of them are: ClickZ, an online advertising and marketing daily news site; Microscope (www.microscope), a weekly banner ad review site; and SearchZ (www.searchz.com), the most complete search engine of online marketing resources. |
| Media Central (www.mediacentral.com) | Advertising and marketing media news, but for online and traditional advertising. |
| Tenagra's Marketing Resources (http://marketing.tenagra.com) | A resource area with lists and links to Internet advertising and marketing books and periodicals, from the company that hosts the online ad discussion list. |
| University of Texas "Advertising World" (http://advweb.cocomm.utexas.edu/world/) | The self-proclaimed "most extensive collection of advertising-related links on the Web!" Includes online and offline resource information. |
| Web Marketing Info Center (www.wilsonweb.com/webmarket) | Wilson Internet Services resource area, with links to hundreds of articles on Web marketing. |

Source: July 1998 Yankelovich Partners

## Learning from Yesterday As We Look Toward Tomorrow

Bob Ivins, SVP (bob_ivins@mediametrix.com)

Media Metrix, Inc. (www.mediametrix.com)

The Web has evolved rapidly in the past few years. It has evolved from its nascent days as a communications tool, used mainly by scientists and researchers, to a well-developed, multidisciplined marketing tool used by marketers around the globe to reach millions of end users. It has given birth to new business models (the virtual store), a new lexicon (hits, page views). It has created new companies who have grown larger than many industrial companies in less than two years. Along the way, it has been driven by consolidation, mainstreaming, and commerce.

### Consolidation

If we look at an early 1996 top 50 list of Web sites and compare them to today's, we see how dramatically the Web has changed since then and why. The 1996 ranking mostly consists of "adult content," technology-related, and university Web sites. And, while the category of adult content has maintained a steady 30 percent reach among all Web users, there are no adult sites among the top 50 today; instead, categories such as news/information and entertainment have increased their presence with a combined reach of over 80 percent. This comparison provides a clear picture of site and traffic consolidation as well as, or, perhaps, *because of,* the mainstreaming of the Web. The top 50 list today consists of many large media properties, and while many of them have grown organically—riding the general wave of Web growth—we have seen many grow through consolidation.

### Mainstreaming

The second significant evolutionary characteristic we have monitored is the mainstream of user demographics. That is, in 1996 Web users were predominantly educated, affluent men age 18 to 34. Today, however, the male/female gender break closely mirrors the U.S. demographic—for the first time ever there are more women than men online in the 18-to-34 age range. Further, with specific segments, such as shopping, women account for more traffic than their male counterparts. This mainstreaming has helped bring new/more commercial investment to the Web as marketers realized that the Web is a cost-effective way to communicate with their customers and prospects.

### Commerce

Last, the Web is a commercial vehicle. It was less than five years ago that news groups and IRC rooms were full of debates about the commercialization of the Internet. Today, online ad spending is projected to grow from $1.5 billion in 1998 to $15 billion in 2003. Industry experts predict e-commerce growth will also soar over the next few years. In fact, the 1998 holiday shopping season, which exceeded even the most optimistic predictions, saw traffic at many sites selling consumer goods double and triple in the week just before Christmas.

### Looking Ahead

Will we see more of the same? Will Web sites continue to grow organically or through consolidation or both? We know that analysts expect there to be more players and more industry consolidation. They also predict Web portals to be all the rage as more traditional media companies enter the fray. Looking back on the last three years, the Internet seems to have evolved very naturally toward profitable business models, and a mainstream audience, but at breakneck speed compared with other media. So, what does this rapid evolution over a relatively short time period tell us? We can't know for sure, but, someone did once say that the only true measure of future behavior is to look at past behavior.

# Buying Online Ads

Many marketers jump into online advertising without a clear plan of action. Internet ad buying entails more than merely calling Yahoo! and placing a few banner ads. An online advertising campaign, like any media campaign, requires strategic planning to ensure that money is well spent and that objectives are achieved.

As in all marketing endeavors, it is best to start with the basics. In the case of an online ad campaign, this means being able to answer the following question in the affirmative: Is the targeted market online, and if so, where online? While there may be discrepancies regarding various statistics on the Internet, no one disputes that there are many millions of online users. However, if none of these surfers fall into your target market, then an online advertising campaign makes no sense; likewise, if the target audience's online whereabouts cannot be pinpointed, an online ad campaign is probably doomed to fail. Thus, the advertiser's challenge is to discover, first, whether there is an online audience for the product or service, and, second, where online this audience congregates.

This chapter is a guided tour through the ins and outs of running an online advertising campaign. It begins by discussing the steps you need to consider before you should spend a single cent on Internet advertising, and then spells out the step-by-step process of buying and running an online ad campaign.

## Determining Campaign Goals

It is impossible to develop an effective marketing campaign if you don't have objectives. Every print, broadcast, or radio campaign has clearly defined goals, and interactive campaigns are no different. The key question you need to ask yourself is, "What do I want my audience to do?" Simply getting people to click on your ad is not enough.

One of the great misconceptions about Internet advertising is that click-through rates are a measure of how well a campaign performed. A company can't gauge a campaign's success by click-throughs alone. As an advertiser, you are looking for something more. You may want to sell products, generate leads, or build brand. When we mention building brand, many marketers think that click-through is an effective measurement of brand impact. This is not true. What if 50 percent of the people who click on your ad leave your site after they get to the home page? You may have a great click-through rate, but we'd argue that 50 percent of the people who clicked may actually be getting a negative brand impact. They're clicking on an advertisement because they expect something. When they get to the jump page they don't see what they expected and may even feel deceived, so they leave. Now, we'll go through various campaign goals and various ways to measure success for each goal.

## Traffic Building

Many campaigns are aimed at driving traffic. For example, Yahoo! wants people to use their Web site, so that they can sell more advertising and boast about their large number of visitors. Of course, their campaign isn't simply looking at the cost per visitor as a metric of success. Their real goal is to maximize the value of each visitor by reaching folks who will frequently return to their site. They try to accomplish these goals with advertisements that mention their customized options, free e-mail, auctions, and other features that tend to give consumers a reason to return. Yahoo! even runs advertising on its own site (called "housed ads") that entices users to try new features (like free e-mail) and to encourage visitors to return frequently (see Figure 9.1).

**Figure 9.1**  Yahoo! advertises its free e-mail service on the top left of its home page.

## Preparing Your Web Site for Increased Traffic from Advertising

After you determine your goals, you still may not be ready to spend money on advertising. If you're planning to use a Web site to achieve your goals—by driving traffic to the site—prior to spending any advertising money, you need to ensure that your site is effective. Before launching a traditional campaign, advertisers test everything related to the campaign to ensure that they're using their budgets efficiently. The same process must be followed on the Web.

"I have spent many hours trying free banner exchanges, low budget promotional offers, link strategies, and yes, I even tried bulk e-mail, only to realize I hadn't spent the time to make my site appealing enough to hold anyone's interest," says Kevin Frazier, VP/ COO of Focus On U (www.focusonu.com). "This should be your primary goal. Develop your own business, cater to your customers, focus on improvements, so when you do get the results from your advertising, your business is there to support the demand. The irony is that many people believe that bigger is better, when the truth is, better will make you bigger."

Here are some ways to ensure your Web site is ready for success:

**Analyze data in your log files.** As we mentioned in Chapter 4, all activity on your Web site is recorded in your log files. You can use this data to test the wording of different buttons. If you want people to register on your site, is it more effective if you say "register" or "register free"? Log data can also tell you what pages are the most frequent exit pages—the pages from which people leave your site—so that you can find out what can be done to retain more visitors. Since you can track how changes to your Web site affect user behavior and navigation, it is important to test and implement the most effective design prior to launching the campaign. Find the design that generates the most orders, leads, and other activity, and then invest in Internet advertising.

**Use a focus group** to see how consumers react to different implementations of your Web site.

**Use an expert panel to review your site.** Find people in your field who are experts on the Web and ask them to review your site and provide feedback.

## Selling Products

E-commerce sites are growing quickly, and sales are one of the leading revenue sources for companies advertising on the Internet. A company selling products doesn't need as many people as possible visiting its Web site. That company needs the right traffic—consumers or businesses who will buy its products.

Businesses selling products also have the opportunity to achieve their goals without having to drive people to their Web sites. For example, Roxy Systems, a reseller of DIRECTV, doesn't always need to drive people to the Roxy Systems Web site. Sports fans are usually good prospects for DIRECTV, because DIRECTV allows them to watch any sports game that is televised. As you can see in Figure 9.2, Roxy Systems has placed its product in the CBS SportsLine store. This is the perfect way to reach sports consumers, who will probably also have a higher comfort level buying the product from a known brand like CBS SportsLine instead of lesser known technology brand like Roxy Systems.

CDnow is another example of a Web property with the goal of selling products. Figure 9.3 shows one of their banner advertisements containing an offer regarding a music sale. CDnow is focused on getting consumers interested in the sale (and purchasing music) and not just on click-through.

## Generating Leads

Many direct marketers have found that it's easier to get prospects to request information online than it is to get them to order. Some consumers are fearful about giving their credit card information online or don't want to make a purchase at the time they see an advertisement or visit an e-commerce site. That has pushed many marketers to use their Web sites for lead generation. Prospects usually have the choice of requesting to receive a phone call, fax, or postal mailer with more information. Like sales, generating leads can be done through a marketer's Web site or through the site on which the marketer advertises. Often it is easier to generate leads through the advertiser's Web site, because you don't have to force consumers to leave the site if they want to request

**Figure 9.2** Roxy Systems sells its satellite TV, DIRECTV, directly through CBS SportsLine by targeting the sports fanatic who wants to have access to all sports channels.

**Figure 9.3**   CDnow banner for "Music Lovers" promoting a discount through text right below banner.

more information. Figure 9.4 is an ad for Star Trek Universe that ran on fastWEB (www.fastweb.com). Consumers were able to request a free set of cards without leaving the fastWEB site. Figure 9.5 is an example of a lead generation banner that brings users to a form on the Star Trek Universe site.

## Building Brand

Many companies are using Web advertising to build the brand recognition of their product or service, which may eventually lead to sales. To measure your brand-building efforts through banner advertising, you can conduct a focus group to determine how your banner ads affect brand recall. If your banner ads positively influence the impression customers have of your brand, you can assign a value to the number of impressions your advertisements receive. You may also decide that a good brand impact is made if someone looks at more than two pages of your Web site, and that a great brand impact is made if someone stays for more than 10 minutes on your Web site. Then you have two more measurements for success.

Building brand recognition does not require driving consumers to the advertiser's Web site. In fact, we believe that some of the most successful branding campaigns have involved advertising that integrates with the editorial and doesn't require a click. Our favorite examples of this type of advertisement are the now classic Dockers' sponsorship of HotWired's DreamJobs (see Figure 2.33), and the Maxwell House Coffee sponsorship of the crossword puzzle on NYTimes.com.

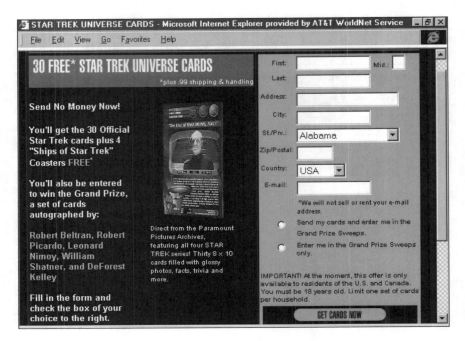

**Figure 9.4**    A lead generation form placed on fastWEB by Star Trek Universe.

Regardless of which goals you choose for your advertising campaign, every aspect of your campaign must be wrapped around those goals: your Web site or jump page design, measurement system, banner design, and site selection.

# The Site Selection Process

There are thousands of Web sites and a variety of methods for paying for advertising on those Web sites. One of the most important factors in reaching your goals is choosing the best places to run your advertising. In this section we'll review some of the factors you should consider when choosing a Web site for your advertising.

## Audience

The first and most important factor is whether or not your target audience can be reached through the Web site. The best advertising in the world won't be successful

**Figure 9.5**    Lead generation banner.

unless it reaches the right people. There are different tools for measuring who is using a Web site, which will be mentioned later in this chapter. We just wanted to point out that although the factors below are important in finding the best placement, they are all secondary to the audience on a site.

# Reporting

A great benefit of the Internet is the flexibility to adjust campaigns to maximize performance. For example, if one banner isn't performing well, you want to be able to remove it from your campaign as soon as possible. To determine what actions will increase performance, you need frequent and timely access to advertising performance reports. We believe it is also critical to have your own method for measuring performance (determining sales and leads and other measures beyond what the clicks and impressions measured by the site). Moreover, you want to make sure that your reporting method works well with the site's system for delivering advertisements.

# Ability to Quickly Rotate Creatives

The fastest ad reports in the world are ineffective if you can't make timely creative changes. Although it seems crazy, some sites require that you wait a certain number of days before they implement a creative change. Also, some sites claim they will make banner changes within one day, but it actually takes them at least a week to make the changes correctly. You'll learn which sites have these problems as you purchase advertising, and you will probably want to negotiate lower rates with these sites or avoid them altogether.

# Banner Size and Placement on the Page

There are many different opportunities to buy advertising. One factor that contributes to the value of an ad placement is the size of the ad and its placement on the page. In each case, test what works best for your campaign. Here are some general guidelines to follow.

First, bigger ads tend to have a greater response rate. This may seem obvious, but sometimes in advertising stating the obvious is important.

Second, ads on the very top of the page, like in Figure 9.6, don't pull as well as those near the top. An ad at the very top can be mistaken for the top of the page instead of a clickable advertisement. Figure 9.7 is an example of an ideal placement: the ad is not the first element on the page but is near the top. Of course, all placements should be within the first fourteen inches of the screen, so that no one has to scroll to see your advertisement. Since many people don't scroll, ads below the fourteen-inch point are not usually worth purchasing. (You want your advertisement to be viewable at 640-by-480 resolution, because that is usually the lowest resolution at which someone will be viewing the Web.)

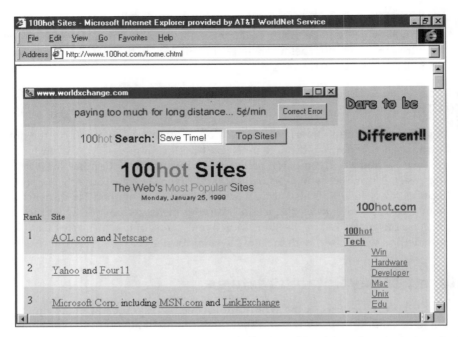

**Figure 9.6**    Ads placed too high on the screen that blend into the page often don't produce significant results.

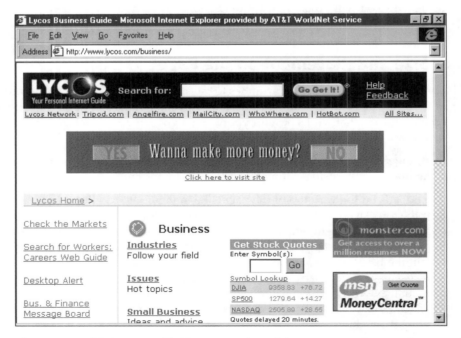

**Figure 9.7**    This banner ad in the top portion of the Lycos page has good eye-catching placement.

In evaluating the placement on the page, you also want to know how visually busy the page is, because that will determine whether or not your ad gets noticed. Figure 9.8 shows Infoseek Spain's layout, an ideal page for placement; the page is very simple, so the ad has a high visibility. On the other hand, Figure 9.9 shows a strategy employed by ClickZ, which has many different advertisements on the page. The high number of ads for a single page makes it difficult for one advertiser to really stand out; but for those who want to reach the niche audience of online advertisers, ClickZ is important as one of the few sites to reach this market; so, the site can place a lot of ads on the page and even charge a premium for ad space.

## Amount of Ad Inventory Available for Purchase

Depending on your goals and the specific site on which you're advertising, you may want to purchase anywhere from 10 to 100 percent of a site's inventory. Someone who is a category leader will want to purchase 100 percent of certain Web site inventory. For example, Claritin is the leading prescription allergy medication. They should purchase all of the allergy keyword inventory on search engines, because they will want anyone searching for allergies to always see an ad for Claritin. There are also allergy areas of medical sites, like the Mayo Clinic's allergy area, that Claritin should "own." These are targeted areas where they will reach their best prospects—people searching for information and solutions regarding their allergies.

**Figure 9.8** Infoseek Spain has a simple layout that helps bring attention to the ads on the page.

**Figure 9.9**   ClickZ has ads to the right, left, and above the site's content.

On the other hand, there are situations where it is inadvisable to purchase more than 10 percent of the available inventory. If you want to sell a product, unless the site is a perfect fit, test the site with a purchase of no more than 10 percent of available inventory. There are a few reasons for this. First, good marketers will always test small amounts before committing more advertising dollars. Second, the response from certain types of sites will drop after more than 10 percent of the inventory has been purchased. This could happen on a site like CNN. CNN has high traffic, but it's reasonable to assume that much of that traffic is from people who check the news every day. So, if you buy a large portion of CNN's inventory, there is a good chance that the same people will see your ad many times. If you're trying to sell a product, your response goes down as your ad is seen multiple times by the same person rather than being seen by different people. Use the 10 percent figure for testing, then see what works—for some campaigns, a buy of 75 percent of a site's inventory will produce the desired results.

## Performance Guarantees

When buying on a site for the first time (actually, anytime, but especially the first time) get some sort of guarantee regarding performance. For example, a site will often promise a certain number of orders or clicks. Not all sites will offer a performance guarantee, but it is worth asking for and certainly makes a site more attractive.

## Technology Capabilities

Depending on your product and target audience, you may be looking to use certain technologies, like HTML banners or Java. Make sure the sites accept these creative formats before you sign the contract. Also keep your eyes open for any sites that try to charge a premium for running HTML and rich media ads. There are sites that charge advertisers an additional $1,000 fee to use HTML advertisements. We imagine that by the time this book has been printed, this practice will stop.

## Targeting Capabilities

In Chapter 6 we mentioned many of the targeting capabilities of the Web. In evaluating a site you want to try to find the placement that helps you best target your audience.

### Tips for Finding the Best Sites for Your Ad Campaign

Think like your audience. Put yourself in the shoes of your target audience. If you were them, where would you go on the Web?

Ask your audience. You can even survey your target audience to get an idea of some sites that they visit.

Look in your log files. As we mentioned in Chapter 4, the log files record activity on your Web site, including the site from which visitors came to your site. Many advertisers think that they shouldn't advertise on sites that already send them a lot of traffic. They don't think they should pay when they're getting free traffic from links already provided. As we already mentioned, we've found that in almost all cases the sites that are already sending traffic to an advertiser are the best sites on which to advertise.

Check online lists. There are Web publications that list sites that accept advertising. Some of those sites are SearchZ (www.searchz.com) and ChannelSeven (www.channelseven.com).

Check subscription databases. The Web publications that list ad sites are okay, but far more comprehensive information is available from subscription databases. The two best are Planner from AdKnowledge (www.adknowledge.com), and Interactive Advertising Source, which is put out by SRDS, the leader in providing ad rates for traditional ad vehicles (www.srds.com). Planner allows advertisers to include Simmons and MRI research as well as Media Metrix data in their site research (if the advertiser subscribes to those services).

Both online planning tools allow media buyers to search Web sites by criteria. Figures 9.10 and 9.11 both show Planner menus from which media buyers can begin researching Web sites that fit their media plans.

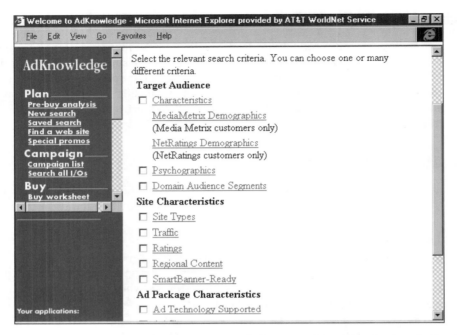

**Figure 9.10** AdKnowledge planner menu helps you select your ad campaign buying profile.

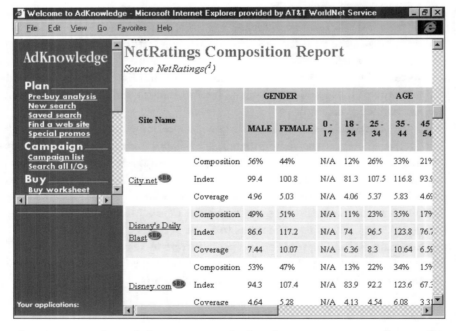

**Figure 9.11** AdKnowledge recommends sites that meet your campaign profile needs.

## Comparing Audience

There are several sources to help advertisers compare site audience. The leading providers of audience measurement information are Media Metrix (www.media-metrix.com) and Nielsen/NetRatings (www.netratings.com). Both of these companies track Web usage through panels. Panel participants have installed software from either of these companies on their computers, and the companies use that software to track the Web usage of these individuals. Advertisers who pay for these services receive reports on the most heavily trafficked Web sites as well as the most heavily trafficked Web sites in specific categories.

Since both of these services cost over $10,000, many small and medium-sized advertisers do not subscribe to them. One alternative is to use 100hot (www.100hot.com, see Figure 9.12), which is a Web site that offers free access to lists of the 100 top Web sites in specific categories—gaming, news, and so on. 100hot gathers its data through ISPs; the aggregate data of the sites users from some of the largest national ISPs visit is used to determine the highest traffic Web sites. We don't believe this is extremely accurate, but it is definitely worth investigating.

## Types of Sites

As we've mentioned, and as you probably already know, there are hundreds of thousands of Web sites. Breaking those sites down into categories is difficult, but we think these categories can be used to classify most sites: (1) well-branded, highly recognizable

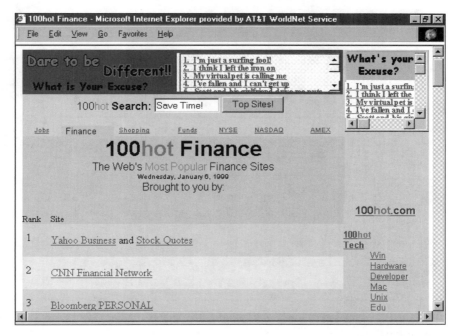

**Figure 9.12** 100hot offers free access to lists of the top 100 Web sites in specific categories.

sites, (2) high traffic sites with less- or non-recognizable brand names, (3) niche sites with low traffic, and (4) hobby and personal sites.

## Well-Branded, Highly Recognizable Sites

These sites include the likes of Yahoo!, ESPN, and other similar sites that most people have heard of, and that receive a large number of visitors. Since these are the most recognizable sites, they are the ones where most advertisers first go to place their advertising. The prices are usually the least negotiable of any of the types of sites. For advertisers, these sites offer a good brand with which to associate their product or services and a sizable audience reach.

## High-Traffic Sites with Less- or Non-Recognizable Brand Names

This category includes sites like Dogpile (www.dogpile.com, see Figure 9.13). If you've got a strong brand, you may not want to associate it with a site named Dogpile. However, the site gets a ton of traffic, so it is perfect for marketers selling products. Sites with low brand recognition and high traffic usually have a lot of unsold inventory that they will offer at a low price.

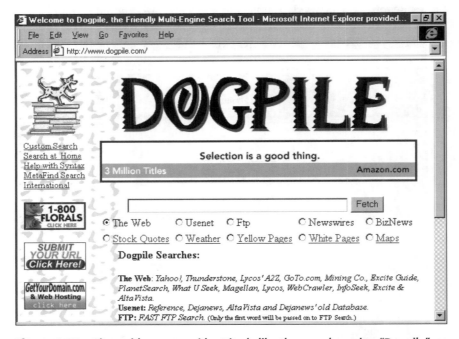

**Figure 9.13** Sites with *names with attitude* like the search engine "Dogpile" can get tremendous traffic.

### Niche Sites with Low Traffic

Sites in this category include ClickZ (www.clickz.com) and ChannelSeven (www.channelseven.com). Both sites are devoted to Internet advertising. They have a very high volume of traffic from Internet advertisers, but that doesn't make them high traffic sites in terms of the Internet. Since they reach such a targeted audience, there is a long line of advertisers willing to pay top dollar to advertise on their sites. ClickZ and ChannelSeven don't have to negotiate as much as other sites, because they offer a great means for reaching advertisers. Well-designed and marketed niche sites that have a good amount of traffic often have so much interest from advertisers that they can even clutter their pages with three or more ads and still be well worth the advertising expense.

### Hobby and Personal Pages

These are often fan pages on a particular topic. They're not as well designed as the niche sites, and usually have much less traffic than them as well. This makes them a very inexpensive buy. Many of these sites are poorly designed, which makes advertisers unwilling to place their messages here. Also, the expense of managing an ad campaign on this type of site can be more trouble than it is worth. You have to decide the minimum amount of impressions that makes it worthwhile to negotiate with a site, deliver ads, check ads, and handle other management overhead.

## Paying for Media Buys

Besides deciding on the type of site you are looking for, you should also look at the different types of media buys. Like any advertising medium, all prices are negotiable. Unless you're making a small buy on a large site, don't forget to negotiate. Below are some of the pricing models that sites are using. Chapter 7 provides a full discussion of pricing.

## CPM

CPM, or cost per thousand, means that the advertiser will pay a set fee for every thousand times an ad banner is delivered. High traffic sites prefer to sell their advertising on a CPM basis. Lower traffic sites may want to price their advertising packages at a fixed sponsor price, since they don't have enough traffic to charge high ad rates based on CPM.

## Cost Per Action

Cost per action means that advertisers pay for every time a specific action is taken. For example, you may pay on a per click or per order basis. Most sites don't like selling advertising on a per action basis. These types of buys compensate the sites for the performance of advertisements, but since the site has no control of the ad copy or the product, it also doesn't have control over how well the advertising works. Sites also feel that if advertisers are only paying on a cost per action basis, there is no compensation for the branding exposure advertisers receive. However, this is a great buy for advertisers, if they can negotiate it.

## Hybrid

A hybrid buy usually means that an advertiser pays a combination of CPM and cost per action. Since sites don't like to sell on a cost per action basis and advertisers clearly want to pay cost per action, a hybrid buy is a nice middle ground upon which both sides can usually agree. In a hybrid, the advertiser will usually pay a reduced CPM as well as some sort of a bonus for every click, sale, or order that is generated from the advertising campaign.

# Pricing for Buys

There are a host of different types of buys with different pricing models. Here we're going to go through some of the basic pricing structures and rate card prices (see Table 9.1). The companion Web site includes sample rate cards to give you an idea of what various sites are charging for advertising space.

## Search Engines and Directories

Sites, like Yahoo!, Lycos, and Excite, have a variety of buys. One is a general rotation buy. This means that the advertisement can appear anywhere in the search engine and at any time. The buy is the lowest priced of the search engine buys, because there is no targeting. The rate card price for these buys is $20 to $30 CPM. However, if an advertiser buys $25K or more for this type of a buy, there is usually substantial room for negotiation.

A more targeted search engine buy is in a topic area. For example, Figure 9.14 is the financial topic area on the GO Network (www.go.com). Marketers can purchase advertisements that rotate throughout topic areas like these. The rate card cost is typically around $40 CPM.

The most targeted search engine ad placement is by keyword. These placements allow for an advertisement to come up whenever a consumer performs a specific search. The price for these is usually between a $40 and a $70 CPM.

## Content Sites

Content sites like Quote.com or CNN are usually more expensive than search engines. But content sites can be great, because you often have a very targeted audience (it's clear that ESPN is a great way to reach sports fans). However, unlike search engines, good content sites are visited to read articles or research information, which makes visitors less likely to click on an advertisement. Content site costs can be anywhere from a $25 to a $75 CPM.

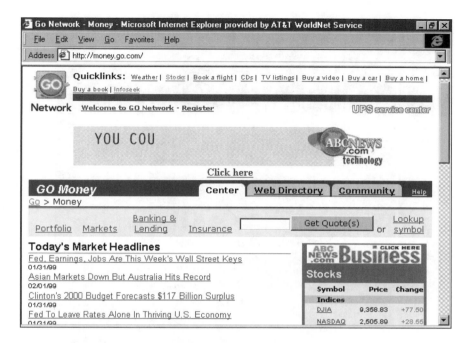

**Figure 9.14**  Financial topic area on the GO Network.

# Network Buys

Networks sell advertising for a number of sites—see Table 10.2 in Chapter 10 for a list of ad networks. The network doesn't usually own the sites, but serves as the ad sales representative. This works well, because sites often don't have the experienced sales force (or the money to hire an experienced sales force) that will be able to sell advertisements to large advertisers and agencies. And, agencies can make large ad purchases on a variety of sites through one entity rather than negotiating with all of the network's sites individually. Another advantage to networks is that they offer great targeting capabilities. For example, if you want to target everyone using the Netscape 4 browser, you can quickly reach a large number of people by advertising across an entire network. Many networks represent enough sites that they actually offer more reach than the large search engine sites.  As we mentioned earlier, network buys can range from a $30 CPM to a $35 CPM depending on targeting.

# Free E-mail Services

Advertisers can purchase advertisements in many of the free e-mail services, which include Hotmail (www.hotmail.com), USA.net (www.usanet.net), Juno (www.juno.com, see Figure 9.15), and most of the major search engines. Many free e-mail services require registration from users; these services can then offer demographic targeting based on users' responses to the questions. For example, advertisers on Juno can target based on zip code, sex, and household income. The cost on these sites can range from a $10 CPM to a $35 CPM depending on how finely the advertising is targeted.

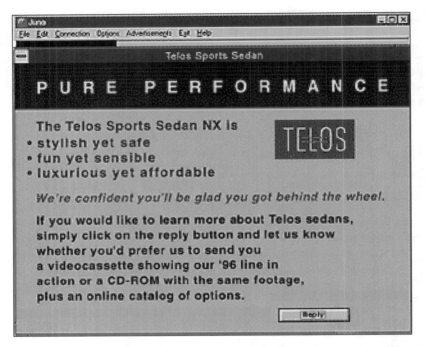

**Figure 9.15**  Juno offers its users free e-mail in return for ads on the e-mail reader.

## Spot Buys

These are ad buys that allow the advertiser to buy advertising space in the open market. Usually, the entity selling the advertising sets a bottom price point, and then advertisers can submit bids. Flycast (www.flycast.com) and Adauction.com (www.adauction.com) both offer these services. Figure 9.16 shows a screen in which an advertiser is offering a price for advertising on Flycast.

So far we've talked about setting campaign goals and some of the differences you'll see between different media buys. Now we're going to cover budget allocation and testing.

# Allocating Your Campaign Budget

We believe that as an advertiser you should commit a maximum of 50 percent of your budget to long-term buys. If you want to dominate a category, you may have to allocate more budget to long-term buys to lock competitors out of the best targeted inventory; otherwise, there is no reason to commit more than 50 percent of your budget up front. So, what should you do with your remaining budget? For starters, once the campaign begins, you will be able to see which sites are performing best. It's nice to have extra budget to allocate to those sites that are top performers. Also, there are constantly new opportunities. The Net is a rapidly changing environment, and you should always have funds

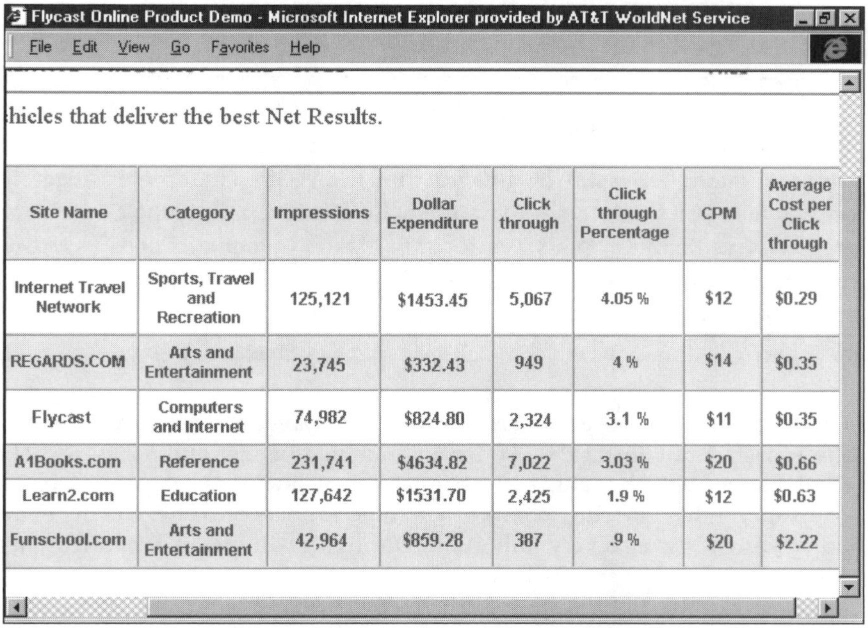

| Site Name | Category | Impressions | Dollar Expenditure | Click through | Click through Percentage | CPM | Average Cost per Click through |
|---|---|---|---|---|---|---|---|
| Internet Travel Network | Sports, Travel and Recreation | 125,121 | $1453.45 | 5,067 | 4.05 % | $12 | $0.29 |
| REGARDS.COM | Arts and Entertainment | 23,745 | $332.43 | 949 | 4 % | $14 | $0.35 |
| Flycast | Computers and Internet | 74,982 | $824.80 | 2,324 | 3.1 % | $11 | $0.35 |
| A1Books.com | Reference | 231,741 | $4634.82 | 7,022 | 3.03 % | $20 | $0.66 |
| Learn2.com | Education | 127,642 | $1531.70 | 2,425 | 1.9 % | $12 | $0.63 |
| Funschool.com | Arts and Entertainment | 42,964 | $859.28 | 387 | .9 % | $20 | $2.22 |

**Figure 9.16** An advertiser is offered a price for advertising on Flycast.

remaining for new targeting opportunities and new ad venues. Last, there are always discounted inventory sales, and there will be nothing more frustrating than having no budget for when the inventory is at half price.

## Cross-Media Promotion

There is a great benefit from advertising your Web property offline as well as online. From billboards to print ads to television commercials, ads for Web sites are appearing everywhere. In 1998 we saw many top Web sites go to TV to build brand awareness. From Amazon.com to HotBot, the irreverent humor of the Web met broadcast TV and it worked. TV advertising increased traffic and stock value.

Hollis Thomases from Web Ad.vantage (www.webadvantage.net) reminds us not to forget using targeted co-op print ads for the sole benefit of promoting Web site URLs. People who surf the Web also participate in other media, so let one help build on the other so that all roads do lead online.

For example, an American Airlines promotion placed by DDB–Dallas on the Broadcast.com site was part of a cross-media blitz that included national radio airtime, a golf "partnering" site, and a site to promote contest entries. It was the marketing mix that made the campaign work, with 93,000-plus visitors in the one-month campaign.

*Continues*

## Cross-Media Promotion *(Continued)*

Maxim Communications International used a Web site as the destination for people responding to print, radio, and online ads about a real estate venture in Stowe, Vermont, www.stowehighlands.com. Even with a moderate budget, they were able to use the Internet to improve the effectiveness of their ads. "It also proves," says Keith Reynolds, president of Maxim Communications (www.maxim-com.com), "you don't need millions of hits to succeed if you have a narrow audience and a high-ticket product."

In addition to media costs, advertisers must also pay for creative. An agency will typically charge about $600 to $1,000 for an animated banner and $1,000 to $2,000 for an HTML banner (which includes the banner, script, and jump pages; resizes cost extra). We'd suggest that you run no fewer than three banners on a site. Having extra creative budget set aside is also very important. During the campaign, you'll learn a lot about

**Table 9.1**    Ad Rates and Offerings

| | |
|---|---|
| Search Engines | $20–$50 CPM |
| Keyword Advertising | $40–$70 CPM |
| Local Advertising | $20–$80 CPM |
| City Guides | $20–$80 CPM |
| Advertising Networks | $10–$70 CPM |
| Auction Sites | $1–$25 CPM |
| Top 100 Web Sites | $25–$100 CPM |
| Opt-In Email Advertising | $.10–$.20 per addess |
| Small Targeted Content Sites | $10–$80 CPM |
| Sponsored Content | $45–$85 CPM |
| Rich Media | $35–$100 CPM |
| Click-Through Pricing | $.20–$1.20 |
| Range of Click-Throughs | .5%–15% |
| Average Click-Through | .5%–2.5% |
| Overall Average CPM | $27 |
| Pay Per Lead | $1–$15 |
| Pay Per Sale | 5%–30% of purchase price |

Compiled by Ad Resource (www.adresource.com) as of 6/9/98.

what creative works best, and you'll want to have the money to change your creative to maximize response.

Don't forget that you'll also have tracking and fulfillment costs. If you offer to mail something to people, you'll have to pay for shipping and handling, not to mention purchasing or manufacturing the product.

## Testing

You've already heard from us about the Internet's great ability to efficiently test campaigns. But, of course, this only works if you actually take the time to test sites, ad placements, and the ads themselves. Two good ad-testing programs are TestIt! (www.doubleclick.net/advertisers/ad_rates/network/testit.htm) and FlyCast (www.flycast.com). A small test flight, a week before your campaign, is good for ensuring that you know as much as possible about what will work before you begin your actual campaign.

## Dump Your Traditional "Partner" Agency Now

Todd Tweedy, Director of Client Services <todd@ webnet-marketing.com>
web-net marketing <www.webnet-marketing.com>

Interactive media shops have dominated the digital marketing arena because they understand that customers control the flow of information and digital agencies also realize how technology can enhance online media placements. These two facts are critical when assessing the value of interactive media pricing. That's why I believe you'll find more direct marketers in the digital marketing game. It's also the reason why the traditional advertising model of pushing messages is dead in the digital age.

Traditional shops have outsourced interactive media planning and placements for one reason: The big shops still don't get it even if say they are "integrated." And although it sounds wonderful for an advertiser and its "partner" agency to have a shared vision of where the advertiser's brand will go, if the partner agency doesn't know where to go online the advertiser's online placement will go nowhere. If you want an effective online media campaign, dump your "partner" agency now.

Why take such a radical step? Because most agencies are behind the curve. They don't have the resources in staff and intellectual capital to provide the service you need and deserve. Getting the most bang for your interactive investment dollar begins with raising the bar on the services your interactive media agency provides. Interactive media planning is more than making recommendations on specific media properties to include in your plan. Your interactive media placement agency should also lead contract negotiations; provide placement verification reports, daily performance reporting, and tracking; and test methodologies to sustain and optimize creative performance, trend reporting, reconciliation of media delivery, and analysis. It's amazing, but I still hear advertisers telling horror stories that the first data they received was after their campaign concluded.

The issue isn't whether the agency is old or new. The issue isn't whether the agency is economically priced. The issue is: Can the agency help you maximize your online investment? Whether the tactic is utilizing high-reach vehicles with run-of-site positioning or site-specific content targeting, the marketing value of online media is not solely driven by media costs. An agency that understands this is worth its weight in gold.

# CHAPTER 10

# Selling Online Advertising

Y ou want to sell advertising on your Web site. Who doesn't? The American Association of Advertising Agencies professes that advertising is the engine of capitalism. And, with the Internet frontier wide open, does everyone want to jump on the bandwagon?

Before you throw all your cards on the table, recognize that conducting business on the Internet is much more than a matter of point and click. Planning, persistence, and hard work are essential. And, even with all that, there is no guarantee you will make a profit from selling ads. It's a buyer's market in cyberspace. There are thousands of sites selling advertising. To succeed, you not only have to be lucky, but cyber-savvy. This means taking steps to:

- Stand out from the multitude of publishers selling advertising
- Offer inventory that meets the needs and interests of your advertisers, whether that's banners, rich media, or sponsorships
- Work to build long-term relationships with advertisers
- Be flexible with pricing and creative

The selling philosophy presented in this chapter is simple: Add value through quality—quality in measurement, management, targeting, and delivery. Whether your site receives 100,000 or 1,000,000 visits per week, whether you cater to college students or car buyers, following this rule of thumb will have your site well on its way to attracting advertising dollars. The suggestions in this chapter will help you make your site advertising-friendly, smart, and successful.

## Identifying and Defining What You Have to Sell

The first step in developing an ad sales program is identifying and defining what you have to sell. As in any sales structure, you need to define your product. When you are selling online advertising, the ads are the product and need to be defined, classified, and inventoried. The entire site needs to be reviewed for ad format acceptance and ad placement possibilities so that site specifications can be determined, including:

**Ad formats.** The types of ads accepted: banners, buttons, logos, reciprocal linking, sponsorships.

**Technical specifications.** File size, dimensions.

**Ad space locations.** Run of site, run of category, section-specific.

**Placement.** Location of ads on each page (this could be literally anywhere on the page, although we recommend placing all advertising within the first fourteen inches of the page). Placement can also refer to how many ads are on a page.

**Type.** Static, animated, rich media.

**Targeting.** Demographic, collaborative filtering, behavioral, etc.

**Special benefits.** Exclusive agreements and other special opportunities.

## Preparing Your Site's Infrastructure

Before you begin accepting advertising, you must set up your site's infrastructure. This means making certain you have the technical applications on your site to fulfill the needs of the professional advertising community, which include monitoring and measuring your site's traffic, deciding which ad models to use, and ad management. Some advertisers may also need an audit of your numbers.

### Monitoring and Measuring Site Traffic

Part of knowing what you have to sell is knowing the traffic on your Web site. It is central that you employ effective measurement tools so that you can precisely calibrate the traffic to and from your site, as well as gauge the traffic patterns within your site. Being able to monitor and measure how many users are visiting your site, where they come from, and what they are doing once they get there will provide you with a blueprint for determining the best pages for placing paid advertising. For a full discussion of measurement software, revisit Chapter 4.

### Ad Models

In designing your site, you must decide which ad models you'll accept: banners, buttons, product placement, interstitials, sponsorship, and so on. You can accept one or several ad types, as well as institute your own innovative ad models to intrigue cutting-edge advertisers. Chapter 2 provides a lengthy overview of all the ad models available for use.

## Ad Management

Media buyers want to be confident that when they buy advertising on a site, the ad will go live at the designated time; that it will remain online for the proper period of time; and that they will receive performance reports as often as possible in an understandable format. Advertisers also like to be able to rotate multiple ads simultaneously. Fulfilling advertisers' ad management needs is a daunting task to perform manually—almost impossible to do well—even for the most organized individual. To ensure that the ads you sell are delivered professionally, it is wise to employ ad management tools; it's very difficult to sell advertising, and, the last thing you want to do is lose an advertiser because you couldn't manage the ad serving. For a full discussion of ad management tools and techniques, refer back to Chapter 5.

## Auditing

If you hope to secure top-billing advertisers, you may have to provide them with the audit services they have come to expect in traditional advertising. Audit reports document the credibility of results in the form of an independent third-party analysis. Although currently, most online publishers do not provide audits, in the near future this will no doubt become standard practice. More about auditing is available in Chapter 4.

# Know Your Audience

The true value of your site is its audience. If your site generates a good volume of traffic—100,000 to 1 million or more visits per month—then one of your site's asset is its traffic volume. Currently, sites with the most traffic receive the bulk of online advertising dollars. Even if getting to 100,000 visits is unrealistic for your site, you need to continually work to increase its traffic.

Increasing traffic sends two messages to advertisers. First, it says that the site is popular and servicing the needs and interests of its audience. Second, increasing traffic ensures media buyers that they will be able to continually expand their reach with the advertising they place on your Web site.

We've mentioned that it's the highest traffic sites that get the lion's share of the advertising dollars. However, even if your site is not in the top 1 percent (or even 10 percent) in traffic, you can still find buyers for your ad space if your site's visitors represent a target market. By catering to a specific audience, you can present yourself as the premier marketing opportunity for a specific consumer product or service. For example, if your site is designed for tennis enthusiasts, then it would be a prime location for advertising tennis products. If your site provides information about a particular disease, such as diabetes, or a medical condition, like high blood pressure, your site would be an excellent location for a pharmaceutical company to promote its new medications.

Advertisers want to know—indeed, they must know—who they will reach by advertising on your site. Consequently, you need to be able to provide a profile of your audience. This profile can be compiled through interactive strategies such as registration, surveys, or even games and contests. You can also implement many of the new technologies available for greater targeting and personalization of ads. See Chapter 6 for more on targeting. The more detail you can include in your audience profile, the more valuable your advertising real estate. If your site can deliver an already targeted consumer market, your real estate has a higher value that generic "land" on another site.

## The Credibility Issue

Credibility is transferable. A site with a loyal following is especially attractive to an advertiser. Advertisers expect that the goodwill and community you foster on your site will inspire response, resulting in sales, brand building, and leads.

Because audience loyalty is of prime importance, publishers must be certain that the advertising they accept won't upset their audience. Therefore, it is important to review ads, not only for spec adherence but also for contextual appropriateness. In most cases, this is a non-issue. But a site might want to establish a policy addressing unacceptable ads. Ads might be deemed unacceptable because they are too sexually provocative or contain other content that might be offensive to the site's particular audience. Or the format of the ad itself might be offensive. For example, there are a number of sites that don't allow advertisers to run banners that resemble computer-generated dialogue boxes with error messages (see Figure 10.1). When such ads ran, consumers thought the banners were actual error messages and clicked on them for that reason. When the users were transferred to the advertiser's site, they realized that they were deceived. Some sites have banned these ads because of the resulting user backlash. Publishers should also be careful not to add too many ads to a page before they are certain that it won't upset their audience.

What is appropriate for one audience may be inappropriate for another. This is especially true for children's sites. By serving an advertisement on your site, you are tacitly endorsing the company, product, or issue. You don't have to accept every ad just because someone is willing to pay for the impressions. Credibility is easier to lose than to regain. And, if you lose credibility with your audience, you may lose traffic and, subsequently, inventory available for sale.

## Pricing Ads—Developing the Rate Structure

Once you know what you have to sell, then you need to decide what rate structure you are going to use. How are you going to charge for your ads: flat fee, CPM (cost per thousand), CPC (cost per click), PPS (pay per sale)? Chapter 7 provides a full discussion of pricing options. You can use one method, or offer a menu of rates for an à la carte approach to pricing. In fact, the rate menu approach is gaining popularity as ad campaigns become more customized and more representative of a partnership between the advertiser and the site property.

**Figure 10.1**   A banner that resembles an error dialogue box.

The primary considerations in determining your rate structure should be the size and diversity of your ad inventory, your revenue needs, and what the advertisers have come to expect and demand from the market.

**Size and diversity of ad inventory.** The size of your site's audience and how much ad space you have to offer are important factors in determining the best rate structure for your site. If your site only has 50,000 page views per month, then charging by CPM might not be in your best interest; if you offer one banner per page, the number of impressions you have on your site is 50,000, and if you charged a $32 CPM, the maximum revenue you could expect is $1,600. For a small site, a flat fee on a monthly, quarterly, or yearly basis offers the site more revenue potential. Also, multiple ad units may allow the publisher to sell more than one impression on a page. For example, the publisher could sell a banner impression on the top, a button on the right, and a text link somewhere else on the page. If the site is extremely well targeted, the publisher may even be able to get away with selling multiple banners on each page. A site's ad inventory (the total number of impressions available for sale) is rarely static. There are many factors that can influence the size of the inventory beyond the number of pages with ads and the number of ads per page. A site's inventory can increase or decrease by fluctuations in the number of visitors, the amount of time each visitor spends on the site, and the number of page views by a visitor. In short, if site traffic drops, ad inventory drops.

**Revenue needs.** This is always a loaded question. Advertising can generate revenue, but few sites rely solely on advertising. Advertising should be part of the site's overall revenue strategy. A diversified revenue approach seems to be the safest strategy on the Web. Putting that aside, keep your expectations realistic. Advertising is not the silver bullet, and only a handful of sites are making serious money. Start by trying to cover the costs of running the advertising program, and build from there.

**Market structure.** With so many sites accepting advertising, every site has competition. Your advertiser is probably reviewing your competition's advertising opportunities as well. Know the rates your competitors are charging and make your competitive advantage value, quality, and aggressive pricing.

As discussed in Chapter 7, there are several pricing models to choose from; CPM, flat-fee, click-through, and cost per action are among the most common. To decide this important issue, publishers need to take a realistic look at the value of the advertising they're offering. If you are building a site that will be in the top one percent of traffic generators with several million impressions per day, you can charge a lower CPM. For such high-traffic sites with broad appeal, the attraction to advertisers is simply volume.

But most sites do not fall into this category. Most cater to an identifiable group: teens with expendable income, golfers, model rocket hobbyists, doll collectors, and so on. And, this is what the Internet does best: provide access and exposure to niche markets. Such targeted sites can charge a higher CPM. They have a limited inventory to sell, but what they have is the best vehicle for reaching a particular audience.

If you are still in the process of building your site and need sponsors to provide working capital, then a flat-fee model would work best. Rob Frankel, marketing executive at Frankel & Anderson (www.frankel-anderson.com), sees a clear advantage for small sites to accept fixed pricing. "Fixed pricing gets you paid. Impression-based takes forever to calculate and collect, and is almost never worth the same as fixed price. Take the money up front, not 'on the come.'" The flat-fee model also works best for small sites that don't generate enough traffic to charge reasonable CPMs. A flat fee of $250 will seem more reasonable to advertisers than a $125 CPM.

If your site generates a lot of response for advertisers, you may be able to charge a higher rate. You might be able to lure advertisers with an attractive test rate for first-time clients. If response on the site is good, the advertisers will be willing to pay a higher rate after the test. If your Web site is having trouble selling inventory, offering per-click-through advertising is usually a good way to get advertisers to test the site.

As noted earlier in the book, the market rate for impressions and click-throughs constantly changes. Therefore, the best way to find out the going rate is to compare your site with the rate sheet for similar sites.

If you are a small to medium-sized site, the best pricing model might be an individual arrangement with each advertiser. If you are a large site, this might be something you can provide only for your major advertisers. As with any sales deal, be flexible with your pricing and be prepared to customize on demand. However, if you offer someone a great deal to test your Web site, make sure he or she is aware that this is a one-time pricing break. You don't want to start a trend in which you lose out on revenues.

Since the Internet was built on barter, and it's a buyer's market, a rate sheet is often viewed as the opening bid, with the buyer and seller negotiating from there.

Once you determine the rate structure, then you are ready to calculate the rate for each ad product. The rate prices are determined by such factors as:

- size of site audience
- content of site
- ad's ability to reach and interact with the audience (targeting and ad format)
- ad placement (top or bottom of page)
- number of ads on a page
- dynamic delivery to targeted audience

## Agency and Sales Commissions

In calculating your rates, don't forget agency commissions (customarily 15 percent). The agency gets their commission from the 15 percent discount that sites give agencies. The agency keeps the 15 percent so that there is no extra cost to the advertiser. This is how many agencies are paid for their services, so not offering this commission could make you a less attractive buy.

## Discounts and Special Deals

As in retail, discounts and special deals work in selling advertising space. Remnant sales and end-of-quarter sales are always welcomed by media buyers.

It is not uncommon for a site to have remaining impressions at the end of month. According to Richard Hoy, moderator of the Online Advertising List, a "PR-centered" answer is to overdeliver. "The client feels like she got a little something for free, and you aren't really losing anything. I mean, what the heck are you going to do with those extra impressions anyway?" For example, if you have 100,000 impressions to sell, you may only sell 95,000 of them. Then, at the end of the month, you can give a client the 5,000 remaining impressions for "free." Because you keep track of the traffic to your site, you know you will have the impressions to deliver your minimum and more. Overdelivery builds goodwill and loyalty, or can be a safety net if something unexpected should occur. For example, if an ad campaign is pulling really poorly, the advertiser may ask for over-delivery to compensate for the poor performance.

Exclusivity is a standard in traditional advertising and a popular strategy in the arsenal of online advertising deals. Exclusivity means that for an increased price, an advertiser is the only advertiser in a specific category or is the only vendor of a type of product or service on a site. For example, a travel firm can be the exclusive travel agency for a site. Or a bookseller can be the exclusive bookstore of a site. The benefit to the advertiser is premium exposure. The benefit to the publisher is increased revenue.

## Selling Day Parts

Day part advertising is starting to take hold online, and being able to offer it could give your site an advantage over competitors who don't. A commonly used tactic by television and radio advertising, careful timing of when an ad appears can result in better response. Auction sites are doing it: iDeal increases its use of banner ads in the hours before the midday bidding deadline for its auction site www.dealdeal.com. "If we get people to bid at the end of an auction," says Jamie Locke, iDeal co-founder, "that helps move prices into an acceptable range for merchants." Internet advertising veteran John Audette of MMG has found that lunch hour advertising can increase click-through rates by 25 percent. Other key times are right after work (5–6 P.M.) and after 10 P.M. In short, "Everything we know from traditional media about day parts must be translated to the Internet," says Laura Berland, of ORB Digital Direct. "There is not just a right place but also a right time to convey your message."

## Competitive Analysis

It is important that you know your competition so that you can anticipate and answer advertisers' questions. Review other sites in your category, and know their audience and advertising program. Your advertisers will. Even if you see a world of difference between your site and the other sites in your category, your advertisers may not. It's best to take the philosophy that those sites are great, but your site is different, and it is that difference that will help advertisers reach their campaign objectives.

The Web offers a veritable cornucopia of tools and services for conducting competitive research and learning from other advertising campaigns. If you want to learn about banner ad and its relation to CTR (click-through rate), check out the CTR Comparison site at www.whitepalm.com/fourcorners/ctrcomparison.shtml and see how banners that ran on Yahoo!, LinkExchange, and other sites performed. If you're interested in following an ad's placement, you can use NetRating's Online Observer (www.netrat-ings.com), which offers ad banner tracking. This service shows you the ad, where it ran on any particular week, how many unique impressions were delivered, the demographics of those impressions, and the click-through rates achieved. You can even drill down to the individual pages on which the ads were posted.

# Media Kit

Whether you are selling advertising for a Web site or an e-mail newsletter, you need a media kit that spells out your advertising opportunities (see the companion Web site for sample media kits). The online version should be a link accessible on every page and titled "media kit," "advertising opportunities," "how to advertise with us," or even just "advertising" or "sponsorships."

What makes a good media kit? One that works. Barbara Feldman, syndicated columnist and publisher of the site "Surfing the Net with Kids" (www.surfnetkids.com), has found that her simple and straightforward online media kit is producing results. "I'm selling at least one ad campaign (of various sizes, of course) per month with *only* in-bound leads. In fact, I can't even use the word 'sell.' I'm just taking orders from those that have already read my media kit."

There are nine key elements that need to be included in an online advertising program media kit. These elements can be presented as separate sections or consolidated into sections of a single page:

1. Site overview and features
2. Contact information
3. Advertising and sponsorship programs
4. Advertising rates
5. Site traffic
6. Audience demographics
7. Production specifications
8. Delivery specifications
9. Reporting

## Site Overview and Features

The media kit needs an introductory page, which serves as a springboard to all of its elements. The page does not need to be lengthy. Its purpose is to set the tone and offer a text overview of the pieces in the media kit as well as a list of links to each of these elements.

Most importantly, this is the page where you put your site's best features forward. In short, this is where the hard sell occurs, with all the other pages serving as supporting documents. For a sample media kit introductory page that uses a road map format, see Figure 10.2 from Women.com. For a sample of a page that spells out the value of advertising on the site, see Figure 10.3 from PriceSCAN.

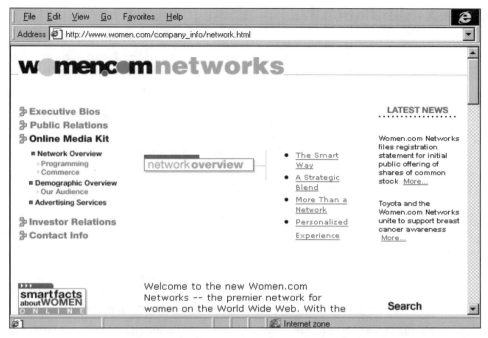

**Figure 10.2**  Women.com media kit uses a road map format listing the sections of the media kit in the left column.

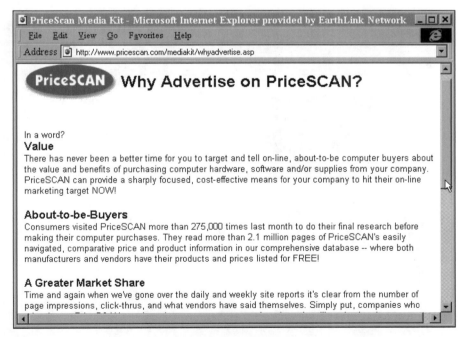

**Figure 10.3**  PriceSCAN media kit spells out the value of advertising on the site on the introductory page.

## Contact Information

This can either be a separate page or incorporated in a page with other information. Wherever this information is placed, it should be easy to find and list full contact information for the person or persons handling the advertising and sponsorship program. Full contact information includes name, title, address, phone, fax, and e-mail (on the Web page the e-mail should be a mailto: link). Keep in mind that people buying ad space often like to deal directly with a person; a generic contact fill-in form may be efficient for you, but sales is about building relationships. There is nothing warm, fuzzy, or personal about a form. A person at the other end of the telephone is the best approach.

## Advertising and Sponsorship Programs

This is where the advertising and sponsorship options are spelled out for potential advertisers. It can be in any design format—tables or text—but keep it simple and provide answers to all question you can anticipate. For example, in the Inc. Online media kit, the banner advertising program is separated out from the sponsorship program, with each receiving its own page (see Figure 10.4). A site offering advertising on many different areas of the site, such as Talk City with its multiple communities, will often spend time going into the value of the offerings in each location (see Figure 10.5).

You might also want to list some of your current advertisers, especially if the list is long and impressive. Nothing motivates an advertiser like competition—not to mention that it indicates that your site is a proven entity. However, it is important to realize that if you list

**Figure 10.4**    Inc. Online media kit has a separate section for banner advertising.

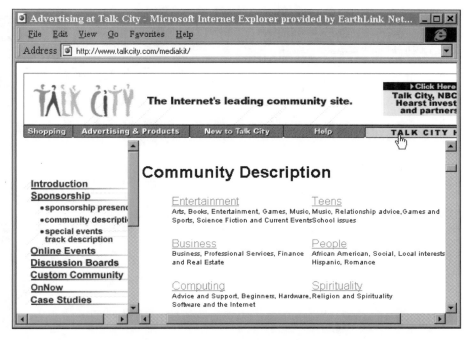

**Figure 10.5**  Talk City media kit has a separate section for each of its community areas.

your advertisers, that information will be accessed by your current and future competitors, who will begin to call on your clients (if they don't do so already).

## Advertising Rates

This is the page where the rates are listed, and it is referred to as the "rate card." Place your rates up front and center; don't make the buyer dig for this information. There should be no mystery as to your fees. Also, date your rate card so the media buyer knows that the rates are for the current quarter or time period. The LATINOLink rate card is simple—one page, no graphics. It lists the CPM, the cost per month, insertion due dates, commission policy, and right of refusal policy, with complete contact information on the bottom of the page (see Figure 10.6). Sample rate cards are provided in this book's companion Web site.

## Site Traffic

This is the area where information from the Web site measurement software is displayed. Charts and graphs work particularly well in this section. Information of particular interest to advertisers includes impressions throughout the site and in all categories where you sell advertising, and traffic growth over the past three to six months. As the saying goes, a picture is worth a thousand words, and nowhere does a chart work better than in reflecting site traffic. In the HomeArts media kit, the one page that is shortest is the one that documents the site traffic; a simple chart and table say it all (see Figure 10.7).

**Figure 10.6**  LATINOLink chose a simple and straightforward rate card format.

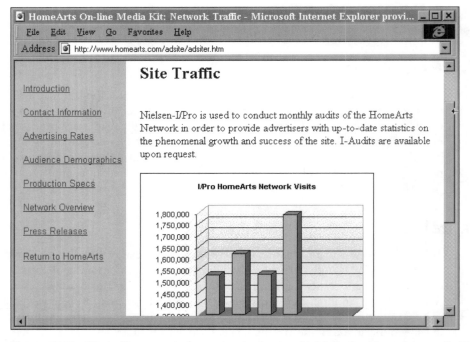

**Figure 10.7**  Site traffic presented as a simple chart and table in the HomeArts media kit.

## Audience Demographics

This is where information on the site's audience is presented, such as age, gender, income, and geographic distribution.

## Production Specifications

This is the area where the design specifications are provided for each ad product. The information needed includes:

**Ad dimensions.** Whether it is a button (120 × 60 pixels), a banner (468 × 60), or other dimensions.

**Ad due date.** How soon before a flight the creative must be delivered.

**File format.** Most common is GIF, with many sites accepting JPEG. Indicate type of looping allowed and rich media rules.

**File size.** Most sites require 12 KB or less.

**ALT text.** The specs for the text that will appear in the ad space before the ad downloads.

## Delivery Specifications

This section delineates how ads need to be sent to the site. Options include e-mail, Web, or ftp.

**E-mail.** Name of the person to whom the e-mail should be sent, and how the ads should be named.

**Web.** Instructions for sending an e-mail with URL for pickup location of banners.

**FTP.** FTP address and file location (name and password as well, if necessary).

## Reporting

This section denotes how you are going to provide the advertiser with reporting on the performance of their ad or sponsorship; whether this information is accessible in real time or on a daily or weekly basis; and whether this information will be e-mailed or is accessible online. Also provide information if your site is professionally audited by one of the industry firms (as discussed in Chapter 4). If your site is audited, publish this information as well. Inc. Online does this on one screen and makes the information short, sweet, and to the point (see Figure 10.8).

## Deciding the Format of Your Media Kit

There is no clear-cut rule as to whether you need both an online and print version of the media kit. Many find an online-only version sufficient. Others find a value in having a print version as well. "We've found that hard copy media kits work better in terms of sales than online only," says Eric Ng of Student.com (www.student.com). Still others don't want to make their rates available online, because of a fear that their competition will see.

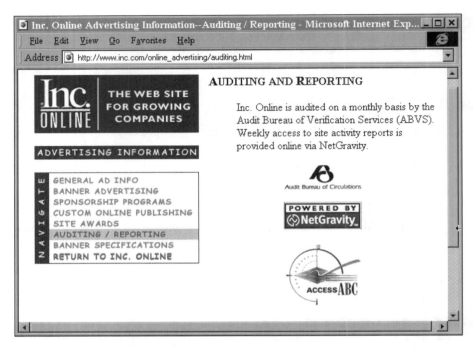

**Figure 10.8** Inc. Online's audit information: short, sweet, and to the point.

Be sure that the media kit is full of good information, and doesn't simply look good on the outside. A fancy design won't answer a media buyer's questions. Dana Blankenhorn, editor of a-clue.com and veteran journalist, puts it this way: "The money spent in packaging a press announcement or media kit is often inversely proportional to its importance. An expensively wrapped announcement of little real news value is a sure sign of a company out of ideas." Whether you go paper or plastic, online-only or online and print versions, it's what's inside that counts. What's a solid media kit? One that works.

A good media kit is essential, but it doesn't substitute for strong sales. "It's hard to say exactly how much of our success had to do with the media kit," says Ann LeRoy, vice president of Marketing and Business Development at PriceSCAN, "and how much can be attributed to my kick-ass determination to make us profitable, by working, calling, writing, and pitching some more." As LeRoy states, it takes a lot more than a media kit to generate ad sales.

# Sign on the Dotted Line

Consult your legal counsel to draw up an insertion order for your advertising space. The insertion order should include the specifications of the ad placement, name of advertiser, duration of the flight, cost, start and stop dates, and any other special orders. The contract should also include a payment schedule, as well as any other terms and conditions of particular importance to you and your business. A sample insertion order from Townonline (www.townonline.com) is given in Figure 10.9, which is an excellent example, but not meant to be a boilerplate. You should consult your legal counsel to have an insertion order developed for your particular needs.

## Information Media Buyers Need to Know

**Size of audience**

**Demographics of audience**

**Targeting capabilities for ads and for content**

**Flight schedules (daily, weekly, monthly)**

**Guarantees and make-goods**

**Reporting and measurement capabilities**

**How the site defines terms like "impression" and "page view"**

**What gets measured**

**Availability of reports and access to data (real time)**

**Rates**

**Inventory available**

**Ad specs**

**Joint marketing opportunities (online and off)**

**Sponsorship (co-branding) opportunities**

**Content integration (product placements)**

# Selling Strategies

Selling can be the most exciting part of the advertising process, but it is also the most difficult to do right. In addition to readying your site to accept advertising, you need to get the right people to sell the ads. Those people may be an in-house sales force, a representation firm, an ad network, or an online ad auction service. It may even be all of them. To determine what will work best for you and your company, examine the benefits of all the different sales strategies; and remain flexible so you can implement an alternative approach if one proves to be ineffective.

## Site Representation Firm

A site representation firm—informally known as a rep firm—specializes in selling advertising and sponsorship packages for a select slate of clients (see Table 10.1). These firms usually have an exclusive agreement with a site to act as its sales representative. Representation firms charge a commission for their services, with fees ranging from 35 to 40 percent. They carefully select properties they represent and often have a monthly impression minimum for their sites (averaging one million impressions per month). It should be noted that the monthly minimum does vary, and firms do occasionally represent sites with smaller monthly impressions if those sites are market leaders of a clearly defined and lucrative target audience. Rep firms also generally require third-party research to validate, identify, and document audience size and demographics.

Representation firms can have different clientele focuses. For example, HerAgency.com (www.heragency.com) focuses exclusively on the female demographic online by partnering with high-quality, female-focused Web sites to assist advertisers in reaching women

## CNC INTERNET INSERTION ORDER/CONTRACT — W00000

Account #

Account Name

Agency

| Date | P.O.# | Rep. # | Rep. Ext. | Rep. Name(s) | Unit |

### BILLING

Payment Options: (attach yellow copy of receipt slip with payments)

☐ Visa  ☐ Discover  ☐ Master Card  ☐ American Express  ☐ Prepayment  ☐ Cash  ☐ Bill  ☐ Check #: _____

Ad Authorized/Contact Name

*Customer signature indicates acceptance of all advertising conditions, policies and standards as specified on the reverse of this form.*

Authorized Signature

Co-op Mfr. | Amount %/$

### ACCOUNT ACCESS   Go to: www.townonline.com/advertisers/login.html   (Minimum 6 letters or numbers, no spaces and case sensitive)

Username/login | Password

*This information is used to allow the Customer access to their account information and to check banner campaign progress.*

| CODE | PRODUCT | START | END | RATE/MO. | # OF MOS. | TOTAL |
|---|---|---|---|---|---|---|
| PREM | Premium Web Site Package  (10 pages) | - - | - - | $ | × | = $ |
| SUPR | Super Web Site Package  (6 pages) | - - | - - | $ | × | = $ |
| VALU | Value Web Site Package  (3 pages) | - - | - - | $ | × | = $ |
| BASC | Basic Web Site Package  (1 page) | - - | - - | $ | × | = $ |
| PROW | Promo Web Site Package  (listing) | - - | - - | $ | × | = $ |
| SETC | Setup Charge | - - | - - | $ | × | = $ |
| XPGS | Additional Web Page(s) | - - | - - | $ | × | = $ |
| YPTS | Yellow Pages - Tile Size Upgrade | - - | - - | $ | × | = $ |
| YPAC | Yellow Pages - Additional Categories | - - | - - | $ | × | = $ |
| YPRU | Yellow Pages - Radius Upgrade | - - | - - | $ | × | = $ |

| CODE | PRODUCT (use layout forms for targeting) | START | END | RATE | QTY | TOTAL |
|---|---|---|---|---|---|---|
| TILE | Tile Impressions | - - | - - | $ | × | = $ |
| SPON | Sponsorship | - - | - - | $ | × | = $ |
| VIRT | Virtual Tour | - - | - - | $ | × | = $ |

**Figure 10.9** Insertion order form from Townonline.

|  |  | | | | |
|---|---|---|---|---|---|
| AVPR | Audio/Video Production | $ | × | = | $ |
| DOMN | Domain Name Registration | $ | × | = | $ |
| EFRM | Email Form | $ | × | = | $ |
| BANR | Banner Impressions | $ | × | = | $ |
| ANIM | Banner Animation | $ | × | = | $ |
| BACR | Banner Creative | $ | × | = | $ |
| ETPC | Extra Text/Photo Change | $ | × | = | $ |
| LAYC | Layout Change | $ | × | = | $ |
| SETC | Setup Charge | $ | × | = | $ |
| CDWK | Custom Design Work | $ | × | = | $ |
| EMAL | Email sponsorship | $ | × | = | $ |
| | | | | | |
| | | | | | |
| | | | | | |
| TOTAL | *Bill 1st ____ month(s) @ $ ____ , then the next ____ month(s) @ $ ____ per month.* | | | = | $ |

White ± Order Entry, Yellow ± Production, Green ± Interactive, Pink ± Salesperson, Gold ± Customer

*Distribution: Give order entry White copy, advertiser Gold copy, keep Pink copy for your records and give remaining copies to the Internet Coordinator.*

**Figure 10.9** *(Continued)*

---

**Terms and Conditions**

1. All Products are subject to and governed by the rates, conditions, standards, terms, guidelines and policies contained in this CNC Internet Insertion Order/Contract ("Contract") and the applicable Rate Card.

2. CNC and Advertiser will cooperatively develop the "Product" specified in this Contract. CNC will accept text, graphics or other information from Advertisers to create "Content" for use with the Product. No Content will be posted unless first approved by Advertiser.

3. CNC may provide Advertiser with a "Design Document." A Design Document approved by Advertiser will become a part of this Contract.

4. Advertiser will use the minimum time period or quantity agreed upon and, if such time period or quantity is not used as specified, Set Up Fee charges will be due and the cost of the Product shall revert to the non-discounted rate retroactive to the Start Date of this Contract. **This Contract in no way binds CNC to specific rates; rather, it applies discounts on the prevailing Rate Card rates. In the event of a rate revision, the Advertiser may, at its option, terminate this Agreement without penalty upon written notice to CNC prior to the effective date of the scheduled rate revision. Advertisers will receive thirty (30) days advance notice of any rate increases. Products canceled after ordering will be charged at the rate for the minimum time period available, or for a cancellation fee as noted on the Rate Card.** Invoices for Products are due and payable upon receipt, and will be considered overdue thirty (30) days from the date of billing. Advertiser, and any third party or agency used in the order of Products, shall be jointly and severally liable for such monies as are due and payable to CNC for Products ordered by such agency or third party. CNC reserves the right to suspend any Product if invoices remain overdue for more than thirty (30) days.

5. The Advertiser shall retain all proprietary rights and interests in any Content submitted for use in the Product. Advertiser hereby grants to CNC a non-exclusive, non-restricted, worldwide license to use, or create derivative works from, all Content it submits or develops for use in providing the Product.

6. All Content is accepted and posted entirely on the representation by Advertiser that it is authorized to publish the Content and subject matter thereof, that all Content submitted is in strict conformance with the Content Guidelines and that the Content is neither unlawful nor violates the rights of any person. In consideration for providing the Product, the Advertiser (and its agent) agrees to defend, indemnify and hold CNC, its affiliates and personnel, harmless from and against any loss or expense (including, without limitation, fees and expenses of counsel), arising out of any claim, actual or threatened, resulting from the posting of Content, including, without limitation, those resulting from claims or suits for defamation, violation of privacy, trade secrets or publicity rights, plagiarism, or copyright, patent or trademark infringement. Advertiser acknowledges that CNC is relying on such indemnity and would be unwilling to enter into this Contract in its absence. CNC reserves the right to suspend any Product for any reason, and may suspend a Product if CNC becomes aware of any potential violation of third party legal rights.

7. Neither CNC, its affiliates, nor any of their personnel, will be liable to the Advertiser for: any failure to include Content, or any delay in providing the Product; any typographical, linking, formatting or other error occurring in providing the Product; any claims or threatened claims relating to Content; the existence, non-existence, functioning or non-functioning of any hypertext links provided through the Product; any material available through any hypertext links requested by Advertiser; and any interruption or unavailability of the Product as a result of technical difficulties, Acts of God or otherwise. In the event of a continuous interruption or unavailablity of the Product in excess of twenty-four (24) hours, Advertiser must notify CNC. Advertiser will be entitled to an extension of the amount of time specified in this Contract for a period of time equivalent to the time from CNC' receipt of such notice until resumption of normal services. This shall be Advertiser's sole remedy in such cases. Advertiser acknowledges that CNC is relying on this limitation of liability and would be unwilling to enter into this Contract in the absence of such limitation.

8. Under no circumstances shall CNC, its affiliates or their personnel be liable to the Advertiser under any theory for any indirect, incidental, consequential, punitive, special or exemplary damages.

**Figure 10.9** Insertion order form from Townonline. *(continues)*

9. This Contract shall remain in effect for the time period specified herein (the "Term"). Either party may renew this Contract, at the then current Rate Card rates, by giving the other party notice thirty (30) days before the expiration of the then current Term.

10. It is expressly agreed that CNC and Advertiser are acting hereunder as independent contractors and neither shall be deemed to be the agent of the other. Under no circumstances shall any of the employees of one party be deemed to be the employees of the other for any purpose. Neither party has any right or authority to assume or create any obligations of any kind or to make any representation or warranty on behalf of the other party, whether express or implied, or to bind the other party in any respect whatsoever. Advertiser and its agency agree not to make promotional, merchandising or advertising references to CNC, its newspapers or Town Online without prior express, written approval.

11. All notices required or permitted under this Contract shall be deemed delivered when in writing and delivered by a reputable mail carrier to the persons on the face of this Contract at the billing address. This Contract represents the final and complete agreement of the parties. It shall be governed by Massachusetts law and shall not be assigned by Advertiser.

12. All advertising is accepted subject to the Advertiser's strict adherence to CNC's credit terms. Advertisers will be required to make application for credit and may be required to pay in advance until such time as credit has been established. CNC reserves the right to cancel advertising at any time without notice for non-compliance with the credit terms. A fifteen dollar ($15.00) charge will be applied for all returned checks.

### Content Guidelines

a. Town Online reserves the right to refuse to post, or to remove after posting, any Content which in its sole judgment is not in conformance with these Content Guidelines. However, Town Online has no duty to review the Content, and Advertiser remains solely responsible for all Content at all times.

b. No Content will be posted without the express permission of Advertiser. Any self-published Content will be presumed to have been reviewed and approved. All Content is subject to federal, state and local laws.

c. The Content may not include any material that: is grossly offensive, including bigotry, racism, discrimination, hatred or profanity; is pornographic or obscene; is defamatory or libelous; results in an invasion of privacy; violates another's rights of publicity; promotes or provides instructional information about illegal activities or physical harm or injury to any group, individual, institution or property; or infringes on a proprietary interest of another, including but not limited to, copyrights, trademarks, servicemarks or patents.

d. Advertiser may not use the Product for any purpose not expressly permitted in this Contract without first obtaining the express, written approval of Town Online.

**Figure 10.9** *(Continued)*

throughout the Web. .TMC (www.dottmc.com) has mostly travel clients. These specialized focuses help the firms tone their expertise in a specific area, benefiting the advertisers and publishers alike.

## *Pros and Cons*

There are both pros and cons to using a representation firm. The number one benefit is that a representation firm can serve as a site's sales force, eliminating the need to hire an internal sales force. Another benefit is for sites with cash flow issues, since payment is based on commission, requiring less cash outlay for staff. On the negative side, representation firms have an exclusivity requirement, such that no internal sales people or ad network can be used in conjunction with them. Also, representation firms only want to represent the top tier sites, making their services inaccessible to smaller sites with more limited budgets.

**Table 10.1** Representation Firms

| REPRESENTATIVE FIRM | CLIENT ROSTER |
| --- | --- |
| 2CAN Media (www.2canmedia.com) | 123 Greetings, 32bit.com, Accountingjobs.com, Accountingnet.com, AFI 100 Top Movies, America's Most Wanted Ameritrade, Arthur Frommer's Encyclopedia of Travel, Bed & Breakfast Online, Body and Mind, Business Financial Network, BusinessWire, Car Wizard, Christian Science e-Monitor, Cinescape Online, City Search, College Club USA, Cool Site of the Day Cyberswap, Developer Shed Discjockey.com, Entrepreneur Magazine Online, FinanceCenter, Frommer's, Fun School, Galaxy, GoRacing, Headbone.com, Historic Wings, IEE Network, Infohiway, Internet Travel Network, IPPA, Kiplinger Online, Lease Source, Live Online, Mamma.com, MCP, Metroville.com, Motor Trend Online, Mysterynet.com, National Enquirer Online, National Geographic Online Net London, NewsBlues, On Money, Oscar Knows, PCGame, Peoplelink, Petersen Events, Pure Baseball.com, Pure Sports games.com, Radcity.com, Realnames, Rick Dees, S&P Personal Wealth, School Sucks, Smart Money, Surflink, Teen Online, The Case.com, The Wedding Channel, TheCase.com/Kids, Total News, Truck Trends, UBL, Ultimate TV, Variety, WebFlyer |
| Cybereps (www.cybereps.com) | Andover Network, CAD InfoNet, Cambridge Information Network (CIN), ClickZ Network, Cool Tool, CYBER Reports, Free RealTime, Hit The Beach!, Inside Dynamic HTML, Nettaxi.com, Stewart Cheifet Productions, Teen.com, The Internet Movie Database, Weather24, Win95 Mag & Go Windows NT, YNot Creations |
| Ken Margolis Associates (www.kenmargolis.com) | Channel A, CLIQCOLLEGE, CLIQFINANCIAL, CLIQGOLF, CLIQHOME, CLIQKIDS, CLIQSPORTS, CLIQTECH, CLIQTRAVEL, CollegeNET, Concentric Network, CyberKids, CyberTeens, Digital Music Network, GamePen, Gavin, MysteryNet, Save The Earth Artrock Auction, Sweet!, Unified Gamers Online, Women's Forum, Yack! |
| Online Media Partners (www.onlinemp.com) | Adletts, Childbirth.org, ClickTV, Disney Nation, Learn2, MDG, New Media Communications, San Francisco Giants, WWWomen |
| .tmc (www.dottmc.com) | BizTravel.com, Consumers Digest Online, LeisurePlanet.com, NetStations, ShopNow.com, TheTrip.com, Travelbase, TravelNow, TravelWeb, |

**Table 10.1** *(Continued)*

| REPRESENTATIVE FIRM | CLIENT ROSTER |
|---|---|
| .tmc *(continued)* (www.dottmc.com) | WebOffers.com; Metropolitan-Networks: Hotelguide, EventGuide, DiningGuide, Retail-Guide, and NightGuide |
| Unique Media Services (www.uniquemedia.net) | Childbirth.org, ClickTV, Learn2, San Francisco Giants, WWWomen |
| WebMedia (www.webmedia-sales.com) | Acclaim.net, Country Music Association, Information Please, Marvel, PGA.com, TalkCity, Traveller |
| WinStar Interactive (www.winstar.com/ims/index.html) | 1travel.com, AllRecipes.com, Biztravel.com, Bloomberg Web Networks, Christmas98.com, Classical Insites, drkoop.com, Film Scouts, Gist TV Listing, HomeShark, Intellicast, Jazz Central Station, Moms Online, Music Boulevard, PGA-TOUR.com, Rocktropolis, SportsFan Online, Student.com, Sundance Channel, Yuckiest Site on the Internet |

# Ad Networks

The ad network universe just keeps growing, both in number of networks and size of networks (Table 10.2). Many of the larger networks' criteria for site selection is short and simple: at least 1 million page views per month, quality content, and a major brand name on the Web. We've touched on ad networks briefly in several other places throughout this book. To recap, an ad network brings together a group of sites with advertising inventory to sell in order to offer greater access and ease to publishers and advertisers. For publishers, this means access to more advertisers through the network's sales force;

**Table 10.2** Top Ad Networks

| | MEMBER SITES |
|---|---|
| LinkExchange (www.linkexchange.com) | 400,000 |
| ContentZone (www.contentzone.com) | 3000 |
| Flycast (www.flycast.com) | 700 |
| Real Media (www.realmedia.com) | 560 |
| DoubleClick (www.doubleclick.com) | 300 |
| 24/7 Media (www.247media.com) | 200 |
| CLIQNOW! (www.clicknow.com) | 85 |
| @dVenture Network (www.adventure.com) | 70 |
| ADSmart (www.adsmart.com) | 33 |

for the advertisers, this means that with one buy they can purchase impressions on a host of sites. As the cliché promises, there is power in numbers, and ad networks bring the power of a selling block to individual sites.

## Benefits of Ad Networks

As already described, participating in an ad network has benefits for the advertiser and publisher alike. Media buyers like working with ad networks for many reasons, which is certainly reason enough to place inventory on a network.

For a Web site publisher, using an ad network provides three primary benefits. First, an ad network can substitute or augment in-house sales departments with the network's dedicated, aggressive, and online ad management sales team. Second, having an ad network carry all of a site's ad inventory can eliminate the need for a site to invest in sophisticated and expensive ad management software. And finally, an ad network can move remnant inventory. To summarize:

**BENEFITS TO THE SITES**

- Substitute or augment in-house sales departments with the network's dedicated, aggressive, and online ad management savvy sales team
- Eliminate the need for a site to invest in sophisticated and expensive ad management software by running the ads off of the network
- Sell leftover or remnant inventory

**BENEFITS TO ADVERTISERS**

- Consistency in ad delivery reporting
- Can work with one sales rep for multiple site buys
- Competitive pricing because of the network's economy of scale
- Targeting options over a slate of sites, reducing the number of wasted impressions

### Simplifying the Buying Process

Media buyers need to purchase enough ads to reach the target audience enough times to get the desired response and be able to measure that response. The typical ad agency represents dozens of clients with dozens of products and dozens of target audiences. An ad network provides a means to buy in large enough volume while controlling the segmentation of the audience, and, in some cases, controlling the frequency and reach for maximum penetration. With an ad network, the media buyer can call in the morning and have an ad running on a slate of sites that same day. For the media buyer, networks help navigate through the high volume of sites offering advertising.

### Experienced Sales Force

Buying ads separately on the ever-growing number of sites can be a daunting task; you have to make your way through separate sales forces, individual rate sheets, and a myriad of audience demographics. When you work with a network, you are in contact with just one experienced sales force made up of people who know the online advertising business. And the ad space offered on the network usually represents prime online real estate. Ad networks function to simplify the ad buying experience for advertisers, who otherwise would face many daunting ad placement challenges on the Web such as overwhelming site choices, lack of legitimate, verifiable information, and inconsistent ad packages, rates, terms, and ad creative specifications. Ad networks streamline the entire process, benefiting the buyer and seller alike. This is not to say that ad networks are the only means through which ad agencies purchase online media. It is just often a part of their media mix.

The benefits to the publisher are equally as great. By participating in a reputable network, a site is in the hands of an experiences sales force. Thus, the publisher is free to devote time and resources to producing the best content possible. In response, some sites choose not to retain an in-house sales force in order to curb costs of hiring, training, and maintaining a sales team. Naturally, other costs are incurred, because networks command a hefty commission on all advertising space that they sell.

### Inventory

Instead of buying piecemeal, an advertiser or an agency can buy large quantities of ad space over several sites. Studies show that results are better for ad placement over a wide variety of sites, in contrast to placing advertising within many layers of the same site. Networks provide a convenient way to implement these far-reaching yet targeted buys. For the publisher, working with an ad network can help move remnant or leftover inventory. It can be a great way to augment the sale of inventory.

### Membership Criteria

What are networks looking for in choosing members sites? First, they want sites that service an identifiable audience, from financial to sports to parenting. Second, they seek sites with large monthly impressions levels. Most networks want a traffic level of a half million to a million-plus monthly impressions. This traffic volume signifies that the site has the draw and can deliver an audience. Third, networks want to know whether the site's audience will respond to ads. And finally, networks are looking for major online brands, because many advertisers want to place their ads on brand name sites.

Here are some issues for site publishers to address when considering working with a network. First, if your site is part of a network, you will have little control over the specific ads shown on the site. You can specify categories of ad types, but you will not receive each ad separately to review. Equally important, an ad network sales force focuses on the selling of categories of sites and not specific sites, so your site will not be receiving individual attention. And, if you are a small site, remember that the major networks are unavailable to sites with less than one million impressions per month.

## *Servicing Small to Medium-Sized Sites*

If your monthly audience is under 500,000 impressions, you can still join an ad network. There are networks where the criteria for inclusion are not based on audience size. These networks cater to the small and medium-sized sites and service hundreds of sites just like yours. For example, Burst Media (www.burstmedia.com) will represent sites that have as few as 1,000 requests per month.

### Targeting Buyers on a Budget

Networks that cater to the small site and the buyers on a budget make it possible to get a good buy whether your Web advertising budget is $25 or $1,000 per month. What, you might ask, can someone get with just $25? At LinkExchange, 2,000 impressions. According to Tony Hsieh, co-founder of LinkExchange, "If you compare that with a $5,000 buy on Yahoo!, the CPM is a better buy on us."

## *Barter Networks*

One of the most popular types of ad networks is one that offers a barter program. Under a barter program, sites exchange ad placements. The equation works as follows: when a site places a certain number of the network's impressions on its pages, the site receives a certain number of its ads on other network properties. One of the first barter networks, and the largest ad network in existence (over 400,000 member sites), is LinkExchange (www.linkexchange.com). Members of LinkExchange can either purchase ad space on the network or participate in the banner exchange program. Link-Exchange members receive an ad placement on the network for every two ads displayed on their site (making it a 2:1 ratio).

Barter networks differ from each other in many ways. Some networks are distinguished by their exchange ratio: 1:1 or 2:1 ratio. Others differ by the size of ads they place: buttons (120 × 90) or banners (486 × 60). Some banner exchanges revolve around a topic or theme, such as sports (Basketball Banner Exchange, www.verticaljump.com/banners/, and SoccerSwap, www.soccerswap.com), gender (The Women's Hyberbanner, women.hyperbanner.net), or age (Kids Hyberbanner, kids.hyperbanner.net). There are banner exchanges for minority-owned sites such as La Camara Hispana (http://camarahispana.com), and networks focusing on European countries like EuroBanner (www.eurobanner.com). Lists of banner exchange programs can be found on SearchZ (www.searchz.com) and Adbility (http://markwelch.com/bannerad/baf_exchange.htm).

# Differences Between Ad Networks and Representation Firms

An ad network and a representation firm both broker ad space, but differ in the focus of the sales process. Both serve as supplemental or replacement sales forces, but a rep firm represents the site itself. An ad network, on the other hand, is usually selling its network categories to an advertiser and presents all of its member sites as a group. In other words, the network may represent four sports-related sites, so they would sell advertisers space on the network's sports category sites, not on one individual site.

A network most often sells its inventory based on the strength of the consolidation of its member sites into categories, such as financial sites or sports sites. A repping firm, on the other hand, represents the individual sites themselves. It is the sales force for a selected group of Web sites. Whereas ad networks are looking for volume of sites, rep firms only represent a small list of sites because of the individual nature of the work. In addition, reps often request exclusive arrangements with sites whereby they are a site's only outside sales force. They do this to limit confusion caused when an advertiser is approached by a site's internal sales force, by an ad network, and by a rep firm—each with different rates and different inventory.

## Auctions

Another means to sell inventory is to auction impressions. In 1998 auctions came of age on the Internet. From consumer goods to impressions, the online community embraces the action, excitement, and potential savings involved in buying through an auction. The leader in the online auction space is Adauction.com (www.adauction.com).

Adauction.com only offers well-branded sites for auction. The auction process is very simple. Using an auction gives Web publishers an easy way to generate incremental revenue from their expiring ad inventory. Adauction.com provides exposure to the industry's top media buyers, who can use the service to save on quality Internet ad space. Adauction.com offers large quantities of banner ad impressions at prices significantly below rate card.

---

### Words of Wisdom on Selling Online Ads from an Internet Advertising Director

**Dave Coyne, Internet Advertising Director,
Community Newspaper Company**

- Motivating existing staff to sell is a slow process due to need for intensive training, extensive handholding and other competing priorities for their time.
- Customers *hate* multiple sales reps from the same company, which is why we continue to try to leverage our existing sales force.
- Unlike even one year ago, we rarely find ourselves beginning an Internet sales call by giving an Internet lesson. What's more, many customers seem to be aware that having a site isn't sufficient and that advertising it is the most important part.
- Customers hardly ever bother to log in to check their banner stats.
- We have seen no cannibalization of our newspapers. Customer who have no more budget for print routinely find more money somewhere to spend on the Internet with us! We've also developed significant new business for the company in terms of new advertising accounts with no history advertising in our papers.
- Compensation issues are a bear!
- We use our standard newspaper advertising agreement with slight modification when we bother to use one at all. Although it has not been a significant issue for us so far, we are moving to tighten up our use of contracts to ensure it never becomes an issue.

Adauction.com's Close-Out Auctions (which occur on the third Thursday of each month) offer single site buys or bundled content category packages, both of which run over a four-week flight period, starting the following month. To participate in an auction, you need to register as a bidder. Auctions are proving to be best way to unload remnant inventory.

# Sales Staff

Selling is an art form, and nothing can replace raw talent, but with proper training, a young sales force can be groomed to become a dynamic team. A key component of this training is learning the medium itself.

Gina Garrubbo, executive vice president of sales at Women.com, is known for saying that her sales force is the hardest working crew at Women.com. Most online ad sales directors would make the same claim about their staff and their company. Selling online ads is tough. Really tough. Not only do you need to know your property, how to sell, and what to sell, but you also need to know the technology.

## Sales Training

Whether you are looking for a job in online sales or hiring sales staff, whether you have experience in sales or are new to selling Web ads, learning the art and science of selling ads is an ongoing process. Online advertising and marketing is a new and burgeoning field, and business schools are only now adding it to the curriculum  A survey conducted by The Laredo Group found that 67 percent of sales reps have under two years of Internet experience, with 22 percent having less that two years of any sales experience at all. Clearly, training is key to ensuring you that your staff is schooled in the skills needed to sell ads efficiently and effectively. Most of the material available for training the sales staff of today and tomorrow exists either online, at conferences, or through publications.

### Distance Learning

Distance learning is a great training tool for busy staff in different locations. Through online courses, staff can take a class at their convenience, whether that is 10 A.M. or 10 P.M. Ziff Davis University (ZDU) offers a course on Internet Advertising as well as online business strategies and Web site promotion (www.zdu.com). These classes are extremely inexpensive: under $10 per month.

### Conferences

One of the best avenues for learning about online advertising is to attend one of the outstanding conferences and seminars held every year. These events are a mix of panel discussions, exhibit hall extravaganzas, and serious industry networking in the hall. Some of the key events can be found in Table 8.4. Another option is to attend the smaller and more focused advertising seminars. These events take more of a skills-building approach:

**"Advertising and Marketing on the Internet."** Inexpensive, one-day conferences held in cities across the country, providing a local and statewide perspective; produced by The Zeff Group (www.zeff.com).

**"How to Buy and Sell Web Ads."** A comprehensive training seminar on buying and selling Web ads for the novice and professional, taught by the online ad sales experts and produced by AdWeek (www.adweek.com) and the Laredo Group (www.laredogroup.com).

## Online Publications

As presented in Tables 8.1–8.3, the online advertising discussion lists and newsletters are where all the cutting edge information in the industry gets discussed on a daily basis. The first step in learning about the industry is to become a member of the online advertising community. And there is no better way to immerse yourself in the community than reading and participating in the industry's key publications.

# The Never-Ending Quest to Keep Good Sales Staff

There used to be an unwritten rule that longevity at a job was the norm. The Internet, with its own sense of time, has turned job security on its head; staff changes jobs at regular intervals. However, sales are built on relationships, and a high turnover rate hurts the bottom line. High turnover in sales positions is common right now. If you want to keep qualified salespeople, you should consider giving them a bigger piece of the equity pie; according to the Laredo Group 1998 survey, 95 percent of respondents said that more equity would decrease their chances of job hopping.

## Compensation Plans

There are a variety of options available for compensating sales staff: salary, base salary plus commission, or straight commission. The most common compensation package is salary plus commission. A survey conducted by the Laredo Group in 1998 found that 55 percent of sales staff are following this model. The study also found that 25 percent are on straight salary, 12 percent on straight commission, and 8 percent receive a salary plus a commission but with a maximum they can earn.

## Finding a Job in Online Ad Sales

Employment is a hot topic online, and no type of job is better marketed online than positions at online companies. You can pursue jobs by going through the front door, or find other means to open doors. The front door method is to post your resume through online resume banks and dutifully surf the online job boards such as Monsterboard.com (www.monsterboard.com), under the category "Advertising/Marketing Media and Media Sales," or CareerPath.com (www.careerpath.com), which not only lists the classified ads from the nation's leading newspapers, but also lists ads taken from the Web sites of leading employers. Online sales job are also listed in the print and online versions of Advertising Age (www.adage.com) and AdWeek (www.adweek.com). Another option is to visit the Web sites of companies you find of interest and check out their job listings. If that doesn't work, then network your way in through the side door. And don't underestimate the value of selling yourself to the company by sending an unsolicited e-mail.

A full list of online advertising periodicals is given in the Resource Directory of the companion Web site.

# Spread the Word about Your Advertising Opportunities

Just because you have ad space available, doesn't mean people will know to look at your site as a place to buy advertising. You need to do some advertising of your own. It is your responsibility to let media buyers know about your site. The following is a list of sites where you can post your rate cards.

You can list your site and rates the way you would in traditional media through SRDS. SRDS (www.srds.com) is the largest compiler of advertising placement information across all media, and has put together two extremely valuable resources for online advertising. The first is the SRDS Interactive Advertising Source, which is available in print and online (www.srds.com/cgi-bin/srds/iasonline/iasonline.cgi). Contact SRDS directly to be including in the source directory. They also have a free online database of 1,500 online media kits and Web sites for business publications and consumer magazines (www.srds.com/cgi-bin/srds/mediakitlink/mediakitlink.cgi).

You should also list your site with AdKnowledge (www.adknowledge.com), a database of Web sites that accept advertising, which is available to advertisers who pay AdKnowledge or use one of their services. And, finally, many online advertising resource sites—for example, SearchZ (www.searchz.com)—list media kits.

And, of course, don't overlook prominently promoting the advertising opportunities on your own site—on your home page and on every page. Make certain that a media buyer can easily find your rate card and contact information. If a prospective advertiser requests information, have a sales representative personally follow up with a phone call. (In spite of—or maybe because of—e-mail and voice mail, people appreciate when someone takes the time to establish personal contact; and it's especially valuable when you want to secure a sale.) In listing your advertising opportunities, itemize the creative opportunities you offer, from banners to full-section sponsorship; inform

---

## Getting Your Ad Opportunities Noticed

With thousands of sites offering advertising opportunities, if you want to get noticed, you need to take extra steps to put your advertising opportunities on someone's radar screen. You can do this by:

- Listing ad opportunities on your site and in appropriate rate card indexes
- Participating in ad networks
- Hiring a Web rep
- Putting together your own sales force

potential advertisers of all that your site can do for them. And, most importantly, make sure you follow up in a timely manner.

Any veteran salesperson will tell you that sales are all based on relationships. Since the Web is a relationship technology, use all the resources at your disposal—both technological and personal—to give your site that "extra something" that will set it apart from the pack. And that "extra something" might just be that your advertising space is listed everywhere making it easy for the media buyer to find the information he needs to purchase ad space quickly on your site.

If you are just starting your ad program, you might want to put up your own "house ads" (ads that you use to advertise your products, services, or information available in specific sections of your site) until your list of paid advertisers grows.

## One Last Word on Client Care and Feeding

With so much technology, how come it's still hard to connect with people? Selling online ads is like selling anything: the sale is in the relationship. The bottom line is take care of your clients. Provide multiple means of contact, not just an online form. Some advertisers still like to hear a human voice. Above all, answer e-mail requests promptly (see Figure 10.10).

This chapter presented the challenges of selling Web advertising in a way that we hope encourages responsible planning while clarifying the many opportunities available in this new medium. As we've pointed out, be flexible and ready to work with buyers; you could be—and should want to be—building the foundation for a profitable long-term advertising relationship.

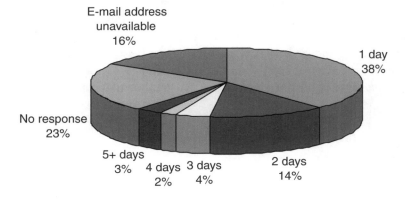

**Figure 10.10** Response time to e-mailed question.

## The Challenges and Future of Selling Internet Ads

Leslie Laredo, President (llaredo@laredogroup.com)

Laredo Group (www.laredogroup.com)

Internet Ad sales is one of the hardest media selling jobs. Sites and advertisers expect reps to know and understand not only their online property and media principles, but they must also be well versed in:

**Technology:** How Internet technology impacts their ability to create, target, and deliver advertising campaigns.

**Media Measurement:** Media measurement and research methodologies and why the numbers are often very different across the services and how caching and proxy servers impact the numbers.

**Ad Delivery:** The necessity and impact of ad operations and ad delivery options, including third-party ad serving by ad agencies and rich media technology enablers.

**Business and Pricing Models:** Various business models from CPM to performance-based pricing, plus hybrid options, and how to measure ROI with each.

**Relationship Marketing:** How to utilize advanced relationship marketing techniques within media campaigns as advertisers look to expand their online presence, improve customer relationships, increase customer involvement over a product life cycle, and increase up-sell opportunities for their brands.

**Database Marketing:** Selling the advantages and availability of database-derived targeting and ad delivery.

**Targeting Technologies:** The emerging ad targeting technologies and their impact on pricing and ROI.

**Creative Technologies:** Utilizing creative and rich media options for banners and evaluating the impact they have on ad effectiveness.

**Ad Production:** The production process for creating new ad units, micro-sites, and integrated ad programs. In traditional media selling, this would be equivalent to understanding the technologies of four-color separation, the economics of print production, the intricacies of broadcast transmission, and more. In addition it means expecting reps to be experts in all media (broadcast, print, direct marketing) and to play high level marketing consultant and technology experts.

Reps are also faced with a fast moving landscape that often means a rate card "du jour." Web sites add and change content and design frequently, and they employ new technologies. Reps must keep up with these changes and relearn the benefits of their media property.

Reps are also faced with a wide ranging and not well defined competitive environment. They are competing with like sites in their category as well as search engines, ad networks, rep firms, and traditional media.

The current shortage of seasoned Internet sales reps will continue and grow over the next five years. Most companies will not be able to hire an entire staff of seasoned Internet sales professionals so they must hire and train sales reps from other sales and media fields.

Many large, traditional media companies are watching their advertising base become more interested in their Internet properties. Advertisers are demanding integrated media proposals. Both the traditional and Internet sales organizations will have to work together and sell integrated programs. Such programs have to reach vertically across media brands (for example, a program that includes multiple Conde Nast and CondeNet properties) and horizontally to reach print and Internet audiences across one brand (for example, an integrated program that reaches Fortune magazine readers and visitors to Fortune.com).

The future of Internet selling means that traditional reps need to be conversant about their Internet properties. Internet reps need to work with their counterparts to jointly meet the needs of their common advertisers. Those companies with separate sales forces must combine their talents, experience, and sales goals—not a small feat.

From the Laredo Group's work (training the sales organizations of both Internet-only publishers and large media firms), we see a growing need to make traditional sales reps Internet literate. We also see the development of a "hybrid" or team selling approach. We believe the future success of large media companies requires training all sales organizations to sell the Internet to meet the needs of their advertisers and promote integrated media selling.

# CHAPTER 11

# Going Local

One of the basic rules of thumb in retail is that people spend 80 percent of their salary within 20 miles of their home. It is not surprising that local online advertising makes up a significant portion of the advertising revenue pie. Of the total 1998 U.S. advertising revenue for traditional media ($187 billion), $73 billion was spent on local and $114 billion on national advertising (see Table 11.1 for a breakdown per medium).

Up until 1998, the Internet offered few options for advertisers to reach a local audience. The ability to locally target Internet advertising has improved significantly. Why? For one thing, there are many more people online covering most cities, states, and towns in the United States. The recent growth of the local content user is fueling this surge in local online ad spending (see Figure 11.1). In fact, an entire genre of locally focused content sites has emerged. Moreover, advances in targeting technology make geographic targeting more accurate, efficient, and cost effective.

Local advertising is predicted to play an even larger role online than in traditional media. Jupiter Communications predicts that by 2002, local online advertising revenue

**Table 11.1**   Local Advertising Revenues in Traditional Media

| MEDIA | PERCENTAGE OF TOTAL U.S. ADVERTISING SPENDING | TOTAL REVENUE |
|---|---|---|
| Television | 20% | $9 billion |
| Yellow Pages | 85% | $10 billion |
| Newspaper | 80% | $35 billion |
| Cable | 85% | $7 billion |
| Radio | 85% | $12 billion |

Source: 1998 Robert J. Coen: McCann Erikson Report; The Kelsey Group

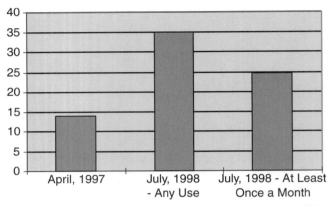

**Figure 11.1**   Recent growth in use of local content (millions of U.S. online adults).
Source: Cyber Dialogue.

will surpass national numbers (see Figure 11.2). In this chapter we'll examine the primary methods for taking your ad campaign to a geographically focused audience.

# Profile of a Local Information User

The local online user is someone who goes online to find geographically determined information such as the local weather or movie theater schedules. As local usage

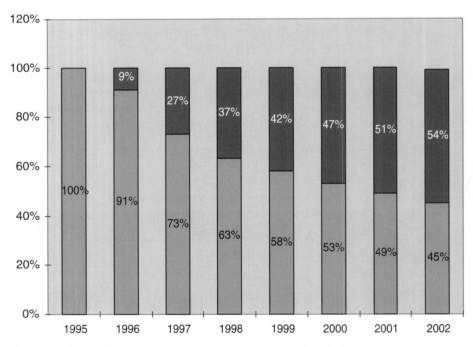

**Figure 11.2**   Online advertising revenues: local vs. national, 1995–2002.

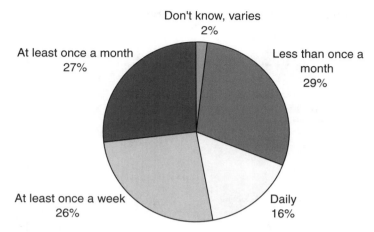

**Figure 11.3** Frequency of local information retrieval.
Source: Cyber Dialogue.

grows, we are better able to understand the actions, tastes, and wants of the local online user. According to Cyber Dialogue (www.cyberdialogue.com), nearly 35 million U.S. adults use local content online, with 71 percent using local content at least once per month (see Figures 11.3 and 11.4). Local content users report weather forecasts and local news as the most useful local content (see Figure 11.5). Local users also retrieve

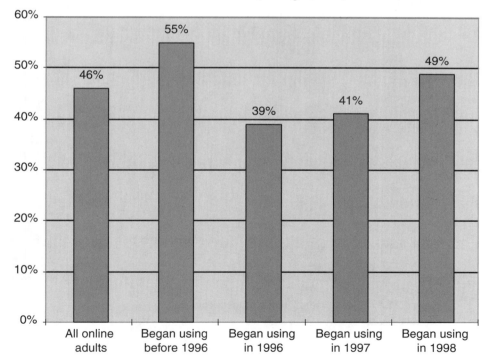

**Figure 11.4** Monthly use of local information by online experience.
Source: Cyber Dialogue.

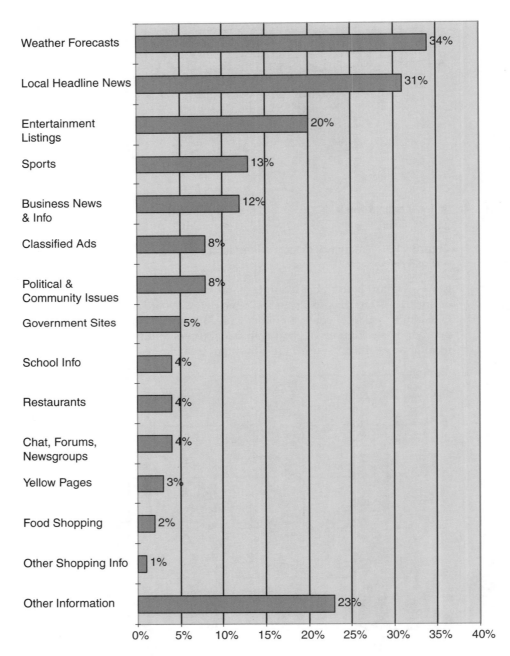

**Figure 11.5** "Most useful" types of local content.

Source: Cyber Dialogue.

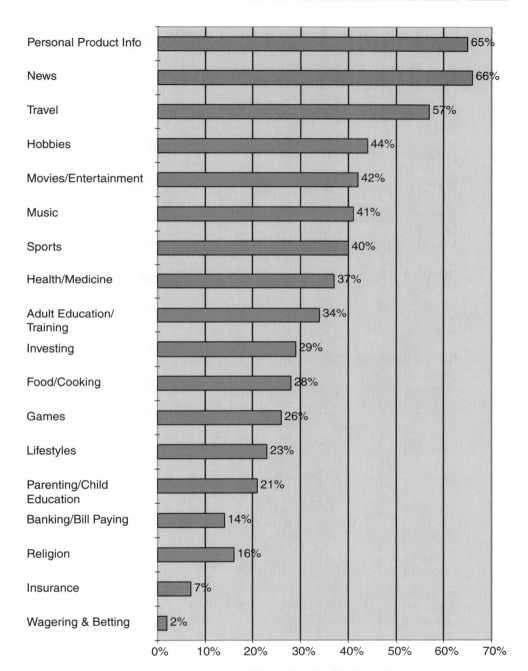

**Figure 11.6**   Personal content areas used by online local information users.

Source: Cyber Dialogue.

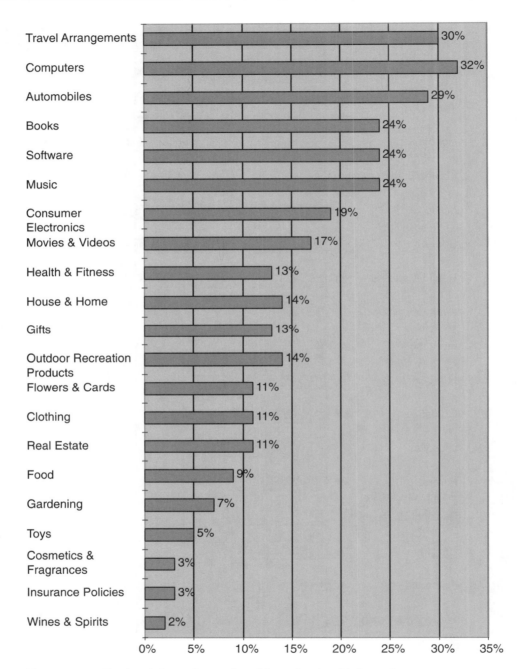

**Figure 11.7** Product information retrieved by online local information users.

Source: Cyber Dialogue.

product information, with travel arrangements, computers, automobiles, and books topping the lists (see Figure 11.6). Cyber Dialogue profiles the adult using local information as follows:

**Gender.**   54 percent men and 46 percent women.

**Age.**   Local information users are slightly younger than average Internet users. Cyber Dialogue places the average age of online users at 38, with users who regularly use local content at 37.

**Hours per week.**   Local information users average nearly 10 hours per week.

**Purchasing activity.**   Over one third of local information users purchase personal products online. Travel arrangements, computers, automobiles, books, software, and music top the list of product information retrieved (see Figure 11.7).

# Targeting by Content

Most local targeting in traditional advertising is done by buying ads in local media. This means the local paper, the local radio, or the local magazine. This same strategy of targeting a local audience by placing your advertisement within a local context works online as well. There are many sites that focus on a geographically determined audience.

## Online Versions of Local Media

Clearly, placing advertising on regionally specific Web sites is the easiest way to successfully target ads locally. Local media are jumping online, from local newspapers to local television to local cable channels to local radio stations even to local disk jockey personalities. These Web sites are great venues to reach a local audience.

### Online Newspapers

One of the first places to look is your regional newspaper. If you are trying to reach the Philadelphia market, placing an ad on the online version of the *Philadelphia Inquirer* newspaper, phillynews.com, is a good first stop (see Figure 11.8). To find the online version of a newspaper, you can contact the paper directly or use online resources. The Newspaper Association of America (www.naa.org) hosts two sites to facilitate locating the online versions of newspapers. NewspaperLinks.com (Figure 11.9) connects you to the online versions of newspapers in all 50 states. If you want to search by topic or geographic area, then the NAA Directory (http://naa.intype.com) provides that service (see Figure 11.10). If you're already advertising in the print edition of the newspaper, you may be able to get your sales rep to throw in an advertisement on the newspaper's Web site as added value.

**Figure 11.8**   Philadelphia Online, the online publication of the *Philadelphia Inquirer*.

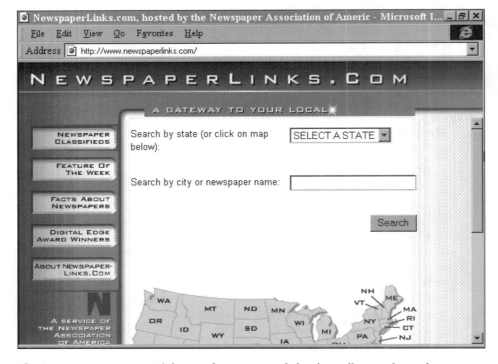

**Figure 11.9**   NewspaperLinks.com lets you search for the online versions of newspapers by city and state.

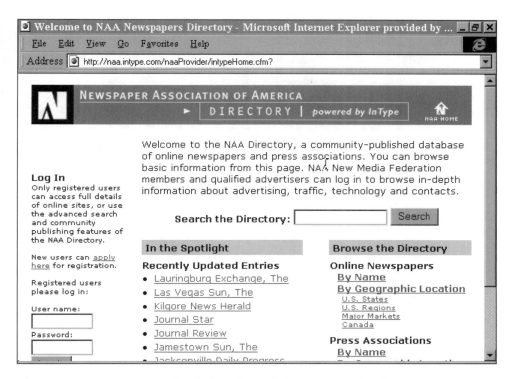

**Figure 11.10** Newspaper Association of America's Directory of online newspapers.

## Online Radio and Television

Local radio and television stations are now hosting their own sites to distribute content, build community, and inform their audiences of upcoming events. The audience for these sites is local by nature.

## City Guides

City guides or local portals offer additional opportunities. From AOL's Digital City sites (www.digitalcity.com Figure 11.11) to Microsoft's Sidewalk (www.sidewalk.com, Figure 11.12) to CitySearch (www.citysearch.com, Figure 11.13), every city has a presence on the Net to help people find local restaurants and events and to connect with the local online community. These are premiere sites for local advertising because they reach the local audience, whether site visitors are just passing through or are permanent residents.

Many of the search engines offer local targeting. For example, you can advertise on a number of local Yahoo! guides. Figure 11.14 shows the Yahoo! Metro sites. As when you advertise in other local guides, you can assume that your advertising will reach consumers living in that area, thinking about moving to that area, or visiting that area. Moreover, you can purchase geographic keywords on search engines such as names of cities or towns.

**Figure 11.11** AOL's Digital City sites service local markets in town around the country such as this hub for Digital City Philadelphia.

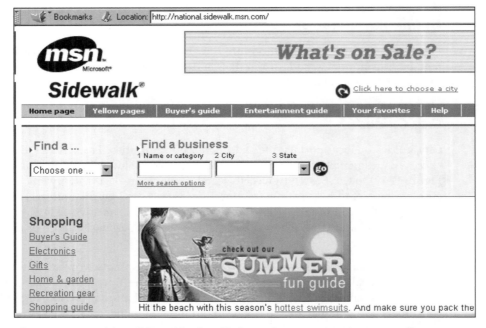

**Figure 11.12** Sidewalk provides local information on entertainment and events.

**Figure 11.13**    CitySearch has local sites in cities. throughout the U.S.

**Figure 11.14**    Yahoo! has Metro Sites in key cities.

Another option is the personalized home page offered by portal sites (for statistics, see Figure 11.15). From Yahoo! to Excite, users can personalize the start-up page so that it is customized to a their own interests and geographic location (see Figure 11.16).

And, of course, every region has local portal sites, which are sparked by local magazines, weeklies, or even local ISPs. For example, in Philadelphia the nonprofit ISP LibertyNet (www.libertynet.org, Figure 11.17) functions as a local portal for reaching the local audience of consumers, businesses, and nonprofit organizations.

## Classifieds

The majority of local advertising revenue in print media comes from classified and directory listings. Classified advertising, which is the bedrock of newspaper advertising and a $5 billion market, has been embraced online. Today, online classifieds (see

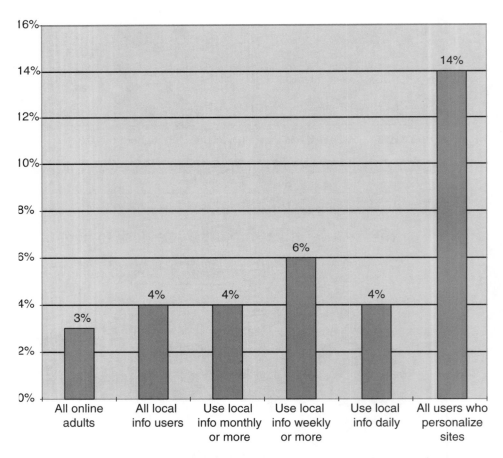

**Figure 11.15** Percentage of users who personalize sites with local news and information.
Source: Cyber Dialogue.

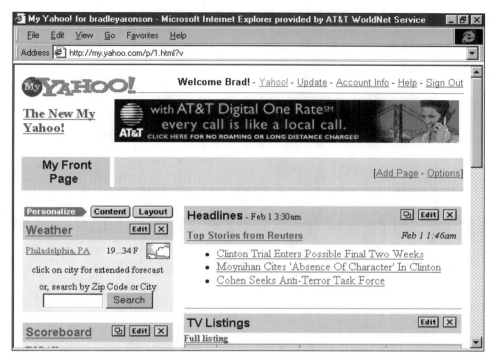

**Figure 11.16**   A personalized Yahoo! home page incorporates local information, such as this personalized page for Philadelphia.

Figure 11.18) are commonplace and a great way to reach a local audience, who may be searching such categories as real estate, automobiles, and employment.

### Yellow Pages and Directories

Online yellow pages are another great means to reach a local audience. In fact, many search engines have bought the classifieds and directory sites and merged them into their own. In the Excite Yellow Pages (see Figure 11.19), an advertiser can target consumers searching for business listings in a specific geographic region. There is no question that online directory advertising is hot. In fact, Jupiter Communication predicts that directory revenues will reach $671 million by 2002 (see Figure 11.20).

## Informational Sites with Regional Focuses

There are a host of informational sites available for local targeting. These sites service the entire U.S. market, broken down on a regional, state, city, or even street level.

**Figure 11.17** LibertyNet is a nonprofit ISP which services the greater Philadelphia area and acts as a local portal site.

**Travel and mapping.** Travel and mapping sites are extremely popular for finding locations and getting driving directions. Local advertising on MapQuest (www.mapquest.com) will reach users requesting travel directions in a specific region (see Figure 11.21).

**Weather sites.** Getting the local weather is one of the top uses of local content sites (see Figure 11.5). Specifically, the Weather Channel, www.weather.com, offers the ability to target on weather results for specific areas. If you advertise on local weather sites, you can assume you're reaching people who live in or are traveling to the geographic areas. For example, Green Mountain Energy is advertising its services to the Pennsylvania region and places banner ads on the Weather Channel targeting Pennsylvania weather (see Figure 11.22).

**Address locators.** Finding addresses and phone numbers of friends and colleagues is a common online action. On Switchboard (www.switchboard.com), when you search for a person, you get ads for local businesses.

## Ad Networks Go Local

There are now ad network options for targeting a specific geographic region (see Table 10.2 for a list of ad networks). Real Media (www.realmedia.com) sells advertising on over 100 online regional newspapers (see Figure 11.23 for a partial list of Real Media

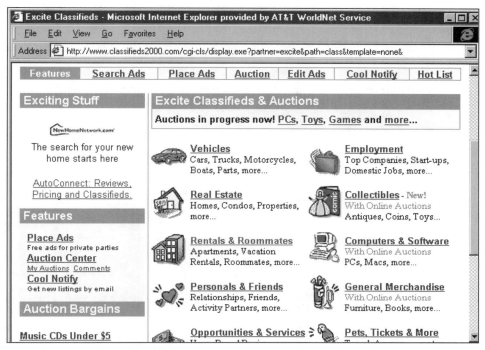

**Figure 11.18** Excite's classified ad section.

**Figure 11.19** Excite Yellow Pages.

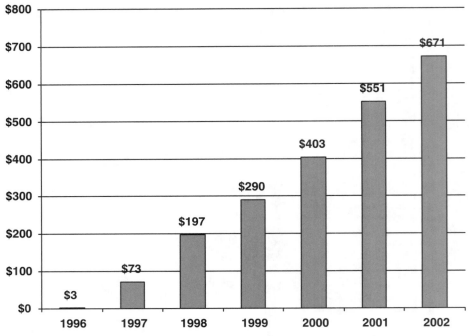

**Figure 11.20** Online directory advertising revenues, 1996–2002 (in millions).

Source: Jupiter Communication.

**Figure 11.21** Local advertising on MapQuest.

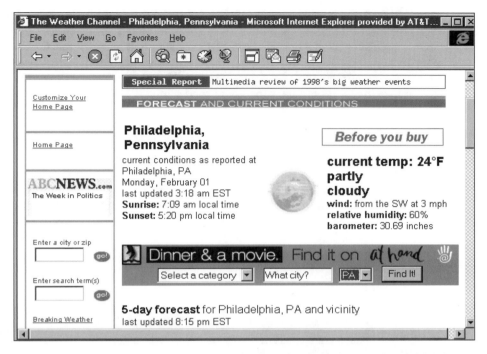

**Figure 11.22** Local advertising on The Weather Channel targeting the Phildelphia area.

| Site name/title | URL | CPM | Page views |
|---|---|---|---|
| **New York, NY** | | | |
| New Jersey Online | www.nj.com | $35 | 6,000,000 |
| *The Star-Ledger* | | | |
| Newsday.com | www.newsday.com | $35 | 5,000,000 |
| *Long Island Newsday* | | | |
| Village Voice | www.villagevoice.com | $30 | 2,000,000 |
| *Village Voice Worldwide* | | | |
| **Los Angeles** | | | |
| Los Angeles Times | www.latimes.com | $35 | 11,000,000 |
| *Los Angeles Times* | | | |
| OC Register | www.ocregister.com | $35 | 1,500,000 |
| *Orange County Register* | | | |
| LA Weekly | www.laweekly.com | $30 | 350,000 |
| *Los Angeles Weekly* | | | |
| **Chicago** | | | |
| Chicago Sun-Times | www.suntimes.com | $35 | 8,000,000 |

**Figure 11.23** Real Media regional newspaper network sites.

network sites). DoubleClick has DoubleClick Local (www.doubleclick.net/advertisers/local) for local targeting capabilities on major brand sites. "You can leverage national brand name sites like Dilbert and AltaVista while only paying for reaching users from your local market," says Brian Hunt, marketing manager, DoubleClick Local. "We've helped everyone from movie theaters to banks reach their market online." DoubleClick determines the locality of the consumer based on the IP address.

## Local Organizations

In each city, there are local organizations that use the digital medium very effectively. Many have Web sites and e-mail discussion lists or newsletters, which can be tapped to reach a local niche audience. For example, if you were trying to target the local Internet community in Philadelphia, you would want to participate in the Internet Business Alliance (www.iba.org) or the Eastern Technology Council (www.techcouncil.org, see Figure 11.24), both of which accept sponsorships for programs and events and send e-mail to their members.

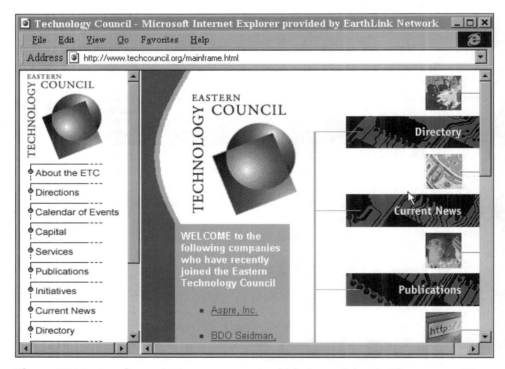

**Figure 11.24** Local organizations are a great vehicle to reach local niche communities. The Eastern Technology Council services Internet business professionals in the greater Philadelphia region.

## Ranking Local Sites

Media Metrix (www.mediametrix.com) has a local market report that tracks national and local market reach. The report demonstrates how national and local Web sites perform within each of 14 top local markets: Atlanta, Boston, Chicago, Cleveland, Dallas–Fort Worth, Detroit, Los Angeles, New York, Philadelphia, Phoenix, San Francisco–Oakland–San Jose, Seattle–Tacoma, Tampa–St. Petersburg–Sarasota, and Washington, D.C.

# Targeting Through Registration Data

Another method of targeting geographically is through sites that collect data from their users. Some sites ask or force consumers to register, and that registration process often asks users for their zip code or address. In these cases the site has a few methods for tracking these users.

The site can force the users to enter their user names every time they return to the site. Then the site will be able to recognize the registrants and deliver them ads based on geographic data entered when they registered.

After a person registers, the site can place a cookie on his or her computer. (For more information on cookies, see Chapter 4 on Web measurement.) That cookie will contain a text string that identifies the user. When the user returns to the site, the site can look at the cookie and correlate the text string to data entered when the user registered—including geographic data.

Services that offer free e-mail or free Internet access will also ask users to provide their zip code. Of course, this also allows for geographic targeting—assuming folks are telling the truth. Figure 11.25 is an example of the New York Times registration page, and Figure 11.26 shows the registration page for the free e-mail service Hotmail.

# IP Targeting

Regional targeting through IP addresses can be effective—when done properly. Every computer connected to the Internet has an identifying IP address, which is a string containing numbers and periods, such as 12.323.3213. If you have a direct connection to the Internet, you probably have an IP address for your computer, or your company's server assigns you an IP address when you access the Internet through your company's network. If you connect to the Internet through an ISP, your ISP will dynamically assign you an IP address when you dial in through their service.

When a person visits a Web site certain information is shared between the visitor's browser and the Web site's server (see Chapter 4 on Web measurement for more details). One of those pieces of shared information is the IP address. As explained in

**Figure 11.25** New York Times uses registration data to target locally.

Chapter 4, every IP address represents a domain name. For example, let's say 12.323.3213 is an i-frontier IP address. The Web site's ad serving software can perform a "lookup," which determines the domain of the IP address. After determining that the IP address is i-frontier, the ad server can perform a "lookup" to determine the geographic location. Here's how that works, and how mistakes are made.

When a domain is registered, it is done through Internic (www.internic.net). In the registration process, the registrant indicates what IP addresses will be associated with its domain names. For example, IBM may list a number of IP numbers that are associated with ibm.com. During that registration process, IBM has the option of associating a geographic region with each IP, but that is optional. So, a site can target using IP addresses, but the site will have to match the IP addresses to geographic information provided to Internic.

When geographic information is not provided to Internic, IP targeting can get pretty inaccurate; there's no way to really know the geographic area of the IP number. If there are a number of IP addresses associated with a company, and the company did not provide regional information for those IP numbers, a publisher can still decide to provide geographic ad targeting based on the company address (given to Internic for contact info). In that case, all users accessing the Internet from a company, regardless of their different geographic locations, are determined to be coming from the geographic location listed for the company address. In most cases this will cause errors. (This is also a

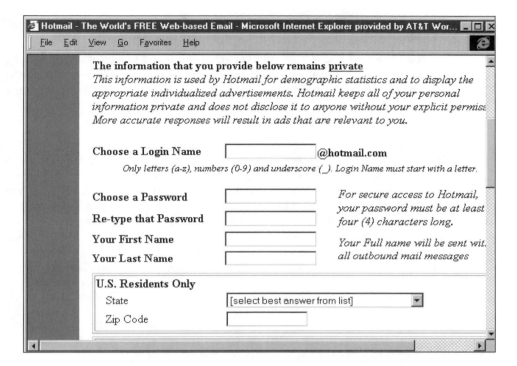

**Figure 11.26**    Hotmail registration page gathers geographic targeting information.

problem with large ISPs that service multiple geographic areas and don't specify the geographic location of their IPs.)

For example, Coca-Cola's main address is in Atlanta. However, Coke may have registered IP addresses for its offices across the United States. If Coke doesn't provide the regional information, and a publisher targets the ads by the company location (when no regional information is provided), all Coke employees will look like they're coming from Atlanta. Needless to say, the folks who are targeting accurately will have to be very careful in how they deal with companies with offices in different geographic locations. Publishers providing accurate targeting usually throw those IPs out of the targeting pool.

As we've mentioned, it is difficult to geographically target customers of large national ISPs. For starters, a large ISP like AOL has an incentive not to provide regional information regarding its IP numbers. AOL sells advertising, and, of course, they want the advertising they sell to be more valuable than that of their competitors. If AOL provided information that allowed their IP numbers to be identified as specific local areas, AOL's competitors would be able to sell high-priced, geographically targeted ads when AOL visitors came to *their* sites. If no one but AOL has the geographic IP information, then advertisers have to buy with AOL to target their 15 million–plus members by geographic area. AOL might sell a publisher a list of their IP numbers broken down by geographic location, allowing the buyer to geographically target AOL users, but they would never provide that information for free.

To accurately target locally, IP numbers from AOL and other national ISPs who don't provide regional information must be disregarded, or the publisher must research and work with these companies to link their IP numbers to specific locations. Otherwise, everyone coming from AOL would be considered to be based in Virginia, which is where AOL is headquartered.

Geographic targeting is great when it works, but can be embarrassing at best when it doesn't. Tom Kuegler, director of operations at Skyline Network Technologies Inc. (www.skyline.com), tells how a friend of his was visiting a major portal/search engine when he saw an ad for a movie theater. The viewer, who lived in Maryland, had never heard of the movie theater. He clicked on the ad, which took him to the theater's site. To his surprise, the theater was located in Los Angeles. It turns out that the ad was being targeted to users in Southern California. The viewer was working in a field office in Maryland for a company headquartered in Los Angeles. Every employee of that company is served by one proxy machine located in LA, so all users appear as if they're originating from an IP in Los Angeles, and the thousands of employees at that company are geographically targeted incorrectly.

## What's It Gonna Take?

**Melinda Gipson, Director of New Media Business Development (gipsm@naa.org)**
**Newspaper Association of America (www.naa.org)**

**According to a Deloitte & Touche survey conducted with the National Retail Federation of the 50 top retailers, 26 percent now have Web sites. While a number of top retailers advertise on the Web without having their own bona fide site, that still indicates that 74 percent of major retailers—and millions upon millions of Main Street merchants—aren't yet taking advantage of the promotional power of the Internet.**

**What's it going to take?**

**How about envy? Added to the list in the 1998 holiday season and just following: Macy's, Nordstrom's, Victoria's Secret, Toys "R" Us. They joined the likes of Wal-Mart, Kmart, Lands' End, Barnes & Noble, and a host of other catalogers and retailers looking to counter their Web-grown competition—folks with names like Amazon.com, eBay, and Bluefly.**

**Greed? Certainly, all these companies were looking to cash in on the attention of the 8.7 million U.S. households that Forrester Research says shopped online for travel and retail goods (other than autos) by the end of 1998. Please note: that's households. Some 16 million people bought books online, just to pick one category. Shop.org, a new association of online merchants, estimates that 1998 online**

sales should top $13 billion. Zona Research Inc. interviewed more than 1,000 Internet users, and reports that their spending online dramatically increased over last year. Whereas last year the survey group's average Net tab was $216, this year it hit $629! Spending by users in the over-50 age group grew at the fastest rate, up 545 percent over last year. E-shopping still represents a low single-digit total of the total retail pie. But many more folks browsed than bought, meaning that the Web contributes to a sizeable portion of sales offline, and is a lynchpin in the buying process of the value-conscious consumer.

As they say, "it's all good." But I'd argue that the real reason your business will want to advertise on the Net this year is growth. That Zona bunch—at least 61 percent of them—says they plan to spend even more in the coming year. They're well-off, well educated, and very, very busy. Some too busy to shop in brick-and-mortar stores, meaning this is a customer with whom you can have a relationship that you didn't before.

And since we're discussing marketing, here's my pitch for my niche. Online newspaper readers are not only better educated with more disposable income than the average Web user; in an age where there's an explosion of new media outlets competing for their attention, 45 percent of online newspaper readers come to their preferred site once a day. One in five visit more than once a day. (These figures come from a fall study by The Laredo Group for RealMedia.) INTECO Research found that online newspaper users book travel online three times as much as the average Web user, and make purchases online more than two and a half times more often. They are more likely to contact an advertiser in an online newspaper classified than one in even a big-name Internet brand. And they're people who can associate your brand—online and in print—with one they trust to run their lives. . . . I'd just like you to think of it this way: You want to be on the Net because your customers are—both the ones you could lose and the ones you haven't met yet. In the case of the former, remind them you exist. In the case of the latter, let a trusted source introduce you.

# CHAPTER 12

# International Online Advertising

If you look at a traffic report from any major U.S.-based branded Web site, 20 to 60 percent of users will be from outside of the home market. Users are coming from the four corners of the globe, and the savvy business is trying to figure out how to fit into the global marketing capabilities of the Internet.

Most of the online advertising dollars spent in 1998 focused on the United States. In 1998, North America accounted for 87 percent of online advertising. Forrester Research predicts that the Internet advertising gap between the U.S. market and the rest of the world will start to shrink and that by 2003, North America will only account for 70 percent, with Europe representing 18 percent, Asia 8 percent, and Latin America 4 percent. The Internet is finally becoming the global market everyone envisioned (see Figure 12.1).

This chapter will look at tips, tools, and concerns involved in advertising online to an international audience.

## Why Go Global?

Just because Internet access can technically take place anywhere on the globe, it doesn't mean that your Web site will reach all potential international customers. Each country, just like any market or community, needs to be targeted strategically. To go global really means going local in each geographic area. People respond to marketing messages through their own cultural glasses. You need to present a message they can understand, relate to, and trust. This is true if you're trying to market to Paris, Texas, or Paris, France.

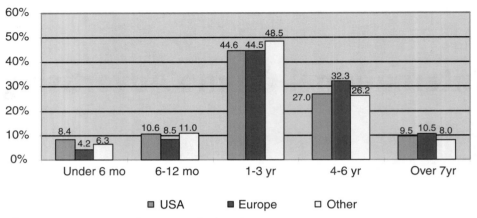

**Figure 12.1** Years on the Internet by location.

Why go global? Just because you can is not a sound business reason. Advertising outside of your home market makes sense on two fronts. First, if you are looking to increase traffic to your site, there are many eyeballs to be had in the global online arena. On the Internet, the English-speaking world represents the majority of users. Computer Industry Almanac (www.c-i-a.com) projects that by the year 2000 this majority will begin to decline and there will be as many Internet users from non-English-speaking countries as from English-speaking countries (see Table 12.1). The primarily English-speaking world (Australia, Canada, Ireland, New Zealand, South Africa, United Kingdom, and United States) represents only 8 percent of the world's population and 30 percent of the world economy, so the movement of the rest of the world to get online is only going to grow the global e-commerce pie.

Second, if you are trying to expand your market in terms of sales, it might make sense to go global. However, although you can reach the online audience in France, Japan, or China, be cognizant of the fact that doing business in other countries brings up all sorts of issues, from units of currency, to shipping charges and country tariffs, to customer service and product support. Is your product really applicable in a specific country? Do you have the resources to distribute goods and services to an international audience? How about the resources to support those clients' customer service needs? If you do want to market and sell products in other countries, do your homework first. The classic story of an international Internet purchasing nightmare is about a product that is purchased online from a business in the United States by someone in Japan. When the product arrives in Japan, the purchaser is charged not only the amount of the product, but also the shipping and country tariff, making the $500 purchase turn into a $2,000 nightmare. Mistakes like this can be avoided by doing your homework first—in this example, researching shipping and tariff fees before deciding to ship to a particular country.

To get users, whether in Moscow or Milwaukee, to buy your product, to use your merchandise, or to contract you for services, means doing so has to be faster, simpler, and more convenient that using traditional channels such as local businesses. "Faster, simpler, and more convenient" means different things in different countries and cultures.

According to the Computer Industry Almanac (www.c-i-a.com), there will be over 579 million computers-in-use by year-end 2000—up from 360 million computers-in-use at year-end 1997. The United States is projected to have over 164 million computers-in-use or 28.3 percent of the total in year 2000. The top 16 countries shown in Table 12.1 account for over 70 percent of the worldwide computers-in-use in year 2000.

**Table 12.1** Top 16 Countries in Computers-in-Use in Year 2000 (projected in November 1998)

| 2000 RANK | COUNTRY | COMPUTERS-IN-USE IN MILLIONS | % SHARE OF TOTAL |
|---|---|---|---|
| 1. | United States | 164.1 | 28.32 |
| 2. | Japan | 49.9 | 8.62 |
| 3. | Germany | 30.6 | 5.28 |
| 4. | United Kingdom | 26.0 | 4.49 |
| 5. | France | 21.8 | 3.77 |
| 6. | Italy | 17.5 | 3.02 |
| 7. | Canada | 16.0 | 2.76 |
| 8. | China | 15.9 | 2.75 |
| 9. | Australia | 10.6 | 1.82 |
| 10. | South Korea | 10.6 | 1.82 |
| 11. | Russia | 9.2 | 1.59 |
| 12. | Brazil | 8.5 | 1.47 |
| 13. | Spain | 8.1 | 1.39 |
| 14. | Netherlands | 7.2 | 1.25 |
| 15. | India | 6.3 | 1.08 |
| 16. | Mexico | 6.3 | 1.08 |
| | Total Top 16 Countries | 408.6 | 70.52 |
| | Europe Total | 154.9 | 26.73 |
| | Worldwide Total | 579 | 100 |

Source: Internet Industry Almanac (www.c-i-a.com/19981103.htm)

Note: These numbers include all computers, from PCs to supercomputers, used in business, educational institutions, and homes.

# Are You a Candidate for Going Global?

Should you go global? You probably already are. On close inspection of your site traffic report, you will undoubtedly find that a percentage of your visitors are originating from outside your home country. Whether you want to do business abroad or just increase your traffic, the first step is determining the makeup of your audience.

**Reviewing your traffic.** One way to determine if you have an international audience is to look at your traffic reports (see Chapter 4 for more information on generating and using traffic reports). If you are receiving a healthy stream of visitors from a specific country, then it makes sense to start customizing your site to visitors of that country and perhaps even to start advertising to Internet users from that country. A list of the domains for each country is available on the companion Web site for this book (www.wiley.com/compbooks/zeff).

**Reviewing your sales.** Another key determining factor is sales. Are the visitors from outside your home market buying your products or services? If so, then it is time to look at servicing these customers in their own language and investigating the logistics of distribution in their country.

# Obstacles to Adoption

The Internet may be global in nature, but in each country there are domestic, economic, and social issues that limit Internet access.

## Connection

Outside the United States and most of Canada, Internet usage is often on a pay-per-minute basis. This may not affect some business users, but it is a great deterrent against random surfing for consumers and many businesses. "In Japan, with no unlimited local call service provided by NTT, everyone has to pay ¥ 10 for every three minutes online. Couple this with ISP fees and it becomes very prohibitive to the casual user," points out Richard Lemmer, an American teacher living in Japan. The situation is even more extreme in China. "The price for one hour on the Internet equals my one day's wages," points out Li Yue of China. "I [would] rather spend half of [the] day to go shopping on [the] street than go '[shopping] on the Internet.'" In this situation, the common usage pattern is to go online to search for information. Once that information is found, it is printed and then read offline.

Moreover, there are still many countries with limited telephone access in general. From parts of Russia to parts of Africa and Central America, if there are no telephones, Internet access is out of the question.

Despite these barriers, more and more Europeans are getting on the Net; and because they are jumping on the wagon later than Americans, many new European users will likely skip the access-by-modem model. Development for high-speed infrastructure is gaining momentum in Europe. For example, Cybercable (www.cybercable.fr) will be offering high-speed Internet access via cable in France for a flat fee, including communication charges. Free Internet access is now available in the United Kingdom through Freeserve (www.freeserve.co.uk), which offers high-speed access, local-call charges for national calls, an unlimited number of e-mail addresses, free Web site space, and free e-mail-based support.

Political momentum is also building in France and other European countries for lower communication charges for accessing the Internet. For example, the 3 million French Internet users as well as users from other European countries boycotted the Internet on December 13, 1998, to protest new taxes on telephone communications. So, although many parts of the world don't yet have a communication infrastructure that promotes Internet usage, they are making progress toward getting there.

## Internet Service Provider

Another barrier is lack of choices for ISPs. This lack of choice keeps prices high and access limited. Moreover, in many countries in Africa and elsewhere in the Third World, the government acts as the ISP. Yet, many more options are quickly becoming available.

## Competing Systems

France has yet another obstacle. The dominance of the Minitel network has resulted in the country's slow adoption of the more open Internet. The good news about Minitel is that the French feel comfortable using an online network to pay bills. The bad news is that there is not a great movement to switch to the more open Internet. Minitel has many advantages: It's inexpensive, already in operation, and localized.

# Turning Access Obstacles into Opportunities

In playing on the international field, identifying and addressing barriers to access will help you turn these obstacles into opportunities and your competitive advantage. Let's be honest: There is not much any one business can do about the issues of lack of telephone service, ISP choice, or competing services. What you can do is make your site as user-friendly as possible to each potential audience. If you are advertising in or have traffic from a country where Internet access is still on a pay-per-minute basis, it's important to provide clear information easily accessible in the native language so they can find what they need, print, and move on. Since most of the material will be printed, make sure each page is printer-friendly (white background, with all material on one page), or have a special page identified as the one to print where all information is consolidated. Moreover, the entire site should download quickly, since every second counts. In short, "The best way to communicate with overseas visitors," says Bill Hunt of the Multimedia Marketing Group, "is to have as many details answered as you can on the Web site."

## Translation Issues

There is no getting around the fact that if you want to market to a country, you have to market in the native language. In the words of former German chancellor Willy Brandt, "If I'm selling to you, I speak your language. If I'm buying, dann müssen Sie Deutsch sprechen [then you must speak German]."

Translation needs to occur on various levels. First, if you are going to service an international audience beyond the English-speaking countries, then you need to have elements of your Web site translated into the languages your audience speaks. Next, if you are going to advertise to increase traffic or generate sales or leads, then you need to develop an advertising campaign that speaks to and resonates with each specific culture. Finally, you need to be able to provide customer service to your users once they come to your site. Anthony Schneider, President of Web Zeit (www.webzeit.com), sums it up best when he says, "If content is king, then language must be queen."

## Translating Your Web Site

It sounds straightforward enough. To reach a market, you need to speak to a market in its own language even if that market knows your language. Bill Dunlap of EuroMktg

---

### Advertising Translation Bloopers

This is a list of advertisements that missed the mark when translated from English to another language. In going through the process of translating your advertising campaign message, make sure you do thorough research to avoid falling victim to a similar cultural *faux pas*. We want to thank everyone who submitted their favorite bloopers, especially Bill Dunlap and the Global Marketing Discussion List (www.euromktg.com/eng/ed/gmd.html).

Coors put its slogan "Turn it loose" into Spanish, where it was read as "Suffer from diarrhea."

The Dairy Association's huge success with the campaign "Got Milk?" prompted them to expand advertising to Mexico. It was soon brought to their attention that the Spanish translation read "Are you lactating?"

When American Airlines wanted to advertise its new leather first-class seats in the Mexican market, it translated its "Fly In Leather" campaign literally, which meant, "Fly Naked" (vuela en cuero) in Spanish.

The ever-popular introduction of Chevy's great car into Latin America: the Nova (= "no go" in Spanish), and Toyota's MR2 into Quebec: MR2 ="em-er-deux" = "merde" = "shit" in French.

Scandinavian vacuum manufacturer Electrolux used the following in an American campaign: "Nothing sucks like an Electrolux."

Clairol introduced the Mist Stick, a curling iron, into German only to find out that "mist" is slang for manure. Not too many people had use for the "manure stick."

asked a group of Swedish users who are very comfortable in English if they surfed in English or Swedish. Dunlap found that the answer was unanimous that they surfed in Swedish. "They feel strongly about their own identity," remarks Dunlap. "Just because they speak a language doesn't mean they want to or feel comfortable surfing in that language. "

Deciding to translate is just the first step. Now, new questions arise. Should you translate all of your Web site or just specific pages? If you only translate selected pages, which pages?

The 1997 Japanese Content Survey conducted by Global Promote (www.globalpromote.com) found that 88 percent of Japanese Web users would like more content translated into Japanese. When asked what information they want translated into Japanese, 68 percent said the order form, 65 percent the terms and conditions, 50 percent said the FAQ, and 8 percent responded with product information. This shows that international users want the meat of a site—hold the marketing.

Just because a person has a working knowledge of a language, doesn't mean that person feels comfortable making or executing a purchase in that language. To put it into perspective, how comfortable would you feel placing an order online using your high school French? That's the situation of many online users conducting business on English-language sites.

---

When Gerber started selling baby food in Africa, they used the same packaging as in the United States, with the beautiful Caucasian baby on the label. Later they learned that in Africa, companies routinely put pictures on the label of what's inside, since most people can't read.

Colgate introduced a toothpaste in France called Cue, the name of a notorious porno magazine.

An American T-shirt maker in Miami printed shirts for the Spanish market that promoted the Pope's visit. Instead of "I saw the Pope" (el Papa), the shirts read "I saw the potato" (la papa).

Pepsi's "Come alive with the Pepsi Generation" translated into "Pepsi brings your ancestors back from the grave," in Chinese.

Frank Perdue's chicken slogan, "It takes a strong man to make a tender chicken," was translated into Spanish as "It takes an aroused man to make a chicken affectionate."

The Coca-Cola name in China was first read as "Ke-kou-ke-la," meaning "bite the wax tadpole" or "female horse stuffed with wax," depending on the dialect. Coke then researched 40,000 characters to find a phonetic equivalent "ko-kou-ko-le," translating into "happiness in the mouth."

When Parker Pen marketed a ballpoint pen in Mexico, its ads were supposed to have read, "It won't leak in your pocket and embarrass you." The company thought that the word "embarazar" (to impregnate) meant to embarrass, so the ad read: "It won't leak in your pocket and make you pregnant."

## Viewing a Site in Another Language

To view a site in another language, especially one that does not use the Roman alphabet, you will need language support software as well as a browser that supports that language. A listing of software options is presented in Table 12.2. MacOS 8.5 has a custom-install option to install Asian and other foreign language characters for the entire operating system, including browsers. When installing 8.5, select "Custom Install."

The other option is to use a multilingual browser like Tango (www.alis.com/internet_products/browser/browser.html) that doesn't require additional software. Tango is compatible with Windows 3.1, 95, 98, and NT.

Microsoft is progressing in localizing its operating system, assisting new users in accessing the Internet in their native language from day one. You can find a full listing of Microsoft language plug-ins for Internet Explorer at www.microsoft.com/ie/intlhome.htm.

**Table 12.2**   Language Software and Browser Support for Asian Languages

| JAPANESE |
| --- |
| **Japanese Language Support Software** |
| Windows 95 |
| AsiaSurf (www.dynalab.com/) |
| Twinbridge (ftp://ftp.aimnet.com/pub/users/chinabus/tbjdemo.zip) |
| UnionWay (www.unionway.com) |
| Win/V (www.interchange.ubc.ca/gregsmit/winvhome.html) |
| Windows 3.1 |
| **Browsers That Support Japanese** |
| Netscape Communicator (http://home.netscape.com/download/client_download.html?communicator4.02) |
| Microsoft Internet Explorer (www.microsoft.com/products/default.asp?divisionid=10) |
| Macintosh users (running System 7.1 or later) need to load the Japanese Language Kit (www.macos.apple.com/macos/easy/intl/langkitsover.html), as well as a browser that supports Japanese, like Netscape Navigator Gold 3.02 (http://home.netscape.com/download/nav_download.html?navigatorgold3.02). |

**Table 12.2** (Continued)

| CHINESE |
| --- |
| **Chinese Language Support Software** |
| NJStar (www.njstar.com) |
| TwinBridge Software (www.twinbridge.com) |
| UnionWay (www.unionway.com/download.htm) |
| Macintosh users |
| Elixir (www.e.kth.se/~e94_lih/html/Elixir.html) |
| Chinese Language Kit from Mac (www.apple.com/macos/multilingual/chinese.html) |

| KOREAN |
| --- |
| **Korean Language Support Software** |
| Win 95 and NT |
| UnionWay (www.unionway.com) |
| AsiaSurf (www.dynalab.com) |
| Windows 3.1 |
| UnionWay (www.unionway.com) |
| **Browsers That Support Korean** |
| Netscape Communicator (http://home.netscape.com/download/client_download.html?communicator4.02) |
| Microsoft Internet Explorer (www.microsoft.com/products/default.asp?divisionid=10) |
| Macintosh users (running System 7.1 or later) need to load the Korean Language Kit (www.macos.apple.com/multilingual/korean.html), as well as a browser that supports Korean, like Netscape Navigator Gold 3.02 (http://home.netscape.com/download/nav_download.html?navigatorgold3.02). |

# Translating Your Ad

Trying to differentiate your marketing message from the clutter is demanding. Add to that the issue of presenting your message to another culture in another language and the task gets even more daunting. Banner ads need to be translated into the native language. But this can be your competitive advantage. Often a translated banner is the only text in the native language on a page. Bill Hunt of Global Promote was in India speaking with a group of Hotmail (free e-mail service) users. He asked the users whether they would respond to an ad that came up in Hindi (one of the main languages of India). The group replied that they rarely click on ads, but any text in their native language would catch their attention immediately and they would probably click on it. Indeed, Hunt has found that his ads get a 5–25 percent boost by using localized banners.

Let's face it, you never see a Toyota ad in Japanese in an American paper; so why would you show an ad in English in Japan? In Holland, where almost everyone speaks English, ads are always in Dutch, the native language. It all boils down to trying to reach your customer. "The background language of the mind is a person's native tongue. The way you target is in the language of the country, always, 100 percent of the time," says Dunlap.

## Localization

Merely translating the text of an ad doesn't mean the language usage is correct or effective from a marketing perspective. A technique used by the Multimedia Marketing Group is to invite people from the target market to critique the ad in a private area of your site. This way the ad is tested in a controlled environment and you can check to make sure the message is clean—no culturally misleading innuendoes—with an applicable call to action for that market. What is appropriate to do and say in one culture, may not work in another. For example, a typical advertising strategy with American consumers is to compare one product with another. But this technique backfires in Japan, where saying your product is better than another is frowned upon. In other words, going global really means going local in each country. See the sidebar on pages 286–287 for a humorous look at translation bloopers in advertising.

## Communicating with International Customers

Marketing is all about building relationships, whether you are dealing with a customer around the corner or across the globe. The process of developing and maintaining a dialogue with your customers presents additional difficulties when dealing with a multilingual customer base. If you're going to market in different languages, be prepared to provide customer service in multiple languages. Building a banner in another language or having multiple language versions of your site is only the beginning. You need to be able to service each customer in the language in which the original advertising proposition was made. Offer multiple channels for communication: e-mail, fax, phone, and snail mail. And, whenever possible, have a local telephone number, fax number, and mailing address. Whether you have a field office or just a virtual office, make it easy for your new customers to communicate with you. Make working with your company convenient— as convenient as working with a local company. If you are going to offer a toll-free number, make sure it is accessible in the countries you are pursuing. An 800 number works in the United States and Canada, but not in Japan or the United Kingdom. In terms of translation issues, there are several options:

- You can have a local sales office in each country, with a local staff that answers the phone, mail, and e-mail, eliminating the need for translation.

- You can offer your international customers e-mail communication only, and run all e-mail out of the home office using automatic translation software such as AltaVista's free service (http://babelfish.altavista.com/) to translate the questions and answers (please note that using translation software leaves room for many mistakes).

■ You can hire native speakers to handle all communication and translate the questions and answers for your staff whenever needed.

## How an Online Marketing Campaign Helped the Swedish Hotel Adlon Use a Multilingual Web Site to Bring in Business

By Bill Dunlap (ema@euromktg.com)
Managing Director Euro-Marketing Associates (www.euromktg.com)

Stockholm is a bit out of the way, when you're traveling around Europe on business, and it takes a little more than usual to attract attention from businesspeople. The Adlon Hotel (www.adlon.se) realized this when they created a Web site to attract a businessperson who is keen to have PC and Internet connections in their room. To get the word out to people around Europe, they translated the main page of their Web site and sent out press releases in German, French, and Spanish. This work is equivalent in price to one month's run of a quarter-page color ad in a magazine. Yet what a difference in the results of their marketing—a print advertisement would need to keep up this monthly budget, whereas the Internet ad (that is, their Web site) continues, and the traffic increases, thanks to being in local indexes and search engines.

When designing the online marketing plan, they had to decide who their target audience was: who comes to Stockholm. Obviously the Germans (Sweden's leading trading partner), but also some French, some Spanish/Portuguese (even from Latin America), and the Italians. Hence, Adlon Hotel's director chose to have their gateway page into the Web site translated into German, French, Spanish, Portuguese, and Italian.

One year later, this is what they have to say, when asked if the multilingual approach helped them build their hotel business:

Yes! We are right now up to over 3,000 visits per week! And it is from the whole world. Please bear in mind that Adlon Hotel is a small hotel in a small city in the northern Europe and it is not a tourist hotel. Only businesspeople (although we keep getting a lot of tourists as well).

From our simple e-mail booking facility we are getting more than 10 percent of our turnover! No discounts, no commissions, etc. The one and only reason for getting this kind of result is the way you are linking your site on Internet.

The winners are the hotels who have understood the importance of being seen on the Web. The cost in money is small. The knowledge how to market your site on the Internet is the key to success.

Bengt G. Lidforss,
Director of Adlon Hotel,
Stockholm, Sweden

*Continues*

## How an Online Marketing Campaign Helped the Swedish Hotel Adlon Use a Multilingual Web Site to Bring in Business *(Continued)*

What is important to keep in mind when one decides to internationalize a Web site is that it takes time to build traffic. The Adlon Hotel's site was not fetching that much traffic internationally 6 months after their translation and promotions, but a year afterward, it was clearly a success. This is partly because the indexes and search engines in each country attract more and more attention, as more people in other countries come online.

The Adlon Hotel made the efforts to translate a home page in 10 languages (see Figures 12 a-c), and actively promote these gateways into their Web site. During the month of August 1998, the breakdown of people using these language gateways to find the site was as follows:

German: 10%
French: 9.6%
Italian: 9.3%
Spanish: 9.2%
Portuguese: 8.9%
Scandinavian languages and English: 53%

Of course, they could handle Scandinavian languages and English themselves, and contracted out the other European languages. It's most interesting that the other European languages are now pulling in 47 percent of the traffic to these language gateways to their site.

Another lesson to be drawn from this example is the separate targeting of the U.K. Instead of going through one of the large American Web site registration services, Adlon Hotel decided to target specifically U.K. search engines and press. The American Web promotion services are excellent when broadcasting a message worldwide to anyone who is conversant in English, but it does not make sense when one is wanting to target only one or two Anglophone countries, as in this case. Many English businesspeople come to Stockholm in comparison with Americans. Hence, the need to target the U.K. alone among Anglophone countries.

Of course, the next step would be to translate their banner ad into these languages and run it in travel sites related to Stockholm. By creating several identical Web pages in each language, each with its own URL—for instance, in French this could be index-fr1.html, indexfr2.html, etc.—the webmaster could test various forms of Web promotion in different countries and see what promotion technique brings in the most people.

The conclusion is obvious: for very little outlay of advertising budget, there can be considerable yield from other countries, just by taking the pains of translating one single page of a Web site, and promoting these language gateways into the site. Let's hope that this technique will grow in popularity as businesses become more aware and interested in getting exposure to those abroad.

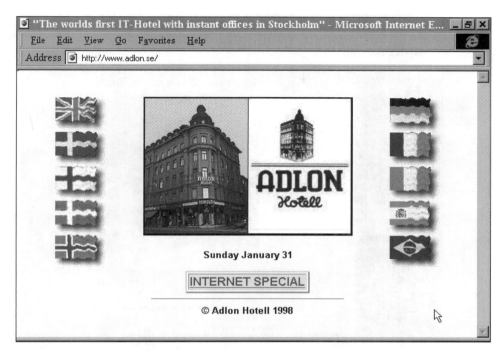

**Figure 12.2a**    Adlon Hotel Web site homepage.

**Figure 12.2b**    Adlon Hotel Web site in German.

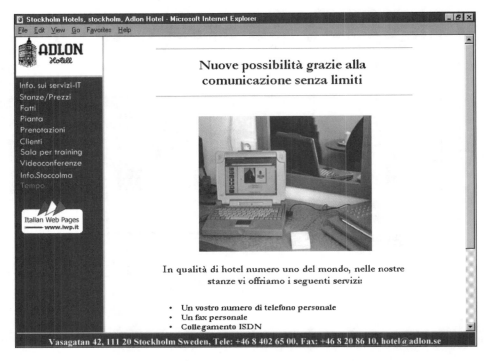

**Figure 12.2c** Adlon Hotel Web site in Italian.

# Locating Appropriate Sites in Other Countries

Where should you advertise? Where your customers and potential customers already congregate. Find out where your audience goes and advertise there. If you are doing a brand-building campaign (where you are after reach and frequency), then you need a site that aggregates a high volume of eyeballs (like a search engine or portal site). However, if you are running a direct marketing campaign, then you want to reach an audience that is already interested in your type of product.

## Portals and Directories

Most of the major search engines and directories have multiple language sites. Yahoo! and MSN are battling it out to reach out and touch the global Internet Community. Yahoo! now has a presence in 14 countries, and Microsoft projects to be in over 30 countries by 2000. Table 12.3 lists the different country and language sites of the major portals and search engines. EuroMktg has a section of its site that lists search engines, directories, and indexes around the world (www.euromktg.com/eng/GR/regis.html), and is a great stop on your search to find Web sites for reaching different countries; it covers Chinese, Danish, Dutch, Finnish, French, German, Italian, Japanese, Korean, Norwegian, Portuguese, the Pacific Rim, Spanish (including the Americas), and Swedish sites.

**Table 12.3** The Major U.S. Portals, Search Engines, and Directories Affiliates Around the World

| EXCITE | |
|---|---|
| Australia | http://au.excite.com |
| Chinese | http://chinese.excite.com |
| France | http://fr.excite.com |
| Germany | www.excite.de |
| Italy | http://it.excite.com |
| Japan | www.excite.co.jp |
| Netherlands | http://nl.excite.com |
| Sweden | http://se.excite.com |
| United Kingdom | www.excite.co.uk |

| INFOSEEK | |
|---|---|
| Brazil | www.infoseek.com/Home?pg=Home.html&sv=BR |
| Denmark | www.infoseek.com/Home?pg=Home.html&sv=DK |
| France | www.infoseek.com/Home?pg=Home.html&sv=FR |
| Germany | www.infoseek.com/Home?pg=Home.html&sv=DE |
| Italy | www.infoseek.com/Home?pg=Home.html&sv=IT |
| Japan | japan.infoseek.com |
| Mexico | mexico.infoseek.com |
| Netherlands | www.infoseek.com/Home?pg=Home.html&sv=NL |
| Spanish language | www.infoseek.com/Home?pg=Home.html&sv=ES |
| Sweden | www.infoseek.com/Home?pg=Home.html&sv=SE |
| United Kingdom | www.infoseek.com/Home?pg=Home.html&sv=UK |

| LYCOS | |
|---|---|
| Belgium | www.be.lycos.de/ |
| France | www.lycos.fr |
| Germany | www.lycos.de |
| Italy | www.lycos.it |
| Japan | www.lycos.co.jp |
| Netherlands | www.lycos.nl |
| Spain | www.es.lycos.de |
| Switzerland | www.lycosch.ch |
| United Kingdom | www.lycos.co.uk |

*Continues*

**Table 12.3** The Major U.S. Portals, Search Engines, and Directories Affiliates Around the World *(Continued)*

| MSN | |
|---|---|
| Australia | ninemsn.com.au |
| Canada | ca.msn.com |
| France | fr.msn.com |
| Germany | http://msn.de |
| Japan | www.jp.msn.com |
| United Kingdom | http://msn.co.uk |

| YAHOO! | |
|---|---|
| **Europe** | |
| Denmark | www.yahoo.dk |
| France | www.yahoo.fr |
| Germany | www.yahoo.de |
| Italy | www.yahoo.it |
| Norway | www.yahoo.no |
| Spain | www.yahoo.es |
| Sweden | www.yahoo.se |
| United Kingdom and Ireland | www.yahoo.co.uk |
| **Pacific Rim** | |
| Asia | www.yahoo.com.sg |
| Australia and New Zealand | www.yahoo.com.au |
| Chinese language | http://chinese.yahoo.com |
| Japan | www.yahoo.co.jp |
| Korea | www.yahoo.co.kr |
| **Americas** | |
| Canada | www.yahoo.ca |

# Ad Networks

One inherently efficient means to reach an audience outside of your home market is to use an ad network. As explained in Chapter 10, ad networks serve both the advertisers and publishers as an efficient means to either sell or buy online ad inventory. The major U.S.-based networks recognized the global nature of the Internet audience and set up shop in the English-speaking countries as well as other high Internet usage countries. An advertiser can use a network to make buys in multiple countries, in multiple languages, that operate under different currencies, without ever changing account executives or exchanging currency. Publishers with content that reaches beyond national borders can offer ad inventory to advertisers they could never reach before. There's no question that ad networks make the process of buying and selling ads easy, efficient, and cost effective for both the advertiser and the publisher.

Most of the major networks have international inventory available. For example, DoubleClick International considers itself a network of networks comprised of 15 local networks in the following countries: Australia, Canada, Denmark, Finland, France, Germany, Ireland, Italy, Japan, Netherlands, Norway, Spain, Sweden, United Kingdom, and United States. Each network is made up of locally branded sites. A local sales force handles each network so that the network is always managed locally, but each sales representative can sell inventory on any of the networks. This means that a customer in France can buy ad space to reach French-speaking users in Canada and pay in francs.

Canadian Airlines used the DoubleClick network for its campaign to educate Web-savvy travelers on new services with the relaunch of the Canadian Plus inter@active site (www.cdnair.ca). The new site offered online reservation services, schedule checking, and frequently flyer point checking. The campaign ran ads on travel sites and other sites that attracted an affluent audience, including keyword buys on AltaVista. Canadian Airlines extended the scope of the campaign to include the position of ads with local content on clearly international sites. "When we initially were planning the Canadian Airlines online campaign," says Debra Lamb, media director at Parallel Strategies, "DoubleClick brought forward the idea of extending the campaign to include a global perspective. The results were that we were able to target Canadian users on sites around the world. This was extremely beneficial in providing more depth to an effective campaign for our client."

Indeed, the reach and immediacy of the Internet is changing the face of doing business internationally. For example, DoubleClick Japan worked with the Mitsubishi media buyer in Japan for a buy in Europe. The buy occurred in Japan; the ads had a localized message and creative for the European audience. The reporting of the campaign was done in Japanese for the advertiser and the costs were presented in yen. If this had been done in traditional media, it would have required three different media buyers in three different countries, resulting in excessive paperwork.

The LinkExchange banner network is the world's largest network, with members representing 34 languages (http://adnetwork.linkexchange.com/international.html; see Table 12.4 for the list of languages).

# Testing the Market

As with all aspects of online advertising, test the waters before jumping in. Portals and search engines are a good place to start. With so many going global, many topic-specific sections, which are locked up for keyword buys and sponsorships in the English-speaking counterparts, are wide open in the other language versions of the sites. Other good starting points are local gateway sites and ad networks. Also look at regional sites. These often have more loyalty from consumers than portals, because the portals are often a U.S. product that is simply translated to try to meet another region's needs. An example of a great international site is StarMedia Network (www.starmedia.com), which

**Table 12.4**    Languages Represented by LinkExchange Members

| | | |
|---|---|---|
| Arabic | French | Polish |
| Bahasa | German | Portuguese |
| Indonesia | Greek | Romanian |
| Bengali | Hebrew | Russian |
| Chinese | Hindi | Slovak |
| Croatian | Hungarian | Spanish |
| Czech | Icelandic | Swedish |
| Danish | Italian | Thai |
| Dutch | Japanese | Turkish |
| English | Korean | Vietnamese |
| Farsi | Malay | |
| Finnish | Norwegian | |

is the largest Internet community for Portuguese- and Spanish-speaking people. Instead of trying to be something for everyone, they've become the best at serving their specific markets (see Figure 12.3).

**Figure 12.3**    StarMedia Network, the leading portal for Portuguese- and Spanish-speaking Web users.

# Targeting by Language, Not Country

Not all targeting of specific language users occurs in countries outside of one's own. In most countries, many languages are spoken. Many U.S. consumers go to U.S.-based language-specific sites. For example, there are numerous sites built in the Chinese language targeting Asian Americans, as shown in Table 12.5. These sites serve Chinese and other expatriates who live in the United States but feel more comfortable surfing in their native tongue. When Virtual Vineyards wanted to target the Chinese American population in the United States, they launched a Chinese-language ad campaign on U.S.-based Chinese-language sites. There are similar sites serving Americans who speak Spanish, Japanese, and so on.

In following the rule that the best strategy is to find out where an audience already congregates and then advertise there, advertisers are starting to follow expatriates online—from American expatriates in Japan to Japanese expatriates in American. Newspaper sites are great for this purpose. Many expatriates visit newspaper sites in their native tongue for news from home. For example, the number-one newspaper in the Philippines found that a great deal of their traffic came from the United States. The newspaper switched its advertising strategy to include American advertisers wanting to reach the Philippine American audience. Likewise, a Norwegian paper found that 60 percent of its traffic came from Norwegian Americans so they started to go after that market through their Norwegian ads.

## *International Advertising and Marketing Agencies*

There are firms that specialize in international online marketing (see Table 12.6). One of the oldest in this field is EuroMarketing (www.euromarketing.com), which is led by Bill Dunlap and headquartered in France. For those trying to reach the Japanese audience, Bill Hunt's Global Strategies (www.globalpromote.com), now part of Multi-Media Marketing Group, is the way to go.

European firms, like U.S. firms, are opening offices in other countries. For example, InterAd (www.interadsales.net/english/index_eng.htm), the London-based European sales representative firm, has an office in California. European companies want to

**Table 12.5**  Sites Targeting Asian Americans

| IN ENGLISH |
| --- |
| ABC Flash (www.abcflash.com) |
| Astyle (www.astyle.com) |
| **IN CHINESE** |
| Chinese Cyber City (www1.ccchome.com/index.htm) |
| SINANET (www.sinanet.com) |
| WebUnion Media (www.webunion.com) |

**Table 12.6**  Sample of International Online Marketing Firms

| FIRM | HOME COUNTRY | COMMENTS |
|---|---|---|
| EuroMarketing (www.euromktg.com) | France | One of the oldest and most well-respected firms specializing in international online marketing |
| i-map (www.i-map.ie) | Ireland | Internet marketing, audience development, and ad placement agency focusing on Ireland |
| Bluesky International Marketing (www.blueskyinc.com) | France | Specializes in Europe |
| Multimedia Marketing Group (www.mmgco.com) | Oregon | Purchased Global Strategies, a firm specializing in Japan |
| Biz-Zone (www.biz-zone.com) | Canada | Specializes in Canada |
| Novawind (www.novawind.com) | Israel | Specializes in the Middle East and Europe |

target the largest consumer market in the world, the United States. If they are handling a European or Asian account for an advertiser, it makes sense that they would want to try and handle the American account as well.

# Educating the International Market

The United States is projected to be anywhere from 12 to 36 months ahead of other markets. To build the industry, a large percentage of the selling process is educational. DoubleClick International is doing this in three ways. First, all of their marketing material has a strong educational element. Second, they run a series of ads that act as public education messages for advertisers focusing on targeting and tracking. Third, they participate in local industry trade shows and events. Moreover, they run their own series of meetings in each country with guest speakers to build and educate the local advertising and marketing community.

"Going global on the Internet is different than in traditional media," says Barry Salzman, president of DoubleClick International. " In traditional media a global presence means an office in New York, Paris, and London. For an Internet business, going global means having a local presence wherever your online audiences dials in." In the words of Anthony Schneider, president of Web Zeit (www.webzeit.com), "The Internet makes molehills out of geographical mountains and fosters virtual communities of far-flung users." Indeed, going international is now a staple of online advertising. From Procter & Gamble (spending more than $3 billion on advertising outside the United States in 1997) to Virtual Vineyards, businesses are using the Internet to

**Table 12.7** Global Web Advertising and Marketing E-mail Discussion Lists

| TITLE | LANGUAGE | URL |
|---|---|---|
| Global Marketing Discussion List | English | www.euromktg.com/eng/ed/gmd.html |
| Marketing en Ligne | French | www.euromktg.com/fr/ed.html#mel |
| Netmarketing | German | www.werbeagentur.de/netmarketing.htm |
| PResent | Dutch | www.prconsult.nl/present/index.htm |
| WebIt | Italian | www-serra.unipi.it/listserver/lists/WEBIT/ |

reach their niche markets in every corner of the globe and through every language. The Internet is all about community, and advertising on the Internet makes it easy, cost effective, and efficient to reach your target community wherever that community resides, and in the language they speak. To keep up on global Web advertising, see Table 12.7, which lists e-mail discussion lists on the topic.

# I'm OK, Euro K

Katherine Randolph (krand@microsoft.com)
Director of International, Microsoft Online Sales (www.microsoft.com)

The Internet is a global phenomenon. In 1998, over half of the estimated 155 million online users lived outside the U.S., and international users were growing at a 30 percent CAGR, compared to 15 percent in North America. The projections for online advertising and e-commerce growth are even greater, with online advertising expected to reach $1.4 billion by the year 2000, and e-commerce $32 billion (178 percent growth). International growth is outpacing the United States, even though international users have to put up with higher local phone charges and comparatively fewer local sites than American users, to be able to join the freedom of the fray in the global Internet village.

All around barriers are coming down. The Euro became a reality on January 1, 1999, and suddenly it's springtime in "Euroland." But it's more than just trade barriers and monetary barriers that are coming down. Language, cultural, and social barriers as eroding as well. What seemed absolutely unthinkable just a few years ago is commonplace, and almost acceptable today. When I lived in Paris as a college student I thought I'd never see the day when Parisians carried knapsacks and wore sneakers. Now they not only carry knapsacks "pour faire du camping" in the mountains and around town, they can and do chose from among dozens of models from REI's French-language Web site. It's not unusual for someone to live in Belgium and work in Paris, or to live in Munich and have their country house in Northern Italy. On the weekends they drive their Ford and Renault minivans to the Toys 'R' Us.

The types of trade restrictions that manufacturers and governments created to limit the flow of goods from market to market have all but disappeared on the Internet. The Internet has suddenly made it possible for consumers to comparison shop like never before. European consumers can now see it's cheaper to buy CD's from American Internet music shops like CDnow than it is to buy them down the street, and that they may get a better deal on that new BMW in Brussels than in Bonn. And the number of consumers who are both comparison shopping and completing transactions on the Internet is growing dramatically.

Europeans will ruminate over the role of the Internet and the impact of technology on their lives and their culture. They'll debate what to do all week, then get in their minivan on the weekend and drive to the Hypermarche, which is their answer to Costco and the category killer. Asians are much less troubled by the changes, and are embracing technology as fast as they can afford it.

So what's the message here? Companies that learn to take advantage of this market will be ahead. But it's not easy. The global elite are the forerunners, who discover the American brands—Barnes & Noble, REI, Bloomingdales—while shopping in America on vacation. When they're in America, they'll put up with only American-speaking sales assistants. But with the Internet, you can easily bring your brand to the consumer in their homes in London, Lisbon, and Kuala Lumpur. And then, they—and the next wave of the mass market—will be expected to provide local services for shipping, payment, and customer services. Because it's not enough to be "just out there" on the Internet. With increasing price comparison, there will be a need for customer service internationally, in the same way that there is in the States. U.S. sites have the technological advantage in the Internet marketing and shopping arena, but the gap is closing as international local competitors wake up and gear up to defend their local territories against the Amazon.coms and E-trades.

The realities of ramping up internationally are real, and numerous. The questions that international or "global marketers" have always faced remain in Internet advertising and marketing. That is, how much can products be marketed similarly around the world? Is there such a thing as a global brand? How much should you tailor marketing strategies to individual countries? And to compound problems, there is little or no systematic market research and assessment. There are few measurements to gauge the actual size and growth of international markets. Third-party market measurement companies like Media Metrix simply don't exist outside the United States. And despite the dedicated effort of the IAB International and Price Waterhouse Coopers to create a Global Revenue Reporting program, the network of global publishers is not yet comprehensive enough across all countries to provide sufficient global revenue figures. So it's difficult to know if you're doing well, or if your "success" is only as good as your market projections. But that's no different than in the United States.

And how do you know which markets are growing fastest and where to expand to next? You do your best to find reliable resources and build your own intelligence network to find out what's *really* happening out there. You get a general idea and hold on for the ride. It's like when you're traveling on the Eurostar from London to Paris. You zip along the English countryside, going at what you think is a fine clip. Then suddenly, *whompf*, you get sucked into the Chunnel, everything gets dark, and things really pick up. When you emerge on the other side, you're absolutely flying. No doubt about it.

Yet despite the challenges, it's surprising how many companies—whether publishers or agencies—have yet to really realize the global impact and potential of the Internet, let alone take advantage of it. Perhaps the Americans are so busy keeping pace with, or acquiring, their competitors in Silicon Valley and Redmond, that they don't have the time to do that *and* expand internationally.

After three years building and managing the international sales organization for Microsoft's Online Sales team, I've concluded that the largest obstacles in this fast-paced technological field are human- and time-based. To succeed globally in the breakneck speed of the Internet, a company must develop a global presence,

*Continues*

## I'm OK, Euro K *(Continued)*

at least in the core markets, which requires a minimum of scale or leveraging partners' scale. At the same time, the company must be nimble and fast, which are usually attributes of small, lean teams. It must also have strong local management which is able to understand and react to local competitors, and a strong centralized management which knows when to promote and enforce consistency and when to respect local autonomy. And those things can only be built and reinforced over time through a strong network of people.

# CHAPTER 13

# Legal Issues Every Internet Advertiser Should Know

**Rochelle Blaustein, Esq. (blaust@patentplus.com; www.patentplus.com)**

In the offline world of marketing, it is accepted practice to collect demographic information, create mailing lists, sell those lists, and use them for unsolicited targeted marketing. The ease of doing all these things in the digital format has raised concerns and campaigns for protecting consumers.

Privacy has become one of the greatest concerns of consumers on the Internet. In response to this, governments have taken various actions to protect the privacy of their citizens. As with many legal issues on the Internet, the global nature of cyberspace means that the various governments have differing laws. Many of the governments have discussed ways to harmonize these laws, but the solution remains a goal for the future.

For now, we must deal with the realities that exist in the law and on the Internet. The areas of concern when marketing on the Internet include:

- collection of personal data, such as for targeted marketing
- distribution of personal data, such as sale of mailing lists
- retaining records and security for databases containing personal data
- unsolicited commercial e-mail (UCE), also known as spam

## The European Experience

European law has been the most aggressive in protecting consumers' personal data on the Internet. The Council of Europe Convention on Data Protection long ago set forth principles intended to protect the rights of individuals about whom information is obtained, shared, processed, or supplied. These principles are central to various European laws, including the UK Data Protection Act of 1984.

## UK Data Protection Act Guidelines, Guideline 4

The following is taken from the "Data Protection Act Guidelines, Guideline 4," published by the UK Data Protection Registrar at http://maga.di.unito.it/security/resources/laws/guide4.pdf. The Registrar permits reproduction of short extracts from the Guidelines in other publications so long as there is acknowledgment of the source of the material.

1. The information to be contained in personal data shall be obtained, and personal data shall be processed, fairly and lawfully.

2. Personal data shall be held only for one or more specified and lawful purposes.

3. Personal data held for any purpose or purposes shall not be used or disclosed in any manner incompatible with that purpose or those purposes.

4. Personal data held for any purpose or purposes shall be adequate, relevant and not excessive in relation to that purpose or those purposes.

5. Personal data shall be accurate and, where necessary, kept up to date.

6. Personal data held for any purpose or purposes shall not be kept for longer than is necessary for that purpose or those purposes.

7. An individual shall be entitled—

    (a) at reasonable intervals and without undue delay or expense—

       (i) to be informed by any data user whether he holds personal data of which that individual is the subject; and

       (ii) to access any such data held by a data user; and

    (b) where appropriate, to have such data corrected or erased.

8. Appropriate security measures shall be taken against unauthorized access to, or alteration, disclosure or destruction of, personal data and against accidental loss or destruction of personal data.

### Sensitive Data

The UK Act is also specific about four types of sensitive personal data:

- racial origin
- political opinions or religious or other beliefs
- physical or mental health or sexual life
- criminal convictions

(See also the Convention for the Protection of Individuals with Regard to Automatic Processing of Personal Data at www.echo.lu/legal/en/dataprot/counceur/conv.html.)

More recently, the European Parliament brought these principles clearly into focus for the Internet and other digital technology with Directive 95/46/EC, a complete copy of which can be found at www2.echo.lu/legal/en/dataprot/directiv/directiv.html.

The European Directive is of particular interest to U.S. businesses, since it directs European Member States to prevent transfer of data to countries that do not ensure an adequate level of protection. Since the United States does not yet have law that protects consumers' data collection and distribution from commercial and non-commercial entities, it is feasible that European Member States could block access to at least select U.S. Web sites.

Fortunately, the Directive also contains some exceptions that Member States can rely on so that business with U.S. and other countries' Web sites can continue, under certain circumstances. These exceptions include transfer of personal data needed to fulfill a contract with the person whose data is being transferred or for the benefit of that person, or if unambiguous consent of that person is received. The latter exception is particularly useful, since measures can be taken to include request for consent as part of a Web site's activities. Posting privacy notices and obtaining agreement from consumers are discussed below.

## Protection of Individuals with Regard to the Processing of Personal Data and on the Free Movement of Such Data

**Article 6 of Directive 95/46/EC of the European Parliament and of the Council**

**1. Member States shall provide that personal data must be:**

**(a) processed fairly and lawfully;**

**(b) collected for specified, explicit and legitimate purposes and not further processed in a way incompatible with those purposes. Further processing of data for historical, statistical or scientific purposes shall not be considered as incompatible provided that Member States provide appropriate safeguards;**

**(c) adequate, relevant and not excessive in relation to the purposes for which they are collected and/or further processed;**

**(d) accurate and, where necessary, kept up to date; every reasonable step must be taken to ensure that data which are inaccurate or incomplete, having regard to the purposes for which they were collected or for which they are further processed, are erased or rectified;**

**(e) kept in a form which permits identification of data subjects for no longer than is necessary for the purposes for which the data were collected or for which they are further processed. Member States shall lay down appropriate safeguards for personal data stored for longer periods for historical, statistical or scientific use.**

*Continues*

**Protection of Individuals with Regard to the Processing of Personal Data and on the Free Movement of Such Data (Continued)**

Article 26 includes exemptions to a European Member State's requirement to prevent transfer of personal data to third countries without adequate privacy protection laws. In summary, transfer may take place on condition that:

(a) the person has consented unambiguously to the transfer;

(b) the transfer is necessary for responding to a request from the person whose data is in question or to follow through on a contract with that person;

(c) the transfer is necessary to follow through on a contract with a third party, but for the benefit of the person whose data is in question;

(d) the transfer is legally required or required for a legal claim;

(e) the transfer is necessary to protect the interests of the person whose data is in question;

(f) the transfer is made from a legal register intended to be open to the public according to laws or regulations.

# The U.S. Situation

In the United States, the laws specifically concerning personal data have been largely focused on what the government can and cannot do with that data. There is, however, legislation being considered, including the Netizens Protection Act of 1997 (HR 1748 105th Cong.), Consumer Internet Privacy Protection Act of 1997 (HR 98 105th Cong.), and the Data Privacy Act of 1997 (HR 2368 105th Cong.).

## Unsolicited Commercial E-mail (Spam)

There is legislation currently pending to update the law on unsolicited advertisements to include electronic means. Even in the absence of federal legislation, Cyber Promotions, one of the larger "spammers" (as those who send electronic unsolicited advertisements are called), has already been found guilty of sending unsolicited advertisements, known as "spam." The existence of this legislation indicates that unsolicited advertising, made easier by technology, is to be approached with caution, and that the legislation should be watched carefully so that it may be complied with should it become law. This is an area where following industry guidelines can be very helpful and limit risks. Some industry guidelines for unsolicited advertising and other privacy issues are discussed below.

## Pending Legislation to Prevent Unsolicited Commercial E-mail (Spam)

- **Unsolicited Commercial Electronic Mail Choice Act of 1997 (S 771)**
- **Electronic Mailbox Protection Act of 1997 (S 875)**
- **Netizens Protection Act (HR 1748)**
- **E-mail Users Protection Act of 1998 (HR 4124)**

# Personal Identifying Information

The Consumer Internet Privacy Protection Act of 1997 is intended to regulate the use by interactive computer services of personally identifiable information provided by subscribers. An interactive computer service, according to HR 98 (105th Cong.), is any information service that provides computer access to multiple users via modem to the Internet, such as an Internet service provider. A related bill, the Data Privacy Act of 1997, identifies the interactive computer service as any information service, system, or access software provider that provides or enables computer access by multiple users to a computer server, including, specifically, a service or system that provides access to the Internet, and an online information service. This definition is extended to any person operating a Web site for commercial or noncommercial purposes, including anyone offering products or services for sale. It will be important to watch the progress and status of these and other legislative actions.

The Federal Trade Commission already has some authority to protect the consumers' privacy on the Internet. In August 1998, the FTC settled a suit it had brought against GeoCities for violating consumers' privacy on the Internet. Although the settlement is not law, it is the first case of privacy violations brought by the FTC, and it can offer a guideline for online conduct concerning privacy. It is particularly helpful, as it shares many principles with the European laws, and Web activity is global.

## Keeping Up to Date

To keep up to date on the status of pending legislation, and to find the text of bills and laws, visit http://thomas.loc.gov to browse the database or to search by word or phrase or bill number.

A listing of "Bills and Regulations Affecting the Interactive Industry" can be found at the Association of Interactive Media's Web site, at www.interactivehq.org/html/bills_regulations.htm.

# Consumers' Personal Identifying Information

The following suggestions concerning collection and distribution of personal data are taken from the settlement. The FTC administrative complaint and proposed agreement are available on the Internet at, respectively, www.ftc.gov/os/1998/9808/geo-cmpl.htm and www.ftc.gov/os/1998/9808/geo-ord.htm.

## Collection of Personal Identifying Information from Consumers

An online service should not make any misrepresentation about its collection or use of personal information, including what information will be disclosed to third parties and how the information will be used. An online service should also not misrepresent the identity of the party collecting any information or the sponsorship of activity on its Web site.

An online service should not collect personal information from any child if the online service or its employees or representatives have actual knowledge that such child does not have his or her parent's permission to provide the information to the online service. (It should be noted that the FTC has obtained an order against GeoCities that places liability on that company if the child has falsely represented that he or she is not a child, although the online service does not knowingly possess information that such representation is false.)

## Notice to Consumers Concerning Collection of Personal Identifying Information—Privacy Notices

An online service should provide clear and prominent notice to consumers, including the parents of children, with respect to the practices of the online service with regard to its collection and use of personal identifying information. Such notice should include disclosure of:

- what information is being collected (e.g., "name," "home address," "e-mail address," "age," "interests")
- its intended use
- the third parties to whom it will be disclosed (e.g., "advertisers of consumer products," "mailing list companies," "the general public")
- the consumer's ability to obtain access to or directly access such information and the means by which he or she may do so
- the consumer's ability to remove directly or have the information removed from respondents' databases and the means by which he or she may do so
- the procedures to delete personal identifying information from the databases of the online service and any limitations related to such deletion

The notice should appear on the home page of the Web sites of the online service and at each location on the sites at which such information is collected.

If the information is limited to tracking information and the collection of the information is described in the notice on the home page, it may be appropriate not to include the notice at the locations at which information is collected.

Adequate notice is likely to be:

- placement of a clear and prominent hyperlink or button labeled PRIVACY NOTICE on the home page, which directly links to the privacy notice screen;

- placement of the disclosure information clearly and prominently on the privacy notice screen, followed on the same screen with a button that must be clicked to make it disappear; and

- placement on the initial screen on which collection of any personal identifying information is collected of a clear and prominent hyperlink which links directly to the privacy notice and which is accompanied by the following statement in bold typeface:

> **NOTICE: We collect personal information on this site. To learn more about how we use your information click here.**

## Concerning Collection of Personal Information from Children

An online service should maintain a procedure for obtaining express parental consent prior to collecting and using a child's personal information.

A screening procedure is likely to be adequate if the online service collects and retains certain personal identifying information from a child, including birth date and the child's and parent's e-mail addresses (hereafter referred to as "screening information"), enabling the online service to identify the site visitor as a child and to block the child's attempt to register with the online service without express parental consent. If the on-line service elects to have the child register with it, the on-line service should:

**Give notice to the child to have his or her parent provide express parental consent to register.**

**Send a notice to the parent's e-mail address for the purpose of obtaining express parental consent.**   The notice to the child or parent shall provide instructions for the parent to go to a specific URL on the Web site to receive information on the practices of the online service regarding its collection and use of personal identifying information from children.

**Provide express parental consent for the collection and use of such information.** The online service's collection of screening information should be by a manner that discourages children from providing personal identifying information in addition to the screening information. All personal identifying information collected from a child should be held by the online service in a secure manner and should not be used in any manner other than to effectuate the notice to the child or parent, or to block the child from further attempts to register or otherwise provide personal identifying information to the online service without express parental consent. The personal identifying information collected should not be disclosed to any third party prior to the receipt of express parental consent. If express parental consent is not received by twenty days after the online service's collection of the information from the child, the online service should remove all such personal identifying information from its databases, except such screening information necessary to block the child from further attempts to register or otherwise provide personal identifying information to the online service without express parental consent.

## Concerning Access to and Removal of Personal Identifying Information

The online service may provide a reasonable means for consumers, including the parents of children, to obtain removal of their or their children's personal identifying information collected and retained by the online service as follows.

For consumers whose personal identifying information has already been collected, the online service may provide a clear and prominent notice to each consumer over the age of twelve concerning:

1. the information that was collected (e.g., "name," "home address," "e-mail address," "age," "interests"); its use(s) and/ or intended use(s); and the third parties to whom it was or will be disclosed (e.g., "advertisers of consumer products," "mailing list companies," "the general public") and with respect to children, that the child's personal identifying information may have been made public through various means, such as by publicly posting on the child's personal home page or disclosure by the child through the use of an e-mail account;

2. the consumer's and child's parents right to obtain access to such information and the means by which (s)he may do so;

3. the consumer's and child's parent's right to have the information removed from the online service's or a third party's databases and the means by which (s)he may do so;

4. a statement that children's information will not be disclosed to third parties, including public posting, without express parental consent to the disclosure or public posting;

5. the means by which express parental consent may be communicated to the online service permitting disclosure to third parties of a child's information; and

6. a statement that the failure of a consumer over the age of twelve (12) to request removal of the information from the online service's databases within twenty (20) days of the notice will be deemed as approval to its continued retention and/or disclosure to third parties by the online service.

For all consumers, including the parents of children, the online service should provide a reasonable and secure method to request access to or directly access their or their children's personal identifying information. Similarly, the online service should provide a reasonable method to request removal of their or their children's personal identifying information from the online service's and/or any applicable third party's databases or an assurance that such information has been removed. The methods may include direct access through password-protected personal profile, return e-mail bearing an electronically verifiable signature, postal mail, or facsimile.

The online service should provide to the parent of a child a reasonable method for communicating express parental consent to the retention and/or disclosure to third parties of the child's personal identifying information. The online service should not use any such information or disclose it to any third party unless and until it receives express parental consent.

If, in response to the notice, the online service has received a request by a consumer over the age of twelve that the online service should remove from its databases the consumer's personal identifying information, or has not received the express consent of a parent of a child to the continued retention and/or disclosure to third parties of a child's personal identifying information within twenty days after the parent's receipt of the notice, the online service should within ten days:

1. Discontinue its retention and/or disclosure to third parties of such information; and

2. Contact all third parties to whom the online service has disclosed the information, if appropriate, requesting that they discontinue using or disclosing that information to other third parties, and remove the information from their databases.

With respect to any consumer over the age of twelve or any parent of a child who has consented to the online service's continued retention and use of personal identifying information, such consumers or parents should have a continuing right to obtain access to their or their child's personal identifying information or removal of such from the online service's databases.

Exception to the above can be made for information that is retained solely for the purposes of Web site system maintenance, computer file back-up, to block a child's attempt to register with or otherwise provide personal identifying information to the online service without express parental consent, or to respond to requests for such information from law enforcement agencies or pursuant to judicial process. Except as necessary to respond to requests from law enforcement agencies or pursuant to judicial process, the online service should not disclose to any third party any information retained in its archived database.

## Retaining Records Concerning Collection of Personal Identifying Information

In the event the Privacy Policy or Notice of the online service becomes an issue with another party, or in a litigation, an online service may wish to retain for five years after the last date of dissemination of a notice a print or electronic copy in HTML format of all documents relating to the notices and privacy policy, including, but not limited to, a sample copy of every information collection form, Web page, screen, or document containing any representation regarding the online service's information collection and use practices. Electronic copies should include all text and graphics files, audio scripts, and other computer files used in presenting information on the World Wide

Web, for five years after the last collection of personal identifying information from a child, all materials evidencing the express parental consent given to respondent.

### Employee Education Concerning Collection of Personal Identifying Information

An online service should deliver a copy of the Privacy Policy and Notice to all current and future principals, officers, directors, and managers, and to all current and future employees, agents, and representatives having responsibilities with respect to the subject matter of this order. The online service should deliver the Privacy Policy and Notice to current personnel within thirty days of its creation and to future personnel within thirty days after the person assumes such position or responsibilities.

An online service should establish an "information practices training program" for any employee engaged in the collection or disclosure to third parties of consumers' personal identifying information. The program should include training about the privacy policies of the online service, information security procedures, and disciplinary procedures for violations of its privacy policies. The online service should provide each current employee with information practices training materials within thirty days of the creation of such materials, and each future employee within thirty days after he or she assumes his or her position or responsibilities.

# Industry Guidelines

It is generally accepted that issues of concern on the Internet, including privacy issues, will require technological, legal, and industry cooperation. There are various methods of protection against cookies and other data collection devices, but that discussion is outside the scope of this topic. Industry Guidelines, however, must be part of our discussion, as they may offer neutral territory on which governments can rely as the harmonization process continues.

The Internet Alliance (IA, formerly Interactive Services Association) has taken stands on Internet privacy and spam. It has made available a "Privacy Tool Kit" for creating and noticing a Privacy Policy. The Tool Kit can be found at www.isa.net/policy/privacy_toolkit.html. IA's Guidelines Concerning Spam can be located at www.isa.net/policy/spamming_guidelines.html. The IA principles and policy are summarized below:

**Potential collection of personal data.**   Those who operate chat areas, newsgroups, and other public forums should indicate to users that information voluntarily disclosed in these areas may result in their receiving unsolicited messages.

**Policy against collecting personal data from forums for unsolicited e-mail.**   Online marketers should avoid collecting personal data (including e-mail addresses) in online forums, such as chat rooms, bulletin boards, and newsgroups, for the purpose of sending unsolicited e-mail, *unless* the forum clearly displays a notice that the collection and use of personal data is permitted.

**Guidelines for e-mail solicitations.**   Online solicitations should:

- be consistent with a forum's or service provider's stated policies
- be clearly identified as solicitations
- disclose the sender's identity
- include notice of consumer privacy practices with e-mail solicitations
- give consumers the ability to exercise choice over whether to receive future e-mails from the sender ("opt-out")
- give consumers the ability to exercise choice over whether their identities are included in any e-mailing list or database used for solicitation ("opt-out")
- give consumers the ability to exercise choice over whether their identities are included in any e-mailing list or database used for solicitation ("opt-out")

There are many laws that affect activities and marketing on the Internet, including copyright and trademark laws, regulations, tax laws, and others. We have chosen to discuss two important areas for advertising on the Internet: collection and use of personal data, and unsolicited advertisements. Information given is accurate at time of writing, but these can be quick-moving issues. Acting with knowledge of the current laws, domestically and internationally, as well as knowledge of pending legislation and court actions, can help limit risks involved in doing business on the Internet. The Internet itself has tools for keeping up with some of the changes. Some sites for doing just that have been mentioned.

# CHAPTER 14

# The Internet Advertising Convergence

W hen online advertising first appeared as a new advertising option, it was dismissed by many in professional advertising circles as a novelty or a fad. What a difference a few short years can make. Today, Internet advertising is a player and recognized as such from the investment firms on Wall Street to the advertising agencies on Madison Avenue. Not only is Internet advertising no longer the new kid on the block, but it has become a force to be reckoned with, influencing, infiltrating, and converging on all forms of communication and advertising.

*Convergence* means the union or merging of technologies, applications, media, world views. The word is often used to describe the inevitable merging of the Internet with TV or the Internet with the telephone. Convergence also occurs within and around Internet advertising. This convergence is taking place between online advertisers and publishers and traditional advertisers. Convergence is occurring in ad forms, their format and delivery. Convergence is also occurring in the types of products and messages being deployed and the selling strategies being used. Indeed, online advertising has taken the advertising world by storm, unabashedly staking its claim.

## Convergence Is *Everywhere!*

**Tony Winders, President (tony@iagency.com)**
**InterActive Agency, Inc. (www.iagency.com)**

**Media, advertising, the Internet, and communication technologies are in the midst of turning life as we know it on its head. Not just in the proliferation of the Internet, but in the consolidation of all media, business, information, and ideas.**

*Continues*

## Convergence Is *Everywhere! (Continued)*

The constant blur of information, entertainment, and news, and their cousins editorial integrity and advertising, have created an endless stream of new challenges and new ways of doing business in the marketing and communications industries. The information revolution is happening right in front of us, and nowhere faster than at the forefront of Internet advertising.

Convergence is happening in the collective skills and like minds of talented people everywhere who are talking about the exhilaration brought on by the rush of the Internet Wave and its infinite possibilities in business and life. Some of the smartest, most ambitious and caring people I have ever met work in the Internet industry and appreciate the medium for much more than for its promise of financial gain, although I've found that to be one of the biggest motivating factors.

The phenomenon of the collapsing of time, or "Internet time," is a real one. As we have connected electronically through our thoughts and words, we have created the time to do more and we're communicating faster. And it's spreading. Six degrees of separation is a thing of the past. Convergence has put us only a few clicks away from everybody; something I call "Two-Click Separation."

The most visibly powerful exhibition of convergence should be when television and the Internet merge all the way. Think about it: all of the interactivity of the Web with the broadcast quality of television and rich 3-D environments. Hello? It's almost here! Tomorrow it will be called "enhanced TV," then "broadband," and perhaps ultimately just "The Network." Couple that with more of the production and broadcasting tools in the hands of "the people" and things could get pretty wacky. And it will all carry some form of advertising. It already does.

Throughout the convergence space, there are amazing pockets of opportunity for savvy online marketers. Mine has been in providing integrated marketing services and demonstrating how messages and brands can consistently traverse multiple media, with various marketing disciplines in play. In the age of convergence, people intercept information at all levels in the information food chain, from the most expensive and highly targeted direct selling opportunity to the ability to stimulate the organic nature of word-of-mouth advertising.

A common language for Internet advertising is emerging, but it's constantly evolving too. Integration is happening quickly at all levels, but not nearly as fast as the good ideas, business relationships, and technology are propelling our industry and the world economy forward. The information revolution is in progress and the dawn of the new millennium will only intensify its effect on business and people in general.

The ultimate convergence will happen when enough people of like minds realize they *can* make a difference, and they use the Internet's potential to bring our collective best interests together in the real world. I'd love to be the agency in charge of that advertising campaign!

## Digital Convergence of All Media

**David Wamsley, CEO and President(dave@adauction.com)**
**Adauction.com (www.adauction.com)**

The convergence of the Web with other forms of mass media has manifested itself in three significant ways over the past two years:

1. **Retailers have created a near-seamless migration of their products sold through:**

   - brick-and-mortar stores and catalogs to e-commerce enterprises

   - Web-based businesses that regularly use traditional media to drive traffic online

   - Marketers—including those representing the Fortune 500—that emphasize their companies' Web presence in all branding and messaging

2. **Online advertising not only has planted itself in mainstream media, but is also proving its worth for building brand awareness and loyalty, testing ad campaigns and creative, and filtering down to reach specific audiences. Advertisers must still compare the benefits of advertising on the Web with television, radio, print, cable, direct mail, and outdoor. The difference today is that media buyers and marketers are integrating the process of buying and selling Web advertising into their core media strategy.**

3. **Online advertising is evolving so fast that it is pushing all forms of media to become digital and more accountable—ultimately collapsing them down into one large platform. This convergence represents a giant step toward simplifying the overall media buying and reporting process. More important, we will soon see the day when all types of media will originate in a digital form—from production to sales to distribution.**

# It's Everywhere, Used by Everyone

"I was quoted five years ago as saying you'd never sell toothpaste on the Internet," remarked G. M. O'Connell, chairman and CEO of True North Communications' Internet advertising unit at the Cannes Advertising Festival's first Cyber Lions awards (as reported in the September 1998 issue of *Small Business Computing & Communications*). G. M. goes on to explain that not only is toothpaste being sold online, but his firm ran a campaign for Mentadent toothpaste in 1998 with a successful sampling and conversion program. Even luminaries in the industry like O'Connell did not foresee that Internet advertising would move at lightning speed from a medium used to sell software and books to a medium used to sell everything from toothpaste to laundry detergent. Online advertising is everywhere being used to sell everything.

As a result, the small group of online advertisers and publishers has become a large group of mainstream advertisers and brand name publishers. Rather, the advertisers are now mainstream, and online publishers have recognizable brand names, with many being part of large media companies. From Procter & Gamble's pivotal role in helping push the industry along through its formation and backing of the Fast Forward organization (as described in Chapter 1) to Unilever's multimillion deal with AOL in 1998, the biggest advertisers in the world are starting to flex their muscles on the virtual landscape. Advertisers, whether trying to reach customers across town or across time zones, are harnessing the power of this digital medium and making it part of their marketing mix.

Every piece of screen real estate is for sale, and the creative talent is constantly figuring out new fun, entertaining, and informative ways to present advertising messages. For example, the online version of the newspaper *USA Today* blended its masthead with the "Got Milk?" campaign, resulting in an animated pitcher pouring milk into the *USA Today* logo (see Figure 14.1). This campaign was deemed innovative by the interactive community and suspect by others. Indeed, Internet advertising, with its technological approach to message delivery, is challenging the old grammar of advertising. With every move, online advertising raises the bar by being more measurable, accountable, targetable, and interactive than any advertising medium before it.

**Figure 14.1**    The "Got Milk?" campaign goes digital on the *USA Today* site.

The Internet is becoming an important part of the arsenal of political campaigning as an outreach and organizing tool. And using the Internet for political advertising is an inevitable extension. As targeting gets more precise, especially in terms of geo-targeting on the Web, we will see more political candidates use of Internet advertising.

How the Internet will be used for political campaign advertising remains to be seen. Since the technology allows for timely and sophisticated message delivery, it has the potential to live up to the greatest ideals of campaigning or the worst we've ever imagined. For example, we might see a banner ad that is literally a mudslinging contest between two candidates similar to the HP Pong game banner ad mentioned in Chapter 2. Or, on the other hand, the Internet might be declared a "no-negative-advertising campaign zone" and only feature ads that promote issues and ideas. The direction is yet to be seen.

We're even seeing the use of the Internet for issue advocacy purposes through Public Service Announcement (PSA) banner ads on everything from educating the public about a health crisis to natural disasters. Some of the best PSA banner ads today come from the American Red Cross (see Figure 14.2), one of the first nonprofits on the Internet.

Indeed, Net companies want to do good work and make a difference as they do well financially. Many of these firms are doing well on paper but are not in the position to make a financial contribution; however, they can donate excess or unsold advertising inventory.

Online publishing powerhouses like HotWired are committed to placing PSAs. Ad networks such as DoubleClick have a PSA program. NetGravity, the ad serving and management technology firm, also has its own program. In fact, the Internet Advertising Bureau helped lay the foundation for this with the Ad Council, which handles public service announcement arrangements for the traditional advertising industry.

**Figure 14.2**   PSA banner ads by the American Red Cross to help raise awareness and generate donations to support their disaster relief work.

## Creative 101: Bandwidth No Magic Bullet for Creative Woes, or "Blue Sky" Thinking Can Obscure Current Weather

**Evan Neufeld, Senior Analyst, Advertising Group (evann@jup.com)**
**Jupiter Communications (www.jup.com)**

The Internet has disappointed some advertisers because, despite the fact that it is digital and interactive, its ad forms don't provide a sensory-heavy experience. Advertisers are accustomed to creating ads, like AT&T's "Rocket Man" spots, that make people cry (it's uncertain if they make anyone switch to AT&T, however), but even the most animated, dynamic, interactive banner won't get a viewer's juices flowing.

Barriers to burgeoning bandwidth—including equipment costs and rollout delays—will impede broadband penetration. It is Jupiter's estimation that, by 2002, only 20 percent of online households will access the Internet via a broadband (i.e., greater than 256 kbps) access solution, equaling only 11.2 million broadband-subscriber households, compared with 45.5 million dial-up households. Advertisers seem to be unaware of this fact, and appear to be willing to trade lack of reach for richness of execution when considering high-speed options as opposed to the

If you are a publisher, you have many options in setting up a PSA program. You can take any PSA ad that requests placement. Or you can designate certain charities that are of particular significance to your company for your PSA program. Or third, you can choose to accept PSAs only from organizations or charities that fit into your corporate mission. In any case, you should demand the same professional process for banner ad development and delivery from such organizations as with any advertiser.

Indeed, advertising may be on everything and everywhere, but a mantra that has continued to ring true in the industry throughout the writing of the first and second editions of this book is that ads need to be built with the technological limitations of the audience in mind. The majority of Web users access the Internet with a 28.8 modem and with a 15-inch screen. Moreover, almost half of all people online in the United States are dialing in through AOL, so that ads, like sites, needs to be built that speak to the lowest common denominator. This advice is heeded by some and dismissed by others.

At the same time, rich media requires greater bandwidth than available to most online users today (as discussed in greater detail in Chapter 2). With greater bandwidth can come more technology-rich ads, ie more television-like ads. We're close, but we're not there yet.

## Watch Out E-mail, Here Comes Instant Messaging

What's faster than e-mail, occurs in real time, and is as popular among teenagers as among business professionals? Instant messaging—an AOL favorite feature—has moved onto the Web en force. With instant messaging, a user can see if a person is

> plain old Web. Such a trade-off is a grave error in judgment. Though experimentation with emerging broadband formats is a savvy move, it should not come at the expense of ignoring the near-term opportunity to reach 60 million "bandwidth-challenged" individuals already online. Games are won by hitting singles and doubles, not by swinging for the fence every time.
>
> Bandwidth + Entertainment = Branding Context. Greater bandwidth provides users with a richer experience that allows for greater usage of the Internet as an entertainment medium. This, in turn, provides the context for more emotionally appealing brand messages, because entertainment activity is generally characterized by longer engagement times and a more captive audience than in the current "quick strike" nature of information gathering online. Users become vested in a narrative or look to an outcome. It is still up to the advertisers, however, to motivate users to interact with their brand in a meaningful way.
>
> The pipe doesn't change the message. Just as early TV commercials were merely scripts read by radio announcers, narrowband ad models, still in the early stages of execution, are simply billboards on the Web. Although bandwidth allows additional creative freedom and richness, it is still the basic concept and message of an advertisement, not the production value, that connects with consumers. Regardless of the size of the pipe, the message must speak to a consumer's needs and emotions.

online and then send a short message in real time, available for an instantaneous response. Whether using AIM or ICQ (both owned by AOL) software (see Figure 14.3), the technologies are free, easily downloadable, and build a tremendous global user base. Watch out e-mail, here comes instant messaging, which blends the best of e-mail, the telephone, and a pager.

The question on everyone's mind is, how will instant messaging incorporate advertising? There is no question that it has the reach and penetration to make the most staid marketer salivate. Ask kids today and they'll tell you that the only way to keep in touch with friends is through instant messaging. To them, this is not just a technology—it's a social necessity.

## Internet, Intranet, and Extranet . . . Oh My!

Online advertising is not just for the Internet anymore. Corporations can now use their intranets (private internal Internet sites, such as for company personnel only) and extranets (semi-private Internet sites often used between companies and their suppliers) to sell corporate programs from training classes to health plans. Internets, intranets, and extranets are all ripe for in-house (internal) advertising, since selling messages works as well inside out as outside in. The government runs ads for its training programs. A company puts up ads for a blood drive. These in-house ads work. It's like the proverbial K-Mart Blue Light Special—when a person is already in your store

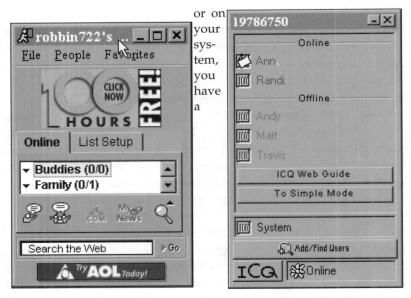

or on your system, you have a

**Figure 14.3** AIM (left) and ICQ (right) instant messaging software hold great advertising potential.

golden opportunity to continue the selling process. Self-promotion works and makes sense and should not be forgotten when going digital.

# Moving Full Speed Ahead

Internet advertising is moving full speed ahead, as is everything Internet. Online advertising has already gone through several stages. It was first met with skepticism, then heralded as full of promise and potential fueled by hype. Today online advertising is making good on its promises and producing results. The long and short of it is that Internet advertising works. And its future looks even brighter.

## Parody: Top Ten Quotes from Top Internet Industry Professionals that ClickZ *Doesn't* Expect to Print in the Near Future

**Ann Handley, Editor in Chief (ann@clickz.com)**
**Andy Bourland, Publisher (andy@clickz.com)**
**The ClickZ Network (www.clickz.com)**

[Note: The Internet industry, with its irreverent sense of wit, finds no greater form of humor than parody. In the spirit of good fun, the ClickZ team put together a "Top Ten Quotes" parody that summarizes the state of the online ad industry. RZ and BA]

1. "Rich media? No problem!"—Bob Pittman, AOL

2. "Our ad inventory is completely sold out. Really. There's nothing left." —Tim Koogle, Yahoo!

3. "Online advertising will represent at least 10 percent of our advertising budget in the coming year."—Denis Beausejour, Procter & Gamble

4. "All the FAST committees have reached consensus and we've accomplished our agenda. My work here is done."—Rich LeFurgy, FAST Forward Steering Committee

5. "Really? I didn't know that!"—The Jacobyte

6. "We have completed the acquisition of . . . "—Avram Glazer, Zapata Corporation

7. "We are pleased to announce a quarterly profit for the first time in our company history."—Jeff Bezos, Amazon.com

8. "To be honest, we have no idea who is on the receiving end of that banner." —Pete Estler, MatchLogic

9. "As I tell site publishers all the time, I'm very comfortable with rate-card pricing."—Brad Aronson, i-frontier

10. "The online ad industry is heading deep South."—Evan Neufeld, Jupiter Communications

# How to Advertise for Free or Almost Free

**Eric Ward (netpost@netpost.com)**
**President, The WardGroup (www.netpost.com)**

First, let me give a personal thanks to Robbin and Brad for inviting me to participate in this book. I've known each of them for several years, and respect their work tremendously. Since I started in this industry back in 1994, I have purposely never written any content for any book publisher, and my decision to author this section is based on my belief in them, not just as Net professionals, but as people. I live in Tennessee and Florida, and had never met Brad until 1995, but in a remarkable coincidence, it turned out that as kids Brad and I lived on the same street in the same town, yet never knew one another.

The following section is a distillation of several presentations I've made around the world on announcing, submitting, introducing, and otherwise promoting a Web site. It is designed so that you can use it yourself to do many of the activities I will be describing. Some of the techniques and activities might seem surprisingly simple, yet they can have a surprisingly positive impact on your site. Spend some time doing some of the things I describe, and you'll see what I mean. The best way to read this section is while you are online, because I will refer to many Web sites you need to see during the process of marketing and promoting your site. Good luck,

Eric Ward

## First Things First: Preparing to Announce and Submit Your Site

Everyone in the world, it seems, has a Web site. In the 10 seconds it takes you to read this sentence, another 100 companies probably will launch Web sites. Like yours, these sites seek an audience. I've said many times that a Web site is nothing but a collection of files on a computer, unless someone decides they want to see them. Then those files come to life. I've been announcing and marketing Web sites since 1994, when I did the first launch awareness building campaign for Amazon.com Books. While my role was not the key to their success, I'd like to think I helped in my own way. There are some Web marketing and promotion techniques that are appropriate for nearly every site, like submitting the site information to Yahoo! for a listing in their well known and highly trafficked directory. To be sure, any decent Web site should be listed with the key search engines and directories. But search engine, directory, and Web guide listings represent just one part of marketing a Web site.

## The Practical, Tactical Approach to Search Engine and Directory Submissions

When a Web site is launched, one of the first tasks the site's owners are faced with is making sure the site is listed with the many search engines and directories that people use to locate Web sites. Submitting a site to search engines and directories is certainly important, but truthfully, it is only one small part of marketing a Web site. Sadly, most site owners don't realize just how many other Web promotion opportunities they've missed. Too often they use a shortcut auto-submission service, and think that's all there is to it.

Think of it this way: For every Web site, there is a perfect collection of search engines, directories, Web guides, site reviewers, announce sites, "What's New" lists, and other places that should be told about it, based on the site's topic, subject, and features.

The frustrating part of this process is finding these perfect places to submit to, once you've pass those easy first 20 or so that we all know about. For example, you may know that you can announce your site at several resources designed just for that purpose. But the value and quality of these types of announce sites varies wildly, as does their impact on your site. While getting your site featured at Netscape's "What's New" (see Figure 1) typically results in tens of thousands of visitors to your site, at the resource called "What's New Too," at http://nu2.com (see Figure 2), your announcement will likely yield only a trickle of visits, maybe none at all. This is my cardinal rule of Web site submissions: All submission sites are not created equal.

In addition, the reality is that the Netscape "What's New" site is heavily reviewed, meaning that just because you submit your site to them does not mean you will be selected.

## You're Ready to Submit Your Site, But Is Your Site Ready to Be Submitted?

If search engines are one of the primary ways people find Web sites, then making sure the search engines can find and properly index your site's HTML is certainly important. One of the most common mistakes I see from the sites I work with is that many of

**Figure 1**   Netscape's "What's New" area announces new sites.

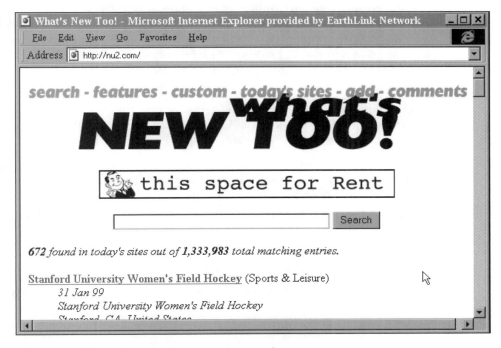

**Figure 2**   "What's New Too" announces new sites.

them tried to launch to the public without realizing they had serious design flaws that kept the search engines from being able to index them properly.

I realize there are some very legitimate reasons why you might not care if the big search engines can index your site, but for most Web marketers, being indexed by search engines, and available to searchers, is very important. What many Web designers don't realize is that many accepted Web designs that look nice to human viewers actually discourage search engines from being able to index them.

Search engines are also called bots, crawlers, and spiders. The key point to understand about them is that they work by accessing your Web server and downloading your site's pages into their huge database. After they've downloaded your site's pages, they use the HTML text they found on them to determine how they will rank your pages for searchers, and for various search terms.

As of January 1999, the three primary hindrances to proper search engine indexing are:

**Pages that use frames.** Most of the major search engines cannot follow frame links. If you use frames, be sure to use an alternative method for search engines to enter and index your site. To learn more about this, go to www.searchenginewatch.com/webmasters/frames.html.

**Pages created "on-the-fly" by database programs.** Generating pages via CGI or database delivery means that some of the search engines won't be able to index the resulting pages that are generated. Possible solution: Consider creating static pages (files) that can augment the database-delivered pages.

**Pages that are made up only, or mostly, of images.** If your site uses mostly images for content and navigation, instead of text, you can expect the search engines will have a harder time determining what your site is about. One possible fix: Make sure that any page that is primarily made up of graphics has a text HTML description of it as well. A great example of this approach can be seen at www.coolshopping.com (see Figure 3).

The bottom line is to make your site as search engine–friendly as possible. There are many sites dedicated to helping you do just that, and here are my personal selections for the most accurate information on this subject:

- Danny Sullivan's Search Engine Watch (www.searchenginewatch.com, Figure 4). Danny is a friend who not only is a nice person, but is also the single most knowledgeable authority on search engines in the world.

- Submit It: Tips for Announcing Web Sites to Search Engines (www.submit-it.com/subopt.htm).

- HTML Unleashed: "Strategies for Indexing and Search Engines" (www.webreference.com/dlab/books/html-pre/43-0.html).

- WebReference.com's search engine tutorial (www.webreference.com/content/search/).

**Figure 3**  The Coolshopping opening page is mostly images, so they include an HTML description.

## Getting Organized: The Web Site Questionnaire

Assuming you are sure your site is search engine–ready, you can begin the process of announcing and submitting your site.

One of the first activities you should engage in is submitting the site's name and URL to the appropriate search engines, directories, Web guides, announce sites, and other outlets. Some people believe that this is an easy and quick process, best performed by an automated multi-submission program or service. Nothing could be further from the truth. After five years of doing it, I can promise you that if you use a shortcut submission service, you will be missing the very submission outlets that matter the most for your site.

Remember my earlier point: For every Web site, there is a perfect collection of search engines, directories, guides, e-zines, Web-zines, site reviewers, announce sites, and other outlets that need to know about it, based on its subject and features.

In other words, no two Web sites should have the same announcement and submission campaign, because every site has a different intended audience and features. Since automated submission services submit to the same batch of places without giving any

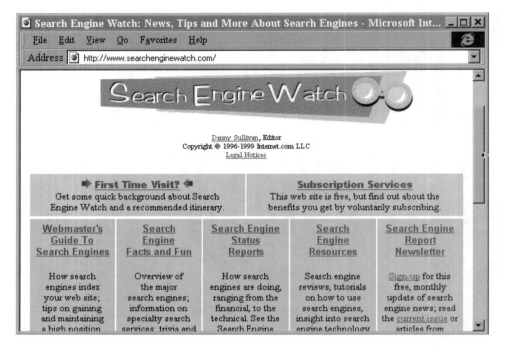

**Figure 4** Search Engine Watch is the premium site for search engine registration information.

consideration to your site's specific subject matter, those directories and search engines that are a perfect match for your subject matter will be completely missed.

There are certain pieces of information about your site that you'll need to have handy as you make submissions. You'll need these bits and pieces of information over and over again during the Web promotion process, because many of the places you will be contacting or submitting to will request them. If you've ever made a submission to a search engine, you know what I'm referring to. All of them require you to submit at the very least the URL for your site, and some submission forms require 20 or 30 fields of information. Yahoo!, for example, has four screens of fields you must fill in, in order to have your site reviewed for a possible listing. Some sites request a contact name and phone number; others request a description of your site in a certain number of words.

I use a tool I created called a Web Site Questionnaire. An abbreviated version of it is included in the sidebar. If you answer each of the questions on the Web Site Questionnaire, and then save the file for future reference, you can use it over and over again during the submission process. When I'm making submissions, I have the Web Site Questionnaire open in my word processor, and open my Web browser as well, so I can cut-and-paste from one to the other as I make submissions. Yes, I know there are some programs and tools that will cut-and-paste for you. Trust me, don't use them. Once you have this sheet finished you can begin making some submissions.

## Web Site Questionnaire

Company name
Address
City
County
State/Province
ZIP/Postal code
Country
Phone number
FAX number
E-mail address
800 number

Contact person for more information about this site
    That person's e-mail address:
    That person's phone number:
    That person's title/position (e.g., Marketing Coordinator):
    What is the time zone for the contact person?

Title of the Web site:
The URL of the Web site:
    http://
The date this site was first made available on the Web:
How often (roughly) is this site's content updated?
    (Daily, weekly, etc.)
This Web site's administrator:
    (Name)
    (Admin e-mail)

Do you sell products or services from your site directly via online transactions?
    (Yes or No)
Are these transactions conducted using a secure server environment?
    (Yes or No)
About how many products do you offer for sale from the site?
FROM what country (or countries) do you ship?
TO what regions of the world do you ship?
Languages spoken other than English:

*Continues*

## Web Site Questionnaire *(Continued)*

**Consumer Protection Databases**
Are you registered with:
BizRate
Public Eye
BBBOnLine

**Satisfaction-refund policy**
What methods of payment do you accept for your products/services?

**Technical information about the Web site**
What is the actual I.P. (Internic) number for your site?
Does your site have any of the following technical or design features?
Frames
A non-frames version
Animated GIFs
Javascript
Java
Shockwave
Flash
VRML
Dynamic HTML
Push
Chat
Does your site offer audio?
Yes or No, and include the type of audio below
Video?
Yes or No, and include the type of video below
Any other Web-specific technical features at the site?

**E-zine/Web-zine questions**
Do you offer an e-zine or Web-zine on a particular topic that users can sign up for?
Description (strict 80 character maximum length):
Directions for how to subscribe:
Is there a fee for this e-zine?
Publication frequency:
Do you accept paid advertising in this zine?
If yes, what is the CPM? (Cost Per Thousand)

**Discussion list/Listserv questions**
Do you offer a discussion list on a particular topic that users can sign up for?
How is your list technically run?
(Majordomo, Listserv, Listproc, etc.)
Name/address of list (brief: the part before the "@"):

Description (strict 80 character maximum length):

Directions for how to subscribe:

Do you accept paid advertising on this list?

If yes, what is the CPM? (Cost Per Thousand)

How many subscribers does the list currently have?

Is this discussion list moderated?

Is there a fee to belong to subscribe to this list?

**Keywords**

List up to 10 keywords below for the site. These words are in case you submit to a search engine or directory that asks specifically for keywords. Most do not. These words do not have to be identical to the words you have placed in your site's META keyword tag. I suggest that you use multiple words and phrases in your site's META keyword tag, but for this list, just give single words, in lower-case plural form: for example, "trips," instead of "trip" or "Trip."

1)

2)

3)

4)

5)

6)

7)

8)

9)

10)

Categories/Headings that you feel are most appropriate for your site to be listed under in directories:

1)

2)

3)

4)

5)

6)

7)

8)

9)

10)

Remember that some sites select the heading they put you under, regardless of what you ask for. Also, most directories are now running 1–5 weeks lag time from when they receive press releases/registration requests to when your site appears.

*Continues*

## Web Site Questionnaire *(Continued)*

### Site Description

Please write four versions of your site description, as you would like it to appear. (Many places allow only these amounts of text, so please stick to the numbers.)

Tip: Make these descriptions have as many of your most important keywords as possible.

Version 1) Description up to 15 words:

Version 2) Description up to 30 words:

Version 3) Description up to 60 words:

Version 4) Description up to 100 words:

### Educational relevancy

If you have content that would be helpful to teachers to use in a classroom setting, what is the appropriate grade level?

Preschool, K–6, 7–8, 9–12

### Press Release

Please include here a press release about your site, along with a contact name, phone number, and e-mail address for that contact person.

# Finding the Most Appropriate Resources to Announce and Submit Your Site

An announcement and submission campaign for a new launch will involve making submissions to many different types of locations. Some of the most obvious are major directories like Yahoo! and search engines such as Infoseek and Lycos. There are hundreds, perhaps thousands of places exist where you could potentially announce your site's existence. The truth is that the majority of these places are useless to you, and will not serve any purpose for your site.

The key tactic I use is to hunt for and submit or announce only to the highest quality edited outlets that are used by the type of people I want to know my site exists. I say "edited" because if a submission outlet allows submissions from any and all sites (not edited for quality), then the quality of many of the sites submitted there will be awful, and the directories will be nearly worthless. While there are thousands and thousands of possible places you can submit and announce a site to, most are not edited, and contain so much spam, junk sites, pornography, and other useless content that you shouldn't waste your time with them. An edited directory like Yahoo! only lists sites that meet criteria set forth internally by its editors. There are services that can make submissions for you, as well as services that can help you find the sites you need to be submitting to, and I will discuss them later, but for now, let's proceed on our own. Also, there are some search engines and directories, like www.GoTo.com, that allow you to buy a high-ranking listing.

## Keeping a History of the Submissions You Make

You have several options you can use to keep up with the many submissions you will be making. I use a paper tracking method. The reason I like a paper method over keeping records only on a PC is that often PCs crash, or get upgraded; or in a corporate setting, you might move to a new office and a new machine, or any one of a number of things. It's a nightmare if you lose a couple years' worth of submission records. If you do opt for keeping records on a PC, then at least make backups and keep a printed copy as well.

## General Search Engines

Currently, the "Big Six" search engines are considered to be:

| | |
|---|---|
| Infoseek | www.infoseek.com |
| AltaVista | altavista.digital.com |
| Lycos | www.lycos.com |
| Webcrawler | www.webcrawler.com |
| Excite | www.excite.com |
| HotBot | www.hotbot.com |

Other lesser-known search engines you should submit to are:

| | |
|---|---|
| PlanetSearch | www.planetsearch.com |
| NorthernLight | www.northernlight.com |
| Anzwers | http://server2.anzwers.ozemail.net/index.html |

Sometime in early 1999 Microsoft is expected to begin accepting direct submissions at their new search engine.

The one thing the above search engines have in common is that they accept listings from sites regardless of the subject matter or topic of the site. This is why it's sometimes impossible to find what you're looking for when you do a search at a major search engine. There are simply too many millions of pages out there being indexed by the major search engines.

What many people fail to recognize is that there are search engines devoted to specific topics and subjects, which are much more focused than the major search engines. For example, there is a popular search engine/directory combo just for Canadian and Alaskan Web sites, called Alcanseek (www.alcanseek.com, see Figure 5). There's even a search engine devoted just to funny Web sites, called HumorSearch (www.humorsearch.com).

These niche search engines and directories have their pros and cons. On the one hand, they get far fewer searchers using them compared to the big boys like AltaVista, but on the other hand, the users of these niche search engines and directories

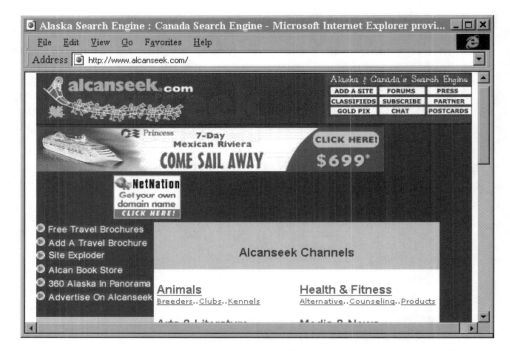

**Figure 5** Alcanseek is a popular search engine/directory combination for Canadian and Alaskan Web sites.

have a far greater likelihood of finding your site, because you're not competing with millions of sites. Of course, the challenge rests in finding these niche search engines. Here's some help.

First, try Yahoo!'s excellent list of Search Engines: www.yahoo.com/Computers_and_Internet/Internet/World_Wide_Web/Searching_the_Web/Search_Engines. Then, you might also try iSleuth: www.isleuth.com (see Figure 6).

Note that almost every search engine now has a human-reviewed site guide along with the search features. If your site gets the attention of the guide editors, the results for your site can be significant.

## General Directories

The big daddy, of course, is Yahoo! (www.yahoo.com), but many other excellent directories exist:

| | |
|---|---|
| MiningCo | www.miningco.com |
| LookSmart | www.looksmart.com |
| Snap | www.snap.com (see Figure 7) |
| Starting Point | www.stpt.com |

**Figure 6**    iSleuth is a good resource for locating niche search engines.

**Figure 7**    Snap is one of the newer search engines on the block.

## "What's New" Announcement Sites

"What's New" announcement sites are designed just for announcing new Web sites, or new content additions to sites that already exist. In the early days of the Web back in 1993, one of the biggest and best places to go to find listings of new sites, or to submit a new site, was the NCSA "What's New" page. Sadly, it was closed down a few years ago. There are still many great places you can use to announce your site. Like directories, though, the best ones are the most heavily edited. An example is the Netscape "What's New" site, located at http://home.netscape.com/netcenter/new.html.

As I mentioned earlier, if the Netscape editors select your site, you could expect thousands and thousands of visits to your site as a result. This is because so many hundreds of thousands of people go to the Netscape "What's New" page daily. The difficulty is that because this site is so popular, they get literally hundreds of new submissions every day, but only feature a tiny percentage of them. Only the best of the best sites get featured here.

This is the opposite of another popular announce site, called "What's New Too" (http://nu2.com). At What's New Too, anyone can submit a site and it will automatically be featured. This sounds great, but realize that this also means the quality of the sites announced varies wildly. This is not to knock the folks at What's New Too, because they are providing a nice free service; however, don't expect that by submitting to What's New Too you will get much—if any—traffic to your site as a result.

Here's a list of some of the better known "What's New" announcement sites:

| | |
|---|---|
| Netscape What's New | http://home.netscape.com/netcenter/new.html |
| What's New Too | http://nu2.com. |
| Net-happenings | http://scout.cs.wisc.edu/scout/net-hap/ |
| What's Nu | http://www.whatsnu.com/index.html |

To find others, and to see if any exist in your specific subject, go to:

www.yahoo.com/Computers_and_Internet/Internet/World_Wide_Web/
Searching_the_Web/Indices_to_Web_Documents/What_s_New/

## Best of the Web and What's Cool Outlets

You may have heard of online (and print) outlets that feature the best of the best Web sites, such as The Cool Site of the Day (http://cool.infi.net), USA Today Hot Sites (www.usatoday.com/life/cyber/ch.htm, see Figure 8), and Yahoo! Picks of the Week (www.yahoo.com/picks/).

There are literally hundreds and hundreds of similar types of outlets. While the above-mentioned "Best Of" sites are excellent and legitimate, many others are useless to you. Over the years, I've tried to become friends with the folks that make the selections at these major edited outlets. I've done so by respecting their time and quality standards. I don't send them sites that I know won't be selected. Back when I did the Amazon.com announcement campaign, it was easy to get the attention of an editor at Yahoo! Picks of the Week. There was not as much competition, and the Amazon.com site was excellent. It was a natural to be featured as a "special pick." Times have changed, though, and the competition is now fierce.

Based on my experience with the "Best of the Web" type outlets, here are my opinions from a Web marketing perspective.

For the high end "Best Of" outlets, like Cool Site of the Day, Project Cool, and Netscape's What's Cool, it is useless to submit a site for consideration unless that site is absolutely exceptional. Glenn Davis, the founder of the original Cool Site of the Day, once told me he gets about 100 junk submissions for every one good one. He also told me that he never selects a site that is submitted to him via an automated submission service. He rightfully feels that if the person submitting won't even take the time to contact him individually, then that person's site isn't likely to be any good anyway.

The bottom line is that if your site is a few pages of company and product information, then it's not going to get selected for coverage or review by the major awards sites. Why should it? This also means you should beware of any Web promotion service that brags about how it will submit your site to 100 Best of the Web or other awards outlets. It really comes down to common sense. No editor who reviews Web sites on a daily basis wants to be spammed by impersonal bulk e-mail submissions announcing a plain vanilla site. I know this to be true, because I review Web sites for several online and print magazines myself, and I always delete e-mail submissions from people who obviously haven't taken the time to know who I am and what types of sites I like to cover.

**Figure 8**   USA Today has its own page that lists top Web sites.

In addition to the major Best Of and awards sites I mentioned earlier, there are many hundreds of other outlets that select, review, or otherwise feature Web sites on a daily, weekly, or monthly basis. The quality of these varies significantly. Some are even scams. One scam I see often is where someone creates an awards site that presumably reviews great Web sites, and then sends e-mail to thousands and thousands of sites the scammer wants to give awards to, asking them to display the awards logo or banner at their site. The scammer does this repeatedly, so that in time she ends up with a nice collection of inbound links to her awards site from all the sites she has given awards to. See the scam here? She really just wants to build a collection of links to her own site.

### How to Find the Best Awards Sites for Submissions

So how do you avoid these types of outlets and identify the ones that make sense for your site? Go to Yahoo!'s section that lists all the top Best Of and awards sites (http://dir.yahoo.com/Computers_and_Internet/Internet/World_Wide_Web/Best_of_the_Web/). Use this to research and identify the most appropriate places you can submit to. As you look at this list, you will see that the key is that you have to take the time to seek out and identify the best outlets to submit to that are a match for your site's content. Submitting to a hundred random awards sites you've never even visited and which have nothing to do with your site's content is a waste of time, and irritates the people you were trying to impress.

## Usenet Newsgroups

Newsgroups often have just the niche you'd like to reach; however, not all accept blatant commercial posts. Also, the specific groups available will vary by service provider. The best way to approach them? Begin by reading the newsgroup charters, and by actually participating. Visit the Usenet Charters site at www.lib.ox.ac.uk/internet/news/faq/by_group.index.html (Figure 9).

If you are new to the world of newsgroups, one of the single best ways to learn about, search for, and participate in them is through Deja News (www.dejanews.com, see Figure 10), which offers a Web-based interface to the most popular Usenet newsgroups.

## Learn Appropriate Internet Marketing Practices

One of my favorite places to recommend people visit to learn about acceptable Internet marketing practices is Tenagra's net.acceptable site at http://marketing.tenagra.com/net-acceptable.html (see Figure 11).

## Sites That Help You Announce Your Site

There are sites that have been created to help you choose places to announce your site. Link Exchange's Directory Guide (www.directoryguide.com, see Figure 12) is an extensive catalog of search engines and directories that accept Web site announcements. They reviewed over 1,000 sites and selected 400 they felt provided the best promotion value to Web marketers. They regularly review and add new listings to keep the guide current. Other useful sites are the Central Registry (www.CentralRegistry.com/thelist.htm), FreeLinks (www.freelinks.com), and The Definitive Search Engine Submission

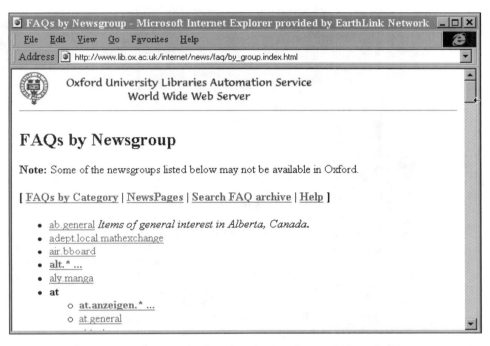

**Figure 9**   The Usenet Charters site lists the charters for operation of all Usenet groups.

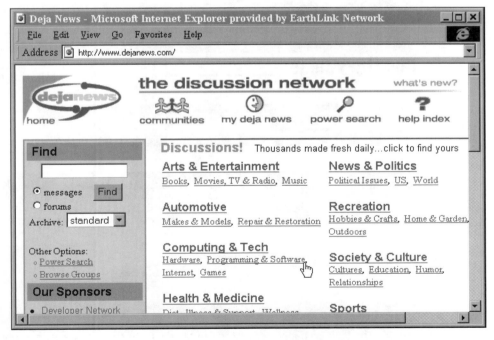

**Figure 10**   Deja News provides a comprehensive listing of newsgroups.

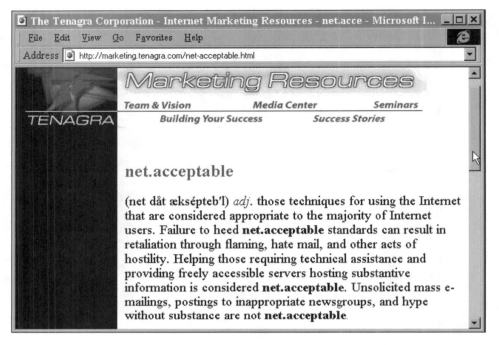

**Figure 11**  Tenagra's net.acceptable site gives examples of appropriate Internet etiquette.

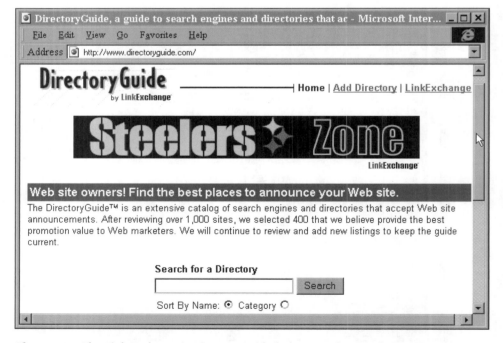

**Figure 12**  The Link Exchange's DirectoryGuide helps you choose places to announce your site.

Page–Finding Site (www.geocities.com/~laisha/submit/index.html). Use these resources to locate useful sites, but never submit your site to any person, search engine, directory, or Web guide without first taking a minute to visit their site and learn who they are and what they want.

# Content Rating, Reciprocal Links, Offline Promotions, and Other Techniques

There are certain Web site promotion options that only the owner or publisher of the site can evaluate and pursue. Many such opportunities exist. Some are better than others, and not all are appropriate for every site.

## Rating Your Web Site's Content

One of the emerging trends on the Web is rated content, where the site owners voluntarily rate the appropriateness of their sites' content for children. Regardless of your beliefs about the ethics of this, it is an issue we all must deal with, and thus I suggest you take a moment and rate the content of your site with the RSACi organization. This requires you to insert a new META tag into your site's HTML on the pages you decide to rate. All details of the RSACi system, including the online form you use to rate your site, can be found at www.rsac.org/homepage.asp (see Figure 13).

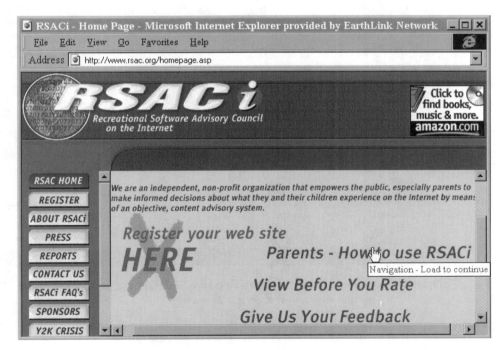

**Figure 13**   RSACi has a system to help you rate your site.

Similarly, an organization called "Family Friendly Sites" offers a service where they will list you in their directory in exchange for placing their "Family Friendly" logo/banner on your site. Details can be found at www.virtuocity.com/family/Index.cfm.

## Offline Promotional Products

You might consider giving away T-shirts with your Web site logo on them, or offering them as an incentive for users who sign up for an e-mail newsletter. I have seen high quality work from one company that produces such T-shirts, called Web T-shirts (www.webtshirt.com). I also like Web Cards (www.printing.com, see Figure 14), which are postcard-sized cards that feature your Web site on one side and copy of your choice on the back. Think of them as extra-large business cards. I've given out hundreds at the various conferences I speak at, and everyone who looks at them loves them.

**Figure 14** Promote your Web site offline with Web Cards, a postcard with your Web site on one side and text on the other.

# Reciprocal Links

If you offer reciprocal links to other sites, meaning you give them a link if they give you a link, there are several directories that want to know about your site. The quality of these directories is often suspect. Use caution.

**Missing Link:** reciprocal link finder (www.igoldrush.com/missing/)

**Link-Me:** A reciprocal links exchange database (www.iwr.com/free/reciprocal.htm)

# Inbound Links

In addition to reciprocal links, you may want to engage in a campaign of requesting links to your site from other sites that are either similar to yours or that offer content that is complementary to yours. For example, if you have a Web site that sells hand-made fly-fishing lures, then you may want to see if you can get a link to your site from sites that have content related to fly fishing but that aren't competing with you for the same type of product sales.

Over the past year or so the climate regarding link swapping or granting inbound links to sites has changed remarkably. While it is definitely still possible to get high-quality inbound links to your site at no cost, it is becoming harder, and the very task of managing an inbound link–seeking campaign is far more complex than it once was. Here's why. Free links are rarer these days, as folks realize that links are worth money, and services are appearing that connect buyers and sellers of links (text-based or otherwise). Let's say you have identified 50 sites that you would like to have links on pointing back to your site. Some are directories with no strings attached, some are topical site guides, some are specific to certain regions, some are even other sites in your industry that look promising. A nice mix, you think, and now you'd like to begin asking them for links.

As you approach these sites, here's what you have to keep up with.

- The name of the site
- The URL
- The name of the person who runs the site
- The e-mail address of that person
- The date you contact that person
- The date he or she responds
- The resulting deal (some will say yes, some no, others will not reply at all, others will want a link back from you, some may want money for links, some will be out of town and take weeks to reply, etc.)
- The status of the deal

- Verification of the link in place

- Checking for links over time (yes some folks swap links and then pull yours for odd reasons)

So, as you can imagine, at any given point in your inbound link–seeking campaign you have many sites and deals to keep up with. (And remember that such campaigns really never end--you should constantly be pursuing them.)

Here are my experienced-based opinions on how to do this well. I do not believe that you can out-source an inbound link–seeking campaign to a third party. There are simply too many areas for abuse and nobody will care as much about your site as you will. The main problem is judging performance. If you try and pay them only for the links they generate for you, then they will be more inclined to look for the sites that are most likely to grant a link, regardless of the quality. Heck, there are a million free-for-all-links-pages out there, but I wouldn't want to be on them, and I'd never pay a cent to be on any of them, because their quality is so bad. So, if you opt to pay based on numbers of links generated, set some quality control standards right up front. And reserve the right of approval for any link deals.

The other challenge with having someone else do your inbound link–seeking campaign is that since each site they contact will have a different demand, your third party will have to be given the right to negotiate on your behalf. Are you willing to give them that authority over your site? I'm not. If they contact someone who says they will give you a link in exchange for a link back to your site, do you want a third party telling them yes, basically giving them the control to add links to your site? And what if the site they contact says that they will give you a link for $10 a month? Do you want some third party spending your money this way?

One option is to reserve the right to say yes or no to any linking agreement someone negotiates for you, and this I encourage. However, if you do this, it slows the process so much that it makes it nearly impossible for anyone to make any money doing your link seeking. If it takes an entire day to negotiate a $25-a-month link (e-mails back and forth, phone calls, return calls, etc.), and you are paying your link seeker $20 per accepted in-link, then your link seeker isn't going to be a very happy person. These are just a couple of the sticking points in having a third party do an inbound link–seeking campaign for you. Others include the verification that the link is up and working right, reviewing the linking site from time to time to be sure the site hasn't dropped the link (it happens) or put up a porno banner right above your link (this I've seen happen). And all this before you even know if that link on their page will generate one single click and deliver someone to your page.

The truth is that an inbound link–seeking campaign is more of an administrative task than a strategic one. I can spend a few days and easily identify 50 perfect sites that I'd like a link on. It will then take weeks, even months, to coordinate and negotiate the deals with each site I located. Without a tracking tool or spreadsheet (what I use), it's impossible to do this efficiently.

All this brings me back to the key point: You must take control of your inbound linking efforts on your own. Do it in-house, yourself. Nobody cares about your site as much as you. The logistics of it are better, as will be the quality of the sites you are linked on and the deals you negotiate on your own behalf. There is one aspect of the campaign you *can* pay a third party for: site discovery. It can take a long time to locate top-quality sites to seek a link on. My clients have me do that part for them, and I provide them with a list of 25, 50, or 100 sites that make the best strategic sense for them to be linked on. Then, they pursue the link seeking in-house, negotiating each one as they go along, using a tracking sheet as they do it. They save time and money, we each use our strengths to their best advantage, and there is no abuse of the system or cracks for things to fall through. Ask yourself this question: Would you rather pay thousands of dollars to have someone negotiate blindly for you, or pay a few hundred for the best link leads and negotiate them yourself?

# Conclusion

Hopefully this section didn't scare you off. Sure, there is a lot to do, but you don't have to do it alone. There are several good third-party services, like my own, that can help you. Also, the techniques I describe above are just a part of an overall process. There are many, many other techniques you can use. Send me an e-mail (TheWardReport@netpost.com) if you'd like to subscribe to my e-mail–based newsletter that reviews the best new Web marketing techniques that you can engage in yourself.

# Resource Directory

Following in the tradition of the first edition, we are including a Resource Directory of contact information of key companies, products, and services in the online advertising industry. We compiled this directory while writing the first edition because we needed the basic contact information for many companies and couldn't find this information in one place on the Net. Today, there are several search engines, directories, and resource sites of online advertising resources, but these services provide links, not straight contact information. The goal of this revised directory is to provide you with valuable contact information in one convenient place. A last word: It should be noted that companies in this industry are constantly forming, merging, and changing. It is inevitable that some of the contact information presented here will change as soon as this book is published. Companies listed here are arranged in the following categories:

- Ad Management Technologies
- Ad Networks
- Alternative Ad Models
- Associations (National)
- Auction
- Auditing Services
- Banner Exchange Programs
- Conferences and Events
- Contests
- Directories of E-mail Discussion Lists and Newsletters
- E-mail List Brokers/Services
- E-mail List Software

- Loyalty Programs
- Market Research Firms
- Measurement Technologies
- Personalization Technologies
- Promotion Services
- Rating Firms
- Representation Firms
- Resources (E-mail Discussion Lists and Newsletters, Informational Sites, and Online Publications)

# Ad Management Technologies

### Accipiter

URL: www.accipiter.com

E-mail: info@engage.com

Company: Engage Technologies / Accipiter

Address: 4000 Wake Forest Rd, Raleigh, NC 27609

Phone: 919.872.7755    Fax: 919.872.5060

Description: Ad serving, management, and personalization software.

### Ad Cafe

URL: www.infohiway.com/adcafe/adcafe1.htm

E-mail: feedback@infohiway.com

Company: Infohiway, a division of Rocky Mountain Internet

Address: 1099 18th Street, 30th Floor, Denver, CO 80202

Phone: 303.313.0872    Fax: 303.672.0711

Description: Ad Cafe works with a simple Web interface to publish, target, track, and manage advertising on your Web site.

### Ad Stream

URL: http://www.realmedia.com/rm_home.html

E-mail: rmsales@realmedia.com

Company: Real Media

Address: 32 E. 31st St., 9th Floor, New York, NY 10016

Phone: 212.725.4537   Fax: 212.725.4573

Description: Web management tool that randomly rotates banner ads throughout a site and provides reports on impressions and click-throughs.

## Adfinity Service Bureau

URL: www.247media.com/techno/te_adfin.htm

E-mail: kforkish@247media.com

Company: 27/7 Media

Address: 1250 Broadway, 27th Floor, New York, NY 10001

Phone: 703.519.6816   Fax: 212.760.1774

Description: The Adfinity Service Bureau is an ad delivery system that offers advanced targeting features, extensive reporting capabilities, and accurate inventory management, giving Web publishers a turnkey ad revenue solution.

## AdForce

URL: www.adforce.com

E-mail: info@adforce.com

Company: AdForce

Address: 10101 North De Anza Blvd., Suite 210, Cupertino, CA 95014

Phone: 408.873.3680   Fax: 408.873.3693

Description: AdForce services both publishers and advertisers with its system of campaign targeting and scheduling to ad delivery, reporting, auditing, and billing.

## Adjuggler

URL: www.adjuggler.com

E-mail: aj@dn.net

Company: digitalNATION

Address: 5515 Cherokee Ave., Alexandria, VA 22312-2309

Phone: 703.642.2800   Fax: 703.642.0261

Description: Banner rotation tool that gives you a full range of powerful management capabilities to ensure complete control of advertising action on your Web site.

## AdKnowledge

URL: www.adknowledge.com

E-mail: webmaster@adknowledge.com

Company: AdKnowledge, Inc.

Address: 2191 East Bayshore Road, Palo Alto, CA 94303

Phone: 650.842.6500    Fax: 650.842.0665

Description: Users can plan, buy and traffic, target and serve, report and analyze all Web advertising through one system.

## AdKnowledge System

URL: www.adknowledge.com

E-mail: mschott@adknowledge.com

Company: AdKnowledge

Address: 2191 East Bayshore Road, Palo Alto, CA 94303

Phone: 650.842.6500    Fax: 650.842.0665

Description: The AdKnowledge System was designed with advertisers and agencies in mind and includes the Planner, Campaign Manager, SmartBanner, Reporter, and Advisor to plan, manage, and deliver an  Internet advertising campaign.

## AdManager

URL: www.accipiter.com

E-mail: info@engage.com

Company: Engage Technologies

Address: 100 Brickstone Square, 1st Floor, Andover, MA 01810

Phone: 978.684.3884    Fax: 978.684.3636

Description: Automates online advertising management for Web sites, automatically delivering inventory, scheduling and targeting ads, and generating up-to-the-minute, customized reports.

## AdServer Enterprise & AdServer Network

URL: www.netgravity.com

E-mail: info@netgravity.com

Company: Netgravity

Address: 1900 S. Norfolk Street, Suite 150, San Mateo, CA 94403

Phone: 650.425.6000    Fax: 650.425.6060

Description: Automates the online advertising management process—from inventory management, to the targeting and delivery of ads, to the generation of performance reports.

## Bannermatic

URL: www.getcruising.com/crypt/banmat.html

E-mail: crypt@getcruising.com

Company: GetCruising

Description: Free CGI scripts that make it easy to set up a banner rotation system on your home page, or set up a counter to see your hits. Not recommended for medium- and high-traffic sites.

## Bondsmith

URL: www.bondsmith.com

E-mail: contact@bondsmith.com

Company: Bondsmith Inc.

Address: One Kendall Square, Bldg. 600, Suite 211, Cambridge, MA 02139

Phone: 816.471.7627    Fax: n/a

Description: Banner advertising management, and exchange for publishers, advertisers, and ad reps.

## Campaign Management

URL: www.matchlogic.com

E-mail: info@matchlogic.com

Company: MatchLogic

Address: 10333 Church Ranch Blvd., Westminster, CO 80021

Phone: 303.222.2000    Fax: 303.222.2001

Description: Third-party ad management tools for publishers and advertisers.

## Central Ad PRO 3.0J

URL: www.centralad.com

E-mail: support@centralad.com

Company: Central Ad Software

Address: 263 Warren St., Waltham, MA 02154

Phone: n/a    Fax: n/a

Description: Banner rotation software.

## Direct Media

URL: www.directmedia.com

E-mail: mbartk@ix.directmedia.com  Contact: Max Bartko

Company: Acxiom

Address: 200 Pemberwick Road, P.O. Box 4565, Greenwich, CT 06830

Phone: 203.532.1000    Fax: 203.531.1452

Description: An Internet ad buying placement and testing service designed for direct marketers.

## DoubleClick DART

URL: www.doubleclick.net

E-mail: info@doubleclick.net

Company: DoubleClick

Address: 41 Madison Ave., 32nd Floor, New York, NY 10010

Phone: 212.271.2542    Fax: 212.889.0062

Description: DoubleClick DART offers complete ad management including targeting, delivering, reporting, and billing.

## MatchLogic

URL: www.matchlogic.com

E-mail: info@matchlogic.com

Company: Matchlogic Inc+G44.

Address: 10333 Church Ranch Blvd., Westminster, CO 80021

Phone: 303.222. 2000   Fax: 303.222.2001

Description: Ad management and measurement solutions for publishers and advertisers.

## NetGravity AdServer/AdCenter

URL: www.netgravity.com

E-mail: info@netgravity.com

Company: NetGravity Inc.

Address: 1900 S. Norfolk Street, Suite 150, San Mateo, CA 94403

Phone: 650.425.6000    Fax: 650.425.6060

Description: Provides software for management of ad delivery as well as a third-party service to manage ad delivery.

### Solbright

URL: www.solbright.com

E-mail: info@solbright.com

Company: Solbright Inc.

Address: 420 Lexington Ave., Suite 300, New York, NY 10170

Phone: 212.673.6100    Fax: 212.673.6166

Description: Developer of software for managing online advertising buys, trafficking, and billing.

### Straight Up!

URL: www.roianalysis.com

E-mail: sales@straightupsoftware.com

Company: Straight Up! Software

Address: 3550 General Atomics Court, Building 15, San Diego, CA 92121

Phone: 619.455.3124    Fax: 619.455.3595

Description: Internet tracking and reporting service that enables a Web marketer to fully measure and understand the impact and effectiveness of Web marketing options including banners, buttons, e-mails, media sites, interstitials, and hyperlinks.

### trueVu

URL: www.matchlogic.com

E-mail: info@matchlogic.com

Company: MatchLogic

Address: 10333 Church Ranch Blvd., Westminster, CO 80021

Phone: 303.222.2000    Fax: 303.222.2001

Description: Solution for advertisers interested in delivering rich media ads. Provides site clearance, compatibility assurance, plug-in determination, targeting, efficient delivery, and centralized reporting on campaign-wide advertising traffic.

# Ad Networks

### @dVenture

URL: www.ad-venture.com

E-mail: sales@ad-venture.com

Company: Venture Communications Electronic Marketing Inc.

Address: 60 Madison Avenue, New York, NY 10010

Phone: 212.684.4800   Fax: 212.576.1129

Description: Places advertising on its network of business-to-business and consumer sites.

## 24/7 Media, Inc.

URL: www.247media.com

E-mail: info@247media.com

Company: 24/7 Media Inc.

Address: 1250 Broadway, 27th Floor, New York, NY 10001

Phone: 212.231.7100   Fax: 212.760.1774

Description: Reaching more than one out of three online users, 24/7 Media, Inc., provides Internet advertising and online direct marketing solutions for advertisers and Web publishers through its national network of sites.

## Ad Club Network

URL: www.adclub.net

E-mail: members@adclub.net

Company: Ad Club Network

Address: 1100 Olive Way, Suite 1270, Seattle, WA 98101

Phone: 888.907.3224   Fax: 206.521.8808

Description: Ad network that offers real-time, online reporting, major advertiser banners, and a dedicated ad serving system, as well as a focused sales force.

## Ad-Net

URL: www.ad-network.com

E-mail: admin@ad-network.com

Company: Victory Information Network

Address: P.O. Box 517, Cleveland, OH 44107

Phone: 216.961.8970   Fax: 216.732.9953

Description: An advertising network with hundreds of affiliated Web sites.

## ADSmart

URL: www.adsmart.net

E-mail: info@adsmart.net

Company: ADSmart Corporation

Address: 100 Brickstone Sq., 1st Floor, Andover, MA 01810

Phone: 888.559.8222    Fax: 978.684.3618

Description: ADSmart.net automates the planning, executing, and managing of campaigns for Web advertisers, and facilitates the advertisers' selection of a highly targeted audience through its national ad network.

## AdSoftware Network

URL: http://E216adnet.aureate.com/advertisers.html

E-mail: info@aureate.com

Company: Aureate Media

Address: 8777 Purdue Road, Suite 225, Indianapolis, IN 46268

Phone: 800.695.5369    Fax: 317.802.5100

Description: AdSoftware Network is a client-side software application. It allows advertisers to target their messages to users who are running the software.

## Area IP

URL: www.areaip.com

E-mail: info@areaip.com

Company: Area Internet Publicidad S.A.

Address: Calle Travesera de Gracia 342-344, Barcelona, Spain 08025

Phone: 34.93.446.50.33   Fax: 34.93.446.50 34

Description: Spanish advertising network with some of the most important Spanish and South American Web sites.

## ASIAD

URL: www.asiad.net/english/

E-mail: service@asiad.net

Company: Asiad Corp.

Address: 7F, 267 HsinYi Road, Sec. 4, Taipei, Taiwan, R.O.C.

Phone: 886.2.2755.1755    Fax: 886.2.2755.2795

Description: Taiwan's largest ad network, providing professional quality advertising and localization services to international clients.

## Burst! Media

URL: www.burstmedia.com

E-mail: bhanna@burstmedia.com

Company: BURST! Media LLC

Address: 10 New England Executive Park, Burlington, MA 01803

Phone: 781.272.5544   Fax: 781.272.0897

Description: A banner brokering service that represents both small and large Web sites both national and local in focus.

## Classified Warehouse

URL: www.classifiedwarehouse.com

E-mail: advertising@classifiedwarehouse.com

Company: AdOne Classified Network

Address: 361 Broadway, Suite 100, New York, NY 10013

Phone: 212.965.2900   Fax: 212.334.3307

Description: Classified Warehouse, from AdOne Classified Network, is one of the largest networks of classified advertising for employment, autos, transportation, and real estate for sale or rent.

## ClickThrough Interactive

URL: www.clickthrough.ca

E-mail: sales@clickthrough.ca

Company: ClickThrough Interactive

Address: 86 Bloor Street West, Toronto, Ontario, Canada

Phone: 416.966.2542   Fax: 416.966.3097

Description: Canadian company with exclusive sales partnerships with many well-known and popular Web sites in Canada and around the world.

## CLIQNOW!

URL: www.clicknow.com

E-mail: admin@clicknow.com

Company: 24/7

Address: P.O. Box 2614, Rome, GA 30164-2614

Phone: 888.213.5635   Fax: n/a

Description: Sells advertising on Web sites.

## ContentZone

URL: www.contentzone.com

E-mail: csupport@contentzone.com

Company: 24/7 Media Inc.

Address: 1250 Broadway, 27th Floor, New York, NY 10001

Phone: 212.752.3928   Fax: 212.760.1774

Description: The ContentZone Network is a community of over 2,000 Web site owners and developers which targets sites by gender, age, income, and other criteria.

## DMN Media

URL: www.dmnmedia.com

E-mail: comments@dmn.com

Company: Digital Music Network, Inc.

Address: 319 Main Street (Suite 1), Stoneham, MA 02180

Phone: 781.279.2895   Fax: 781.279.3507

Description: Online advertising network for music-oriented sites.

## DoubleClick Direct

URL: www.doubleclick.net

E-mail: info@doubleclick.net

Company: DoubleClick

Address: 41 Madison Ave. 32nd Floor, New York, NY 10010

Phone: 212.271.2542   Fax: 212.889.0062

Description: A cost-per-action (per click, per lead, and per download) ad network.

## DoubleClick Network

URL: www.doubleclick.net

E-mail: info@doubleclick.net

Company: Doubleclick

Address: 41 Madison Ave., 32nd Floor, New York, NY 10010

Phone: 212.271.2542   Fax: 212.889.0062

Description: An Internet advertising network that has local, national, and international audiences for its top brand name sites.

## eAds

URL: www.eads.com

E-mail: info@eAds.com

Company: Electronic Advertising

Address: 5200 Keller Springs Road, Suite 1012, Dallas, TX 75248

Phone: 214.696.2252    Fax: 214.696.5726

Description: An ad network where the host site gets paid based on the number of responses the ad generates, not the number of impressions provided.

## Flycast Network

URL: www.flycast.com

E-mail: info@flycast.com

Company: Flycast Communication Corporation

Address: 181 Fremont St., San Francisco, CA 94105

Phone: 415.977.1000    Fax: 415.977.1009

Description: Ad Network with over 700 member sites targeting national and local audiences.

## HyperAsia

URL: www.hyperasia.com

E-mail: info@hyperasia.com

Company: HyperAsia

Address: 805 Third Avenue, 8th Floor, New York, NY 10022

Phone: 212.832.7000    Fax: 212.751.8888

Description: Develops targeted Chinese ads and places them strategically through-out its network of leading Chinese Web sites.

## InterAd

URL: www.interadsales.net

E-mail: corporate@interadsales.net

Company: InterAd Holdings Ltd.

Address: 49-51 Carnaby Street, London, UK WIC 1PF

Phone: 44.171.287.7300        Fax: 44.171.437.0780

Description: Provides global representation for leading European and international Web sites, giving top quality services to advertisers and Web site clients alike.

## LinkExchange

URL: www.linkexchange.com

E-mail: admin@linkexchange.com

Company: Microsoft

Address: 217 Second St., San Francisco, CA 94105

Phone: 415.543.4435    Fax: 415.543.1483

Description: Largest ad network in the world.

## Medius Network

URL: www.mediusnetwork.com

E-mail: media@medius.net

Company: Medius Interactive

Address: 830 4th Ave. S., Seattle, WA 98134

Phone: 206.442.9099    Fax: 206.442.9199

Description: Ad network of sports-related sites.

## NarrowCast Media

URL: www.narrowcastmedia.com

E-mail: info@narrowcastmedia.com

Company: NarrowCast Media

Address: 12304 Santa Monica Blvd., Suite 101, Los Angeles, CA 90025

Phone: 310.979.4638    Fax: 310.979.4633

Description:  NarrowCast Media is an advertising space brokerage and exchange service that sells banner advertising space on a click-through basis. Sites can earn cash or barter for their banner ad space inventory.

## Net AD Net

URL: www.netadnet.com

E-mail: NetADNet@pobox.com.au

Company: Net Ad Net

Address: P.O. Box 521, Brentford Sq., Victoria, Australia 03131

Phone: 61.3.9803.3886 Fax: 61.3.9886.3990

Description: Australian ad banner network.

## PennyWeb

URL: www.pennyweb.com

E-mail: sales@pennyweb.com

Company: PennyWeb

Address: 468 N. Camden Dr., #200, Beverly Hills, CA 90210

Phone: 888.867.3669   Fax: 213.939.9591

Description: PennyWeb allows advertisers to have their own click-through banner campaigns.

## Real Media

URL: www.realmedia.com

E-mail: rmsales@realmedia.com

Company: Real Media

Address: 32 E. 31st St., 9th Floor, New York, NY 10016

Phone: 212.725.4537   Fax: 212.725.4573

Description: Sells advertising on newspaper Web sites.

## Safe-Audit

URL: www.safe-audit.com

E-mail: admin@safe-audit.com

Company: Global Market Ltd.

Address: 29 Fairholme Gardens, London, UK N3 3ED

Phone: 44.0181.346.8316   Fax: 44.0181.346.0770

Description: Banner ad network with audited statisics. Also offers banner design services.

## TeknoSurf Adwave

URL: www.teknosurf.com

E-mail: john@teknosurf.com

Company: TeknoSurf Teknologies, Inc.

Address: 2315 Velvet Ridge Dr., Owings Mills, MD 21117

Phone: 410.825.6143   Fax: 410.825.6147

Description: Pay-per-click banner network.

### ValueClick

URL: www.valueclick.com

E-mail: robyn@valueclick.com

Company: ValueClick

Address: 1333 De La Vina Street, Suite E, Santa Barbara, CA 93010

Phone: 805.965.0543    Fax: 805.564.7151

Description: Pay-per-click banner network with premium quality ad space on over 10,000 sites.

### WebCounter

URL: www.digits.com

E-mail: questions@digits.com

Company: Computer Networking Services Inc.

Address: 322 Mall Blvd., Suite 306, Monroeville, PA 15146-2229

Phone: n/a    Fax: n/a

Description: Provides ad banner opportunities on the sites of its 300,000-plus active subscribers.

### The Women's Forum

URL: www.womensforum.com

E-mail: jodi@womensforum.com

Company: Women's Forum

Address: 253 E. Delaware Place, Suite 21 C, Chicago, IL 60611

Phone: 312.475.0100    Fax: 312.475.0116

Description: Ad network containing sites for women of all ages.

# Alternative Ad Models

### Alexa

URL: www.alexa.com

E-mail: info@alexa.com

Company: Alexa Internet

Address: The Presidio of San Francisco, P.O. Box 29141, San Francisco, CA 94129-0141

Phone: 415.561.6900    Fax: 415.561.6795

Description: A free advertising-support Web navigations service that provides Web site recommendations as the user surfs.

### Aureate Media

URL: adnet.aureate.com

E-mail: info@aureate.com

Company: Aureate Media Corp.

Address: 8777 Purdue Road, Suite 225, Indianapolis, IN 46268

Phone: 800.695.5369   Fax: 317.802.5110

Description: An electronic media company that distributes free software. The software is supported by advertisements.

### Comet Cursor

URL: www.cometsystems.com

E-mail: info@cometsystems.com

Company: COMET Systems

Address: 180 Maiden Lane, 20th Floor, New York, NY 10038

Phone: 212.231.2000   Fax: 212.809.0926

Description: Allows customization of cursors (e.g., NBA players, Spice Girls, animals, instead of a flashing line). The user must download a plug-in to be able to see custom cursors that a site may use.

### NetZero

URL: www.netzero.com

E-mail: feedback@netzero.net

Company: NetZero, Inc.

Address: 3835 R. East Thousand Oaks Blvd., #338, Westlake Village, CA 91362

Phone: 818.879.7250   Fax: n/a

Description: Offers free Internet access and e-mail through an advertising interstitial window.

# Associations

### Ad Council

URL: www.adcouncil.org

E-mail: info@adcouncil.org

Company: Ad Council

Address: 261 Madison Ave., New York, NY 10016

Phone: 212.922.1500   Fax: 212.922.1676

Description: A volunteer organization that conducts advertising campaigns for the public good and is the largest source of Public Service Advertising (PSA) in the country. The Ad Council's campaigns include the online industry with Internet PSAs.

## American Association of Advertising Agencies (AAAA)

URL: www.commercepark.com/AAAA

E-mail: aaaa@commercepark.com

Company: American Association of Advertising Agencies (AAAA)

Address: 405 Lexington Ave., New York, NY 10174-1801

Phone: 212.682.2500   Fax: 212.682.8391

Description: National advertising agency trade association.

## CASIE (Coalition for Advertising Supported Information & Entertainment)

URL: www.casie.org

E-mail: donahue@aaaa.org

Company: CASIE (Coalition for Advertising Supported Information & Entertainment)

Address: 405 Lexington Ave., New York, NY 10174-1801

Phone: 212.850.0702   Fax: 212.682.2028

Description: The CASIE mission is to create an environment where consumers have the broadest possible array of high-quality media options at the lowest possible cost.

## Direct Marketing Association (DMA)

URL: www.the-dma.org

E-mail: webmaster@the-dma.org

Company: Direct Marketing Association

Address: 1120 Avenue of the Americas, New York, NY 10036-6700

Phone: 212.768.7277   Fax: 212.302.6714

Description: National organization for direct marketing professionals.

## FAST

URL: www.fastinfo.org

E-mail: misc.im@pg.com

Description: An organization formed out of the Future of Advertising Stakeholders (FAST) Summit hosted by Procter & Gamble in August of 1998 and dedicated to "accelerating the development and broad use of digital advertising."

## Internet Advertising Bureau

URL: www.iab.net

E-mail: barbara@iab.net

Company: Internet Advertising Bureau

Address: 1500 Broadway, 25th Floor, New York, NY 10036

Phone: 914.921.6988   Fax: 914.967.2538

Description: Association founded in 1996 to promote and foster advertising on the Internet.

## Internet Direct Marketing Bureau (IDMB)

URL: www.idmb.org

E-mail: idmb@idmb.org

Company: Internet Direct Marketing Bureau

Description: Organization formed in 1998 to promote the maximum effectiveness and acceptance of direct marketing on the Internet.

## Internet Society

URL: www.isoc.org

E-mail: isoc@isoc.org

Company: Internet Society

Address: 12020 Sunrise Valley Dr., #210, Reston, VA 20191

Phone: 703.648.9888   Fax: 703.648.9887

Description: A non-governmental international organization promoting and facilitating global cooperation on the Internet.

## Newspaper Association of America

URL: www.naa.org

E-mail: freec@naa.org

Company: n/a

Address: 1921 Gallows Rd., Suite 600, Vienna, VA 22182

Phone: 703.902.1600   Fax: 703.902.1800

Description: NAA focuses on strategic issues of vital importance to newspapers: marketing, public policy, diversity, industry development, and newspaper operations.

# Auction

## *Adauction*

URL: www.adauction.com

E-mail: chris@adauction.com

Company: Adauction.com

Address: 188 Embarcadero, Third Floor, San Francisco, CA 94105

Phone: 415.597.4830   Fax: 415.597.4840

Description: Adauction.com is a planned buying opportunity for premium ad space at value pricing, through a real-time auction for top-branded sites.

# Auditing Services

## *ABC Interactive*

URL: www.abcinteractiveaudits.com

E-mail: hepnerea@accessabc.com

Company: ABC

Address: 900 North Meacham Rd., Schaumburg, IL 60173-4968

Phone: 847.605.0909 x282        Fax: 847.605.0483

Description: Provides independent third-party audits of Web site activity.

## *BPA International*

URL: www.bpai.com

E-mail: info@bpai.com

Company: BPA International

Address: 270 Madison Ave., 2nd Floor, New York, NY 10016

Phone: 212.779.3200   Fax: 212.779.3615

Description: Provider of third-party interactive auditing.

### I/AUDIT

URL: www.ipro.com

E-mail: info@ipro.com

Company: I/PRO

Address: 1400 Bridge Parkway, Suite 202, Redwood City, CA 94065

Phone: 650.226.2700   Fax: 650.226.2701

Description: A standard auditing solution provided by I/PRO and Nielsen Media Research.

## Banner Exchange Programs

### Click2Net Network

URL: www.click2net.com

E-mail: sales@click2net.com

Company: Click2Net, Inc.

Address: 1321 Birchcliff Drive, Oakville, Ontario, Canada L6M 2A5

Phone: 905.469.6680   Fax: 905.469.3327

Description: Canadian banner exchange program that provides members with a full array of reporting features for tracking site visitors..

### HyperBanner

URL: www.hyperbanner.net

E-mail: info@hyperbanner.net

Company: HyperBanner

Address: 49a Ider St., Haifa, Israel 34752

Phone: 972.4.8340.936   Fax: 972.4.8346.783

Description: Free banner exchange for 33 countries and topic-based communities.

### Internet Banner Network

URL: www.banner-net.com

E-mail: ibn1@savvy.com

Company: Internet Banner Network

Address: 55 Maple Avenue, Rockville Centre, NY 11570

Phone: 516.255.0500　Fax: n/a

Description: Targeted banner advertising.

## LinkExchange

URL: www.linkexchange.com

E-mail: admin@linkexchange.com

Company: Microsoft

Address: 217 Second St., San Francisco, CA 94105

Phone: 415.543.4435　Fax: 415.543.1483

Description: A free service that allows publishers to advertise their Web site through the reciprocal exchange of banner ad displays with thousands of other sites. This is the granddaddy of all banner exchange programs, with over 200,000 members.

## SmartClicks

URL: www.smartclicks.com

E-mail: info@smartclicks.com

Company: SmartAge

Address: 1515 Mockingbird Lane, Suite 207, Charlotte, NC 28209

Phone: 704.522.1999　Fax: 704.522.9131

Description: Free banner exchange with targeting options. When you join you are also subscribed to the SmartAge newsletter via e-mail.

## TradeBanners

URL: www.resource-marketing.com/banner.shtml

E-mail: chris@resource-marketing.com

Company: Resource Marketing Inc.

Address: 61 Covert Place, Ft. Thomas, KY 41075

Phone: 606.441.8700　Fax: 606.441.8795

Description: A free banner trading program that advertises: "Do you need more hits? Don't get knocked out on the information highway—advertise your site by trading hot-link banners free!"

# Conferences and Events

### @d Tech

URL: www.ad-tech.com

E-mail: skip@emarketworld.com

Company: eMarketworld

Address: 700 East Franklin St., 12th Floor, Richmond, VA 23219

Phone: 800-535-1812   Fax: 804-643-8376

Description: Semi-annual conference covering the latest trends and issues in Internet marketing, public relations, and media.

### Advertising & Marketing on the Internet

URL: www.zeff.com

E-mail: info@zeff.com

Company: The Zeff Group

Address: 1821 N. 21st St., #5, Arlington, VA 22209

Phone: 703.516.9091   Fax: 703.516.4357

Description: Locally and regionally focused one-day training events on online advertising and marketing held in cities throughout the United States.

### AdWeek Forum at Internet World

URL: www.adweek.com/adweekconf

E-mail: mpollock@adweek.com

Company: Adweek

Address: 1515 Broadway, 12th Floor, New York, NY 10036

Phone: 212.536.6527   Fax: 212.536.5353

Description: Two-day forum about marketing, advertising, and branding on the Web.

### Camp Interactive

URL: www.4interactivemarketing.com/camp99/index.html

E-mail: jjacobsen@4interactivemarketing.com

Company: Interactive Marketing, Inc.

Address: 32545 B Golden Lantern #244, Dana Pt., CA 92629

Phone: 949.249.0625   Fax: 949.249.6821

Description: A retreat for senior marketers to discuss products, services, and capabilities in interactive marketing.

### Online Advertising Forum

URL: www.jup.com

E-mail: jupiter@jup.com

Company: Jupiter Communications

Address: 627 Broadway, New York, NY 10012

Phone: 212.780.6060    Fax: 212.780.6075

Description: Conference on latest developments in the online advertising industry.

### Variety's Interactive Marketing Summit

URL: www.4interactivemarketing.com

E-mail: mpubentz@4interactivemarketing.com

Company: Interactive Marketing, Inc.

Address: 32545 B Golden Lantern #244, Dana Pt., CA 92629

Phone: 888.880.0625    Fax: n/a

Description: Information on how interactive marketing strategies are reshaping the future of entertainment marketing.

### Web Advertising

URL: www.thunderlizard.com

E-mail: tlp@thunderlizard.com

Company: Thunder Lizard Productions

Address: 1619 Eighth Ave., North, Seattle, WA 98109

Phone: 800.221.3806    Fax: 206.285.0308

Description: Conferences on Internet advertising that stress in-depth, real-world techniques. Hands-on learning events.

## Contests

### High Altitude Promotions

URL: www.highaltitude.com

E-mail: info@highaltitude.com

Company: The Integer Group

Address: 10455 West 6th Ave., Lakewood, CO 80215

Phone: 303.384.3177    Fax: n/a

Description: Manages all aspects of sweepstakes and contests via any medium.

### Pickem Sports

URL: http://corp.pickem.com

E-mail: info@pickem.com

Company: Pickem Sports Inc.

Address: 3260 Hillview Ave., Pao Alto, CA 94304

Phone: 650.858.2711    Fax: 650.858.3660

Description: Developers of online interactive contests and games.

### Prizes.com

URL: www.prizes.com

E-mail: bauxier@prizes.com

Company: RealTIME Media

Address: 15 Haverford Station Road, Haverford, PA 19041

Phone: 610.896.9400    Fax: 610.896.9416

Description: RealTIME Media develops online sweepstakes and also operates prizes.com.

### Webstakes

URL: www.webstakes.com

E-mail: curious@webstakes.com

Company: Webstakes

Address: 11 West 19th St., 10th Floor, New York, NY 10011

Phone: 212.242.8800    Fax: 212.242.8825

Description: Prize and savings club with 11 targeted consumer channels. Webstakes uses dialog marketing, which enables online merchants and consumers to interact.

# Directories of E-mail Discussion Lists and Newsletters

### The List of Lists

URL: http://E175tile.net/lists

E-mail: info@lyris.net

Company: Lyris Technologies

Address: 174 Santa Clara Avenue, Oakland, CA 94610

Phone: 800.768.2929    Fax: 510.597.0159

Description: Reference to all the Listserv, ListProc, and Majordomo e-mail discussion and announcement lists on the Internet.

### Liszt

URL: www.liszt.com

E-mail: liszt@liszt.com

Company: Liszt

Address: n/a

Phone: n/a    Fax: n/a

Description: Directory of Internet discussion groups, mailing lists, newsgroups, and IRC chat channels.

### Publicly Accessible Mailing Lists

URL: www.neosoft.com/internet/paml

E-mail: arielle@taronga.com

Company: PAML

Address: P.O. Box 720711, Houston, TX 77272

Phone: n/a    Fax: n/a

Description: A list of publicly accessible mailing lists.

# E-mail List Brokers/Services

### Acxiom DirectMedia

URL: www.directmedia.com

E-mail: mbartk@ix.directmedia.com

Company: Acxiom Direct Media

Address: 200 Pemberwick Road, Greenwich, CT 06830

Phone: 203.532.1000    Fax: 203.531.1452

Description: Off- and online solutions for direct marketers.

### BulletMail

URL: www.bulletmail.com

E-mail: sales@bulletmail.com

Company: BulletMail

Address: 3215 East River Rd., Rochester, NY 14623

Phone: 716.292.6189    Fax: n/a

Description: BulletMail offers targeted opt-in direct e-mail marketing services.

## CMG Direct

URL: www.cmgdirect.com

E-mail: mdrislan@cmgi.com

Company: CMG

Address: 187 Ballardvale St., Suite B110, P.O. Box 7000, Wilmington, MA 01887-7000

Phone: 978.657.7000  Fax: n/a

Description: Database management services, analytical services, and targeted opt-in e-mail lists.

## DeliverE

URL: www.matchlogic.com

E-mail: info@matchlogic.com

Company: MatchLogic

Address: 10333 Church Ranch Blvd., Westminster, CO 80021

Phone: 303.222.2000  Fax: 303.222.2001

Description: Delivers sales and branding messages to pre-qualified, highly receptive opt-in e-mail audiences.

## Digital Impact

URL: www.digital-impact.com

E-mail: sales@digital-impact.com

Company: Digital Impact

Address: 1730 S. Amphlett Blvd., Suite 217, San Mateo, CA 94402

Phone: 650.286.7300  Fax: 650.286.7310

Description: Customized electronic marketing campaigns.

## Direct Marketing Online

URL: www.directmarketing-online.com

E-mail: dmonline@directmarketing-online.com

Company: Grizzard Communications Group

Address: 229 Peachtree St. NE, Suite 900, Atlanta, GA 30303

Phone: 404.522.8330  Fax: n/a

Description: Full array of online and offline direct marketing services such as opt-in e-mail list rental.

## eGroups

URL: www.egroups.com

E-mail: info@egroups.com

Company: eGroups.com

Address: 5214-F Diamond Heights Blvd., #731, San Francisco, CA 94131

Phone: n/a   Fax: n/a

Description: eGroups provides organizations and groups of people, such as alumni and sports teams, an integrated package of services for effective group communication. Also a good place to find lists of e-mail lists.

## MatchLogic

URL: www.matchlogic.com

E-mail: info@matchlogic.com

Company: Matchlogic INC.

Address: 10333 Church Ranch Blvd, Westminster, CO 80021

Phone: 303.222.2000   Fax: 303.222.2001

Description: Service includes fielding target e-mail audiences, coordinating e-mail content and URLs, managing the campaign push, and monitoring the life cycle of the campaign.

## PostMaster Direct Response

URL: www.postmasterdirect.com

E-mail: contact@netcreations.com

Company: Netcreations

Address: 379 West Broadway, Ste. 202, New York, NY 10012

Phone: 212 625 1370   Fax: 212.625.1387

Description: Offers e-mail list rental, list management/brokerage, and e-mail list delivery.

## Sift, Inc.

URL: www.sift.com

E-mail: Sales@sift.com

Company: Sift, Inc.

Address: 155-A Moffett Park Dr., Suite 210, Sunnyvale, CA 94089

Phone: 408.541.7633   Fax: 408.541.7637

Description: Sift's Net-Lists opt-in e-mail network allows clients to reach more than 3,000,000 recipients in thousands of categories—business-to-business or consumer.

### WebPromote

URL: www.webpromote.com

E-mail: manager@webpromote.com

Company: WebPromote

Address: 565 Lakeview Parkway, Suite 135, Vernon Hills, IL 60061

Phone: 847.918.9292   Fax: 847.918.9296

Description: Sends clients' e-mail messages to a targeted list of individuals who have requested announcements about sites that cater to their interests.

# E-mail List Software

### Cuenet

URL: www.cuenet.com

E-mail: Info@cuenet.com

Company: Cuenet Systems

Address: P.O. Box 1134, Ben Lomond, CA 95005

Phone: 408.246.3388   Fax: n/a

Description: Provides list servers, auto-responders, document distribution, and other services.

### Listserv

URL: www.lsoft.com/listserv.stm

E-mail: sales@lsoft.com

Company: L-Soft International

Address: 8401 Corporate Dr., Landover, MD 20785

Phone: 301.731.0440   Fax: 301.731.6302

Description: System that allows the creation, management, and control of electronic mailing lists on corporate networks or the Internet.

### Lyris

URL: www.lyris.com

E-mail: sales@lyris.com

Company: Lyris Technologies

Address: 174 Santa Clara Avenue, Oakland, CA 94610

Phone: 888.248.9519    Fax: n/a

Description: Software for running Internet e-mail mailing lists, such as newsletters, announcements, and discussion lists.

### MailKing

URL: www.mailking.com

E-mail: webmaster@revnet.com

Company: Revnet Systems

Address: 3304 Westmill Drive, Huntsville, AL 35805

Phone: 888.519.4000    Fax: 256.519.9973

Description: MailKing offers an e-mail merge tool for Windows. It allows companies to open most popular databases directly, filter data into targeted e-mail lists, and send personalized e-mail to members of the list.

### Revenet Express

URL: www.revnetexpress.net

E-mail: webmaster@revnet.com

Company: Revnet Systems

Address: 3304 Westmill Drive, Huntsville, AL 35805

Phone: 888.519.4000    Fax: 256.519.9973

Description: Full range of e-mail management and delivery functions as well as advanced options for targeting, personalizing messages, and tracking click-through.

## Loyalty Programs

### BonusMail/MyPoints

URL: www.intellipost.com

E-mail: sales@intellipost.com

Company: Intellipost Corp.

Address: 565 Commercial Street, 4th Floor, San Francisco, CA 94111

Phone: 415.676.3700    Fax: 415. 676.3720

Description: Companies can  send targeted e-mail offers and offer Rew@rd points to an opt-in audience of consumers. MyPoints members earn points by filling out surveys, visiting sites, and making purchases. Points are redeemable for merchandise.

### ClickRewards

URL: www.clickrewards.com

E-mail: customerservice@clickrewards.com

Company: Netcentives, Inc.

Address: 690 Fifth Street, San Francisco, CA 94107

Phone: 415.538.1888   Fax: 415.538.1889

Description: Members can earn ClickMiles for shopping at a network of retail sites. ClickMiles are redeemable for airline miles and other rewards.

### Cybergold

URL: www.cybergold.com

E-mail: n/a

Company: Cybergold

Address: 2921 Adeline Street, Berkeley, CA 94703

Phone: 510.845.5000   Fax: 510.845.5257

Description: Allows marketers to pay consumers for viewing ads, visiting Web sites, or purchasing products.

### FreeRide

URL: www.freeride.com

E-mail: webmaster@freeride.com

Company: FreeRide Media, LLC

Address: 460 Park Ave. South, New York, NY 10016

Phone: 212.340.3800   Fax: 212.576.1436

Description: Members collect points by browsing sponsor Web sites, answering surveys, and shopping in stores. Points are redeemable for Internet access and other products.

# Market Research Firms

### Aberdeen Group

URL: www.aberdeen.com

E-mail: webmaster@aberdeen.com

Company: Aberdeen Group

Address: One Boston Place, Boston, MA 02108

Phone: n/a   Fax: n/a

Description: Computer industry market research, analysis, and consulting organization.

## ACNielsen

URL: www.acnielsen.com

E-mail: webmaster@nielsen.com

Company: ACNielsen

Address: 177 Broad St., Stamford, CT 06901

Phone: 203.961.3000    Fax: 203.961.3190

Description: Provides television ratings and will shortly be providing Web site ratings.

## ActivMedia

URL: www.activmedia.com/headlines.html

E-mail: research@activmedia.com

Company: ActivMedia

Address: 182 Hancock Rd., Peterborough, NH 03458

Phone: 800.639.9481    Fax: 603.924.2184

Description: Conducts custom and syndicated studies of online commerce.

## Arbitron NewMedia

URL: www.arbitron.com/newmedia.html

E-mail: NewMedia@Arbitron.com

Company: The Arbitron Company

Address: 9705 Patuxent Woods Drive, Columbia, MD 21046-1572

Phone: 410.312.8429    Fax: n/a

Description: A provider of consumer intelligence for cable systems, advertisers, telephone companies, advertising agencies, and content developers. Partners with Next Century Media on the CyberMeasurement Index (CMI).

## CalibratE

URL: www.matchlogic.com

E-mail: info@matchlogic.com

Company: MatchLogic

Address: 10333 Church Ranch Blvd., Westminster, CO 80021

Phone: 303.222.2000    Fax: 303.222.2001

Description: CalibratE gives MatchLogic clients the ability to conduct primary research online, including the testing of creatives and brand awareness studies.

## Cowles/Simba Net

URL: www.simbanet.com

E-mail: info@simbanet.com

Company: Simba Information

Address: P.O. Box 4234, 11 River Bend Dr. South, Stamford, CT 06907-0234

Phone: 203.358.9900    Fax: 203.358.5825

Description: Market intelligence and forecasts in the media industry.

## Cyber Dialogue

URL: www.cyberdialogue.com

E-mail: info@cyberdialogue.com

Company: Cyber Dialogue, Inc.

Address: 304 Hudson St., 6th Floor, New York, NY 10013

Phone: 212.255.6655    Fax: 212.255.6622

Description: Specializing in one-to-one marketing, online database marketing, and online market research.

## Dataquest

URL: www.dataquest.com

E-mail: dpginquiry@dataquest.com

Company: GartnerGroup

Address: 251 River Oaks Parkway, San Jose, CA 95134

Phone: 800.419.3282    Fax: 408.468.8088

Description: Computer market research firm.

## Dialogue Telescope

URL: www.cyberdialogue.com

E-mail: info@cyberdialogue.com

Company: Cyber Dialogue

Address: 304 Hudson St., 6th Floor, New York, NY 10013

Phone: 212.255.6655    Fax: 212.255.6644

Description: Offers primary research reports, briefs, and consulting services on consumer and small business issues for digital content, products, and services.

## E Stats

URL: www.estats.com

E-mail: salfstad@eMarketer.com

Company: Emarketer

Address: 821 Broadway, 3rd Floor, New York, NY 10003

Phone: 212.677.7137    Fax: 212.777.1172

Description: Information on ad revenues, usage patterns, geography, market size and growth, demographics, e-commerce, and e-trends.

## Forrester Research

URL: www.forrester.com

E-mail: info@forrester.com

Company: Forrester

Address: 1033 Massachusetts Ave., Cambridge, MA 02138

Phone: 617.497.7090    Fax: 617.868.0577

Description: Conducts market research and produces reports on the Internet and Internet advertising for the business-to-business market.

## GartnerGroup

URL: www.gartner.com

E-mail: inquiry@gartner.com

Company: GartnerGroup

Address: 56 Top Gallant Rd., Stamford, CT 06904

Phone: 203.316.1111    Fax: 203.316.1100

Description: GartnerGroup Inc. is an independent advisor of research and analysis to business professionals making information technology (IT) decisions, including users, purchasers, and vendors of IT products and services.

## GVU User Surveys

URL: www.cc.gatech.edu/gvu/user_surveys/User_Survey_Home.html

E-mail: www-survey@cc.gatech.edu

Company: GVU's WWW Survey Team

Address: GVU Center, College of Computing, Georgia Institute of Technology, Atlanta, GA 30332-0280

Phone: n/a   Fax: n/a

Description: Surveys about the Web.

## INTECO Corp.

URL: www.inteco.com

E-mail: inquiry@inteco.com

Company: INTECO

Address: 200 Connecticut Ave., Norwalk, CT 06854

Phone: 203.866.4400   Fax: 203.852.1599

Description: Conducts primary market research every 4–5 months concerning consumer usage of interactive products and services.

## IntelliQuest

URL: www.intelliquest.com

E-mail: info@intelliquest.com

Company: IntelliQuest

Address: 1250 Capital of Texas Hwy., Bldg. One, Suite 600, Austin, TX 78746

Phone: 512.329.0808   Fax: 512.329.0888

Description: Market research firm that specializes in the technology industry.

## International Data Corporation (IDC)

URL: www.idc.com

E-mail: idcinfo@idcresearch.com

Company: International Data Corporation (IDC)

Address: 5 Speen St., Framingham, MA 01701

Phone: 508.872.8200   Fax: 508.935.4015

Description: Market research firm. Publishes the Internet Factbook.

## Internet Domain Survey

URL: www.nw.com/zone/WWW/top.html

E-mail: info@nw.com

Company: Network Wizards

Address: P.O. Box 343, Menlo Park, CA 94026

Phone: 415.326.2060   Fax: 415.326.4672

Description: Conducts the Internet domain survey.

## Internet Facts

URL: www.parallaxweb.com/interfacts.html

E-mail: postmaster@parallaxweb.com

Company: Parallax Solutions

Address: 350 Cherry Hill Rd., Princeton, NJ 08540

Phone: 609.279.9299    Fax: 609.279.9406

Description: A concise compilation of statistics and research on Internet and World Wide Web demographics, usage, and growth.

## Jupiter Communications

URL: www.jup.com

E-mail: jupiter@jup.com

Company: Jupiter Communications

Address: 627 Broadway, New York, NY 10012

Phone: 212.780.6060    Fax: 212.780.6075

Description: A research, consulting, and publishing firm specializing in emerging consumer online and interactive technologies.

## Kelsey Group

URL: www.kelseygroup.com

E-mail: tkg@kelseygroup.com

Company: Kelsey Group

Address: 600 Executive Dr., Princeton, NJ 08540-1528

Phone: 609.921.7200    Fax: 609.921.2112

Description: Market research firm specializing in local market analysis.

## Killen & Associates Inc.

URL: www.killen.com

E-mail: info@killen.com

Company: Killen & Associates, Inc.

Address: 1212 Parkinson Ave., Palo Alto, CA 94301

Phone: 650.617.6130    Fax: 650.617.6140

Description: Conducts studies on the Internet such as "Internet: Global Penetration 1996 and Forecast for the Year 2000" and "Impact of the Internet on the Global Network Information Service Business."

## Laredo Group

URL: www.laredogroup.com

E-mail: info@laredogroup.com

Company: The Laredo Group, Inc.

Address: 4 Wildwood Avenue, Newton, MA 02460

Phone: 617.559.0200    Fax: 617.559.0202

Description: Research, training, and consulting firm dedicated to Internet advertising and revenue generation. Primary research conducted regarding ad sales professionals.

## Market Facts

URL: www.marketfacts.com

E-mail: webmaster@marketfacts.com

Company: Market Facts, Inc.

Address: 3040 West Salt Creek Lane, Arlington Heights, IL 60005

Phone: 847.590.7000    Fax: 847.590.7010

Description: Directed marketing information company. Market Facts performs custom market research services.

## Matrix Information & Directory Services (MIDS)

URL: www.mids.org

E-mail: sales@mids.org

Company: Matrix Information and Directory Services, Inc.

Address: 1106 Clayton Ln., #501W, Austin, TX 78723

Phone: 512.451.7602    Fax: 512.452.0127

Description: Examines the composition, content, and users of the Internet and presents the findings in textual and graphical representations.

## Millward Brown Interactive

URL: www.mbinteractive.com

E-mail: rex@mbinteractive.com

Company: Millward Brown Interactive

Address: 425 2nd St., 6th Floor, San Francisco, CA 94107

Phone: 415.538.8300    Fax: 415.538.8305

Description: Millward Brown Interactive designs, executes, and analyzes interactive advertising research. Services include the Voyager Profile for determining the reach and frequency of online ad campaigns.

### The Netcraft Web Server Survey

URL: www.netcraft.co.uk/survey/

E-mail: survey@netcraft.co.uk

Company: Netcraft

Address: n/a

Phone: 44.0.1225.447500          Fax: 44.0.1225.448600

Description: Survey of Web server software usage on Internet connected computers.

### Nielsen Media Research

URL: www.nielsenmedia.com

E-mail: interactive@nielsenmedia.com

Company: Nielsen Media Research

Address: 299 Park Ave., New York, NY 10171

Phone: 212.708.7500    Fax: 212.708.7795

Description: Market research firm. Partnership with I/PRO on Web measurement and auditing services.

### NPD Online Research

URL: www.npd.com/corp/interactive/interact_online.htm

E-mail: info@npd.com

Company: NPD Group, Inc.

Address: 900 West Shore Rd., Port Washington, NY 11050

Phone: 516.625.0700    Fax: 516.625.2347

Description: Offers services from Web site visitor profiling and site evaluation surveys, to more traditional marketing concerns such as concept testing, attitude and usage studies, and focus groups.

### NUA Internet Surveys

URL: www.nua.ie/surveys

E-mail: web@nua.ie

Company: Nua Ltd.

Address: 400 Lafayette St., 5th Floor, New York, NY 10003

Phone: 212.358.1775    Fax: 212.358.1760

Description: Comprehensive surveys of Internet news, demographics, and use.

## Roper Reports

URL: www.roper.com

E-mail: info@roper.com

Company: Roper Starch Worldwide

Address: 205 E. 42nd St., 17th Floor, New York, NY 10017

Phone: 212.599.0700   Fax: 212.867.7008

Description: The reports provide ongoing tracking of technology consumers, including Internet users and their attitudes and behaviors regarding the Internet.

## SIMBA Information Inc.

URL: http://simbanet.com

E-mail: info@simbanet.com

Company: Cowles/Simba

Address: Box 4234, 11 Riverbend Dr. So., Stamford, CT 06907

Phone: 800.307.2529   Fax: 203.358.5824

Description: Conducts studies, publishes reports, and hosts conferences.

## SRI International

URL: www.sri.com

E-mail: Inquiry_Line@sri.com

Company: SRI International

Address: 333 Ravenswood Ave., Menlo Park, CA 94025-3493

Phone: 650.859.4771   Fax: 650.859.4111

Description: Multidisciplinary research and consulting. Surveys users of the Web with a questionnaire at future.sir.com.

## Statistical Research Inc.

URL: www.sriresearch.com

E-mail: sri@sriresearch.com

Company: Statistical Research, Inc.

Address: 111 Prospect St., Westfield, NJ 07090-4003

Phone: 908.654.4000   Fax: 908.654.6498

Description: Research on television and other media including the Internet.

## Survey-Net

URL: www.survey.net/

E-mail: webmaster@survey.net

Company: Icorp/InterCommerce Corp.

Address: n/a

Phone: 504.780.9717    Fax: 504.779.5100

Description: Surveys that provide information, opinions, and demographics from the Internet community. Compiled results can be seen instantly.

## Vanderbilt University Project 2000 on Internet Marketing

URL: www2000.ogsm.vanderbilt.edu

E-mail: hoffman@colette.ogsm.vanderbilt.edu

Company: Owen Graduate School of Management

Address: 401 21 Ave., Nashville, TN 37203

Phone: 615.343.6904    Fax: 615.343.7177

Description: A five-year research effort devoted to the scholarly investigation of the marketing implications of commercialization of the World Wide Web.

## WebCMO

URL: www.webcmo.com

Description: Completely virtual market research firm that explores Web marketing movements, opportunities of the Web market, and Web marketing strategies.

## Yankelovich Partners Inc.

URL: www.yankelovich.com

E-mail: NuBusiness@yankelovich.com

Company: Yankelovich Partners

Address: 101 Merritt 7 Corporate Park, Norwalk, CT 06851

Phone: 203.846.0100    Fax: 203.845.8200

Description: A marketing research and consulting organization with an extensive client list and experience in many industries. Their research and consulting services focus on syndicated research services and strategic market research.

## Zona Research

URL: www.zonaresearch.com

E-mail: info@zonaresearch.com

Company: Zona Research, Inc.

Address: 900 Veterans Boulevard, Suite 500, Redwood City, CA 94063

Phone: 650.568.5700    Fax: 650.306.2420

Description: Qualitative and quantitative information and advice on market trends via syndicated subscriptions, services, and reports.

# Measurement Technologies

## Accesswatch

URL: www.accesswatch.com

E-mail: n/a

Company: Accesswatch

Address: P.O. Box 183, Fairfax, VA 22030

Phone: n/a    Fax: 703.491.0996

Description: Web site traffic analysis tool designed to be easily installed and create comprehensive reports.

## ARIA

URL: www.andromedia.com

E-mail: sales@andromedia.com

Company: Andromedia Inc.

Address: 818 Mission Street, Second Floor, San Francisco, CA 94103

Phone: 415.365.6700    Fax: 415.365.6701

Description: Andromedia's ARIA RecorderReporter is a tool for high-performance Internet and intranet activity tracking and analysis.

## FlashStats

URL: www.maximized.com/products/flashstats/

E-mail: info@maximized.com

Company: Maximized Software

Address: 55 Santa Clara Avenue, Suite 250, Oakland, CA 94610

Phone: 888.629.7638 in U.S. and Canada only;
       510.433.1903 outside U.S. and Canada    Fax: 510.433.1904

Description: Server-side software for analyzing log files, for small- to medium-sized sites.

## Hit List

URL: www.marketwave.com

E-mail: info@marketwave.com

Company: Marketwave

Address: 601 Union Street, Suite 4601, Seattle, WA 98101

Phone: 206.682.6801    Fax: 206.682.6805

Description: The Hit List product line consists of four products. Hit List Professional and Commerce are inexpensive log analysis solutions for the vast majority of Web sites. Hit List Enterprise and Live are high-end Web mining solutions.

## LandscapE

URL: www.matchlogic.com

E-mail: info@matchlogic.com

Company: MatchLogic

Address: 10333 Church Ranch Blvd., Westminster, CO 80021

Phone: 303.222.2000    Fax: 303.222.2001

Description: Capable of generating demographic reach profiles at the click, site, and campaign levels, LandscapE provides online advertisers with a "picture" of who sees and responds to a particular message, without requiring site registrations.

## Net.Analysis

URL: www.netgen.com

E-mail: sales@netgen.com

Company: Net.Genesis

Address: 215 First St., Cambridge, MA 02142

Phone: 617.577.9800    Fax: 617.577.9850

Description: A powerful tool for analyzing the traffic patterns on your Web site.

## NetLine

URL: www.ipro.com

E-mail: info@ipro.com

Company: I/PRO

Address: 1400 Bridge Parkway, Suite 202, Redwood City, CA 94065

Phone: 650.226.2700    Fax: 650.226.2701

Description: This service provides an outsourced solution for understanding site traffic and user behavior including path-tracking presentation-ready reports.

## SurfReport

URL: www.netrics.com/SurfReport/

E-mail: surf@netrics.com

Company: NETRICS.COM Inc.

Address: 3511 Northeast 22nd Avenue, Suite 200, Fort Lauderdale, FL 33308

Phone: 954.567.0477    Fax: 954.567.0479

Description: Web traffic analysis software that provides data on site visitors and statistics to analyze site performance.

## TrueCount

URL: www.matchlogic.com

E-mail: info@matchlogic.com

Company: MatchLogic

Address: 10333 Church Ranch Blvd., Westminster, CO 80021

Phone: 303.222.2000   Fax: 303.222.2001

Description: Technology for measuring all ad impressions (including cached impressions).

## TruEffect

URL: www.matchlogic.com

E-mail: info@matchlogic.com

Company: MatchLogic

Address: 10333 Church Ranch Blvd., Westminster, CO 80021

Phone: 303.222.2000   Fax: 303.222.2001

Description: TruEffect tells advertisers which ads actually generate the most online sales by tracking user behavior after a user clicks on an ad or other element.

## WebResults Accelerator

URL: www.ipro.com

E-mail: info@ipro.com

Company: I/PRO

Address: 1400 Bridge Parkway, Suite 202, Redwood City, CA 94065

Phone: 650.226.2700   Fax: 650.226.2701

Description: WebResults Accelerator integrates traffic data, customer profiling, and transaction data.

## WebTrends

URL: www.WebTrends.com

E-mail: sales@webtrends.com

Company: WebTrends Corporation

Address: 621 SW Morrison, Ste. 1300, Portland, OR 97205

Phone: 503.294.7025   Fax: 503.294.7130

Description: WebTrends analyzes Web site traffic and generates tables and graphs that show the site's marketing and technical effectiveness. One of the most powerful and inexpensive tools on the market. Popular with small- to mid-sized sites.

### Wusage 6

URL: www.boutell.com/wusage/

E-mail: wusage@boutell.com

Company: Boutell.Com Inc.

Address: P.O. Box 20837, Seattle, WA 98102

Phone: 206.325.3009    Fax: 206.325.3009

Description: A server-based Web traffic measurement system for Linux, Solaris, and many other versions of Unix, MacOS, and Windows 95/NT.

# Personalization Technologies

### Art Technology Group (ATG)

URL: www.atg.com

E-mail: info@atg.com

Company: Art Technology Group

Address: 101 Huntington Avenue, Boston, MA 02199

Phone: 617.859.1212    Fax: 617.859.1211

Description: Provider of Internet products and services that enable major corporations to conduct business online.

### BroadVision

URL: www.broadvision.com

E-mail: n/a

Company: BroadVision

Address: 585 Broadway, Redwood City, CA 94063

Phone: 650.261.5100    Fax: 650.261.5900

Description: Supplier of Internet application solutions for one-to-one relationship management.

### Firefly

URL: www.firefly.com

E-mail: Noreen_Sewell@firefly.net

Company: Firefly Network, Inc.

Address: One Broadway, 6th Floor, Cambridge, MA 02142

Phone: 617.528.1000    Fax: 617.577.7220

Description: Personalization software that uses collaborative filtering. Sites that are Firefly enhanced distribute Firefly Passports to users to develop personal profiles inorder to give users access to personalized content and recommend products.

## GuestTrack

URL: www.guesttrack.com

E-mail: info@GuestTrack.com

Company: GuestTrack, Inc.

Address: 3532 Jasmine Ave., Los Angeles, CA 90034

Phone: 310.558.3599   Fax: n/a

Description: Personalization products that add database interactivity to clients' Internet strategies.

## Net Perceptions

URL: www.netperceptions.com

E-mail: info@netperceptions.com

Company: Net Perceptions, Inc.

Address: 7901 Flying Cloud Drive, Eden Prairie, MN 55344-7905

Phone: 612.903.9424   Fax: 612.903.9425

Description: Net Perceptions Realtime Recommendation Platform can be used for ad targeting, e-commerce, and call centers.

## SelectCast

URL: www.aptex.com

E-mail: info@aptex.com

Company: Aptex Software Inc.

Address: 9605 Scranton Rd., Suite 240, San Diego, CA 92121

Phone: 619.623.0554   Fax: 619.623.0558

Description: Intelligent server software that uses behaviorial targeting techniques to maximize online and direct mail response rates and selectively target audiences based on real-time user behavior.

## TrueSelect

URL: www.matchlogic.com

E-mail: info@matchlogic.com

Company: MatchLogic

Address: 10333 Church Ranch Blvd., Westminster, CO 80021

Phone: 303.222.2000   Fax: 303.222.2001

Description: Advanced one-to-one targeting product allows marketers to target anyone anywhere in the digital channel using traditional demographics.

# Promotion Services

## *Exploit Submission Wizard*

URL: www.exploit.com/wizard/

E-mail: admin@exploit.com

Company: Exploit Information Technology

Address: 10 York Road, Heaton Moor, Stockport, UK SK4 4PQ UK

Phone: 44.0.161.432.0394   Fax: 44.0.161.431.6140

Description: Automated submission software tool that will submit your URL automatically to hundreds of search engines.

## *Pointers-to-Pointers*

URL: www.homecom.com/global/pointers.html

E-mail: pointers@homecom.com

Company: Homecom Communications

Address: 3535 Piedmont Rd., 14 Piedmont Center, Suite 100 3035, Atlanta, GA

Phone: 404.237.4646   Fax: 404.237.3060

Description: A fully automated submission tool to promote a URL to over 200 search engines directories and Web award sites both general and specialized. Both free and fee versions are available.

## *PositionAgent*

URL: www.positionagent.com

E-mail: sales@positionagent.com

Company: MSN LinkExchange

Address: 217 Second St., San Francisco, CA 94105

Phone: 415.543.4435   Fax: 415.543.1483

Description: PositionAgent automatically monitors where your Web site ranks in the 10 most important search engines. Using the keywords/phrases you enter, it generates reports showing where your Web site is listed by page and position within each of the major search engines and directories.

### PostMaster URL Announcement Service

URL: www.netcreations.com/postmaster/

E-mail: postmaster@netcreations.com

Company: Netcreations

Address: 379 West Broadway, Suite 202, New York, NY 10012

Phone: 212.625.1370    Fax: 212.625.1387

Description: Online site registration to hundreds of search engines. Both free and paying versions available.

### Promote-It!

URL: www.iTools.com/promote-it/

E-mail: webmaster@iTools.com

Company: iTools

Address: n/a

Phone: n/a    Fax: n/a

Description: Comprehensive listing of free Web advertising and classified promotion sites on the Net.

### Sponsor of the Day/Sponsored Site of the Day

URL: www.cris.com/~raydaly/sponsors.shtml

E-mail: ray.daly@mailcall.com

Company: MailCall

Address: P.O. Box 324 Dunn, Loring, VA 22027

Phone: 703.560.3259    Fax: n/a

Description: Daily publication that highlights the sponsors of Internet publications, resources, information, and other sites.

### Submit It!

URL: http://submitit.linkexchange.com

E-mail: n/a

Company: LinkExchange

Address: 217 Second Street, San Francisco, CA 94105-3105

Phone: n/a    Fax: n/a

Description: Site promotion software that aids sites to post to directories, search engines, guides, and announcement services.

## The Ward Group/Netpost

URL: www.netpost.com

E-mail: inquiries@netpost.com

Company: The Ward Group, Inc.

Address: 1015 Kenesaw Ave., Knoxville, TN 37919

Phone: 423.637.2438    Fax: 423.971.1523

Description: High-end personalized site promotion services. Non-automated approach to URL submissions and online awareness-building.

## TrafficPack

URL: www.smartage.com/cgi-bin/traffic_home.pl

E-mail: info@smartage.com

Company: SmartAge

Address: 3450 California Street, San Francisco, CA 94118

Phone: 415.674.3787    Fax: 415.674.3782

Description: Packaged solutions for increasing traffic to your site, including search engine registrations, site ranking, position checking, and more.

## Webstep Top 100

URL: www.mmgco.com/top100.html

E-mail: top100@mmgco.com

Company: Multimedia Marketing Group Inc.

Address: 600 SW Columbia, Bend, OR 97702

Phone: 888.699.6939    Fax: n/a

Description: Free index of the 100 best free places to list a Web site.

## Webster Group International

URL: www.wgi.com

E-mail: speterson@wgi.com

Company: Webster Group International

Address: 413 Fee Fee Rd., St. Louis, MO 63043

Phone: 314.209.1005    Fax: 314.209.1126

Description: Promotion service that secures top positioning in search engines. Develops custom promotional programs to reach your target market and be included in industry product and service-specific sites and directories.

# Rating Firms

### Media Metrix

URL: www.mediametrix.com

E-mail: info@mediametrix.com

Company: NPD

Address: 900 West Shore Rd., Port Washington, NY 11050

Phone: 516.625.2357    Fax: 516.625.2347

Description: The online industry's first and larget market research information and analysis service providing demographic data on home PC usage patterns, including time spent on specific pages of the World Wide Web and on AOL. In 1998 Media Metrix merged with Relevant Knowledge.

### NetRatings

URL: www.netratings.com

E-mail: info@netratings.com

Company: NetRatings, Inc.

Address: 830 Hillview Court, Milpitas, CA 95035

Phone: 408.957.0699    Fax: 408.957.0487

Description: Nielsen and NetRatings count traffic and research Web usage to rate sites based on traffic.

# Representation Firms

### .tmc F

URL: www.dottmc.com

E-mail: webguru@dottmc.com

Company: Targeted Marketing Concepts

Address: 17194 Preston Road, Suite 123-110, Dallas, TX 75248

Phone: 972.716.9616    Fax: 972.716.9621

Description: Online interactive marketing.

### 2CAN Media

URL: www.2canmedia.com

E-mail: info@2canmedia.com

Company: 2CAN Media, Inc.

Address: 380 Lexington Ave., Suite 1700, New York, NY 10168

Phone: 212.551.1156   Fax: 212.551.1171

Description: Site-focused sales and advertising representation. Also includes WebRep, ECG, Pinnacle Interactive, MediaPlus, and Grupo NetFuerza.

## Cybereps

URL: www.cybereps.com

E-mail: sales@cybereps.com

Company: Cybereps

Address: 80 Liberty Ship Way, Suite 22, Sausalito, CA 94965

Phone: 415.289.5040   Fax: 415.289.1589

Description: Advertising sales and marketing organization specializing in representation of Internet-related properties.

## CyberFirst

URL: www.cyberfirst.com

E-mail: mail@cyberfirst.com

Company: CyberFirst, Inc.

Address: 2535 152nd Avenue NE, Suite B-2, Redmond, WA 98052

Phone: 425.869.1303   Fax: 425.869.5033

Description: Represents Web sites in the sale of advertising space, including sales, scheduling, serving, tracking, reporting, billing, and collections.

## Future Pages

URL: www.futurepages.com/solutions/

E-mail: emailus@futurepages.com

Company: Future Pages, LLC

Address: 817 North Vandalia Street, Suite 200, P.O. Box 130068, St. Paul, MN 55113

Phone: 651.631.2255   Fax: 651.644.9379

Description: Future Pages is an Internet-specific National Advertising Rep Firm for college media Web sites.

## Ken Margolis Associates

URL: www.kenmargolis.com

E-mail: info@kenmargolis.com

Company: Ken Margolis Associates

Address: 140 2nd Street, Suite 602, San Francisco, CA 94105

Phone: 415.284.1444   Fax: 415.284.1482

Description: Online advertising, marketing consulting, and promotional activities.

### *Unique Media Services*

URL: www.uniquemedia.net

E-mail: wizard@uniquemedia.net

Company: Unique Media Services, LLC

Address: 151 Pleasant View Road, Blythewood, SC 29016

Phone: 803.333.9700    Fax: n/a

Description: Internet marketing advertising representative firm.

### *WebMedia*

URL: www.webmedia-sales.com

E-mail: sales@webmedia-sales.com

Company: WMS Worldwide, Inc.

Address: 301 Grant St., 1 Oxford Center, Ste. 1500, Pittsburgh, PA 15219

Phone: 412.255.3773    Fax: 412.362.2611

Description: Aids Web site publications in generating revenue via advertising, sponsorship, branding, and e-commerce.

### *WebRep*

URL: www.wwwebrep.com

E-mail: nmonnens@webrep.net

Company: WebRep LLC

Address: 704 Sansome, San Francisco, CA 94111

Phone: 415.772.3640    Fax: 415.772.3599

Description: WebRep is a national advertising sales representation firm representing Web sites interested in generating revenue from online advertising.

## Resources

The resources category is divided into three sections. The first section presents the e-mail discussion lists and newletters for the Internet advertising and marketing industry. The second section lists the search engines, directories, and resource sites on Internet advertising. And the third section includes the online versions of the major online advertising and Internet publications.

## E-mail Discussion Lists and Newsletters

### *Banner Tips*

URL: www.whitepalm.com/fourcorners/

E-mail: scanlin@whitepalm.com

Company: Four Corners Effective Banners

Address: P.O. Box 391446, Mountain View, CA 94039

Phone: 650.961.1957   Fax: 650.961.1621

Description: Tips on creating effective banners.

## ChannelSeven NarrowCast Newsletter

URL: www.channelseven.com

E-mail: risse@channelseven.com

Company: ChannelSeven.com Business Alliance Network

Address: 55 John Street, New York, NY 10038

Phone: 212.962.7777   Fax: 212.962.7784

Description: A networking resource for Internet developers, marketers, and advertising executives.

## ClickZ

URL: www.clickz.com

E-mail: andy@clickz.com

Company: Click Z Network

Address: 8 Liberty Street, Andover, MA 01810

Phone: n/a   Fax: n/a

Description: Resource for doing online business. Covers everything from e-commerce, to a directory of marketing-related sites, to online advertising, and more.

## FrankelBiz

URL: www.robfrankel.com/frankelbiz/fbintro.html

E-mail: rob@robfrankel.com

Company: Rob Frankel

Address: 17645 Royce Drive, Encino, CA 91316

Phone: 818.990.8623   Fax: n/a

Description: List devoted to doing business on the Web. List members exchange discounts, offer business leads, and do business with each other.

## Global Marketing Discussion List

URL: www.euromktg.com/eng/ed/gmd.html

E-mail: ema@euromktg.com

Company: Euro-Marketing Associates

Address: 1850 Union St., #1229, San Francisco, CA 94123

Phone: 415.680.2423   Fax: n/a

Description: Advice and information for preparing Web sites (and companies) to address the world market.

## ICONOCAST

URL: www.iconocast.com

E-mail: ICONOCAST

Company: ICONOCAST

Address: 150 No. Hill Dr., Brisbane, CA 94005

Phone: 415.468.4684   Fax: 415.468.4686

Description: Online newletter with analysis of Internet advertising and marketing industry trends as well as hot insider information on companies and industry leaders.

## Internet Advertising Discussion List

URL: www.internetadvertising.org

E-mail: ab@internetadvertising.org

Company: The Internet Advertising Discussion List

Address: 1730 SW Skyline Boulevard, Suite 201, Portland, OR 97205

Phone: 503.292.6987   Fax: 503.614.2026

Description: E-mail discussion of various aspects of the Internet advertising industry. Directed towards businesses with a monthly or annual budget for paid advertising.

## Internet Advertising Report

URL: www.internet.com

E-mail: info@internet.com

Company: Alan Meckler and Penton Media, Inc.

Address: 20 Ketchum St., Westport, CT 06880

Phone: 203.226.6967   Fax: 203.454.5840

Description: Weekly wrap-up of Internet advertising news.

## Internet-Sales Discussion List

URL: www.mmgco.com

E-mail: info@mmgco.com

Company: Multimedia Marketing Group Inc.

Address: 220 Oregon Ave., Studio C, Bend, OR 97701

Phone: 541.330.1527   Fax: 541.330.1654

Description: Moderated discussion list on online sales issues; comprised of over 11,000 subscribers from more than 70 countries.

## Larry Chase's Web Digest for Marketers

URL: www.wdfm.com

E-mail: Chase@wdfm.com

Company: Chase Online Marketing Strategies

Address: 847A Second Ave., Ste. 332, New York, NY 10017

Phone: 212.876.1096   Fax: 212.876.1098

Description: A bi-weekly zine containing 25 short reviews of the latest marketing-oriented sites.

## LinkExchange Digest

URL: http://digest.linkexchange.com

E-mail: aa@le-digest.com

Company: LinkExchange

Address: 217 Second St., San Francisco, CA 94105

Phone: 415.543.4435   Fax: 415.543.1483

Description: Moderated discussion list for LinkExchange members focused on Web site promotion and driving traffic to sites.

## Online Advertising Discussion

URL: www.o-a.com

E-mail: owner-online-ads@o-a.com

Company: The Tenagra Corp.

Address: 1100 Hercules, Suite 120, Houston, TX 77058

Phone: 281.480.6300   Fax: 281.480.7715

Description: Discussion of online advertising strategies, online promotion, and public relations.

## Web Digest for Marketers

URL: www.wdfm.com

E-mail: info@wdfm.com

Company: Chase Online Marketing Strategies

Address: 847A Second Ave., Suite 332, New York, NY 10017

Phone: 212.876.1096   Fax: 212.876.1098

Description: Newsletter that provides information for marketers. Categories include research, sales support, finance, e-commerce, and others.

### Webmarketing Online

URL: www.wilsonweb.com/wmt/

E-mail: rfwilson@wilsonweb.com

Company: Wilson Internet Services

Address: P.O. Box 308, Rocklin, CA 95677

Phone: 916.652.4659   Fax: n/a

Description: Online newsletter with links to articles on Internet advertising and editorials on e-commerce and marketing.

## Informational Sites

### Acceptable Internet Advertising Practices

URL: http://E350arganet.tenagra.com/Tenagra/net-acceptable.html

E-mail: info@tenagra.com

Company: Tenagra

Address: 1100 Hercules, Suite 120, Houston, TX 77058

Phone: 281.480.6300   Fax: 281.480.7715

Description: FAQ on acceptable advertising behavior.

### Ad Resource

URL: www.adresource.com

E-mail: info@adresource.com

Company: Ad Resource

Address: 5854 N. Keating Ave., Chicago, IL 60646

Phone: 312.201.0488   Fax: n/a

Description: A site full of Web marketing and promotional resources and articles.

### AdsGallery.com

URL: www.adsgallery.com

E-mail: mail@warp10.com

Company: Warp10

Address: 9120 Leslie St., Suite 101, Richmond Hill, Ontario, Canada L4B 3J9

Phone: 800.303.WARP   Fax: 905.763.1360

Description: An online interactive gallery of top ads, ad campaigns, and interactive agencies.

## *Advertisers Internet Directory*

URL: www.zenithmedia.com/mapuse00.htm

E-mail: info@zenithmedia.com

Company: Zenith Media

Address: Bridge House, 63-65 North Wharf Road, London, UK W2 ILA

Phone: 44 171.224.8500    Fax: 44 171.255.2187

Description: Provides an Internet directory of useful sites for marketers.

## *Advertising Law Internet Site*

URL: www.webcom.com/~lewrose/home.html

E-mail: lewrose@netcom.com

Company: Arent Fox Kintner Plotkin & Kahn

Address: 1050 Connecticut Ave. NW, Washington, DC 20036

Phone: 202.857.6012    Fax: 202.857.6395

Description: Articles and other resources on advertising law.

## *Advertising Media Internet Center*

URL: www.telmar.com

E-mail: corporate@telmar.com

Company: Telmar

Address: 148 Madison Ave., New York, NY 10016

Phone: 212.725.3000    Fax: 212.725.5488

Description: A site of links for Net advertising resources.

## *ChannelSeven*

URL: www.channelseven.com

E-mail: risse@mercuryseven.com

Company: Mercury Seven

Address: 55 John Street, New York, NY 10038

Phone: 212.962.7778    Fax: 212.962.7785

Description: A network of interactive sites built for the Internet marketing and advertising industry.

## Clickthrough Comparison Page

URL: www.photolabels.com/clickthroughcomp.shtml

E-mail: web@photolabels.com

Company: Photolabels

Address: P.O. Box 390634, Mountain View, CA 94039

Phone: 415.961.1957    Fax: 415.961.1621

Description: This page shows the click-through ratio of Link Exchange member banners and is meant as a design tool to assist in the development of more clickable banners.

## The Conaghan Report

URL: http://www.naa.org/marketscope/

E-mail: conaj@naa.org

Company: Newspaper Association of America

Address: 1921 Gallows Rd., Suite 600, Vienna, VA 22182

Phone: 703.902.1757    Fax: 703.902.1751

Description: The Newspaper Association of America's top researcher shares his thoughts and findings on online research.

## CyberAtlas

URL: http://cyberatlas.internet.com

E-mail: feedback@cyberatlas.com

Company: internet.com LLC

Address: 20 Ketchum St., Westport, CT 06880

Phone: 203.226.6967    Fax: 203.454.5840

Description: The site is a consolidation of Internet marketing research.

## Directory of Public Relations Agencies and Resources on the World Wide Web

URL: www.webcom.com/impulse/

E-mail: impulse@impulse-research.com

Company: Impulse Research Corporation

Address: 8829 National Blvd., Suite 1006, Culver City, CA 90232

Phone: 310.559.6892    Fax: 310.839.9770

Description: A directory of public relations agencies and other resources on the Net.

## E-marketer's Gateway

URL: www.egateway.com

E-mail: contactus@egateway.com

Company: ClickThrough Interactive

Address: 86 Bloor Street West, Toronto, Ontario, Canada M5S 1M5

Phone: 416.966.2542   Fax: 416.966.3097

Description: Dedicated to helping Canadian marketers find useful advertising, marketing, and research information on the Web.

## Media Central

URL: www.mediacentral.com

E-mail: editor@mediacentral.com

Company: PRIMEDIA Intertec

Address: 9800 Metcalf, Overland Park, KS 66212

Phone: 913.341.1300   Fax: n/a

Description: News and information for media and marketing professionals.

## Microscope

URL: www.microscope.com

E-mail: claudia@clickz.com

Company: Click Z Network

Address: 8 Liberty Street, Andover, MA 01810

Phone: n/a   Fax: n/a

Description: A weekly review of top online ad campaigns.

## Online Advertising Glossary

URL: www.247media.com/resource/re_gloss.htm

E-mail: info@247media.com

Company: 24/7 Media Inc.

Address: 1250 Broadway, 27th Floor, New York, NY 10001

Phone: 212.231.7100   Fax: 212.760.1774

Description: List of terms related to online advertising for beginners.

### Tenagra's Marketing Resources

URL: http://marketing.tenagra.com

E-mail: info@tenagra.com

Company: The Tenagra Corp.

Address: 1100 Hercules, Suite 120, Houston, TX 77058

Phone: 281.480.6300    Fax: 281.480.7715

Description: Links to Tenagra's marketing resources for marketing, PR, and advertising on the Internet.

### University of Texas "Advertising World"

URL: http://advweb.cocomm.utexas.edu/world/

E-mail: advertising@mail.utexas.edu

Company: Department of Advertising at UT Austin

Address: Advertising Department, CMA 7142, The University of Texas at Austin, Austin, TX 78712

Phone: 512.471.1101    Fax: n/a

Description: Extensive collection of advertising related links for advertising and marketing professionals, students, and teachers.

### Web Marketing Info Center

URL: www.wilsonweb.com/webmarket/

E-mail: rfwilson@wilsonweb.com

Company: Wilson Internet Services

Address: P.O. Box 308, Rocklin, CA 95677

Phone: 916.652.4659    Fax: n/a

Description: Links to online articles on Web marketing and online business resources. Probably the largest collection of links to articles on Web marketing, advertising, and e-commerce.

### WWW Consumer Survey Results

URL: www.cc.gatech.edu/gvu/user_surveys/

E-mail: www-survey@cc.gatech.edu

Company: GVU Center College of Computing

Address: Georgia Institute of Technology, Atlanta, GA 30332

Phone: n/a    Fax: n/a

Description: WWW user surveys. Nine surveys have been conducted since January 1994.

# Online Publications

### Advertising Age

URL: www.adage.com

E-mail: webinfo@adage.com

Company: Advertising Age

Address: 220 East 42nd St., New York, NY 10017

Phone: 212.210.0100   Fax: n/a

Description: Web site of weekly *Advertising Age*. Also home of supplement *Netmarketing*.

### BackChannel

URL: www.commercepark.com/AAAA/bc/

E-mail: tforbes@tforbes.com

Company: American Association of Advertising Agencies

Address: 405 Lexington Ave., New York, NY 10174

Phone: 212.682.2500   Fax: 212.682.8391

Description: The interactivity newsletter of the AAAA.

### Digital Edge

URL: www.digitaledge.org

E-mail: gipsm@naa.org

Company: Newspaper Association of America

Address: 1921 Gallows Rd., Suite 600, Vienna, VA 22182

Phone: 703.648.1000   Fax: 703.620.4557

Description: Online publication of the Newspaper Association of America.

### Direct Marketing News

URL: www.dmnews.com

E-mail: editor@dmnews.com

Company: Direct Marketing Association

Address: 100 Ave. of the Americas, New York, NY 10013

Phone: 212.925.7300   Fax: 212.925.8754

Description: The online edition of the New York–based weekly newspaper for the direct marketing industry.

## *The Industry Standard*

URL: www.thestandard.com/metrics/

E-mail: webmaster@thestandard.com

Company: The Industry Standard

Address: 315 Pacific Ave., San Francisco, CA 94111

Phone: 415.733.5400   Fax: 415.733.5401

Description: The news magazine of the Internet economy.

# Glossary

The only thing harder than keeping up with what the Internet can do is keeping up with what things are called. Indeed, no one is shy in the online world when it comes to making up new words for tools, techniques, and technologies. The following glossary covers most of the terms and buzzwords presented in this book. However, by the time you flip through it, another new word will have entered the online vernacular. Recognizing the organic nature of Internet vocabulary terms, we encourage you to bookmark some online glossaries that will keep you up to date on the latest terms to hit the industry:

- The Marketing Manager's Plain English Internet Glossary (www.jaderiver.com/gloss1.htm)
- WebPromote Glossary (www.webpromote.com/tools/glossary.asp)

**Ad request.**   When an ad is requested from the server. This happens when someone visits a Web page that has an advertisement and the surfer's browser asks the server to deliver the ad. For a variety of reasons the ad may not always be successfully served.

**Ad view.**   Technically this is when an ad is delivered. However, it is often used to mean ad request.

**ALT tag.**   Code that tells your browser to show specific text while a graphic is loading. When a banner is downloading, the ALT text can be reinforcing the ad's message with a simple line of text.

**Auditor.**   A third party that verifies ad delivery and site traffic.

**Bandwidth.**   How much information can be transferred through an Internet connection at a given time, usually measured in seconds.

**Banner.**   A rectangular ad usually appearing at the top or the bottom of a Web page, commonly 468 x 60 pixels in size.

**Bookmark.** A Web browser feature that serves as an address book for Web addresses.

**Browser.** The software that runs on your computer that translate the information transferred on the Internet into the Web pages that you see.

**Button.** A small, usually square or rectangular ad in the following dimensions: $125 \times 125$, $120 \times 90$, $120 \times 60$, $88 \times 31$, or $120 \times 240$ pixels.

**Cache (pronounced *cash*).** The temporary storing of a Web page on your computer following the page downloading. This speeds up downloading on repeated use, so that the next time you request that page, it is accessed from the cache on your computer instead of from the Web server. Proxy servers and ISPs may also cache pages to make access easier for their customers.

**Click-through.** The number of times an ad is clicked; when a user clicks on an ad that is linked to another page and that page downloads on to the user's browser.

**Click-through rate (CTR).** The percentage of times the ad is clicked on divided by the total number of times an ad is viewed.

**Closed loop reporting.** Measuring the achievement of goals beyond simple click-through—orders, leads, etc. that are generated from specific banners on specific sites.

**Conversion.** The rate at which a goal is achieved (for example, orders or leads).

**Cookie.** A text string that is placed on your computer (in your cookie file) by a Web site. The Web site can view the cookies it places when you move through the site, and use cookies as a means of tracking return visits and interests. (See Chapter 4.)

**Cost per click (CPC).** The price of placing an ad on a site based exclusively on how many times the ad is clicked on by users.

**Cost per lead (CPL).** The price of placing an ad on a site based on how many leads the ad generates.

**Cost per sale (CPS).** The price of placing an ad on a site based on how many sales result from the ad.

**Counter.** A program that a Web site uses to count the number of visits to a Web page.

**CPM (cost per thousand).** The cost of an ad for every 1,000 times the ad is shown on a Web page. (The "M" stands for the Latin mille, meaning "one thousand.")

**Directory.** A listing of Web sites organized into categories. The Yahoo! site is a directory.

**Discussion list.** An e-mail forum for people to discuss a particular topic. Discussion lists usually have a moderator who guides the discussion and ensures that it is pertinent to the discussion list's topic.

**Domain name.** A naming system that translates the numeric name given computers on the Internet into user-friendly addresses. Domain names are read from left to right and go from specific to general. For example, the Web address for Yahoo is www.yahoo.com and is dissected as follows. The Web addresses (URL) starts with the type of machine (www denotes a World Wide Web server), then the general domain name, which is yahoo, and then the top-level domain (.com for commercial). There are two types of top-level domains: categories (com, edu, org, etc.) and countries (uk—United Kingdom, au—Australia, etc.).

**Dynamic rotation (or dynamic delivery).** Ads delivered on a rotating or random basis, allowing different users to see different ads on a given page and for an ad to appear on more than one page. Ads can also be dynamically rotated through a particular section of a site or can be called up as part of a keyword search. (Contrast with *hardwired*.)

**E-mail list.** Similar to a mailing list, except that it contains e-mail addresses.

**Exposures.** The number of times that an advertisement is viewed. Commonly used interchangeably with *impressions*.

**Extranet.** A private network of networked computers that uses Internet protocols to share information between businesses. It is often part of a company's intranet that is shared with vendors and customers.

**File.** A computer document.

**Firewall.** A security barrier that separates a company's internal systems from outside systems.

**Flame.** A hostile note either posted in a discussion list or sent as an e-mail message.

**Flame war.** The exchange of hostile messages between two or more people.

**Flight.** An advertising campaign on a specific Web site for a specific time period. Also, to send out a creative to a Web site.

**GIF or .gif (Graphic Interchange Format).** A format for saving images for use on the Web. Mostly used for line art and simple logos and not meant for high quality art or photographic images, which require the more robust *JPEG* format.

**Gross exposures.** This is another term used to define an advertisement that is viewed.

**Hardwired.** Manner of placing an ad in a fixed position on a particular Web page so that it is delivered each time the page is downloaded (in contrast with *dynamic rotation*).

**Hit.** A line that is recorded in a log file when something is requested of a Web server. For example, if someone goes to a Web page that has five graphics, six hits will be recorded in the log file: one hit for the HTML page and one for each of the graphics. Hits are considered an inaccurate way to measure traffic and are no longer used by savvy advertisers.

**HTML (HyperText Markup Language).** The coding language used to make Web pages. HTML works by surrounding text with codes, called tags, that identify how the text should appear. For example  this designates that the word **example** should be bold. HTML also lets you link one file to another.

**Hypertext.** Text that when clicked on causes the browser to jump to another file either on the same Web site or in another location on the Web. Browsers generally display hypertext by underlining, with the cursor changing into a hand when placed over hypertext or linked images.

**Impressions.** The number of times an ad is delivered. When an advertiser buys advertising on a CPM basis, the advertiser is paying for every 1,000 impressions that the site can deliver. Different sites measure an impression differently. Some sites count an impression when an ad is requested, others only when an ad is fully downloaded, and there are other definitions that are used as well. A savvy advertiser will ask publishers how they define impressions.

**Internet.** The global network of networked computers.

**Interstitial.** An advertisement that interrupts the user. This can be a full page ad that pops up on the user's screen or a pop-up window.

**Intranet.** A network of networked computers that is contained within an enterprise. In other words, it is a private Web site usually servicing a single company. Its primary purpose is to share company information and computer resources with staff.

**Java.** The programming language developed by Sun Microsystems to create self-running applications that can be easily distributed through networks like the Web.

**Java applets.** Small Java programs used on Web pages to operate animation, calculators, and other tasks.

**JPEG or .jpg (Joint Photographic Experts Group).** A format for saving photographic and high quality images for use on the Web.

**Keyword.** A word or series of words that describe a page or site.

**Link.** A hypertext entry that lets a reader jump from one Web page to another page or file either on the same site or on another Web site.

**Log file.** A text file that records all activity on a server: the items that are requested (Web pages, graphics, etc.), the times they are requested, the browser used by the surfer, and other information (see Chapter 4). Traffic analysis software crunches log files to produce traffic reports that are easy to understand and use as a basis for measuring Web site success.

**Meta tag.** A tag that appears in the head portion of an HTML page after the title tag where you can list a series of keywords for your site.

**Netiquette.** Proper Internet behavior.

**Newsgroup.** A Usenet discussion group that talks about a specific topic

**Page view.** A common metric for measuring Web site traffic, usually representing the viewing of all of the elements that comprise a Web page (graphics, text, etc.). It is generally agreed that if someone looks at a Web page that has frames, a page view will be looking at all of the elements of the page. However, some advertisers will count each frame as a separate page view to boost their numbers for level of traffic.

**Pay per click (PPC).** An ad pricing structure by which the advertiser pays the publisher according to how many times an ad is clicked on by users (see *Cost per click*).

**Pay per lead (PPL).** An ad pricing structure by which the advertiser pays the publisher according to how many leads are generated by an ad, often determined by information submitted directly into the banner ad.

**Pay per transaction (PPT).** An ad pricing structure by which the advertiser pays the publisher according to the number of sales generated by an ad.

**Plug-in.** A small application file that is added on to a browser to allow it to play certain applications such as Shockwave and flash files. Microsoft Internet Explorer uses the term *ActiveX controls* instead of plug-in.

**Reciprocal link.** A link provided from one site to another in exchange for a link back.

**Response rate.** The percentage of impressions of an ad that result in the ad being clicked.

**Rich-media ads.** Ads incorporating video, audio, and other technology components beyond simple animation. Rich media is considered higher bandwidth advertising that delivers more of a brand impact than an animated banner advertisement.

**Robot.** A program that automatically surfs the Web. Search engines use robots to surf the Web and catalog different Web sites in their databases. This allows the Web pages to be found when someone performs a search. Robots are commonly referred to as bots and spiders.

**Search engine.** A tool for finding information on the Web. Users can type in exact text, or *keywords* representing their interests, to initiate the search. Popular search engines include Lycos, AltaVista, InfoSeek, and HotBot.

**Shockwave.** A program (see *Plug-in*) that allows Macromedia Director animate files to be played on a browser.

**Signature.** Text often appended to the end of someone's e-mail message to identify them. It can contain name, company name, and contact information. Many people use it as a form of advertising themselves when they post to an e-mail discussion list.

**Site traffic.** The amount of activity on a Web site. This is usually measured in page views or visitors.

**Spam.** On the Internet, not processed meat but unwanted and unsolicited messages, either on a discussion list or as an e-mail message.

**Unique users.** Individual visitors who have been to a Web site within a given amount of time.

**URL (Uniform Resource Locator).** A Web address.

**Usenet.** The Internet's bulletin board system of discussion groups on specific topics. There are more than 25,000 Usenet discussion groups today.

**Visitor.** A person who goes to a specific Web site. Sites often define their traffic levels in terms of the number of visitors they've had in a given time period.

**Visits.** Another way to compare and measure Web site traffic. A visit is activity on a Web site from a specific individual. That activity usually counts as a new visit if the individual has been away from the Web site for a period of fifteen minutes or longer.

**Web page.** A page of a Web site.

**Web site.** A collection of documents made available to users by a publisher on the Internet. These can include news and entertainment centers as well as corporate information sites.

# Illustrations Used with Permission

The following figures were courteously supplied by the companies indicated.

| | |
|---|---|
| *Figure 1.1* | © *Jupiter Communications. Used by permission.* |
| *Figure 1.2* | *Source: Forrester Research, Inc.* |
| *Figure 2.1a* | *"Car Talk" is a registered service mark of Tom and Ray Magliozzi. "cartalk.com" is a joint production of Public Interactive and Dewey, Cheetham & Howe. Contents copyright 1999 Dewey, Cheetham & Howe.* |
| *Figure 2.1b* | *"Car Talk" is a registered service mark of Tom and Ray Magliozzi. "cartalk.com" is a joint production of Public Interactive and Dewey, Cheetham & Howe. Contents copyright 1999 Dewey, Cheetham & Howe.* |
| *Figure 2.2* | © *The Proctor & Gamble Company. Used by permission.* |
| *Figure 2.5* | © *ClickZ, Inc. 1999.* |
| *Figure 2.15* | *Reproduced with permission by Hewlett-Packard Company.* |
| *Figure 2.16* | © *1-800-FLOWERS.COM, Inc.* |
| *Figure 2.17* | © *Cobra Golf, Inc.* |
| *Figure 2.19* | *Reproduced with permission by Hewlett-Packard Company.* |
| *Figure 2.20a* | *Source: Eddie Bauer.®* |
| *Figure 2.20b* | *Source: Eddie Bauer.®* |
| *Figure 2.22a* | © *CDnow, Inc. 1999. All rights reserved.* |
| *Figure 2.22b* | © *CDnow, Inc. 1999. All rights reserved.* |
| *Figure 2.22c* | © *CDnow, Inc. 1999. All rights reserved.* |
| *Figure 2.38* | *Reproduced with permission by Hewlett-Packard Company.* |
| *Figure 3.1* | © *1999 Internet Direct Marketing Bureau.* |
| *Figure 4.7* | © *BPA International 1999. All rights reserved.* |
| *Figure 6.6* | © *Jupiter Communications. Used by permission.* |
| *Figure 6.8a* | © *CDnow, Inc. 1999. All rights reserved.* |
| *Figure 6.8b* | © *CDnow, Inc. 1999. All rights reserved.* |
| *Figure 6.10* | © *Jupiter Communications. Used by permission.* |
| *Figure 7.8* | © *Women.com Networks.* |
| *Figure 8.6* | © *Jupiter Communications. Used by permission.* |
| *Figure 9.3* | © *CDnow, Inc. 1999. All rights reserved.* |
| *Figure 9.9* | © *ClickZ,Inc. 1999.* |
| *Figure 10.2* | © *Women.com Networks.* |
| *Figure 10.10* | © *Jupiter Communications. Used by permission.* |
| *Figure 11.1* | *Source: 1998 Cyber Dialogue.* |
| *Figure 11.2* | © *Jupiter Communications. Used by permission.* |
| *Figure 11.3* | *Source: 1998 Cyber Dialogue.* |
| *Figure 11.4* | *Source: 1998 Cyber Dialogue.* |
| *Figure 11.5* | *Source: 1998 Cyber Dialogue.* |
| *Figure 11.6* | *Source: 1998 Cyber Dialogue.* |
| *Figure 11.7* | *Source: 1998 Cyber Dialogue.* |
| *Figure 11.8* | © *1999 Philadelphia Newspaper, Inc. All rights reserved.* |
| *Figure 11.13* | © *1999 Ticketmaster Online—CitySearch, Inc. All rights reserved.* |
| *Figure 11.17* | © *LibertyNet 1999.* |
| *Figure 11.20* | © *Jupiter Communications. Used by permission.* |
| *Figure 11.25* | © *1999 The New York Times Company. Reprinted by permission.* |
| *Figure 14.1* | © *1999 USA TODAY, a division of Gannett Co., Inc.* |
| *Figure 3* | © *1999 The Infotique.* |
| *Figure 8* | © *1999 USA TODAY, a division of Gannett Co., Inc.* |

# About the Authors

**ROBBIN ZEFF, PH.D.** (robbin@zeff.com) is president of The Zeff Group (www.zeff.com.), an Internet advertising and marketing research, training, and consulting firm located in Arlington, Virginia. When Robbin isn't writing books (author of such Internet classics as *The Nonprofit Guide to the Internet* [Wiley, 1996]) or research reports (author of Jupiter Communications' *1998 Online Advertising Report*), producing the regionally focused conference series "Advertising & Marketing on the Internet" (find out when it's coming to a city near you at www.zeff.com), or consulting, she's riding her horse or surfing the Web with one of her cats on her lap. Robbin, who holds a doctorate in Folklore and American Studies from Indiana University, has taught business in Siberia, marketing in Bulgaria, and Web advertising and marketing in North and South America.

**BRAD ARONSON** (brad@i-frontier.com) is president of i-frontier (www.i-frontier. com), a Philadelphia-based Internet advertising agency. i-frontier was named one of the top 100 Internet advertising agencies in the country by DoubleClick and ChannelSeven, and was recently awarded a Best of Business Online Award from the Internet Business Alliance. Brad is a recognized expert in the field of Web advertising and marketing and is a frequent speaker at Internet business conferences. He was a judge for the Tenagra Awards and has been asked to judge the Advertising Design Club of Canada's annual advertising design awards (interactive category). The *Philadelphia Business Journal* has chosen Brad as one of the city's top 40 leaders under the age of 40. Brad writes an "Expert Advice" column for *Interactive PR and Marketing News*.